Ronsard's ordered chaos

To my parents
and my own *discordia concors*
NETTA, TAMSIN, FINN

MALCOLM QUAINTON

Ronsard's ordered chaos

Visions of flux and stability
in the poetry of Pierre de Ronsard

Manchester University Press

Published by
Manchester University Press
Oxford Road, Manchester M13 9PL

British Library Cataloguing in Publication Data

Quainton, Malcolm
  Ronsard's ordered chaos.
  1. Ronsard, Pierre de – Criticism and
  interpretation
  I. Title
  841'.3   PQ1678

  ISBN 0–7190–0760–7

184 301

Printed in Great Britain by
WILLMER BROTHERS LIMITED
Rock Ferry, Merseyside

CONTENTS

ILLUSTRATIONS

PREFACE

Grateful thanks are due to those many colleagues and friends who have assisted in the preparation of this book. I am particularly indebted to Professor Ian McFarlane who has suggested valuable lines of enquiry and methods of approach and whose stimulating advice over the years has been without equal. I am also greatly obliged to Dr Terence Cave for reading the entire typescript of this book at an early stage and for offering constructive criticism and generous encouragement. A debt of gratitude is also owed to Professor C. A. Mayer and Professor R. Niklaus for their advice and support during the supervision and examination of the thesis on which this book is based, and to John Randall for his help concerning matters of classical scholarship and translation. In so far as this present study has merit it is in large measure thanks to these scholars and friends: its weaknesses, and the responsibility for the final result, are of course mine.

I should like to thank the following bodies for financial assistance which enabled me to carry out the research for this book: the French Government, the British Council, the Centre National de la Recherche Scientifique and, especially, the British Academy whose generous award allowed me to work in Paris during a sabbatical leave of absence granted in 1977 by the University of Lancaster.

I would like to thank also the authorities and the staff of the libraries where I have worked, especially the British Museum, the Bibliothèque Nationale, the Taylor Institution, the Bodleian, the University of Exeter Library and the University of Lancaster Library.

The author and publishers are grateful, finally, to the following for permission to reproduce photographs: the British Museum (plate 1); the Bodleian Library (plate 2); the Brera Gallery, Milan (plate 3).

Lancaster   MALCOLM QUAINTON
October 1978

ABBREVIATIONS

BHR   Bibliothèque d'Humanisme et Renaissance.

CAIEF   Cahiers de l'Association Internationale des Etudes Françaises.

JWCI   Journal of the Warburg and Courtauld Institutes.

LCL   Loeb Classical Library (classical texts and English translations published London, Heinemann; Cambridge, Mass., Harvard University Press). English translations of Latin texts not accompanied by LCL page references are my own.

PMLA   Publications of the Modern Language Association of America.

RHLF   Revue d'Histoire Littéraire de la France.

RPL   Paul Laumonier, *Ronsard, poète lyrique*, 2nd edn., Paris, Hachette, 1923.

STFM   Société des Textes Français Modernes.

THR   Travaux d'Humanisme et Renaissance.

TLF   Textes Littéraires Français.

Biblical references throughout are to the Vulgate.

Italics used in quotations to draw attention to specific lexical, stylistic or structural aspects are mine unless otherwise stated.

PRINCIPAL EDITIONS OF PLÉIADE POETS USED

BAÏF   *Euvres en rime de Jan Antoine de Baïf*. Edition de Charles Marty-Laveaux, 5 vols., Paris, Lemerre (La Pléiade Françoise), 1881–90.

BELLEAU   *Œuvres Complètes de Remy Belleau*. Nouvelle édition publiée d'après les textes primitifs avec variantes et notes par A. Gouverneur, 3 vols., Paris, Franck; Nogent-le-Rotrou, Gouverneur, 1867.

DU BELLAY   *Œuvres poétiques*, édition critique par Henri Chamard, 6 vols., Paris, Droz (STFM), 1908–31.

JODELLE   *Les Œuvres et Meslanges poétiques*, éd. Charles Marty-Laveaux, 2 vols., Paris, Lemerre (La Pléiade Françoyse), 1868–70.

RONSARD   *Œuvres Complètes*, édition critique par Paul Laumonier, 20 vols., Paris, Hachette, then Droz, then Didier (STFM), 1914–75. Vols. XVII-XX revised and completed by I. Silver and R. Lebègue.

TYARD   *Œuvres Poétiques Complètes*, édition critique par John C. Lapp, Paris, Didier (STFM), 1966.

The orthography and punctuation of these editions have been retained throughout with the exception that I have replaced 'i' and 'u' by 'j' and 'v' where necessary.

INTRODUCTION

The importance of the theme of transience in the poetry of Ronsard has been acknowledged by several eminent scholars of the sixteenth century. As early as 1901 Paul Laumonier wrote: '... les coups aveugles de la mort ... la vanité des grandeurs ... la fragilité de l'être humain, trois thèmes lyriques qui remplissent les deux tiers de ses vers.'[1] In his turn Pierre Champion referred to 'l'idée païenne de la fuite du temps ... qui dominera toute sa vie, sur laquelle il écrira tant de variations',[2] whilst in the first volume of his *Ronsard, poète de l'amour*, Fernand Desonay draws attention to 'cette philosophie du muable dont Pierre de Ronsard sera comme obsédé'.[3]

Nevertheless in spite of the acknowledged importance of this 'philosophie du muable', there has never been a comprehensive study of the different themes of flux in the work of Ronsard. Such research as has been published in this respect has tended to concentrate on Ronsard's attitude to death. Even here, however, the interesting articles by A. H. Krappe, Marc Bensimon and Françoise Joukovsky-Micha,[4] as well as the chapters devoted to Ronsard in more general accounts of the changing conception of death in medieval, Renaissance and baroque literature,[5] have still left ample scope for further research into source material and for additional consideration of the rich complexity of Ronsard's different attitudes and visions of death. Similarly, of the major studies devoted to Ronsard's conception of immortality by Henri Franchet, R. J. Clements and Françoise Joukovsky,[6] only the last named has endeavoured to place the poet's discussion of *gloire* in the context of his constant obsession with the notions of flux and stability and to analyse and evaluate the poetic expression of the theme.

Besides Death, the other concepts which have been collected here under the general heading of flux or transience—namely Change, Fortune and Time—have received surprisingly little attention from scholars. In 1955 and 1960 respectively, Dr Dudley Wilson published two articles entitled 'The Forces of Flux and Stability in Sixteenth Century Thought and Literature in France'[7] and 'Contraries in sixteenth century scientific writing in France',[8] but whilst these studies have directed the scope of this present enquiry in certain respects, they are not specifically related to the poetry of the Pléiade and indeed contain only very limited reference to Ronsard. In 1965 Professor Isidore Silver contributed several pages of an article on Ronsard's cosmology to a discussion of the poet's reflections on Time.[9] Subsequently I replied to this article in a study entitled 'Ronsard's philosophical and cosmological conceptions of time',[10] and this paper finds its natural place in a modified and developed form in our present section on Time. The recently-published book by Ricardo J. Quinones, *The Renaissance Discovery of Time* (Harvard University Press, 1972), whilst containing studies of Rabelais and Montaigne, makes no reference to the work of the Pléiade. Most of the research in this respect has been focused almost exclusively on the Pléiade's treatment of the theme of *la fuite du temps* and on the accompanying epicurean refrains of *carpe diem* and *carpe florem*, and this emphasis has tended to obscure the thematic richness of Ronsard's conceptions of time. The discussion of the epicurean themes below will concentrate not only on the popular appeal of the *carpe diem*, but also on the neglected allegorical and philosophical statements and on the role of Seneca as a major source. Similarly, apart from brief references in general studies of Ronsard's cosmology,[11] no discussion of Ronsard's conception of Fortune exists.

More recently (1973), in a collection of essays by English *seiziémistes*, Ian McFarlane and Odette de Mourgues devote several pages to a demonstration of Ronsard's continuing interest in aspects of change and movement,[12] whilst Marcel Raymond has studied the thematic, structural and stylistic implications of Ronsard's preoccupation with change in so far as concerns the concepts of the baroque and mannerism.[13] Professor McFarlane's suggestion that the notion of flux forms part of Ronsard's essential poetic vision happily coincides with the aim of this present study and with its general conclusion concerning the importance of such a consideration throughout his work.

Whilst the following discussion is indebted to the research of these earlier scholars in so far as it has suggested insights and certain lines of approach, it is apparent that no detailed analysis of Ronsard's treatment of the concepts of flux and stability exists in any language. The present study seeks to remedy this situation : its aims are to demonstrate the importance and widespread ramifications of this antithesis in so far as it influences Ronsard's conceptual and imaginative structures, to illustrate the multiple visions and attitudes associated with this duality, to analyse and evaluate its poetic expression and, as far as possible, to establish sources. This task of establishing sources has been greatly facilitated not only by the work undertaken by Paul Laumonier in his *Ronsard, poète lyrique* and in his magnificent edition of Ronsard's *Œuvres Complètes*, but also by the numerous scholarly studies of Professor Isidore Silver. Sometimes, however, the attribution of precise sources is rendered difficult owing to the commonplaceness of certain themes—those concerning, for example, the omnipotence and equality of death, the destructive nature of time and the inconstancy of Fortune. This commonplace vision obviously tends to a repetition of a common stock of themes and *topoi* inherited from classical and medieval traditions, although, as a study of the commonplaces of death will reveal, Ronsard, perhaps not surprisingly considering his humanist aesthetic and his categorical (and unjust) condemnation of previous French poetry, clearly favours direct classical sources rather than intermediary medieval and national models.

As these commonplaces are perhaps the least interesting and original part of Ronsard's treatment, these aspects have not been dwelt upon unnecessarily. However, since the poet returns consistently and emphatically to these commonplace themes throughout the entire corpus of his work, they have been included in this study not only in the interest of thoroughness, not only to demonstrate the way Ronsard poetically transcends the received ideas or often adds a personal dimension to them, but also because their very consistency and emphasis suggest they form part of his essential inspiration. Indeed this whole question of the relationship between imitation and originality is a complex one and has wide methodological implications. The distinguished Ronsardian scholar Professor Isidore Silver has already pointed to the difficulty of determining the substantive originality of a humanist poet imbued deeply with classical literature: 'To begin with, it must probably, and in the case of Ronsard, certainly, lead us into a *regressus ad infinitum*. For if we deny to Ronsard any claim to originality in the initiation of ideas on the ground that, in the given contexts, he is merely reiterating thoughts which he had read in Horace or Virgil or Lucretius, are we not bound by the terms of that denial to point out that Horace's debt to the lyric poets of Greece, Virgil's debt to Homer, that of Lucretius to Epicurus, was in each case similar in nature to Ronsard's debt to all of them?'[14]

Again, might it not be suggested that the *very choice* of a specific model itself reveals a commitment, a personal attitude, a degree of affinity of outlook, a certain sympathy of vision? Whilst a poet might choose a particular model for a host of reasons, be they aesthetic, ideological or biographical, it seems unlikely that he would imitate a text, consciously or unconsciously, if its ideas were opposed to his own attitude. There is, of course, no legislation possible for the creative act, and one can never know an author's motives, but bearing in mind that in the *Deffence et Illustration* du Bellay states that an aesthetic of imitation must be based on a close sympathy of views and outlook, one might argue that, in the case of the Pléiade especially, the very choice of a model suggests approval of, and indeed affinity with, the source's ideas. This point of view, which has been adopted throughout this study, is supported by both Professor Silver—'We shall, therefore, do well not to become engaged in the vain endeavour to distinguish the horizons that Ronsard saw with his own eyes from those which were opened in his mind by the frequentation of the visions of other poets and thinkers'— and by Fernand Desonay: 'La question des influences littéraires, la question des sources, n'est que secondaire: au fond, on n'imite que ce que l'on est déjà prêt d'avouer comme sien.'[15]

The following study is limited to Ronsard because his work clearly provides the most original and poetic treatment of the themes of flux and stability, and because it is he, rather than his fellow poets of the Pléiade, who will introduce the reader to the fullest range of perspectives and attitudes. Moreover one might argue that the other Pléiade poets deserve to be studied in their own right and not, as frequently happens, as mere appendages to Ronsard. For these reasons Ronsard's fellow poets have been excluded except in those cases where they provide interesting comparisons and contrasts and enable the reader to define Ronsard's own position more precisely. Similarly a proliferation of examples drawn from the work of minor figures of the sixteenth century would offer nothing new to the discussion of the themes, and would serve only to repeat *ad nauseam* the more commonplace of their aspects, detracting thereby from what is more rewarding and original in the attitudes of Ronsard. Whilst the volume of evidence would be swollen considerably by such illustration, the conclusions and import of the analysis would not benefit proportionately.[16]

The format of this study has been determined not by strict attention to chronology but rather by Ronsard's essential visions and attitudes, for a detailed preliminary analysis of composition/publication dates and statements relating to the themes of flux led at an early stage to the conclusion that, if one were to remain faithful to the complexity and abundance of material and not to simplify or distort by convenient selectivity, there is generally little overall development or significant evolution of attitude, and that certain inconsistencies in the treatment of themes are not easily resolved by chronological reference. I have, therefore, heeded the warning of Professor Silver who has expressed reservations concerning 'a too meticulous attention to chronological considerations' when studying Ronsard's poetry, and who has noted that 'the advantages of a strictly chronological order are sometimes illusory'.[17] Similarly André Gendre has remarked on the limitations of a strictly chronological approach when applied to Ronsard's work and has argued in favour of a *vue d'ensemble*.[18] Consequently I have preferred to follow this line of more recent research, which is synchronic and synthetic in nature, and concentrate on what Professor Silver calls elsewhere the 'authentic voice' of Ronsard,[19] that is those attitudes and visions which are permanently and emphatically expressed throughout the poet's career even beyond the momentary rejections, contradictions and ambiguities which abound in his verse. His eclecticism is well known and of fundamental importance, being the response of an intellectual curiosity to the often contradictory views of a century teeming with ideas and characterised by what Françoise Joukovsky has termed a 'recherche faustienne', a 'perpétuelle remise en question' (*La Gloire*, p. 595). Ronsard, it will be seen, proudly formulates his self-confessed eclecticism into a poetic theory, an aesthetic principle, which has important parallels with his cosmic and social visions. These inconsistencies found in Ronsard's verse can also be explained by the fact that poets, unlike philosophers (or indeed philosopher-poets like Lucretius), are not essentially interested in rigid systems of thought: indeed as Terence Cave has remarked, 'Ronsard's theory allows for such ambiguities . . . in that the *fureur* of poetic inspiration frees the poet from rational constraints and allows him to explore universal experience intuitively'.[20] On more than one occasion attention will be drawn to these ambiguities, to a duality or a tension in the poet's vision between on the one hand a more optimistic and reasoned apprehension of reality, which favours order and strict control, and on the other an anxious and emotional response which is expressed via powerful images, symbols and allegories.

Thus these dominant visions and attitudes which constitute Ronsard's 'authentic voice' will best guide the reader not only through the complexity and abundance of material and enable him to reach a synthesis and form general conclusions, but they will also help him to plot his course through the ambiguities and eclecticism of the poet and through the problem, posed above, concerning imitation and originality. Within this general criterion of the 'authentic voice' it is hoped, nevertheless, to take into consideration, firstly, Ronsard's different interpretations and attitudes at different times where such exist, and secondly, any marked evolution concerning particular themes and visions. In this last case illustration and argument will, of necessity, be by chronological reference.

NOTES TO INTRODUCTION

1 'La Jeunesse de Pierre de Ronsart', *Revue de la Renaissance*, I (1901), 179.
2 *Ronsard et son temps* (Paris, 1925), p. 33.
3 *Ronsard, poète de l'amour* (3 vols., Brussels, 1952–9), vol. I, p. 14.
4 A. H. Krappe, 'Pierre de Ronsard's *Hymne de la Mort* and Plutarch's *Consolatio ad Apollonium*', *Modern Language Review*, XVII (1922), 150–6; M. Bensimon, 'Ronsard et la Mort', *Modern Language Review*, LVII (1962),

183–94; F. Joukovsky-Micha, 'Tombeaux et offrandes rustiques chez les poètes français et néo-latins du XVIe siècle', *BHR*, XXVII (1965), 226–47.

5   See in particular, E. Dubruck, *The Theme of Death in French Poetry of the Middle Ages and the Renaissance* (The Hague, 1964).

6   H. Franchet, *Le poète et son œuvre d'après Ronsard* (Paris, 1923), pp. 43–175; R. J. Clements, *Critical Theory and Practice of the Pléiade* (Harvard Univ. Press, 1942), chapter II; F. Joukovsky, *La Gloire dans la poésie française et néolatine du XVIe siècle* (Geneva, 1969).

7   *Durham University Journal*, XLVIII (1955), 13–20.

8   Published in *Essays presented to C. M. Girdlestone* (Durham, 1960), pp. 351–68.

9   'Ronsard's Reflections on the Heavens and Time', *PMLA*, LXXX (1965), 359–64. This article has contributed substantially to the argument and illustration of my own section on the cosmological vision of time in chapter 4.

10 *French Studies*, XXIII (1969), 1–22.

11 H. Busson, *Le Rationalisme dans la littérature française de la Renaissance*, 2nd edn. (Paris, 1957), pp. 372, 377. A recent book on Montaigne and Fortune (D. Martin, *Montaigne et la fortune: essai sur le hasard et le langage*, Geneva, 1977) contains a valuable historical survey of the origins and role of Fortune from the classical period until the Renaissance.

12 *Ronsard the Poet* (London, 1973), pp. 26–34, 288–302.

13 See in particular, *Baroque et Renaissance poétique* (Paris, 1955); 'La Pléiade et le Maniérisme', in *Lumières de la Pléiade* (Paris, 1966), pp. 391–423.

14 I. Silver, *The Intellectual Evolution of Ronsard: (I) The Formative Influences* (St Louis, Washington Univ. Press, 1969), p. xiii.

15 Silver, *ibid.*; Desonay, *Ronsard, poète de l'amour*, vol. II, p. 68. Cf. A. Gendre, *Ronsard poète de la conquête amoureuse* (Neuchâtel, 1970), pp. 34–5.

16 One of the longest prose treatises on this theme is by Louis Le Roy, *De la Vicissitude ou varieté des choses en l'univers* (Paris, L'Huilier, 1576). Le Roy devotes pages to the flux of the four elements (fol. 3r–5r), the idea that 'toutes choses en l'univers sont temperees et conservees par contraires & dissemblables' (fol. 5r–6r), 'De la variete et vicissitude humaine' (fol. 9v–14r), 'Vicissitude des peuples' (fol. 14r–14v), 'Vicissitude des villes' (fol. 14v–15r), 'Vicissitude des republiques, royaumes, & empires' (fol. 15r–15v). Book II (fol. 16r–23v) is devoted to a study of 'Vicissitude et variete des Langues', whilst Books III–XII deal with the theme of *translatio studii* and are used to demonstrate the principle of progress ('les choses humaines variables [sont] montees au plus hault').

17 *The Intellectual Evolution of Ronsard*, vol. I, pp. xi–xii.

18 *Ronsard poète de la conquête amoureuse*, pp. 29–33.

19 'Ronsard's Ethical Thought', *BHR*, XXIV (1962), 105.

20 'Ronsard's mythological universe', in *Ronsard the Poet*, p. 185.

CHAPTER ONE

The cosmic and social framework

This chapter will deal not only with Ronsard's description of the physical universe[1] and with his view of society, but also with the formulation of a framework of reference within which cosmic, social and aesthetic considerations are seen to centre on the general principle of a balance of opposites (a *discordia concors*) and on a common core of poetic concerns—the microcosm-macrocosm relationship and the moral concept of *hubris*; the cycle of creation, conservation and destruction and the associated polarities of movement/stagnation, order/chaos, peace/discord, unity/diversity, health/illness—and these concerns of Ronsard, once established, will receive more precise definition and more detailed illustration during the subsequent chapters devoted to the specific thematic areas of change, Fortune, time and death.

The creation of an ordered universe from the original chaos of warring elements provides both the cosmic framework and the point of departure for Ronsard's vision of the world as a fragile balance of opposing forces of flux and stability. Whilst his conception of the structure of the universe remains the geocentric system of Plato, Aristotle and Ptolemy, and whilst his accounts of the pacification of chaos and the separation of the elements conform to the general principles of Genesis 1, and Plato's *Timaeus*, Ronsard is more frequently attracted to the poetic descriptions of Ovid, Virgil and Claudian for his own details of the creation of the world.[2] In the following passage from *La Paix* of 1559, the essential features of Ovid, *Metamorphoses*, 1, 5–37, are complemented, Laumonier notes, by a reminiscence of Claudian, who introduces the allegorical figure of *Clementia* into his account and suggests the role of Peace to the French poet. Typical of Ronsard is the way in which the cosmological perspective is accompanied by a personal aesthetic statement, for chaos is associated in his mind with the absence of measure and movement and these are important and lasting aspects of his conception of beauty as will be seen later:

Avant l'ingenieuse ordonnance du monde,
Le feu, l'air, & la terre, & l'enfleure de l'onde
Estoyent dans un monceau confusement enclos,
Monceau que du nom grec on nomme le Chaos,
Sans forme, sans beauté, lourde & pesante mace,
Comme un corps engourdi ne bougeoit d'une place :
...
Mais la bonne Nature, & le grand Dieu qui est,
A qui tousjours la guerre & le discord desplaist,
Chassa l'inimitié de leurs guerres encloses,
Par l'ayde de la Paix mere de toutes choses :
Loing au rond de la terre elle fist escumer
A part en leur vaisseau les vagues de la mer,
Et plus loing de la mer separa la closture
Du Ciel, qui va bornant les œuvres de nature,
Et du feu tressubtil, & du ciel etheré
L'air le plus espaissi en bas a retiré.

(IX, 107)

In other contexts the harmonising role is given alternately to the goddess Peace (III, 5–7; IX, 25), to God (VIII, 209) or to the Hesiodic or Platonic Eros.[3] The order of the universe, however, does not merely depend on the balanced superimposition of the elements and on a separation of those elemental properties which are antipathetic, but, according to ideas which have their ultimate authority in Aristotelian physics,[4] it also demands the activation of those qualities which are common and therefore apt for combination. Each element possesses two of the primary qualities, and it is through the combination of these common virtues that matter is formed and things created, whilst it is as a result of the repulsion of those properties which are antipathetic that movement occurs and matter ultimately dissolves and things die. Thus the creation and cyclic transmutation of matter, all sublunar movement as well as the stability and balanced perfection of the universe are dependent on the precarious and complex harmony of opposing yet attracting elemental properties, of 'contraires acords', 'accords discordans', 'discord melodieux', 'paisible contrainte', as the Pléiade poets write echoing Horace, Ovid and Manilius.[5]

This delicate equilibrium of contrary forces has its counterpart in the diversely rotating and perfectly ordered movements of the heavens. It is in the *Hymne du Ciel* (1555) that a passage occurs in which the 'Esprit de l'ETERNEL' is equated with the Platonic World Soul, that vital breath which first set the outer globe of the heaven (the Prime Mover) in eternal circular motion and which is infused throughout the cosmos to maintain harmony. In lines which combine scientific clarity with poetic beauty, Ronsard evokes the ordered diversity of the universe where opposing movements are choreographed, dissonances harmonised, shapes regulated into the perfect unity of the all-embracing and eternal spherical form, and sounds, typified by the music of the heavenly spheres, orchestrated and rendered unisonant. The vision is simultaneously cosmological and aesthetic:

> L'Esprit de l'ETERNEL qui avance ta course,
> Espandu dedans toy, comme une grande source
> De tous costez t'anime, & donne mouvement,
> Te faisant tournoyer en sphere rondement,
> Pour estre plus parfaict, car en la forme ronde
> Gist la perfection qui toute en soy abonde:
> De ton bransle premier, des autres tout divers,
> Tu tires au rebours les corps de l'Univers,
> Bien qu'ilz resistent fort à ta grand' violence,
> Seulz à-part, demenans une seconde dance,
> L'un deçà, l'autre là, comme ilz sont agitez
> Des discordans accordz de leurs diversitez:
> Ainsi guidant premier si grande compagnie,
> Tu fais une si douce & plaisante harmonie,
> Que noz lucz ne sont rien aux prix des moindres sons
> Qui resonnent là haut de diverses façons.[6]

The preservation of the universe in this 'paisible contrainte', this fragile stability of opposing elemental forces and celestial movements, becomes in turn a major concern of Ronsard. Whilst both Eros and Bacchus are endowed with cosmic functions of conservation in his verse,[7] more frequently, however, as in the passage from the *Hymne du Ciel* just discussed, he turns to the pantheistic conception of a World Soul for his vision of a binding and harmonising power infused throughout the entire world-system 'comme une grande source'. The idea of an *Anima Mundi* is an essential feature of Platonic, neo-Platonic and Stoic cosmology, as well as being an aspect of the pantheism of the Paduan school of Averroists such as Cardano and Pomponazzi.[8] Ronsard's own conception of the World Soul, however, owes a more direct textual debt to Virgil, *Aeneid*, VI, 724-7, where Anchises expounds the theory of metempsychosis to Aeneas: 'First, the heaven and earth, and the watery plains, the shining orb of the moon and Titan's stars, a spirit within sustains, and mind, pervading its members, sways the whole mass and mingles with its mighty frame' (LCL, 1960, vol. I, p. 557).

Ronsard's earliest expression of a tendency towards pantheism appears in the *Ode de la Paix* of 1550, where the Ovidian account of the pacification of chaos is accompanied by the introduction of the allegorical figure of Peace from Claudian. However, the infusion of the stabilising power of Peace into the entire world structure is developed to such a degree that it becomes equated with an animism which is totally foreign to the Latin texts. This diffused spirit is linked more directly to matter than to a Christian God and acts as a kind of World Soul, binding and balancing the universe:

> Adonq mélant dans ce grand monde
> Sa douce force vagabonde
> Le bien heura d'un dous repos,
> Elle fit bas tumber la terre,
> Et tournoier l'eau qui la serre
> De ses bras vagues & dispos.
>
> (III, 6)

This 'douce force vagabonde' is echoed in the 'du grand Tout l'ame en tout vagabonde' of sonnet XXVI of the *Amours* of 1552 (IV, 29), and Muret's commentary note to this line is significant: 'Selon les Platoniques, qui constituent une ame de l'Univers epandue par toutes les parties du monde: de laquelle Virgile parle ainsi . . .' The passage from *Aeneid*, VI, 724–7, is then cited.[9]

Besides the other brief recollections of this Virgilian passage in his verse (cf. VI, 170), there are three important occasions on which Ronsard uses the Latin text to incorporate a wholly pantheistic conception of a World Soul into his vision of cosmic harmony. The first of these occurs, as has been seen, in the *Hymne du Ciel*. A similar conception, developed at greater length and with greater emphasis, appears in *Le Chat* of 1569, where God is heretically confused with the stabilising and regenerative force of the *Ame du Monde*. Whilst religious conformity could be safeguarded by considering the *Anima Mundi* as 'elle-même analogue au Saint-Esprit des chrétiens' (Schmidt, p. 100), the danger in making God Himself a Universal Soul is that Ronsard at the same time divinises nature and man, and substitutes the principle of immanence for the Christian notion of transcendence. The resulting animism is suspiciously unorthodox:

> Dieu est par tout, par tout se mesle Dieu,
> Commencement, la fin, & le millieu
> De ce qui vit, & dont l'Ame est enclose
> Par tout, & tient en vigueur toute chose
> Come nostre Ame infuse dans noz corps.
>   Ja des longtemps les membres seroient morts
> De ce grand Tout, si cette Ame divine
> Ne se mesloit par toute la Machine,
> Luy donnant vie & force & mouvement:
> Car de tout estre elle est commencement.[10]

Unlike Pontus de Tyard, who, although tempted by the identification of the *Anima Mundi* with God, nevertheless expressed Christian reserva-

tions about the heretical implications of this theory for practical theology,[11] Ronsard seems unaware of the dangerous consequences of his
pantheism. Indeed when he returns for the third time to the notion of a
World Soul in Hyante's speech from the *Franciade* (1572), Ronsard
blandly paraphrases Anchises' reply to Aeneas in order to introduce the
Pythagorean idea of metempsychosis, and leaves it to Amadis Jamyn to
excuse this heresy on the grounds of poetic necessity. Here, as in the
lines from *Le Chat* quoted above, Ronsard insists on a comparison between microcosm and macrocosm with the help of a well-known text of
Manilius, and suggests that the primary functions of the *Ame du Monde*
are to vitalise and preserve the world and to stabilise the apparent flux
of matter.[12]

On other occasions the unifying and preservative functions of a
World Soul are equated with the Sun, which Ronsard alternately describes as the eldest son and the lover of Nature.[13] Whilst the idea of the
sun as eternal source of cyclic change and generation is a feature of
Aristotelian cosmology,[14] Ronsard's animistic conception of the Sun infused throughout the world structure as a controlling and creative
energy owes a more direct textual debt to an eloquent passage of Pliny
the Elder (*Natural History*, II, iv, 12–13). The clearest demonstration of
the influence of this Pliny text, and the most developed description of
the Sun as an *Anima Mundi*, appear in these lines from the *Remonstrance au peuple de France* of 1563 : here too familiar lexical clusters
(*vertus, tournoyer, vagabond, repos*) echo the pantheistic tone of poems
already discussed, and the juxtaposition of antithetical patterns (*entre
ou sort; vagabond, & ferme; En repos, sans repos; oisif, & sans sejour;
Fils . . . & le pere*) again suggests the concept of *discordia concors* which
is so fundamental to Ronsard's vision of cosmic harmony and to his conception of beauty. For present too in these lines from the *Remonstrance*
are certain aesthetic principles and stylistics which will be more fully
defined and illustrated throughout the course of this study, namely the
tendency to multiply lexis and to repeat strong structures (the *qui* and
de ses patterns of ll. 1–4; the numerous antithetical items and the linking *et* formula; the accumulation of present participles and adjectives),
and it is these techniques which give Ronsard's verse its characteristic
libre contrainte, its movement and measure, its diversity and unity
(verse which, it will be seen, is *rond, vagabond, & ferme; En repos, sans
repos*) :

> Je dy ce grand Soleil qui nous fait les saisons
> Selon qu'il entre ou sort de ses douze maisons,
> Qui remplist l'univers de ses vertus cogneues,
> Qui d'un trait de ses yeux nous dissipe les nues,
> L'esprit, l'ame du monde, ardant & flamboyant,

En la course d'un jour tout le ciel tournoyant,
Plain d'immence grandeur, rond, vagabond, & ferme,
Lequel tient dessoubs luy tout le monde pour terme,
En repos, sans repos, oisif, & sans sejour,
Fils aysné de Nature, & le pere du jour.[15]

Reminiscences of Pliny, *Natural History*, II, i–iv, had been evident eight years earlier in Ronsard's *Hymne de la Justice*: here Nature and the *Ame du Monde* have usurped the prerogatives of a transcendental God —referred to by an ambiguous periphrasis ('celuy qui nous feit immortelz les espritz')—and the emphasis, as in Pliny, is on the universal order of a natural immanent force.[16] Similarly it is another passage from Pliny which provides the central inspiration—together with possible echoes from Lucretius, I, 250–64; II, 991–8—for a 1587 addition to the *Hymne du Ciel* (1555), in which Ronsard traces the world's preservation to the fertilisation of the elements and first seeds by 'Une ame, une vertu, une vigueur' emanating from the Heaven:

Du grand & large tour de ta celeste voûte
Une ame, une vertu, une vigueur degoute
Tousjours dessur la terre, en l'air & dans la mer,
Pour fertiles les rendre et les faire germer :
Car sans ta douce humeur qui distille sans cesse,
La terre par le temps deviendroit en vieillesse :
Mais, arrosant d'enhaut sa face tous les jours,
Jamais ne s'envieillist non plus que fait ton cours.
(VIII, 147, var.)

A comparison of these lines with Pliny's text, '. . . from seeds of all these objects, falling from the sky in countless numbers, particularly in the sea, and usually mixed together, monstrous shapes are generated' (*Nat. Hist.*, II, iii, 7: LCL, 1958, vol. I, p. 175), clearly demonstrates the full measure of Ronsard's personal contribution, for the animistic emphasis given to the 'ame . . . vertu . . . vigueur' (Ronsard's substitution for the Latin 'rerum omnium seminibus innumeris'), as well as the generative and rejuvenating powers attributed to this 'ame', are foreign to Pliny. Here the 'vertu' and 'vigueur' is seen both as a seminal fluid and as a liquid akin to water, and elsewhere in Ronsard's verse water is seen, after the manner of Thales, as the original generative and preservative principle activating nature :

. . . le vielliard Ocean
Pere de tout, & non-seulement pere,
Mais nourricier, & donnant comme mere
A ses enfans la mamelle, à cell' fin
Que sans humeur ce grand Tout ne prist fin.[17]

Two other themes form part of this vision of sexual pantheism and of this same conception of water as the primary generative element. The first is the idea that humidity and heat together create life and fecundate the 'semences', the 'germes' of the world,[18] and the second relates to Ronsard's use of the myth—recounted in Hesiod, *Theogony*, ll. 170–202 —concerning the birth of Aphrodite from water fertilised by Uranus's testicles after his castration by his son Cronos (below, pp. 133–4).

On the whole Ronsard prefers the Platonic hypothesis of a self-generating World Soul to the Aristotelian conception of God as the Unmoved Mover, for the former related more directly to his dynamic pantheistic vision of the cosmos as a unified diversity, as aesthetic perfection, '... son nombre egal / Discordant en melodie' (III, 75). In spite of this preference, however, Ronsard is familiar with Aristotle's ideas on the Unmoved Mover from a reading of the *Metaphysics*,[19] or, as Henri Busson suggests (*Le Rationalisme*, p. 364), either as a result of attendance at the lectures given by Francisco Vicomercato at the Collège Royal (1542–67) or from a study of his translation and commentary on the relevant parts of the Greek text. For Ronsard it is essentially 'l'ordre, la raison et la suite des causes et choses créées'[20] and the preservation of the universe in a state of stability which prove the existence of 'Le vray Manouvrier des cieux' (III, 45), evoked in this text of 1563 by a fusion of Christian and Aristotelian terminology:

> J'ay le chef eslevé pour voir & pour cognoistre
> De ce grand univers le seigneur & le maistre,
> Car en voyant du ciel l'ordre qui point ne faut,
> Je suis tresassuré qu'un Moteur est là haut,
> Qui tout sage & tout bon gouverne cest empire,
> Comme un Pilote en mer gouverne son navire :
> Et que ce grand Palais si largement vosté
> De son divin Ouvrier ensuit la volonté.[21]

Associated with this notion of the Unmoved Mover is the Homeric myth of the golden chain on which Zeus suspends the world (*Iliad*, VIII, 13–27); a myth interpreted by Aristotle (*De Motu Animalium*, 699b35–700a3) to prove that the Unmoved Mover exists outside the physical universe. Ronsard also recounts the Homeric myth (VIII, 89–90), and on several occasions uses the chain metaphor to emphasise the cosmic hierarchy, the links of which can be traced back to Aristotle's Unmoved Mover, with the difference, however, that for Ronsard (VIII, 146) God inhabits the world:

> Dieu commande par tout comme Prince absolu
> . . .
> Son ordre est une chene aimantine & ferrée
> Qui se tient l'une à l'autre estroictement serrée.[22]

Elsewhere the verb *encheiner* is used to suggest the same myth and meta-phor, and in the following passage devoted to the order and binding embrace of the elements it is Pliny, once more, who provides certain textual details. Present too are strong suggestions of sexual pantheism and a now-familiar obsession with aspects of movement, order and vital-ity—an obsession operating here on both thematic and stylistic levels (note the accumulative energy, the structural cohesion and the rhyth-mical measure provided by the *Et ... Et comme ... Et ... Et comme* pattern and by the repetition of lexical items: *embrasse, mer, air*):

> Et la mer qui d'un cours sans paresse coulant
> Va dedans son giron nostre terre acollant,
> Et comme l'air espars toute la mer embrasse,
> Et l'air est embrassé du feu qui le surpasse,
> Et comme tous ensemble en leurs ordres presséz
> De la voute du ciel s'encheinent embrassez.[23]

This precarious equilibrium of opposing forces of flux and stability in the world system has its counterpart in a developed allegory involving the principal figures of Peace and Discord. After the creation of cosmos from chaos Ronsard describes how Peace imprisons Discord in hell,

> Apres avoir par ordre arrangé la machine,
> Et lié ce grand Corps d'une amitié divine,
> Elle fist atacher à cent cheines de fer
> Le malheureux Discord aux abysmes d'Enfer
> (IX, 108)

and variations of this allegorical vision, often accompanied by the Hora-tian detail of the iron chains (*Odes*, III, iv, 79–80), are found throughout the verse of Ronsard (VIII, 250; IX, 132; XIII, 62, var.; XV, 350). The victory of Peace over Discord, however, remains tenuous and tempor-ary, and the allegory is seen to have a moral dimension in that not only does God release Discord from prison as a punishment

> Quand les pechez d'un peuple, ou les fautes d'un Roy,
> En rompant toute honte ont violé la Loy,
> Et le sang innocent la vengeance demande
> (IX, 108)

but Jupiter sent 'la méchante Discorde' in the form of the fratricidal Theban war followed by the Trojan conflict, in order to alleviate the burden of humanity on Earth after she had complained 'Du fais qui ... accabloit *son* échine si fort' (IX, 20–1). Discord makes frequent appear-ances in the verse of Ronsard, alternately seen in the undesirable com-pany of abstract personifications and gods symbolising upheaval (*Noise,*

Ire, Creinte, Propos, Colère, Vice, Mars) or worshipped by the evil Iron Age race of men prior to Justice's flight to heaven and to mankind's punishment by God (VI, 182; VIII, 53–4; IX, 132; XVIII, 137). Following his tendency to multiply his allegorical figures after the manner of the *Grands Rhétoriqueurs* and to integrate them into his cosmology as forces of preservation and order, Ronsard gives *Eternité* two deities—*Puissance* and *Vertu*—whose sole function is to combat Discord and ensure that the universe does not slip back into elemental chaos (VIII, 249–50), and for this vision the French poet owes as much to inconographical sources as to the passage of Marullus which is its immediate inspiration (cf. Lafeuille, pp. 46–53).

Allegorically conceived as a constant struggle between Peace and Discord, this stability of opposites not only conforms to a large corpus of contemporary scientific and philosophical writing (D. B. Wilson, 'Contraries . . .', pp. 351–68), but relates closely to the conception of Empedocles, who pictured all cosmic activity as a balance between Love, the principle of generation and order, and Strife, the principle of disorder and corruption. Thus Ronsard's 'Ainsi par l'amitié la vie s'entretient, / Et la mauvaise mort par la noise survient' (IX, 113) clearly has its ultimate philosophical authority in Empedocles' hypothesis as defined in recent neo-Platonic texts.[24] Indeed these two lines from Ronsard's *La Paix* (1559) form the conclusion to a lengthy movement which may well owe a more direct debt to a passage of Ficino (*Commentary on Plato's 'Symposium'*, p. 150), in which the Italian quotes the authority of Empedocles and illustrates the universal pattern of harmony and disharmony by reference to the humours in our bodies and the elements of the world. Ronsard also seeks correspondences between microcosm and macrocosm in his vision of the delicate order of *Amitié* and *Discord* in the universe, where an imperfect balance of the elements—a surfeit of one property[25]—is sufficient to upset the cosmic mechanism in the same way as a disturbance of bodily humours causes illness and death :

> . . . les astres du ciel . . .
> Sont tous remplis d'amour, & par luy s'entretiennent?
> Quand pour trop abonder, les elemens divers
> L'un à l'autre ont discord, tout ce grand Univers
> Languist en maladie, & nous montre par signe
> Qu'une hayne nouvelle offence la machine,
> . . .
> Ainsi quand les humeurs qui nostre corps composent
> En tranquille amitié dedans nous ne reposent,
> Mais en se hayssant, abondent en Discord :
> Lors vient la maladie, & bien souvent la mort,
> Si le bon medecin ne treuve la maniere
> Par art de les remettre en amitié premiere,

Ainsi par l'amitié la vie s'entretient,
Et la mauvaise mort par la noise survient.

(IX, 112–13. Cf. III, 24–5)

Similarly any variation or innovation in the established pattern of cosmic activity can disturb the precise balance of the world system, for its perfect functioning depends, it has been seen, on a disciplined hierarchy in which every part keeps rigidly to its allotted place and acts as a link in a chain which leads back to the Supreme Will. Man is introduced into the chain of being a little lower than the angels and is modelled on the same universal balance of opposing forces, being at once divine and animal, immortal and mortal, rational and sensual, spirit and body, good and evil (XI, 19–20; XV, 39–40; XVI, 285–6). This balance in the microcosm is as fragile as that in the macrocosm, for man's reason and insatiable intellectual curiosity constantly tempt him towards the divine and, determined to 'Decouvrir les secretz de Nature & des Cieux' (VIII, 246), he is ever ready to trespass beyond his allotted place in the scheme of creation and to commit the sin of the Giants. Indeed for Ronsard the very division of the universe into sublunar and extralunar worlds not only represents a line of demarcation between immortality and mortality, stability and flux, blissful serenity and misery (X, 308–9; XIII, 137), but, more significantly, he sees the division as a fundamental aspect of cosmic order, for it is designed to thwart man's ambitions to divinity and to restrain him within the prescribed limits of his condition :

Nostre mere Nature entre les Dieus & nous
Que fist Deucalion du get de ses caillous,
Mist la Lune au milieu qui nous sert de barriere,
A fin que des mortels l'imbecille lumiere
S'exerce à voir la terre, & d'art audacieux
N'assemble plus les monts pour espier les Cieux.[26]

The division of the universe into sublunar and extralunar worlds is a cosmological commonplace,[27] but the idea that the moon was specifically created to act as a barrier against human *hubris* and titanism would appear to be Ronsard's significant personal commentary on an accepted idea.

This relationship between *hubris* and sublunar flux will be further analysed during the course of this study, but a brief discussion of Ronsard's conception of Destiny will establish at this stage a general framework of reference and definition. Although Ronsard constantly tempers his vision by affirmations of free will and by periodic rejections of the more extreme consequences of astral fatalism,[28] he nevertheless sees Destiny and the stars, which hold 'es mains le fil des Destinées' (VIII,

154), as intermediaries of cosmic order through which the predetermined expression of the Divine Will is made manifest (VIII, 64; 153–4; 248; XV, 254; XVI, 42; XVII, 40). Destiny fulfils a command of God and Nature—whose functions and status Destiny appears to usurp on occasions[29]—and orders everything terrestrial to follow certain natural universal cycles encompassing birth, growth, maturity and death. Such cycles ensure that all things have a definite purpose and move towards a predetermined goal, and it is this which constitutes the perfection and stability of the sublunar world:

> Dequoy servent les fleurs, si les fruicts ne meurissent?
> Dequoy servent les bleds, si les grains ne jaunissent?
> Toute chose a sa fin, & tend à quelque but,
> Le destin l'a voulu, lors que ce Monde fut
> En ordre comme il est: telle est la convenance
> De Nature & de Dieu, par fatalle ordonnance.
>
> (XII, 44)

The moral implications for man of this 'fatalle ordonnance' are thoroughly investigated in the *Hymne des Astres* (1555). Here Ronsard insists that originally the stars 'n'avoient noz destins en soucy'; they were 'Eparses, sans vertu' (VIII, 151), and were not given their cosmic functions until after Jupiter's victory over the Giants, in which they played an important part. From the moment the stars were given 'le fil des Destinées' as a reward for services rendered during the war against the Titans,

> ... tous les oyseaux qui volent, & qui chantent,
> Tous les poissons muetz, qui les ondes frequentent,
> Et tous les animaux soit des champs, soit des bois,
> Soit des montz caverneux, furent serfz de leurs loix:
> Mais l'homme, *par sur tout,* eut sa vie sujette
> Aux destins que le Ciel par les Astres luy jette,
> L'homme, *qui le premier comprendre les osa,*
> Et telz noms qu'il voulut au Ciel leur composa.
>
> (VIII, 154)

So man *above all other creatures* is subjected to the rigorous law of Destiny. The reason for this is implied in the same passage by the use of the word *osa,* for man was the only creature in the world who dared to understand the secrets of the heavens, which are denied to him by virtue of his mortal condition. Thus, in seeking knowledge and status beyond that allowed by God, man committed the sin of *hubris*—a sin tainted with both pagan and Christian implications—and as a punishment he was emphatically subjected to the cosmic forces of order. In this passage there is the clear suggestion that Destiny is a weapon used by God and

His intermediary powers to ensure man's constant subordination within the world-pattern.

This is by no means an isolated statement of the close association between *hubris* and Ronsard's philosophic and moral conception of Destiny. In an ode of 1550 he had already developed two Horatian texts in order to condemn those who seek to interpret their individual destiny and to understand the divine mysteries which lie beyond their station, and he had illustrated this principle by the examples of Phaethon and Bellerophon (II, 109–10).

This relationship between Destiny and *hubris* is clarified and further emphasised in Phineus's speech to Jason in the *Hymne de Calaïs, et de Zetes* (1556). Here it is Destiny who has forbidden Phineus to foretell the future and to prophesy the fortunes which await man, just as in *La Franciade*, published sixteen years later, Juno personally intervenes to terminate Helenin's account (XVI, 83–6) and Hyante refuses to interpret all of the gods' meaning to Francus for fear of angering 'les puissances celestes' (XVI, 270). The heavens like their secrets well guarded and place obstacles in the path of human knowledge and progress so that man is forever suppliant and subordinated to their will. In this way Destiny is the cosmic force which refuses man the very information, the knowledge, which would enable him to challenge the Divinity and to transcend the limitations imposed on the human condition :

> Que vous diray-je plus? le destin me deffend
> De vous prophetiser voz fortunes de rang,
> Ny comment vous voirez vostre vie gardée
> Des arts Hecateans de la jeune Medée.
> J'ay peché lourdement autrefois de vouloir
> Faire aux hommes mortels de point en point sçavoir
> La volunté des Dieux, qui veullent leurs oracles
> Estre tousjours voilez de ne sçay quels obstacles,
> Et manques en partie, afin que les humains
> Dressent tousjours au Ciel & le cœur & les mains,
> Et qu'humbles envers Dieu, à Dieu secours demandent,
> Quand au sommet du chef les miseres leur pandent.
> (VIII, 285–6)

It is true, as Laumonier suggests, that the general tenor of these lines, like the greater part of the material for Ronsard's poem, comes from *The Argonautica* of Apollonius Rhodius,[30] but a close comparison of the Greek and French texts clearly shows that Ronsard has brought a subtle, but original and important, emphasis to a commonplace of Greek religious dogma which forbade the knowledge of the future to man. He insists heavily on the implications for mankind of such a decree and emphatically develops the idea of the human consequences of man's subservience to the gods (ll. 9–12 of quotation). The thought that Destiny ensures man's obedience to a cosmic pattern is foreign to the Greek text, the influence of which ends at line 7 of the French extract.

A poem of the 1584 edition returns to this association of Destiny and *hubris* in order to demonstrate why 'l'homme qui est humain, / Ne tient de Dieu le secret en la main' (xviii, 168). Although astrological influence receives a Christian justification in Ronsard's verse in that God is said to have written the individual destinies of all living creatures in the sky and the stars are the characters wherein we must read our fates, prophesy the future and interpret His will (viii, 159; xviii, 34–5; 168), nevertheless it is precisely because of the original sin of *hubris* and the fall from grace—because men are 'chargez de terre & du trespas'—that they are blind to the significance of the divine writing of the stars and to the mysteries of Heaven:

> ... les astres du ciel qui sont ses characteres,
> Les choses nous predit & bonnes & contraires:
> Mais les hommes chargez de terre & du trespas
> Mesprisent tel escrit, & ne le lisent pas.[31]

Whilst Ronsard's ideal society is nostalgically associated with the natural order of the Age of Gold,[32] he also establishes a more practical and contemporary social and political model based on the same principles which govern cosmic harmony. Indeed the same allegorical figures (Peace and Love) which stabilised chaos, promote cultural activity and ensure civil, social and political order (iii, 23–5; ix, 25; 111; xv, 101). Moreover, Ronsard accepts the hierarchical scheme of an ordered universe as the foundation of a well balanced social system in which each class, like each astral body, keeps rigidly to its allotted place: in the following lines this emphasis on cosmic and social order is supported on the stylistic level by the strong major structure of the simile (*car, comme ... Ainsi*) and by the cataloguing effect produced by the repeated pattern *au premier, au second, Au tiers, au quart*:

> ... car, comme en une ville
> Où chacun garde bien la police civile,
> On voit les Senateurs au premier rang marchans
> Tenir leur gravité, au second les Marchans,
> Au tiers les Artizans, au quart le Populace:
> Ainsi dedans le Ciel les astres ont leur place,
> Et leur propre degré, grands, petits, & moyens,
> De la maison du Ciel eternels citoyens.
>
> (x, 103)

In du Bellay's *Ample Discours au Roy sur le faict de ses quatre estats* (published 1567),[33] the Monarch is seen to serve the same function as the World Soul in a social context, for he stabilises and binds together the four different estates—Populace, Nobility, Justice and the Church— into a perfect unity and sets in motion the entire body politic:

> Le Prince, qui voudra regner heureusement,
> Liera ces quatre estats d'une telle harmonie,
> Que de ce grand esprit la puissance infinie
> Accorde l'univers, & luy l'esprit sera
> Qui mouvoir tout le corps egalement fera.
>
> (ll. 606–10)

The result, as in the universe, is a perfect balance of opposites, the harmony of which is not unlike a miniature version of the music of the spheres:

> Cestuy-la, qui voudroit, pour monstrer cest accord,
> Dire qu'il est semblable à l'accordant discord
> D'un Luth bien accordé, auroit par adventure
> Desseigné d'un tel corps la vive protraiture.[34]

Similarly society, like the world system, has its forces for preservation and cohesion, namely those institutions, beliefs and values which have the stabilising authority of tradition—the Monarchy, the Catholic Church and Law. The passage has already been quoted from du Bellay's *Ample Discours* in which the king is compared to a World Soul: elsewhere in the same *Discours* (ll. 23–32) his preservation of the harmonised diversity of the four estates of society is likened to the human body under the guidance of the head (reason). The four estates serve the same function as the four bodily humours, and society depends not only on each estate keeping to its allotted place and performing its specific role, but ultimately on the king's ability to nourish each part of the civil body so that its organism preserves a healthy and proportioned balance (ll. 49–58). In a text published in the same year (1567) Ronsard employs an identical image of the king as 'le chef, où la raison repose' in order to draw attention to the way his moral laxity can endanger the health of the entire social fabric, and, as in the cosmic context (IX, 112–13; quoted pp. 15–16), this developing illness is described in terms of a loss of vital motion and energy ('tout le corps ... se sent / Morne ou perclus, ou tombe en lethargie, / Et tout d'un coup perd la force & la vie': XIV, 186). Elsewhere du Bellay establishes correspondences between the workings of the cosmos and the ideal ruler of a just and ordered state by adapting a motif found originally in Plato. Throughout *The Republic* (cf. pars. 500E, 540A, 592) Plato had emphasised the idea that the perfect body politic must follow a pattern, an image, found in the heavens and to which the ideal ruler must relate for guidance. Plutarch borrows this

Platonic idea in his *Ad principem ineruditum* and develops it on several occasions by comparing the ruler to the divine light of the sun and moon: 'Now just as in the heavens God has established as a most beautiful image of himself the sun and the moon, so in states a ruler ...'[35] Castiglione is clearly indebted to this text of Plutarch for his own account of the ideal ruler in *Il Cortegiano*, IV, xxii. Du Bellay in his turn suggests the same idea in two posthumously published poems to Diane de Poitiers (1568),

La garde des provinces
Est en la main des Dieux,
Et l'image des Princes
Est peincte dans les cieux:
Dieu tourne à son plaisir
Les Rois & leur desir
(V, 367. Cf. V, 379)

and in both cases the contexts develop the comparison of the prince with the sun, moon and light in a manner reminiscent of Plutarch and Castiglione.[36] Ronsard too develops at length this cosmic and political association in his *Comparaison du Soleil & du Roy* of 1571 (XV, 349–51), and the same collection includes a *Cartel pour le Roy habillé en forme de Soleil* (XV, 352–3).

Like the Monarchy the established Church is a binding and stabilising power, and being 'le plus digne estat' it links the other three together 'D'une saincte musique & parfaite harmonie' (du Bellay, VI, 195), maintaining order by its laws and by the 'cement' of its unity:

«Tout Sceptre, & tout Empire, & toutes regions
«Fleurissent en grandeur par les religions,
«Et par elle ou en paix ou en guerre nous sommes,
«Car c'est le vray ciment qui entretient les hommes.
(Ronsard, XI, 84. Cf. XI, 138)

More particularly for Ronsard it is Law which restrains man's inconstancy and natural inclination to change and innovation. For man is a creature of flux, forever solicited by novelty to reject the established order of things (II, 1; XI, 65; XIII, 248–9). Public opinion—the sum total of this individual variability—is therefore characterised by its fickleness and instability: it is a 'monstre testu, divers en jugement', a 'monstrueux Prothé, qui se change à tous cous' (VII, 116). Thus, although we carry within us 'la Loy naturelle / Escrite dans nos cœurs par une encre eternelle' (XVIII, 86), it is the stabilising authority of civil law which has the task of regulating human conduct and controlling the inconstancy which is man's essential characteristic and the greatest threat to social cohesion. Apparent once again in the following extract are the aesthetic principles of movement and measure, of controlled energy, for the long complex sentence simultaneously receives its momentum and its unity and organisation from common stylistic features—the repetition of lexical and structural patterns, especially that of balanced pairing (*sert . . . au navire, . . . sert aux Citez & au peuple; Inconstant . . . & n'a jamais d'arrest . . . Et jamais . . . certains; aujourdhuy une opinion . . . Le l'ende-main une autre; qui volle . . . voleroient; Cà & là; qui est . . . qui volle . . . qui . . . bride*), the alternation of affirmative and negative verbs, and the linking *et* formula:

> Car cela de quoy sert un pillote au navire,
> La Loy sert aux Citez & au peuple qui est
> Inconstant en pensée, & n'a jamais d'arrest :
> Il auroit aujourdhuy une opinion folle,
> Le l'endemain une autre, & comme un vent qui volle
> Cà & là voleroient les espritz des humains,
> Et jamais ne seroient en un propos certains,
> Sans la divine Loy, qui leurs volontez bride,
> Et, maugré leur desir, à bon chemin les guide.[37]

This social order, like its cosmic model, remains fragile, however, and is constantly menaced by the same elements of instability which threat-ened the harmony of the universe, namely *hubris* and the danger of in-novation to the established authorities upon which society's preserva-tion largely depends. It is in Ronsard's polemic against the Reformist movement that these discordant aspects of *hubris* and novelty receive their clearest definition and their most emphatic and poetic interpreta-tion.

The Protestant Reformists are consistently associated with the sin of *hubris* in the verse of Ronsard, for they not only seditiously challenge the Monarchy—God's earthly representative—but arrogantly trespass on God's prerogatives and sanctity by presumptuously seeking to ex-plain His mysteries and secrets (XI, 64). The Protestants are referred to frequently as 'braves vanteurs controuvez fils de Dieu', 'arrogans & men-teurs', 'audacieux', 'vanteurs, & arrogans / Superbes' who have 'le cœur si haut, si superbe & si fier' and 'l'ame surprise / D'arogance & d'orgueil', and their heresy is invariably compared to that of the Giants.[38] Further-more their *outrecuidance* is illustrated by the developed allegory of Opinion,[39] the monster of discord fathered by the Divinity in anger

> . . . contre la race
> Des hommes, qui vouloient par curieuse audace
> Envoyer leurs raisons jusqu'au Ciel pour scavoir
> Les haults secrets divins que l'homme ne doit voir.
>
> (XI, 26)

Conceived by *Dame Presomption*, fostered by *Cuider* and educated by 'orgueil ... fantasie & ... jeunesse folle',[40] Opinion 'un Vuiclef aletta', 'un Jehan Hus enfanta', 'se logea sur le haut de la porte / De Luther son enfant' (XI, 78) and now frequents the Protestant Reformers in France, 'Afin de les punir d'estre trop curieux / Et d'avoir eschellé comme Geants les cieux' (XI, 27). It is this monster of *hubris* who is the sole cause not only of the social, religious and civil upheaval, but of the destruction of cosmic harmony and beauty. In the following passage references to the loss of the world's 'reigle & ... forme ancienne' clearly demonstrate that aesthetic considerations are never far from Ronsard's mind, whilst the rhetorical device of anaphora—*De là* (*vient que*)— here gives the verse its characteristic qualities of movement, rhythmical measure and structural stability:

> De là toute heresie au monde prist naissance,
> De là vient que l'Eglise a perdu sa puissance,
> De là vient que les Roys ont le Sceptre esbranlé,
> De là vient que le foyble est du fort violé,
> De là sont procedés ces Geants qui eschellent
> Le Ciel, & au combat les Dieux mesmes appellent,
> De là vient que le monde est plain d'iniquité,
> Remply de defiance, & d'infidelité,
> Ayant perdu sa reigle & sa forme ancienne.
>
> (XI, 81)

Similarly, although the political and religious conservativism of Ronsard is to some extent motivated by self-interest and expediency in that it is an expression of his financial and social dependence on the Church–State axis, it is also based on the conviction that innovation is of itself an element of disorder, 'Bref, tout se change en vent & en risée, / Quand des ayeulx la Loy est mesprisée'.[41] Neither is there any question of assimilating new institutions or of accepting a coexistence of diverse authorities and values, for in the social context as in the cosmic, unity is equated with harmony and order, plurality with disorder and anarchy (XVIII, 348). The Protestants demonstrate the full measure of their disruptive influence and the heresy of their beliefs by their internal divisions of opinion and the diversity of their sects (XI, 49–50; 65–6). Thus, when the traditional authorities and stabilising forces (Law, Religion, the Monarchy) are questioned in the name of *hubris* and overthrown in favour of novelty and change, the result is a diseased society (XV, 159–60).

Using vocabulary which clearly parallels that found in cosmological contexts, Ronsard explains that by 'Rompant toute amitié, & denouant la corde / Qui tenoit doucement les peuples en concorde'[42] the Reformers

have broken society's cohesive strength : the binding knot and the hierarchical chain are destroyed, and nothing keeps to its allotted place :
'Et tout à l'abandon va sans ordre & sans loy' (XI, 28). There is a total
dislocation of the civil order; values are inverted and normality turned
upside down :

> Le monde, ensorcelé de vaine piperie,
> Ne pourra resister : tout va de pis en pis
> Et tout est renversé des grands jusqu'aux petits !
>
> (XI, 79. Cf. XII, 298)

People do not keep to their social class :

> . . . le pompeux habit
> D'un gentilhomme, au bourgeois interdit,
> Pare un marchant
>
> (XV, 159)

or perform the functions for which they are destined :

> L'artizan . . . a laissé sa boutique,
> Le pasteur ses brebis, l'advocat sa pratique,
> Sa nef le marinier, sa foyre le marchand,
> Et par luy le preudhomme est devenu meschant.
>
> (XI, 28. Cf. XI, 93)

Family ties are forgotten and the social contract broken, as if a new Age
of Iron had returned :

> . . . le fils fait la guerre à son pere,
> La femme à son mary, & le frere à son frere,
> A l'oncle le nepveu.[43]

Vices have upended the world,

> Au vice desreiglé la licence est permise,
> Le desir, l'avarice, & l'erreur incensé
> Ont sans-dessus-dessoubs le monde renversé
>
> (XI, 28–9)

so that nothing is what it seems ('le faux controuvé semble estre verité :
XI, 93. Cf. XI, 98; 100; 165), and identities and values are confused ('Le
crocheteur s'egalle au citoyen' : XV, 153).

The disorder, however, is not restricted to the social or moral spheres
or limited to forceful descriptions of the carnage of war (cf. XI, 37; 56–7),
but is extended into the sympathetic natural world and finally attains

cosmic proportions. Famine, plague, flood, tempest, inexplicable meteorological and astrological apparitions, monstrous deformities at birth, premature deaths, perversions of human conduct: these all herald and accompany the social disorder and, in a vision in which Old Testament theology mingles with reminiscences from Ovid and Virgil, Ronsard sees this total dislocation of the physical world as an expression of divine displeasure and as a punishment for man's sin. Evident once more in these lines is the now familiar tendency to accumulate and repeat structures, often linked by the *et* formula, and here these gather momentum with increasing density (*le Soleil; & la Lune; La Seine; La nourrice Ceres; Le bon Pere . . . & Pales; Et le sel; La famine & la guerre & la peste*) before the final resolution of the sentence is reached:

> . . . le Soleil de despit
> Abominant la Terre, en vestit noir habit:
> Il se rouilla la face, & la Lune argentée
> De taches eust long temps sa corne ensanglantée.
> La Seine oultre ses bords sa rage deslia,
> La nourrice Ceres son bled nous denya,
> Le bon Pere ses vins, & Pales son herbage,
> Et le sel si commun nous nya son usage:
> La famine & la guerre & la peste ont monstré
> Que Dieu avoit son peuple en fureur rencontré.[44]

Even the natural elements are seen to be in revolt against the Reformers (XVII, 408–11): cosmic harmony is itself threatened: 'La Guerre, le Discord, meinte Secte diverse, / Et le monde esbranlé tomber à la renverse' (XIII, 104). Wearied by twenty years of continuous civil strife interspersed with meaningless truces and peace negotiations (XVIII, 37), one of Ronsard's final visions is of the world's return to its primal state of chaos, for it is as if God, having demonstrated his love of order and peace by creating cosmos from elemental confusion (XI, 65),

> . . . vouloit punir en son ire,
> Faire un autre Chaos, & son œuvre destruire
> Par le fer, par la peste, & embrazer le sein
> De l'air, pour étouffer le pauvre genre humain.
> (XVIII, 39–40)

It is within this cosmic and social context of flux and stability—and within an associated common core of preoccupations (the microcosm-macrocosm relationship, the concept of *hubris*, the cycle of creation, preservation and destruction, aspects of movement and lethargy and other richly suggestive antithetical patterns)—that certain recurrent themes of Ronsard's poetry, which have been gathered under the headings of Change, Fortune, Time and Death, receive their full significance. At the same time it has become clear that aesthetic matters are central to Ronsard's considerations, and certain creative principles, already seen to be at work in his verse (movement and measure, accumulation and order, controlled energy), will receive a more precise definition and further illustration in the following chapter within the context of this same idea of a harmony of opposites, a *discordia concors*.

NOTES TO CHAPTER ONE

1 On Ronsard's cosmology, see especially H. Busson, 'Sur la philosophie de Ronsard', *Revue des Cours et des Conférences*, XXXI (1929–30), 32–48, 172–85; *Le Rationalisme dans la littérature française de la Renaissance* (1533–1601), 2nd edn. (Paris, 1957), pp. 362–92; A.–M. Schmidt, *La Poésie scientifique en France au seizième siècle* (Paris, 1938), pp. 71–107; I. Silver, 'Ronsard's Reflections on Cosmogony and Nature', *PMLA*, LXXIX (1964), 219–33; 'Ronsard's Reflections on the Heavens and Time', *PMLA*, LXXX (1965), 344–64; G. Lafeuille, *Cinq hymnes de Ronsard* (Geneva, 1973); L. Keller, *Palingène, Ronsard, Du Bartas. Trois études sur la poésie cosmologique de la Renaissance* (Bern, 1974), pp. 61–106.

2 Cf. Ronsard, I, 19; III, 5–7; IX, 107.

3 IV, 45, s. XLII; XII, 27–8; XIII, 218; XVI, 142. Cf. Hesiod, *Theogony*, l. 116ff.; Plato, *Timaeus*, 29A–31A; *Symposium*, 178A–B; *Marsilio Ficino's Commentary on Plato's 'Symposium'*. The Text and a Translation, with an Introduction by S. R. Jayne (Columbia, University of Missouri, 1944), Speech I, chapt. 3. On the cosmogonic role of Eros in Ronsard, see I. Silver, *The Intellectual Evolution of Ronsard*: vol. I, *The Formative Influences* (St Louis, Washington Univ. Press, 1969), pp. 189–95. For the Platonic influence in the Pléiade's accounts of creation, consult R. V. Merrill and R. J. Clements, *Platonism in French Renaissance Poetry* (New York Univ. Press, 1957), chapt. I.

4 F. Solmsen, *Aristotle's System of the Physical World* (Ithaca, Cornell Univ. Press, 1960), index of topics: *Elements* and *Transformation of elements*.

5 Baïf, II, 4; du Bellay, II, 282, s. XXXIII; V, 38; Ronsard, III, 6. Cf. Horace, 'concordia discors' (*Epist.*, I, xii, 19); Ovid, 'discors concordia' (*Metam.*, I, 433); Manilius, 'discordia concors' (*Astronomica*, I, 142). Cf. Seneca, *Naturales Quaestiones*, VII, xxvii, 4. On this question, see Merrill and Clements, *Platonism . . .*, pp. 4–10, and Ronsard, XIX, 110.

6 VIII, 142–4. Cf. III, 75; VIII, 251. For the cosmological idea of line 9 of the quotation, cf. Plato, *Timaeus*, 36D; 38C–39B; *Republic*, X, 617A; Aristotle, *De Caelo*, II (especially chapters iii–vi, viii, x, xii); Pliny, *Natural History*, II, vi; Cicero, *Somnium Scipionis, De Re Publica*, VI, 17. Ronsard could have found the idea of the dance of the heavenly bodies under their choragus (God) in pseudo-Aristotle, *De Mundo*, VI, 399a 12–21. It is a figure which appears frequently in Ronsard's verse in such contexts (see P. Moreau, 'Ronsard et la danse des astres', in *Mélanges d'histoire littéraire (XVIe–XVIIe siècle) offerts à Raymond Lebègue* (Paris, 1969), pp. 75–82). For other references to the harmony of the spheres in Ronsard, cf. III, 6; 75; VIII, 91; XVIII, 480–2. This idea is found in Plato, *Timaeus*, 35Bff.; *Republic*, X, 617B–C (cf. Cicero, *Somnium Scipionis, De Re Publica*, VI, 18–19): it is hotly contested by Aristotle, *De Caelo*, II, ix, 290b12–291a9. Pliny, *Nat. Hist.*, II, iii, 6, is sceptical.

On this question, consult I. Silver, 'Ronsard's Reflections on the Heavens and Time', pp. 355–7.

7 References to the Platonic Eros, XIII, 218; XV, 101; 115; XVI, 142. Cf. Plato, *Timaeus*, 29A–31A; *Symposium*, 178A–B; Ficino, *Commentary on Plato's 'Symposium'*, pp. 149–50, 152–3; Leone Ebreo, *Dialoghi d'Amore* (second dialogue); Castiglione, *Il Cortegiano*, IV, lxx. References to cosmic role of Bacchus, V, 74; VI, 190. Cf. Marullus, *Hymni*, I, vi, *Baccho*, ll. 49–54. On Ronsard's Bacchic verse, see T. Cave, 'The Triumph of Bacchus and its interpretation in the French Renaissance: Ronsard's *Hinne de Bacus*', in *Humanism in France at the end of the Middle Ages and in the early Renaissance*: edited by A. H. T. Levi (Manchester Univ. Press, 1970), pp. 249–70; 'Ronsard's Bacchic poetry: from the *Bacchanales* to the *Hymne de l'autonne*', *L'Esprit Créateur*, X (1970), 104–16.

8 J. Moreau, *L'Ame du monde de Platon aux Stoïciens* (Paris, 1939). For the ideas of Cardano and Pomponazzi in this and other respects, see Busson, *Le Rationalisme*, pp. 46–64, 212–20; H. Weber, *La Création poétique au XVIe siècle en France* (2 vols., Paris, 1956), vol. I, pp. 44–6.

9 *Les Amours de P. de Ronsard Vandomois, commentées par Marc Antoine de Muret*. Nouvelle édition publiée d'après le texte de 1578 par Hugues Vaganay (Paris, 1910), p. 55.

10 XV, 39–40. A. W. Satterthwaite, *Spenser, Ronsard, and du Bellay: a Renaissance Comparison* (New Jersey, Princeton Univ. Press, 1960), pp. 227–8, stresses the devotional nature of these lines: however, he seems oblivious of the deeper philosophical implications of this poem, and is unaware of other interpretations by Busson, pp. 384–8; Schmidt, p. 102; and Weber, vol. I, pp. 45–6.

11 *The Universe of Pontus de Tyard*, edition by J. C. Lapp (Ithaca, Cornell Univ. Press, 1950), pp. 143–4. Ficino, *Commentary on Plato's 'Symposium'*, Speech IV, chapt. v, refers to certain impious men (Marcus Varro and Marcus Manilius) who have sinned by identifying God with 'a kind of World-Soul'.

12 XVI, 284–5. Cf. Manilius, *Astronomica*, IV, 880–9. Du Bellay (VI, 440–2) translates these Latin lines for Le Roy's commentary on Plato's *Symposium* of 1558. Jamyn is quoted by Laumonier in his edition of Ronsard, XVI, 17–18. On the theory of man as microcosm, see G. P. Conger, *Theories of macrocosms and microcosms in the history of philosophy* (New York, 1922).

13 XI, 67; XII, 38–41. Cf. G. Gadoffre, 'Ronsard et le thème solaire', in *Le Soleil à la Renaissance: sciences et mythes* (Brussels and Paris, 1965), pp. 501–18.

14 *De Generatione et Corruptione*, II, 10. Cf. Solmsen, pp. 393–4, 422, 424–6, 436.

15 XI, 66–7. Cf. XII, 33; 38; 52–3. Besides the Pliny text noted above, see also the influence of *Nat. Hist.*, II, iii, 9, in the extract from the *Remonstrance*.

16 VIII, 68. Note also the influence of Ovid, *Metam.*, I, 32–75, and Psalm CIII (Vulgate). Pliny's presence is seen not only in Ronsard's pantheism, but he also refers to the world's beauty (*Nat. Hist.*, II, iii, 8) in exactly the same terms as the French text (ll. 459–60). Moreover, in the following lines 472–6, Ronsard suggests that the mythological divinities are personifications of God's 'divers effectz' (same idea, XIV, 6; XVI, 345), and this may well be a distant echo of Pliny's discussion of the single Deity and multiple deities in *Nat. Hist.*, II, v, 14–27.

17 VIII, 94. Cf. III, 126; IX, 60–1; XII, 85; XVII, 335, s. LVI. On the theory of Thales, see Aristotle, *Metaphysics*, I, iii, 983b22; *De Caelo*, II, xiii, 294a 28–31; Seneca, *Naturales Quaestiones*, III, xiii–xiv. Thales's idea that the earth floats on water is echoed in Ronsard, III, 74. Cf. Silver, 'Ronsard's Reflections on Cosmogony and Nature', pp. 220–1.

18   IV, 69–70, S. LXVIII; XII, 238–9; XV, 371–2.

19   *Metaphysics*, XII, vi–vii, 1071b3–1073a13. Cf. *Physics*, VIII, v–vi, 256a4–259b1. Cf. Solmsen, pp. 222–49. On this aspect see also Silver, 'Ronsard's Reflections on the Heavens and Time', pp. 347–50.

20   Richelet's commentary note quoted by Laumonier, VIII, 90, n.2.

21   XI, 135. Cf. VIII, 246; IX, 159. The idea that God's power is demonstrated by the ordered heavens and the miracle of creation, is a biblical commonplace (cf. Psalms 18.1–7; 32.5–9; 103; 135.4–9). On this theme in Ronsard, see A. Py, *Ronsard* (Paris, 1972), pp. 38–41, 87.

22   XVII, 80, var. Cf. VIII, 148. On this Homeric myth and its fortunes, see P. Lévêque, *Aurea catena Homeri: une étude sur l'allégorie grecque* (Paris, 1959). For the associated idea of the 'chain of being', see A. Lovejoy, *The Great Chain of Being* (Cambridge, Harvard Univ. Press, 1936); E. M. W. Tillyard, *The Elizabethan World Picture* (Harmondsworth, Penguin Books, 1963), pp. 37–102.

23   IX, 33. Cf. XVI, 284. Ronsard's emphasis on the embrace of the elements is developed from Pliny, *Nat. Hist.*, II, iv, 10–11, especially, '. . . air—this is the principle of life, and penetrates all the universe and is intertwined (*consertum*) with the whole; . . . Thus the mutual embrace (*mutuo conplexu*) of the unlike results in an interlacing (*nexum*)' : LCL, vol. I, p. 177.

24   *Philosophie d'Amour de M. Leon Hebreu, Traduicte . . . par le Seigneur du Parc* (Lyon, 1551), pp. 143–4; Tyard, *Le Premier Curieux* in *The Universe of Pontus de Tyard*, pp. 56–7. Cf. also a passage from Pico della Mirandola's commentary on a love song by Benivieni in *Opere di Girolamo Benivieni . . .* (Venice, Zopino & Vincentio, 1522), fol. 22. On Empedocles' theory of Love and Strife, see D. O'Brien, *Empedocles' Cosmic Cycle* (Cambridge Univ. Press, 1969), especially chapts. 5 and 6.

25   Cf. *Philosophie d'Amour de M. Leon Hebreu*, p. 410 : '. . . car la corruption vient par la superation d'un des contraires . . .'.

26   XVIII, 97. The entire poem is centred on the theme of *hubris* and contains references to Phaethon and Icarus (ll. 95–108).

27   Cf. Aristotle, *Metaphysics*, XII (especially, vi–x); pseudo-Aristotle, *De Mundo*, VI, 397b10–401a11; F. Vicomercato, *In eam partem duodecimi libri metaphys. Aristotelis . . .* (Paris, 1551), p. 6; Lucretius, III, 18–30; Claudian, *De Raptu Proserpinae*, II, 294–9; Cicero, *Somnium Scipionis*, *De Re Publica*, VI, 17.

28   Like Ficino, whose attitude is typical of sixteenth century humanists in this respect (J. Seznec, *La Survivance des dieux antiques* (London, 1940), p. 60), Ronsard limits astrological influence to the body, and by emphasising the liberty of the soul, he allows man free will (VIII, 154; XVII, 40). He restricts the power of the stars to man's birth, giving him moral responsibility for his conduct throughout life (VIII, 160; XVI, 225), and makes an orthodox and emphatic defence of man's 'franc arbitre' in the *Franciade* (XVI, 224–5). He acknowledges God's right to intervene and cancel the decrees of Destiny (VIII, 154), and thereby achieves a definition of divine grace. He recognises that the superstitious belief in omens and presages is a mark of ignorance, and praises Philosophy for revealing Nature's secrets and for explaining cosmic phenomena in a way that calms the terrors of man's imagination (VIII, 90–2). In 1569 he categorically denies the influence of the stars on the destiny of empires and human affairs, and traces the destruction of kingdoms to a set of natural causes (XV, 160–1), whilst in 1575—the same year as he publishes *Les Estoilles!*—he attacks astrologers and their interpretations of Destiny (XVII, 79–80). On this question see also Schmidt, pp. 87–92; D. B. Wilson, *Ronsard, Poet of Nature* (Manchester Univ. Press, 1961), pp. 5–8 and chapt. IV.

29 Cf. Schmidt, p. 87; Wilson, pp. 4, 7. Destiny appears to occupy the position usually reserved for Nature, that of second-in-command to God (xv, 254; xvi, 42), and in the *Hymne des Astres* Jupiter unequivocally places Nature under the control of Destiny and the stars (viii, 154). For the cosmic role of Nature, see below, pp. 39–45.

30 *The Argonautica*, LCL, 1921, pp. 123, 129. These ideas have no equivalent in the account of Phineus's prophecy in Valerius Flaccus, *Argonautica*, iv, 553–624, which is largely imitated from the Greek poem of Apollonius and which Laumonier suggests as a secondary source for Ronsard's *Hymne*. Similar ideas to those expressed by Ronsard and Apollonius can also be found in Virgil, *Aeneid*, iii, 374–80. On the more general question of Ronsard's debt to Apollonius Rhodius throughout his work, see I. Silver, *Ronsard and the Hellenic Renaissance in France*, vol. i: *Ronsard and the Greek Epic* (St Louis, Washington Univ. Press, 1961), pp. 346–412.

31 xviii, 35. Similarly it is on God's authority that man's destiny is written in the lines of his hands and face, but he is not allowed to interpret them (viii, 159).

32 G. Demerson, 'Le mythe des Ages et la conception de l'ordre dans le lyrisme de la Pléiade', in *Humanism in France*, pp. 271–94, has shown that the Pléiade frequently emphasise aspects of social, moral and political order in their interpretations of the Age of Gold myth. On this myth, see especially E. Armstrong, *Ronsard and the Age of Gold* (Cambridge Univ. Press, 1968). Cf. also, Lafeuille, pp. 91–9, 124–6.

33 vi, 189–237. Du Bellay has been included at this stage because certain of his texts—and especially the *Ample Discours*—will enable us to define more precisely this association of cosmic and social perspectives. For other implications of this same correspondence in the sixteenth century, see H. Leclerc, 'Du Mythe platonicien aux fêtes de la Renaissance: 'L'Harmonie du Monde'. Incantation et Symbolisme', *Revue d'Histoire du Théâtre*, xi (1959), pp. 115, 131, 146; M. McGowan, *L'Art du ballet de cour en France*: 1581–1643 (Paris, 1963), pp. 159, 249; Tillyard, pp. 108–11.

34 Lines 43–6. The idea that an ideal society should be based on a balance of opposite forces is not uncommon in contemporary political writers: cf. Jean Bodin, *La Méthode de L'Histoire*, in *Œuvres Philosophiques de Jean Bodin*, vol. i: texte établi, traduit et publié par P. Mesnard (Paris, 1951), p. 412.

35 *Plutarch's Moralia*, vol. x: LCL, 1936, p. 59. Cf. also, pp. 65, 69.

36 v, 368–71, ll. 25–6, 67–72, 83, 97–108; v, 378–9, ll. 10, 20, 31–40. On these texts of Du Bellay and their sources, see Merrill and Clements, *Platonism* . . . , pp. 40–1. For this comparison between royal power and the sun, see also H. Leclerc, 'Du Mythe platonicien aux fêtes de la Renaissance', pp. 131–2, 166, 168.

37 viii, 69–70. Cf. viii, 95–6; xviii, 459–60. For an account of human conduct when man exchanges law for liberty, see xv, 381.

38 Cf. xi, 27; 36 (var.); 37 (var.); 46 (var.); 56; 81; 96; xv, 37; 159; 225; xvii, 5; xviii, 3 (var.). In the same way the nobles who side with the Protestants have lost their former 'simplicité' and 'humilité' and are tainted with the same sin of *hubris* and ambition (xi, 89).

39 Cf. xi, 26–9; 76–80. On this allegory, see J. Pineaux, 'Transformations protestantes d'un thème ronsardien: La naissance d'Opinion, fille de Jupiter et de Présomption', *CAIEF*, x (1958), 30–43. On the wider question of Ronsard's political poetry, consult F. M. Higman, 'Ronsard's political and polemical poetry', in *Ronsard the Poet*, pp. 241–85, and its bibliographical references.

40   XI, 26. 'La présomption et l'orgueil ... sont les caractères essentiels du Cuider' (Laumonier's note).

41   XV, 153. For statements concerning Ronsard's conservatism and his suspicion of innovation, cf. VI, 42; 195; X, 352; 355–6; XI, 7; 20–1; 45; 67; 133; 137–9; 144; XIII, 130. For du Bellay, historical example demonstrates that the transience of former kingdoms is due to novelty, and, more precisely, to the weakening of religious authority (III, 19; VI, 219).

42   XI, 148–9. The lexis (amitié, concorde) and the metaphor of love as the 'perpetual knot and binder of the world' (cf. Ficino, Commentary on Plato's 'Symposium', p. 152) are commonly associated with the cosmogonic role of Eros in the Pléiade's verse (cf. Ronsard, IX, 112–13; du Bellay, V, 38; Baïf, I, 17 (I); II, 77–9; 100–1; 224; Jodelle, II, 25–6; Belleau, I, 142; 143; 216).

43   XI, 81. Cf. XI, 28; 133. Source of idea in St Matthew 10.21, 35; Lucan, Pharsalia, II, 148–51; Virgil, Georgics, II, 510; Ovid, Metam., I, 144–8. For Iron Age vision in similar terms, cf. Ronsard, VI, 206; XII, 89.

44   XVII, 77. Cf. Exodus 32; Ovid, Metam., XV, 785–90; Virgil, Georgics, I, 463ff., especially ll. 466–8, 481–3. Also, Horace, Odes, I, ii. Similar visions in Ronsard, IX, 108–9; X, 359; XI, 21; 24–5; XVIII, 39–40; 165–8.

CHAPTER TWO

Ronsard and the concept of change

Whilst there is a continuing interest in the human consequences of change throughout the entire corpus of Ronsard's work, the most developed and poetically sustained expression of this concept appears in a poem of his maturity, the *Discours a Maistre Juliain Chauveau* of 1569 (retitled *Discours de l'alteration et change des choses humaines* in the 1584 edition), for it is here that many of his most consistent attitudes and obsessions are introduced as well as the widest range of his source material and visions. After an opening movement (xv, 152–4) evoking the social upheaval caused by the enfeeblement of the traditional stabilities of Law and the Church, there is a passage in which Ronsard defines mortality in terms of a transformist philosophy of matter (already poetically prefigured in line 36: 'Ny de renaistre au double par sa mort'):

«Tout est mortel, tout vieillist en ce monde,
«L'Air, & le Feu, la Terre mere & l'Onde
«Contre la mort resister ne pourront,
«Et vieillissant comme nous ilz mourront.
Le Temps mangeard toute chose consomme,
Villes, chateaux, Empires: voire l'home,
L'home à qui Dieu a promis sa maison,
Qui pense, parle & discourt par raison,
Duquel l'esprit s'envole outre la nuë,
Changeant sa forme en une autre se muë.
    Il est bien vray qu'à parler proprement,
On ne meurt point, on change seulement
De forme en autre, & ce changer s'apelle
Mort, quand on prend autre forme nouvelle.
                            (ll. 45–58)

The multiple textual reminiscences from Ovid throughout this *Discours*—so precisely catalogued by Laumonier in his excellent notes—

suggest that the central ideas and illustrations of this passage, although Aristotelian in origin, are primarily inspired from *Metamorphoses*, xv, where the Pythagorean doctrine of metempsychosis is expounded. As Laumonier has shown Ronsard's opening lines invert the order of Ovid where an imprecation against devouring Time and envious Age (ll. 234–6) precedes a passage (ll. 237–51) demonstrating the ever-changing, incessantly-renewing, pattern of the four elements. Similarly Ronsard's reference to the disappearance of cities and empires is a condensed borrowing of *Metamorphoses*, xv, 420–30, whilst the association of death with change and the cyclic regeneration of matter is based on the same Ovidian text, and especially line 165, 'All things are changing; nothing dies,' and lines 252–8:

Nothing retains its own form; but Nature, the great renewer, ever makes up forms from other forms. Be sure there's nothing perishes in the whole universe; it does but vary and renew its form. What we call birth is but a beginning to be other than what one was before; and death is but cessation of a former state. Though, perchance, things may shift from there to here and here to there, still do all things in their sum total remain unchanged.

(LCL, 1916, vol. ii, pp. 377, 383)

Although Ovid is clearly the principal source for Ronsard's transformist vision here, the possible secondary influences of Seneca and, more especially, of Lucretius, need to be recorded in this respect. Both here in the *Discours* and elsewhere in Ronsard's other numerous statements of this philosophy of change, there may well be an assimilation of passages from the *De rerum natura*—a presentation copy of which was in the poet's possession, complete with the signature of the editor, Lambinus.[1]

In spite of this assimilation of essentially Ovidian material, on close analysis it will be seen that Ronsard establishes a distinctive originality both in these verses quoted above and in the wider context of the *Discours*. He emphatically condenses the lengthy Latin developments, rejecting at this stage the detailed description of the intermovements of the elements and the theme of *translatio imperii* in favour of an original development specifically designed to define the relationship between the human condition and this philosophy of change. This departure from his source is by no means accidental, for one of Ronsard's constant considerations is to integrate microcosm with macrocosm, to seek correspondences and links of sympathy between man and those forces of flux in the universe which threaten to engulf him, and his ability to achieve such a fusion will frequently be seen to determine his mood of optimism or momentary pessimism and will partially explain the duality or tension in his work to which reference was made in the introduction. In this passage, for example, the melancholy reflections on death and time are swiftly alleviated by introducing man into the whole transformist pattern of the world, by submitting him to a wider cosmic scheme of changing forms and enduring matter. Moreover, by mitigating the pagan materialism of his sources by prudent religious details, Ronsard finds further consolation for mankind and strikes an acceptable compromise between classical doctrine and orthodox Christian belief.

In the following lines of the *Discours* Ronsard continues to find consolation in this philosophical alliance of change and death, and insists both on Christianising his material and emphasising the naturalness of these transformist cycles by copious illustrations from Ovid.[2] In utilising his source material, however, Ronsard constantly demonstrates independence and originality, nowhere more in evidence than in his adaptation of lines 372–4 of Ovid's text, 'And worms that weave their white cocoons on the leaves of trees (a fact well known to country-folk) change into funereal butterflies' (LCL, vol. II, p. 391), where Ronsard found the example of the silk worm which assumes numerous forms during its pattern of change from an egg to a butterfly. Here Ovid provides nothing more than the basic idea and his remark in parenthesis was sufficient to sharpen Ronsard's memory and to evoke a scene from his personal communion with nature. The following description (ll. 65–78) owes none of its picturesque detail or its visual realism to classical reminiscence, but springs almost entirely from the poet's observation and experience. Here too a subtle use of lexis (*fasché, ennuyé de soy, se faschant*) betrays a fundamental attitude of Ronsard, who clearly equates movement and change with life and interest, whilst immobility is associated with boredom, 'tiredness' and death :

> Voys-tu le Ver, honneur de la Touraine,
> Qui de sa bouche avecq les piedz ameine
> Le fil sur fil en tirant allongé?
> Estoit un œuf, qui en ver s'est changé :
> Apres avoir vomy toute sa soye
> (Qu'un bon ouvrier en meinte estroite voye
> Doibt joindre à l'or pour les habitz d'un Roy),
> Ce ver fasché, comme ennuyé de soy,
> Soudain se change, & vole par les prées
> Fait papillon aux æles diaprées
> De rouge, verd, azur & vermillon.
> Puis se faschant d'estre tant papillon
> Devient chenille & pond des œufs, pour faire
> Que par sa mort il se puisse refaire.

After a prudent repudiation (ll. 87–94) of the Pythagorean theory of metempsychosis as expressed in *Metamorphoses*, XV, Ronsard returns to this Ovidian text for inspiration in lines which attain a genuine epic and heroic quality and which embrace, within the broadening canvas of illustration and a wide temporal framework of alternating present and past tenses, a whole philosophy of history. What characterises these lines too is their abundance and energy, qualities imparted to the verse by the several imperative and interrogative forms (*Leve . . . Voy . . . Voy . . . Qu'est devenu?*), by the multiplicity of examples within the two major areas of flux—natural phenomena and empires—and by the constant tendency to embroider and accumulate by means of simile (lines 12–14, 20–1 of the quotation), periphrasis (ll. 15–19), visual detail and repeated patterning of structural and lexical items (most evident in lines 23–4, but note also *Voy . . . C'estoient jadis . . . Voy . . . Ce fut jadis; Cela n'est pas . . . Car c'est; de Nature & de Dieu; en sa force & vigueur; en vieillesse & langueur; Ce grand, ce fort, cet Empire; Ou vent ou foudre; De tant d'honeurs . . . de tant de villes . . . De tant de mers, de portz & de rivieres; de sa perte, / Et de sa plume; du grand . . . le petit; s'amoindrir & faillir*):

> Leve, Chauveau, de tous costez les yeux,
> Voy ces rochers au front audacieux,
> C'estoient jadis des plaines fromenteuses :
> Voy d'autre part ces grands ondes venteuses,
> Ce fut jadis terre ferme, où les bœufz
> Alloient paissant par les patiz herbeux,
> Ainsy la forme en une autre se change,
> Cela n'est pas une merveille estrange,
> Car c'est la loy de Nature & de Dieu,
> Que rien ne soit perdurable en un lieu.
> Qu'est devenu l'Empire d'Assyrie?
> Du Mede & Grec? Come une herbe fleurie,
> Qui trois mois dure en sa force & vigueur :
> Ilz sont tombez en vieillesse & langueur.
> Cette merveille espouvantable au Monde,
> Qui commandoit des le rivage où l'onde
> De l'Ocean baigne le bord Anglois,
> Jusques au bord des vieux peuples Indois,
> Ce grand, ce fort, cet Empire de Rome
> Est trebuché de sa grandeur, & come
> Ou vent ou foudre en la Terre passa,
> Qui de ses mains luy mesmes se cassa,
> Car nul que luy ne le pouvoit desfaire,
> N'autre que luy ne le sçauroit refaire :
> Lors s'espanchant un si large monceau,
> Du sceptre bas chacun prist son morceau,
> Si que les Rois de l'Europe, couverte
> De tant d'honeurs, sont riches de sa perte,
> Et de sa plume un chacun se vestit :

«Ainsy du grand s'enrichist le petit.
Le Turc, seigneur de tant de villes fieres,
De tant de mers, de portz & de rivieres,
Qui ose seul une Europe assaillir,
Doibt quelque jour s'amoindrir & faillir.

The first six lines of the passage may have been suggested by similar ideas in Horace (*Ars Poetica*, ll. 63–8) and Seneca (*Epist.*, LXXI, 15; XCI, 11), but it is much more likely, in view of the similarity of structure ('Voy . . . voy . . . C'estoient jadis . . . ce fut jadis'; and 'Vidi ego, quod fuerat . . . vidi . . . quodque fuit . . . eque . . . quaeque . . .'), that they are inspired, as Laumonier remarks, from *Metamorphoses*, XV, 259–72, and especially, 'I have myself seen what once was solid land changed into sea; and again I have seen land made from the sea . . . What once was a level plain, down-flowing waters have made into a valley; and hills by the force of floods have been washed into the sea. What was once marsh is now a parched stretch of dry sand, and what once was dry and thirsty now is a marshy pool' (LCL, vol. II, p. 383). Ovid also provides Ronsard's second definition of the transformist philosophy of matter (ll. 7–10 of the extract), which is here restated in such a way that the themes of nature's mutations and the flux of empires evoke no deep feeling of disaster, for cyclic regeneration is seen as part of a natural process, and as such should inspire admiration not fear. It is in the same spirit that Ronsard discounts the influence of the stars on the duration and destruction of empires later in the *Discours* (ll. 169–88), and instead relates their destiny to the same natural pattern of growth and decay as that governing trees. Again, whilst the *translatio imperii* theme and the *ubi sunt?* formula are commonplace aspects of classical and medieval literature,[3] in the context of such persistent Ovidian influence it is doubtlessly, as Laumonier states, from *Metamorphoses*, XV, 420–35, that Ronsard takes the essential ideas, although not the actual details, for the final movement of the extract.

Once more, however, Ronsard takes little beyond his general arguments from Ovid and his original contribution is considerable. For example the 'plaines' become 'fromenteuses', and the image of the cows grazing in the fields and the comparison between the 'herbe fleurie' and the duration of kingdoms—distantly suggested by biblical texts (Psalm 101.5, 12; 102.15; Job 8.11–12)—give visual and poetic colour to a basic principle borrowed from Ovid. Indeed much of the detail of the Latin passages is sacrificed in order that Ronsard can develop the example of Rome as a more accessible and evocative symbol of the transience of empires, before closing with a prophetic allusion to the contemporary strength of the Turks. Although it is true that Ovid also mentions the Roman Empire (ll. 431–5), the French poet is primarily using du Bellay's

Antiquitez de Rome as a source for his reflections on the destiny of the Eternal City in the latter half of the extract. His description of the immensity of Rome (ll. 15–18 of the quotation) recalls *Les Antiquitez*, sonnet XXII, 1–4, whilst the idea of the inferior powers looting the glories of Rome in her downfall (ll. 25–30) is a reminiscence of *Les Antiquitez*, sonnets XXII, 8; XIV, 11–14, and XXX, 10–12. In this context Ronsard adapts the idea of the minor European powers strengthening their own empires at the expense of Rome's dying glory both as an illustration of the continuity of matter and as an example of a philosophy of history based on the principle of *translatio*. This cyclic vision of history is illustrated in the *Franciade* by the Trojan origins of France, and is defined both in the concluding lines of this epic poem, '«Princes et rois et leurs races s'en vont, / «De leurs trespas les autres se refont',[4] and in a 1587 addition to the *editio princeps* (1575) of the *Tombeau de Marguerite de France* (XVII, 80, var.).

Similarly Ronsard's commentary on the thought that civil war was the cause of Rome's ultimate decay, since no outside force was strong enough to destroy her (ll. 19–24), has its counterpart in *Les Antiquitez*, sonnets XXII, 5–8; III, 7, 10 and XXI, whilst the construction and rhythm of lines 23–4 of the extract are closely modelled on sonnet VI, 9–10 of du Bellay's collection—'Rome seule pouvoit à Rome ressembler, / Rome seule pouvoit Rome faire trembler'—themselves a reminiscence of Horace, *Epodes*, XVI, 2: 'suis et ipsa Roma viribus ruit' ('. . . and Rome through her own strength is tottering': LCL, 1952, p. 403).

Ronsard's departure from Ovid at this stage and his emphasis on Rome are by no means accidental, for this passage acts as a transition to the poem's polemic conclusion by introducing a lengthy moral discussion of the causes and symptoms of decadence in a country which lead to its enfeeblement and downfall (ll. 129–68). In fact the present religious wars which divided France provided such an exact parallel with the civil conflict which finally destroyed Rome, that literary echoes and humanist sympathies are to be expected. However, the comparison between France and Rome, frequently used by sixteenth-century writers for polemic purposes,[5] should not be thought of as a mere literary conceit, for it is prompted by a genuine attempt to awaken France to her folly, to establish correspondences in the realm of historical experience which would universalise and enforce the lesson of sanity and provide the rational factual basis for predominantly emotional arguments.

Certainly Ronsard's poem is developed with this patriotic end in view. Adapting a Platonic argument of the *Republic* and *Laws*, the poet suggests a correlation between a people's music and their customs (ll. 133–40; cf. XI, 84) and notes with powerful eloquence that the symptoms of an ailing country are manifest in its moral laxity, its neglect of social hierarchy, its complete disregard for old established laws and justice, and in its adherence to new 'mœurs' and religious beliefs (ll. 141–59). Death comes in two ways '. . . à toute chose humaine, / Par accidentz de dedans ou dehors': so also with kingdoms, where destruction results either from outside attack or from internal civil conflict (ll. 201–8). Significantly the poem returns to the preoccupations of the opening movements and ends with a patriotic plea to God for sanity and protection in these times of religious upheaval and civil chaos (ll. 219–28).

This *Discours* is, therefore, a perfect example of an aesthetic, based on a balance of opposing principles—*copia* and measure, diversity within unity—which will be more fully defined and discussed in section three of this chapter. The poem ranges widely over a variety of subject areas and visions (philosophical, moral, social, political, historical, mythological, contemporary) and, by means of an abundance of illustration and a profusion of detail, it gives the impression of growing organically, of possessing its own momentum and dynamism. In spite of these techniques of *copia*, diversity and energy, Ronsard never moves far away from his central obsessions—change and death—and the rich strands of the poem are tightly organised into a unity—a unity emphasised by the enclosed circular structure where the final movements echo the themes of the opening lines. As the poem progresses Ronsard thus moves from a general statement to a particular national plea for stability, and the philosophical arguments on the duration of matter and the meaning of death, the illustrations of change, the vision of history and the comforting theory of cyclic regeneration are momentarily replaced by a note of urgency, a sudden realisation that because of her present precarious position France too is on the brink of possible extinction. It is this interdependence of social, moral, political, historical and philosophical perspectives, and this structuring of borrowed material to strike a personal note of contemporary relevance, which lend a deeper import to the notion of change and transform the commonplace themes and illustrations.

This poem of 1569 is the most comprehensive statement of Ronsard's vision of change and it provides the reader with the key to certain consistent attitudes and techniques —namely, the consolation which accompanies the rhythmic order of transformation and renewal, the reliance on Ovid, *Metamorphoses*, xv, for many of the illustrations, the cautious Christian reservations regarding borrowed classical doctrines, the aesthetic principle of diversity within unity. The *Discours*, however, in no way represents a momentary or isolated flirtation with literary and philosophical commonplaces. Ronsard's earliest expression of the transformist principle that 'la generation / Se fait de la corruption' appears in 1554 (VI, 20–1), and a year later the *Hymne de la Mort* contains a grandiose cosmic interpretation of his philosophy of change (VIII, 177–8). In his mature years Ronsard turns with increasing frequency to this

theory of enduring matter, and the principles of change and regeneration reappear in a sonnet of 1578 lamenting the death of Charles IX
(XVII, 383–4), in an elegy published in 1584 (XVIII, 146–7), and even more
frequently in texts of the posthumous 1587 edition (XVI, 353; XVIII, 249;
250; 268; 290).

It is in certain of these poems of the 1587 edition that the *direct* influence of Aristotle is evident for the first time. The transmutation and
combination of the four elements and the perpetual transformation of
forms within the eternal cycles of matter are fundamental aspects of
Aristotelian physics, and are found especially in the treatise *De Generatione et Corruptione*.[6] In spite of this, until the 1587 edition the primary
sources for these transformist ideas in Ronsard are clearly those passages of Ovid, Lucretius and Seneca referred to above, and if Aristotle remains the ultimate authority for such theories, nevertheless his influence
is only *indirectly* expressed through these Latin intermediaries and there
are no textual similarities to suggest a first-hand contact with any precise Aristotelian work. However, in two poems of the 1587 edition
Ronsard's debt to the Greek philosopher appears direct and there are
textual signs which point to a knowledge of Aristotelian terminology.
In the *Epitaphe de feu Monsieur le President de sainct André* Ronsard
expresses a basic tenet of a materialist philosophy of change when he
writes:

> Apprens que la matiere eternelle demeure,
> Et que la forme change & s'altere à toute heure,
> Et que le composé se rompt par son discord,
> Le simple seulement est exempt de la Mort.
>
> (XVIII, 290)

Ronsard even attempts to assess the temporal distinction between the
general and the particular, the compound and the simple, in an elegy to
Philippe Desportes, 'Le general est ferme, & ne fait place au temps, / Le
particulier meurt presque au bout de cent ans' (XVIII, 249). Ronsard had
expressed this idea before on frequent occasions but he had never used
quite the same vocabulary. For this philosophical concept of 'le général',
'le particulier', 'le composé' and 'le simple', Ronsard has borrowed and
simplified the distinctions from Aristotle's *De Generatione et Corruptione*, Book I, 6–10 and II, 1–8, where the Greek thinker explains his
ideas of combinations and simple and compound states. Certain references to Aristotle in the *Sonets pour Helene* of 1578 (XVII, 316, s. XXXVI)
and in the elegy *Six ans estoient coulez* of the 1584 edition (XVIII, 33)
point to a recent re-reading of the Greek philosopher's works, and this
similarity of terminology suggests that his study included the treatise
De Generatione et Corruptione.

This discussion of the concept of change is closely associated in Ronsard's mind with the role of Nature and the idea of natural order, for in the same way as inconstant man needs the stabilising effect of Law, so Ronsard submits the world's flux to a universal decree which links it to the cosmic design of things. In this respect Ronsard is adopting a philosophical attitude advocated by Seneca, who, on frequent occasions, depicts the transience of the terrestrial regions, traces a universal law of Nature which dictates this mobility and preaches a moral of total submission to this law (*Ad Polybium De Consolatione*, I, 1–4; *Epist.*, LXXI, 12–16; XCI, 4–16; CVII, 6–10).

Such an attitude is first evident in the ode *A Anthoine Chasteigner* of 1550 (II, 62–4), where Ronsard illustrates the notion of change by a series of commonplace examples developed from Horace and Ovid[7]— the movement of time and seasonal flux, the cyclic transference of knowledge and culture (the *translatio studii* theme),[8] the destruction of kingdoms, the changing seasons of man's life, the vicissitudes of nature. This rapid enumeration of examples, totally bereft of personal commentary or emotional involvement, is clearly designed to suggest a rhythmic order beyond momentary change and to illustrate the poem's opening and closing philosophical statements, based on Horatian precepts, which express the idea that human happiness is to be found in the stoical acceptance of life's fluctuating variety. The catalogue of illustrations also serves to define a law of Nature, formulated in the distant days of man's creation, which is seen to encompass him within the pattern of cosmic order:

Telles lois feit dame Nature guide,
  Lors que par sur le dos
Pyrrhe sema dedans le monde vuide
  De sa mere les os :

A celle fin que nul homme n'espere
  S'oser dire immortel
Voiant le tens qui est son propre pere
  N'avoir rien moins de tel.
          (ll. 29–36)

Laumonier has already demonstrated that these two stanzas are composed of a contamination of multiple texts from Virgil, Ovid, Horace and Pindar. Ronsard's method of adapting his reminiscences in this context is one which he frequently uses in his early odes, and one which is here fundamental to the originality of his interpretation concerning man's relation to change. The poet transposes recollections from diverse models, which he has so well assimilated from his reading that his reminiscences are spontaneous rather than conscious imitations. His art and originality are that he juxtaposes his reminiscences to create a new idea, which owes nothing to the immediate sources he is using and which is so adapted to the content of the poem that the material is given a different significance and emphasis.

Here, for instance, the myth of Deucalion and Pyrrha, which Ronsard will again associate with Nature's law of change in an ode of 1553 (V, 166), is fairly closely remembered from the classical texts, but the relation between change and human *hubris* in Ronsard has no parallel in his models. It is true that the myth has associations of sin and punishment, and that Ronsard may well have found his inspiration for the principle of *hubris* in the Horatian 'immortalia ne speres' (*Odes*, IV, vii, 7) or in several passages of Pindar,[9] but the classical references are flat statements of a tenet of religious dogma and, more significantly, nowhere do Pindar and Horace specifically link this idea to illustrations of the world's change and to the human implications of a universal law of time. Horace uses the words *speres* and *spem* in separate passages and Ronsard borrows this idea, but by adding the verb *oser* he emphasises the notion of *hubris*, as he does in other similar contexts (V, 253; VIII, 87; 154), and introduces a moral tone, not in the original Latin, which the personification of Time and the 'father' metaphor enhance. In this early text the material may be largely a pastiche of classical reminiscences and the poetic value of it limited, but Ronsard has already learnt to reshape his borrowings in order to add ideas and a personal interpretation not found in his models.

At this stage Ronsard sees the world's inconstancy as a law of Nature so devised that nothing of human endeavour can obtain perfection or immortality. This immutable law of change renders man humble, ensures his subservience to the ruling forces of the universe and stifles any semblance of overweening arrogance on his part. It is a law carefully formulated to retain man within the bounds of his fragility, within his agreed place in the hierarchy of the universe. Any deviation from this norm, any demonstration of human *hubris*, as the poet was aware from the classical examples of Prometheus, the Giants, Phaethon, Icarus and Bellerophon,[10] was to transgress this hierarchical scheme and to endanger this fragile order. In this same cause of cosmic harmony man must submit to this rule of change and find consolation in the knowledge that the mortal human condition is a small but essential part of the creation and mechanism of the world-system.

In yet another text of 1550 (I, 104–5) Ronsard submits the pattern of flux to Nature, and although on rare occasions change is attributed to God (II, 171; XV, 155) or Eternity (VIII, 246), throughout his subsequent poetry the function of regulating the transience of the world by means of a complex system of laws is given, after the manner of Seneca, to Nature. Whilst Ronsard's conception of Nature undergoes a marked evolution towards a more extreme stoical pantheism in the later years of his life,[11] and although Nature is at times an ambiguous immanent force, whose role and prerogatives are frequently associated, and at times confused, with those of a Christian God, her function of controlling the fluctuating sublunar regions and of encompassing the world's diversity within unity is similar to that defined in the writings of other contemporary humanists.[12] In Ronsard's verse Nature not only joins with Peace to harmonise chaos and to create the universe (IX, 107), but it is she who presides over the preservation of life and the species by acting as the intermediary of Venus (VIII, 178; 252). Nature renews life through death in a constant cyclic pattern so that 'Tout tel qu'au paravant sera tousjours le Monde' (XVI, 355), and, as controller of the *Anima Mundi*, she ensures that each element, each living creature, keeps to its place and contributes to the harmony and beauty of the world (VIII, 68).

The palace of Nature described in the *Hymne de l'Autonne* (1563) contains 'les semences de toutes choses'—an idea already present in the *Ode a Michel de l'Hospital* of 1552 (III, 126)—and it is Nature who preserves the universe and procreates these 'semences' which the *Ciel* then distributes to each creature (VIII, 148):

> Là sont dedans des pots sur des tables, encloses
> Avecq' leurs escriteaux, les semences des choses,
> Que ces jeunes garsons gardent, à celle fin
> Que ce grand Univers ne preigne jamais fin,
> Les semans tous les ans d'un mutuel office,
> Affin qu'en vieillisant le Monde rajeunisse.
>
> (XII, 62)

Earlier in this *Hymne* (XII, 52)—and throughout Ronsard's verse, as in contemporary emblems and iconography—it is the omnipotence, the sexual fecundity and the regenerative power of Nature which are stressed:

> ... de Nature le sein
> Est tousjours tetineux pour tout le genre humain:
> Chacun le peut succer, & sa vertu feconde
> Ne se vieillist jamais non plus que fait le monde.[13]

Elsewhere Nature's rule of infinite variety is seen to balance virtues and resolve dissonances in such a way that it parallels the *concordia discors* of the cosmic, social and aesthetic perspectives:

> Immitant en ce poinct Nature ingenieuse,
> Qui mect en mesme pré une herbe venimeuse
> Tout aupres d'une bonne, & mect dedans les Cieux

Un astre qui est bon pres d'un malicieux :
Et mesmes Juppiter le bien & le mal donne
De ses pipes là hault à chacune personne,
Afin qu'homme ne soit parfaict en ce bas lieu :
«Car la perfection appartient seule à Dieu.

(VII, 230)

In these lines from an elegy of 1556, Man and the dilemmas of his condition are once again fused with the more powerful cosmic forces, for
the harmony of Nature's rule is seen to have a counterpart in Jupiter's
attitude to humanity. Although Laumonier notes that Ronsard employs
the detail of Jupiter's two urns from Homer, *Iliad*, XXIV, 527–32, the
idea that the vicissitudes of human fortunes are designed as part of a
divine plan to retain Man within the limitations of his imperfection, of
his inferiority to God—this idea is Ronsard's own significant interpretation of the concept of *hubris* and is a restatement of the attitude already
expressed in the ode to Chasteigner of 1550.

In the same way Nature demonstrates her powers of order to mortals,
for it is she who controls the different ages of Man and 'compose tout
d'une meure sagesse' (XVII, 52–3). Nature's fecundity also preserves
poetic inspiration and portions out creative genius in such a manner
that each century and country has its talented poets, writers and
thinkers. Just as Nature renews its strength by alternating periods of
growth with periods of fallow,

Ainsi les bons esprits ne font tousjours demeure,
Fertils, en un pays, mais changent d'heure en heure,
Soit en se reposant, soit en portant du fruit.[14]

In this way Nature preserves the spiritual forces of the universe as
well as the physical, and in the following lines her vitalising energy is
described once again in terms of sexual fertility, whilst the wide temporal framework of her activity is evoked by diverse patterns of past,
present and future tenses :

Tels du vieil Apollon les Ministres estoient,
Ou fust sur le trepied, ou fust lors qu'ils chantoient :
Et tels ceux d'aujourd'huy : car l'antique Cybelle
(La Nature j'entens) n'a tary sa mammelle
Pour maigre n'allaiter les siecles avenir,
Ny ne fera jamais : ce seroit devenir
Une mere brehaigne en lieu d'estre feconde.
Tout tel qu'au paravant sera tousjours le Monde.

(XVI, 355)

This piece is a verse rendering of a prose passage which had already appeared as the conclusion to the *Art Poëtique* of 1565 (XIV, 35). The same argument recurs in the *Preface sur la Franciade*, published posthumously in 1587, where the theme of the permanence of Nature's forces is employed to defend the use of modern languages and to elaborate a theory of imitation based on the principle of *translatio studii* (XVI, 339–40; 349–50; 353).

It is when Ronsard considers the human consequences of Nature's rule in an *epistre* to Charles de Pisseleu (1555) that the presence of Seneca becomes more directly apparent:

> «Certes, mon PISSELEU, il n'est pas de besoing
> «Que l'homme soit tousjours delivré de tout soing:
> «Mais il faut quelquesfois qu'à son tour il endure,
> «Apres un doux plaisir, une tristesse dure,
> «S'il veut bien longuement son estre conserver:
> «Car qui voudroit tousjours en un point se trouver
> «Il ne pourroit durer: telles loix feit Nature
> «Des le commencement à toute creature.
> «On ne voit pas tousjours en mesme estat les Cieux,
> «Quelquesfois ilz sont beaux, quelquesfois pluvieux,
> «Apres le Renouveau vient l'Esté, puis l'Autonne,
> «L'Hyver l'Autonne suit, puis le Printemps retourne.
> «Si donq tout est suget à se muer souvent,
> «L'homme qui n'est sinon que fumée, & que vent,
> «Comme le filz du Temps, ne doit trouver estrange
> «Si quelque fois d'estat comme son pere il change:
> «Et nous voyons cela, pour mieux l'homme assurer
> «Que rien ferme ne peut en ce monde durer.
> «Quand il nous survient donq une fortune amere,
> «Il la faut prendre ainsi que s'elle estoit prospere,
> «Et ne murmurer point, mais paciens souffrir
> «Tout ce qu'il plaist à DIEU pour present nous offrir.
>
> (VIII, 225–6)

It is possible that this passage—which recalls arguments and images already used in an ode to René d'Oradour of 1550 (I, 208–11)—is inspired from Plutarch's *Consolatio ad Apollonium*, chapters 4–6 and 29, and from a contamination of Horatian and Pindaric lines.[15] However, a much closer textual comparison can be made with a passage from Seneca, *Epistulae ad Lucilium*, CVII, 6–9. Not only is Ronsard's attitude to Nature's rule of change reminiscent of the philosophy advocated by Seneca on those occasions when he defines the mutability of the world in terms of a universal law and teaches a lesson of stoical acceptance, but the similarity of the seasonal and climatic imagery, and the verbal

parallels of the final lines of both extracts, would suggest direct knowledge of this Latin passage:

We should not manifest surprise at any sort of condition into which we are
born, and which should be lamented by no one, simply because it is equally
ordained for all ... And an equal law consists, not of that which all have
experienced, but of that which is laid down for all. Be sure to prescribe for
your mind this sense of equity; we should pay without complaint the tax of
our mortality.

Winter brings on cold weather; and we must shiver. Summer returns, with
its heat; and we must sweat. Unseasonable weather upsets the health; and we
must fall ill ... And we cannot change this order of things; but what we can
do is to acquire stout hearts, worthy of good men, thereby courageously enduring chance and placing ourselves in harmony with Nature. And Nature
moderates this world-kingdom which you see, by her changing seasons:
clear weather follows cloudy; after a calm, comes the storm; the winds blow
by turns; day succeeds night; some of the heavenly bodies rise, and some set.
Eternity consists of opposites.

It is to this law that our souls must adjust themselves, this they should
follow, this they should obey. Whatever happens, assume that it was bound
to happen, and do not be willing to rail at Nature. That which you cannot
reform, it is best to endure, and to attend uncomplainingly (*sine murmura-
tione*) upon the God under whose guidance everything progresses.

(LCL, 1925, vol. III, pp. 227–9)

In the French poem this stoical attitude is complemented both by the example of Pisseleu, who has successfully put the philosophical theory
into practice (ll. 39–42), and by the opening lines of the *epistre*, which
reproduce a commonplace argument of the classical *consolatio* and state
that, by activating latent virtues, human misery and adversity have a
moral value and are more beneficial than harmful. By this method the
consolation of the remedy succeeds in alleviating any feeling of melancholy which the development on the theme of transience may have
evoked—not that this central passage provokes sadness on the part of
the reader for the whole tone of it is designed to reassure (even the
cyclic flux of the seasons ends on an optimistic note with the return of
life-giving spring!). Here, as in the ode to Chasteigner, the poet is able to
fuse Man with an equitable cosmic law and with the more powerful
forces of Nature, in such a way that Ronsard is not only resigned but
comforted. In this *Epistre* Ronsard's original contribution to his trans-
position of classical attitudes and ideas is to welcome Nature's law of
change and time's movement as evidence of the world's richness, its
interest, its vitality, as prerequisites for the continuation of life and the
species, and to exhort his fellow man to be assured and find consolation
in the knowledge that his own ephemeral condition is an inevitable and

necessary part of the universal pattern. This lesson of resigned sub-mission to a dynamic natural order of change and preservation remained with Ronsard throughout his life, for a similar idea is found in a variant of the posthumous 1587 edition (XVII, 80).

THE MYTHOLOGY OF CHANGE

Another important dimension of Ronsard's interest in the concept of change is to be found in his frequent recourse to myths which illustrate human metamorphosis and which, for the most part, have their common source in Ovid, *Metamorphoses*. For Ronsard, as for Ovid, these myths of metamorphosis form part of an animistic vision of matter in move-ment, and illustrate the notion of cyclic transformism.[16] However, whilst Ronsard consistently expresses this theme of human metamorphosis with a multiplicity of examples,[17] it is in his longer mythological narra-tive poems that the most interesting and personal interpretations are to be found. In this respect two odes of 1550 are early indicators of certain ideas and attitudes which will become central to his treatment of the theme of metamorphosis in later collections. In the *Complainte de Glauce* (1550: II, 57–60. Cf. I, 158) the metamorphosis of Glaucus is envisaged as a triumph over time and man's fragility,

Thetys pour effacer cela qu'avoi d'humain,
Et d'homme au tens subject, m'a versé de sa main
    Cent fleuves sur la teste
           (ll. 40–2)

whilst in *La Defloration de Lede* (II, 67–79) suggestions of death and human frailty (ll. 191–2, 197–9) are replaced by references to Leda's participation in an eternal, natural order of fertility and generation (ll. 217–28). In both odes metamorphosis is associated with a movement from death to life, with the transcending of human limitations.

This idea, in embryonic form at this stage, will be developed in *Le Narssis* (1554: VI, 73–83), and here Ronsard's independence of his Ovid-ian source (*Metamorphoses*, III, 402–510) will result in a more precise definition of certain original and lasting attitudes. The structure of the poem is important, for the metamorphosis of Narcissus is placed within the framework of two long descriptive passages. The first (ll. 1–44), which has no parallel in the Latin model, opposes the sterility and death of winter with the regeneration of spring, associated here with creative activity ('... ta musette, / Qui durant tout l'hyver avoit esté muette': ll. 1–2), sound, colour, warmth, youth, fecundity, the universal love of nature and with those rustic divinities and gods (Bacchus and Ceres) representing joy, renewal and plenitude. The second descriptive setting (ll. 45–57, 122–6) is extensively developed from Ovid (ll. 407–12), and depicts the fountain in which Narcissus sees his reflection with similar lexical patterns suggesting abundance, beauty, spring, purity and life. The fountain is also related—as indeed was the spring setting (ll. 35–6) —to love and metamorphosis (ll. 50–4), details foreign to the Ovidian account. The metamorphosis of Narcissus in Ronsard's poem,

> ... une petite fleur
> Qui d'un jaune safran emprunta la couleur,
> Laquelle n'oubliant sa naissance premiere
> Hante encor aujourd'hui la rive fonteiniere,
> Et tousjours aparoist pres des eaus, au printans
>
> (ll. 171–6)

develops a brief statement in Ovid ('In place of his body they find a flower, its yellow centre girt with white petals': LCL, vol. I, p. 161), and it is here that the French poet demonstrates the full measure of his originality. In Ronsard's version Narcissus, the flower, returns every spring to haunt the fountain, its birthplace, and is thereby integrated into the seasonal cycle and into the same natural order of plenitude, activity and rebirth he had evoked in the two descriptive settings which opened the poem. Ronsard's personal contribution to his source is to consider metamorphosis as a victory over time, sterility and death, a victory rendered even more emphatic because Ronsard had described Narcissus as 'Comme un froid simulacre, en attendant la mort' (l. 156) prior to his change. In a variant of 1584 (p. 82) Ronsard refines his reflections even further with the help of a distant Horatian reminiscence (Odes, III, i, 14–15: '... with impartial justice Necessity allots the fates of high and low alike': LCL, 1952, p. 162): here, in lines which reveal once again a tendency to accumulate balanced patterns (du matin ou du soir; l'ordre ... et la nécessité; Allonge ou raccourcist; Non ce que ... mais cela que), he embraces the brief life-span of flower and man within a natural equitable order, within the demands of cosmic necessity:

> Aux arbres la Nature a permis longue vie:
> Ceste fleur du matin ou du soir est ravie.
> Ainsi l'ordre le veut et la nécessité,
> Qui dés le premier jour de la nativité
> Allonge ou raccourcist nos fuseaux, & nous donne
> Non ce que nous voulons, mais cela qu'elle ordonne.

In Le Houx of the following year (VI, 135–46) Ronsard returns to the theme of human metamorphosis in a vision which has clear affinities with that of *Le Narssis*. The transformation of the nymph into a holly tree does not destroy the picture of her as a living force of beauty and youth which had been carefully built up in the earlier part of the poem (ll. 35–54; and by association with the cave in which she seeks protection, ll. 55–102). It is not only that her soul continues to animate the tree (ll. 163–72) and that she has human senses after metamorphosis (ll. 219–22), but Ronsard insists on associating the holly tree throughout the poem with symbols of life—love, wine, water, birds, dew, honey, manna (ll. 183–7, 229–38, 246–57). Since the metamorphosis was an act of protection against violation (ll. 159–62), the properties and virtues of holly are essentially life-saving: it guards against evil and poison (ll. 179–82), against the cold winter wind (l. 192) and excessive heat (ll. 194–8). This idea of protection against heat, which parallels the nymph's earlier refuge in the cave (ll. 55–62), has suggestive resonances in Ronsard's verse: it not only recalls the 'excessive ardeur' which kills the flower in the beautiful *Comme on voit sur la branche* (XVII, 125), but it calls to mind the choice of the poet's own tomb, described as being shaded from the wilting sun (cf. II, 98–9). Similarly the holly tree must be related to the opening lines of the poem (ll. 1–13) where trees are linked to the transcendental values of poetry, divination, love and wine (the four Platonic furies: cf. III, 143; XV, 18). Ronsard stresses the connection between Brinon's 'Houx domestique' and the immortalising power of the creative mind, and with poetry and divination in particular (ll. 22–8, 191–3, 208–22, 239–42, 246–8, 258–62). Even the references to the sustaining values of 'rosée, manne, miel' (ll. 253–7) equate the holly tree with poetry and immortality, for these same life forces frequently appear in Ronsard's evocations of the rustic tombs of poets (II, 101; VI, 28).

Several important texts of the *Sixiesme et Septiesme livre des Poëmes* (1569) are subtle and poetic variations on similar themes concerning human metamorphosis. The change of a nymph into a juniper tree in *Le Rossignol* (XV, 186–90) is occasioned, as so often in Ronsard, by excessive desire and the rejection and suffering of love ('. . . desir / Qui en vivant en cent formes me muë': XV, 198, s. v): it is within this context of unbridled passion that the multiple metamorphoses of Jupiter are invariably situated.[18] In *Le Rossignol* (ll. 35–42), as in *Le Houx* (ll. 147–62), it is Ovid's account of Daphne's transformation[19] that provides Ronsard with the idea of describing the actual stages of change in realistic and visual detail:

Ses doigtz longuetz, ses bras veneux & beaux,
A longs fourchons se fendent en rameaux,
Son pied devint une morne racine,
Et une escorce entourna sa poitrine.

Ses longs cheveux, de crainte reboursez,
En feuilles sont piquantes herissez,
Et la palleur qu'elle avoit en sa fuite
Vit sur l'escorce & toujours y habite.

In an animistic vision frequent in Ronsard's work (cf. XVII, 343, s. VIII; XVIII, 144) the juniper is seen throughout the poem as a living force ('... soubz l'escorce une Nymphe ... vit': l. 24) which can even materialise into human form again (ll. 43–7). Moreover, the nightingale which nests and sings in the juniper associates the metamorphosed tree with spring, movement, sound, abundance, beauty, birth and renewal (ll. 1–26, 46–54, 65–70). Although there are suggestions in the poem that Ronsard's serious illness of 1567–9 during his stay at Saint-Cosme is linked in his mind with creative sterility (ll. 17, 71–6) and with physical and mental inactivity ('... la fievre me tient / Reins, teste, flanc': ll. 79–80), more prominent are those references which connect the metamorphosis of the tree with the immortality and therapeutic value of poetry (ll. 80–4). This parallel is established by the nightingale's association with poetry (ll. 11–17, 71–4) and by the word *pucelle* which directly links Ronsard's Muse (ll. 80–1) with the nymph (ll. 24–6: var.). It is interesting to note that an elegy of 1571 (XV, 326–38) describes Ronsard's own metamorphosis into a juniper as a change from death (ll. 171–5) to regeneration, plenitude and growth (ll. 176–98).

Le Pin, which precedes *Le Rossignol* in the 1569 collection (XV, 178–85), is also ostensibly inspired by Ronsard's illness (ll. 165–70) and similarly associates human metamorphosis with life, love, poetry and immortality in an even more positive manner. Before his castration Attis is portrayed in terms of his youthful beauty, his sociability, his physical and mental prowess (ll. 35–6, 68–71, 92–6), and the adjectives chosen ('jeune ... gaillard') recall those applied to certain natural forces in the seasonal *hymnes* of 1563 (the Sun is described as 'jeune, doux, & gaillard': XII, 39). The castration of Attis on the other hand links him to ideas of isolation, inactivity, sterility, old age and death (ll. 48–52, 68–72, 80–2, 85–96). His metamorphosis into a pine tree (an idea not found in Catullus, LXIII, but available to Ronsard via a brief reference in Ovid, *Metamorphoses*, x, 103–5), is seen as part of a natural cycle, a rebirth, for the tree is associated with abundance, life and love (ll. 1–4, 116–17) and with a vitalistic conception of matter (the tree bleeds and actually contains the living form of Attis: ll. 11–12, 15–22, 25–6).

These considerations, which owe very little debt to any classical treatment of the legend,[20] culminate in Ronsard's personal interpretation of 'cette vieille fable' in the final movement of the poem (ll. 131–64). Here Attis is equated with the philosopher-poet, and the myth is seen to signify the necessity of seclusion, contemplation and detachment from the limitations of physical existence in order to concentrate all one's energies on the creative mind, which alone assures immortality and elevation to the divine world 'pour heureusement vivre'. Ronsard (ll. 160–4) poetically associates his own immortality with the sound of the wind in the pine:

Qu'au vent ton Pin puisse siffler mon nom.
Me chante doncq la cyme non muëtte
D'un Pin parlant, non un mauvais Poëtte,
Car j'ayme mieux ses sifflemens divers
Que le froid son de quelques meschans vers.

Whilst *Le Chat* (xv, 42–3)—and, to a lesser degree, *Le Soucy du Jardin* (xv, 173–7)—also create a dense synthesis of the themes of illness, human metamorphosis, love, poetic immortality and divination within a vision of the world which is totally animistic, it is the poem *Hylas* of the same year (1569: xv, 234–53) which will more suggestively envisage change as a conquest over human fragility. The transformation of Hylas into a 'source d'eau' (ll. 385–8: var.) is placed within a setting conducive to metamorphosis, a

... fonteine ... tout à l'entour
Riche de fleurs, qu'autrefois trop d'amour
De corps humain fit changer en fleuretes
(ll. 211–13)

and is described as the absorption of one natural life force into another —Hylas is evoked throughout as youthful, beautiful, active (ll. 87, 181–3, 257–60, 285–8), and both the fountain (ll. 211–48) and the palace of Printine (ll. 273–82) are pictured in terms of plenitude, fecundity, love, movement, purity and rustic joy. Thus the metamorphosis of Hylas integrates him into the eternal, natural world and, as a god endowed with the gift of divination (ll. 397–414), he is specifically described as transcending human misery, mortality and time (ll. 315–17, 395–6). Not only is there no Ovidian authority for the metamorphosis of Hylas, but Ronsard's interpretation of the myth in those areas referred to above reveals a substantial independence of the classical sources he uses elsewhere in the poem (Theocritus, Apollonius Rhodius, Valerius Flaccus, Propertius).

These myths concerning human metamorphosis are thus constantly associated in Ronsard's mind with a conquest of time and death, with the integration of man into an eternal, natural order and with his participation in the divine world. This mythology of change is also seen to have intimate connections with the surpassing of human mortality by

the transcendental values of the creative mind, and in particular with
divination and poetic immortality.

TOWARDS THE DEFINITION OF AN AESTHETIC OF CHANGE

The mythological examples of metamorphosis studied above demonstrate the personal nature of Ronsard's interpretations of received
material (largely of Ovidian origin), and reveal his interest in exploring
the descriptive possibilities and the human consequences of that crucial
moment—synonymous with life in the context of his transformist definitions—when 'la forme en une autre se change'.[21] Ronsard is clearly
fascinated by matter in movement, by the visual painting of fluctuating
phenomena, be it water (III, 45–6; XI, 134; XVIII, 34), smoke (VIII, 289),
the monstrous shapes assumed by clouds (V, 48–52; VIII, 120; XIII, 268–
70; XVI, 101), the rhythmical fluidity of the winnower (XI, 159–60) or of
dancing and balletic movement (XVII, 172; 270–1, s. XXX; XVIII, 111), the
elusive chase of a skylark by a hound (IX, 151–2), the changing forms of
démons (VIII, 119–21) or of dogs in a dream (XVIII, 73), the reflected
flickering of sunlight, moonlight or an *ignis fatuus* on water (XVI, 211;
357; XVII, 172), the play of wind on the shadows of trees on the surface
of a pool (XIV, 244), the waving motion of Cassandre's hair (evoked in
terms of water lexis and imagery: IV, 77, s. LXXVI), the sinuous movement of the snake and the motif of the annual slough of the serpent's
skin (VIII, 288–9; XVI, 184; 358), or the complex architecture on three
simultaneous levels of the opening lines of the *Elegie à Marie Stuart*
(XIV, 152–4), in which the billowing of garments and sails and the
motion of the boat taking the queen from France are interwoven to form
a study in movement where the structure is at once fluid and tightly
organised, diverse and unified.

Marcel Raymond and Ian McFarlane have both pointed to Ronsard's
fascination with undulating, swirling movement and to his frequent use
of a lexis evoking curves, counter-curves and spirals, whilst Odette de
Mourgues has demonstrated the poet's obsession with certain stylistic
and structural devices designed to express the mobility and diversity of
the natural world.[22] Frequently one has the impression that the thought
expressed is secondary to the artistic evocation, to the demands of an
aesthetic exercise. In the following passage from an elegy of 1559, the
images attain an autonomous, plastic existence and, using poetic techniques he favours elsewhere in similar contexts, Ronsard multiplies his
rhythmical effects, develops his similes in triplicate (each supported by
a well chosen adverb), balances his lexis and structures in pairs (frequently in antithetical patterns), and repeats word clusters and active
verbs centred on the idea of mobility (often foregrounded in stressed

positions)—all this in an attempt to wed style and sense and to seize the diversity and movement of the changing phenomena themselves. What characterises these lines at first reading is their decorative richness, the abundance of illustration—the three similes give the extract a multiplicity of centres—and a creative energy not unlike the pictorial dynamism of a mannerist or baroque painting. At the same time the diversity, fluidity and descriptive vitality are to some extent offset by a sense of regularity, by the metronomic movement of the 'deux vens tous contraires' and by certain associated stylistic and structural effects—the firm framework provided by the repeated similes, the traditional caesura breaks of a good number of the lines, the balance of numerous antithetical items. Once again the poetic manner is midway between the unrestrained exuberance of the baroque imagination and the measured discipline of a classical vision:

Tout cela qui depend de nostre vie humaine»
Est sujet à douleur, à tristesse, & à peine»,
Au change & au rechange, & n'a rien tant certain»
Qui ne soit ebranlé du soir au lendemain» :
Comme un arbre planté sur des mons solitaires,
Batu diversement de deux vens tous contraires,
L'un le soufle deçà, & l'autre de rechef
Le resoufle de là, les fueilles de son chef
Volent de tous costez, qui jusque en terre ondoye :
Caché de sous un roc le pasteur s'en efroye :
Ou comme on voit les blez espessement plantez
Branler au moys de May leurs tuiaux eventez,
Deçà delà pliez sous le vent de Zephyre,
Ou sous l'Austre moiteux, l'un à gauche les vire,
L'autre les soufle à dextre, & poussez en avant,
Et poussez en arriere obeyssent au vent :
Ou comme un tourbillon qui chassé du tonnerre
Premier en limaçon vient baloyer la terre,
Puis venteux & poudreux s'elance dans la mer,
Et faict l'un de sur l'autre horriblement armer
Les flots, qui maintenant aux estoilles s'egallent,
Maintenant jusque au fond de l'arene devallent,
Avecques un grand bruict pesle-mesle fuians
Bossez, voultez, courbez, escumans & bruyans,
L'un se voute davant, l'autre se courbe arriere,
L'autre roule à costé : presque en telle maniere
S'ebranle nostre vie, & rien n'est en ce lieu
Ferme sinon l'amour que nous portons à Dieu.[23]

The figures of the sea and cornfield disturbed by wind are found in a passage of Homer (*Iliad*, II, 144–8), and Virgil in turn borrows the double simile, and adds a brief reference to wind in tree-tops (*Georgics*, III, 196–201). However, the allusions in Homer and Virgil are laconic and lacking in descriptive emphasis, and although Ronsard recalls reminiscences of another Virgilian passage in his painting of the wind-tossed waves (*Georgics*, III, 237–41), the realistic detail and the poetic techniques of this visual account are his own original contribution. In such a context the Christian notion of the stability of God—although poetically pre-figured by certain lexical items (*depend, certain, planté, plantez, ferme*) —is merely an unconvincing and artificial addendum to the long central development, for what primarily interests Ronsard is the artistic possibilities of his similes. Ronsard's reaction to flux here is aesthetic and not religious. Change invigorates him rather than terrifies him, and although he envisages God as the ultimate principle of cosmic order, there is little feeling in his verse of the personal presence and comfort of God as a stability.

Ronsard visualises change as the demonstration in time of an eternal, cyclic order; it is the equivalent of diversity, vitality, continuity, and as one of those people who 'De leur nature aiment le changement' (II, 1), he believes that man must actively involve himself in the processes of life and in the fluctuating diversity of the physical world rather than in the contemplation of the immutable and divine (XVIII, 248; 459–60). It is precisely this diversity that he constantly evokes, be it the variety of man's opinions, occupations, customs and temperaments (II, 1–4; VIII, 155–8; XV, 372–3; XVII, 40–2), the many different forms of hunting (VI, 236–8), the cornucopian abundance of France's natural riches (I, 24–35; XIII, 111–16) or the fecundity, abundance and 'formes diverses' of nature (X, 362; XVIII, 33). For Ronsard perfection and beauty are synonymous with variety, and the proof of man's divinity is in his diversity :

> L'homme est vrayement divin, savant, ingenieux,
> Et sur tous animaux le plus semblable aux Dieux,
> Parfaict en son divers.
> (XV, 372)

Similarly in the elegy *L'Excellence de l'esprit de l'homme* (1559) there is a statement, which is again both aesthetic and metaphysical in nature, of how God demonstrates his power and unity through variety in both the macrocosm and microcosm (X, 101–2), and this text is one of many in which Ronsard associates divine omnipotence and excellence with the demonstration of a diversity of effects (VIII, 69; X, 25; XIV, 6). Again, for the Ancients, Nature's perfection and beauty were linked to her fluctuating variety and 'faits divers', and it is the role of poetry, according to Ronsard, to mirror that diversity, richness and inconstancy :

Je suis de cette opinion que nulle Poësie se doit louer pour acomplie, si elle ne ressemble la nature, laquelle ne fut estimée belle des anciens, que pour estre inconstante, & variable en ses perfections. (I, 47)

We thus arrive at a definition of beauty and the formulation of an aesthetic based on Nature's inconstant variety, a conception not uncommon in contemporary neo-Platonic writing.[24] Ronsard considers change and diversity as important aesthetic criteria : Pindar's excellence is linked to his 'admirables inconstances' and his 'copieuse diversité' (I, 47; 48); Horace's 'nombres divers' and Virgil's 'style nombreux' equally appealed to him (I, 265; XVI, 338), whilst the distinction between *poésie*,

Poësie est un pré de diverse apparence,
Orgueilleux de ses biens, & riche de ses fleurs,
Diapré, peinturé de cent mille couleurs,

and *poème* ('Poëme est une fleur . . .') is based on a definition of diversity within unity (XVIII, 283–4). Poets are 'vrais peintres de la nature' (I, 146), honey-bees who flit from flower to flower, theme to theme, style to style, in order to construct their own work after the manner of Nature (VII, 229; XI, 161; XV, 252; XVI, 336). Ronsard's self-confessed eclecticism is thus based on the principle of *copia* and is the result of an aesthetic of mobility :

Ma painture n'est pas mue
Mais vive, & par l'univers
Guindée en l'air se remue
De sus l'engin de mes vers.[25]

The epic poet in particular, '. . . ne peut longuement traicter un mesme subject, mais passer de l'un à l'autre en cent sortes de varietez' (XVI, 343), and Homer and Virgil have already given examples of the perfect epic which should be 'Varié d'argumens & d'accidens divers' (XVI, 354). In describing his own work it is precisely its richness and diversity that Ronsard constantly highlights. He compares the multifariousness of his verse to '. . . un paisage champestre, / D'assiette different, de forme & de façon', and again to '. . . ces tables friandes / Qu'un Prince faict charger de diverses viandes' (X, 362–3), whilst du Bellay equates this copious variety with an 'energie' synonymous with the Latin *genius* (*Deffence*, I, vi).

At the same time this aesthetic of changing diversity and abundance presupposes measure, unifying control and harmony : as in nature multiplicity must be reconciled with unity, and variety must be ordered and accompanied by balanced selection and discipline for the result to be artistically pleasing:

J'amasse, trie & choisis le plus beau,
Qu'en cent couleurs je peints en un tableau,
Tantost en l'autre : & maistre en ma peinture,
Sans me forcer j'imite la Nature.

(xv, 252)

The sound of the poet's lyre and the dance of the Muses bear witness to these same aspects of measure and balance ('mesurer ses pas, accordez par compas' : I, 162, var.), whilst the poet/bee metaphor and the symbolism of the crown illustrate the aesthetic principle of diversity within unity (III, 23; 118–19. Cf. xv, 185). There must be an ordered arrangement of material (xIV, 16; xVI, 4; 337) and a firm control of the poetic imagination, '... la bride de la contrainte arreste & refreint la premiere course impetueuse des fureurs & monstrueuses imaginations de l'esprit ...' (xVI, 348), for variety and change are not synonymous with extravagant abuse: 'Tu enrichiras ton Poëme par varietez prises de la Nature, sans extravaguer comme un frenetique' (xVI, 334. Cf. xVI, 337–8). A free imagination will produce '... inventions fantasticques & melencoliques, qui ne se rapportent non plus l'une à l'autre que les songes entrecoupez d'un frenetique, ou de quelque patient extremement tourmenté de la fievre ... mille formes monstrueuses sans ordre ny liayson' (xIV, 13): and Ronsard emphasises the necessity of 'inventions ... bien ordonnées & disposées ... une elegante et parfaicte collocation & ordre des choses inventées' (xIV, 13–14). Virgil is 'plus parfaict que tous les autres' because he is 'plus rond, plus serré' (xVI, 339). A poem, like the cosmos and society, is a living organism and depends on a healthy, proportioned balance of its component parts (xIV, 10; xVI, 343): in the aesthetic context, as in the social and cosmic, abuse, excess and licence breed illness and deformity (xVI, 4; 334).

When his poetry is accused of being without order and art by the *Predicans & Ministres de Geneve*, Ronsard's reply insists on both the 'libre contrainte' of his control and the diversity of his inspiration (xI, 159–61). If the expression 'libre contrainte' recalls 'une paisible contrainte' of the *Ode de la Paix* of 1550 (III, 6) and the many antithetical terms relating to cosmic order already noted, it is not altogether gratuitous, for many contemporary neo-Platonic writings associated cosmological and aesthetic principles by employing an identical lexis of this sort.[26] Indeed Ronsard envisages his creation as a world composed of atoms (I, 55), and in the *Elegie du Verre* (1555) the art of glass blowing is not only related to the variety and perfection of the *Anima Mundi*, but is specifically used as a parallel for the diversity within unity principle of the creative process (VI, 170).

If God the creator and Nature reveal their unity, perfection and ultimate stability through variety and movement, the work of art is a sort of *discordia concors* held in 'libre contrainte' by the poet-creator, a microcosm whose beauty depends on a controlled energy, a unified and harmonised variety and dissonance, a balanced proportion of multiple forces. The model of excellence and 'beauté pure' is found in the balanced diversity of the opposing movements of the heavenly bodies ('discordans accordz de leurs diversitez': VIII, 142–4), in the proportion and 'ordonnance' of the cosmos ('un compas bien reiglé ... une juste mesure': VIII, 68; 145) and in the perfect unity and all-embracing control of its circular form:

> ... faisant tournoyer en sphere rondement,
> Pour estre plus parfaict, car en la forme ronde
> Gist la perfection qui toute en soy abonde.[27]

If cosmic order is synonymous with beauty, Chaos is specifically described as 'sans forme, sans beauté, lourde & pesante mace' because it is without art, proportion and motion (IV, 45, S. XLII; IX, 107). Even the civil disorder within France is seen to have aesthetic and cosmic implications for it is associated with the loss of the world's 'reigle & ... forme ancienne' (XI, 81).

That Ronsard constantly put these aesthetic theories into practice in his own compositions can be readily demonstrated. Valuable work has already been done in this respect both by Marcel Raymond, who has recently drawn attention to analogies between mannerist art and the themes and techniques of the poetry of the Pléiade, and by Terence Cave, who has studied the concept of *copia* in Ronsard's verse, has noted his continuing interest in variety, abundance and ornate texture and has established parallels with the decorative richness of contemporary visual arts.[28] The focus of earlier pages of this study has been slightly different in that it has pointed to Ronsard's preference for compositions in which an aesthetic *discordia concors* operates (a controlled mobility, *copia* within measure), and this process has been illustrated by a number of texts and especially by the structure of a *Discours* to Juliain Chauveau (1569) and by a lengthy fragment from an elegy of 1559. Indeed as early as the Pindaric *Ode de la Paix* of 1550 (III, 3–35) these same principles of diversity within unity and of *paisible contrainte* are defined

> Tousjours un propos deplaist
> Aus oreilles attendantes,
> Si plein outre reigle il est

De parolles abondantes.
Celui qui en peu de vers
Etraint un sujet divers,
Se mét au chef la couronne :
De cette fleur que voici,
Et de celle, & celle aussi,
La mouche son miel façonne

Diversement . . .   (ll. 291–301)

and the poem itself is a perfect illustration of the manner in which Ronsard weaves together a vast spectrum of thematic material and imagery to form a single rich fabric, an organic whole.

The 'copieuse diversité' which he so admired in Pindar's verse and which was to become a constant feature in his own creative process, is everywhere in evidence in this ode. The wide range of subject matter includes the circumstantial and the contemporary (the recent peace between England and France, eulogies of Henri II and Anne de Mont-morency), the allegorical (the cosmic, social and civic roles of Peace), the mythological (references to the Age of Gold, Mars, Cadmus, Juno, Prometheus and Epimetheus), the moral and gnomic (the vulnerability and fragility of man), the historical and legendary (the Trojan War, the story of Francus, founder of Paris, France and the French monarchy), the political (advice to Henri regarding good and bad counsellors) and the aesthetic (the *fureur* of poetry and prophecy, an outline of the *Franciade*, a statement of aesthetic principles, the status of poetry at court with references to the *Grands Rhétoriqueurs* and the Marotic poets, the distinction between good poets and poetasters, the immortality of poetry, appeals for patronage). This multiplicity of themes has as its backcloth a vast temporal fresco and a dynamic vision of history, for allusions to contemporary events are intermingled both with recollections of mythology, legend and past ages and, in the final lines of the ode, with an anticipation of the future reign of Henri's son. The temporal energy of this poem—supported throughout by lexical clusters centred on aspects of time[29]—is in turn paralleled by other features of vitality and momentum: note especially the use of dialogue and prophecy (ll. 101–50, 201–68) to advance action, to bring the supernatural and the workings of destiny within the ode's panoramic scope[30] and to provide a complex multi-dimensional structure which introduces a 'Chinese-box' technique of episodes within episodes, poem within poem (the story of Francus is thus introduced into the mainstream narrative). Similarly animation and *élan* are imparted to the poem by the tendency to focus attention on episodic action rather than a few richly worked scenes, and by the central position given to the wanderings and exploits of Francus (ll. 107–50, 157–286) and to verbs and imagery associated with movement, action and gesture.[31] On at least four occasions (ll. 287–90, 361–8, 395–406, 461–72) Ronsard insists on describing his poetry by means of images of movement, and indeed the distinction he makes between good and bad poetry is one between mobility and lethargy (ll. 462–5).

At the same time this rich symphony of material is orchestrated into a tonal unity, and certain refrains heard throughout give the poem a coherence and measure both at the level of theme and style. The closer one looks at the thematic development and its apparent 'admirables inconstances', the more one is impressed by the way the ode grows organically, the way themes are interrelated and interdependent, linked often by processes of prefiguration, association and paralleling. For example allegorical, historical, mythological, contemporary and aesthetic dimensions interlock in that the Trojan War, which illustrates the destructive power of Mars (l. 85ff.) within the Peace versus War pattern of human activity, introduces the legend of Francus and the Trojan origins of France (ll. 101–286), which in turn contains a eulogy of Henri II (ll. 245–68) as the culmination of the destiny of the nation and the royal lineage founded by Francus. Later in the poem (l. 372) a discreet mention of Cadmus, founder of Thebes, suggestively recalls this legend of Francus. Similarly the more direct reference to Ronsard's *Franciade* (ll. 285–6) prepares the aesthetic statement of lines 287–301 quoted above, and this has been prefigured earlier by the cosmic vision where chaos and diversity are stabilised and perfected (ll. 45–50). Again the panegyric on Montmorency (l. 349ff.) and the reference to his fall from favour and his exile from court (l. 379) are developed within a statement relating to life's vicissitudes (ll. 369–74), and this in turn anticipates a later passage (l. 387ff.) devoted to human fragility and, by contrast, to the conquest of death and time by poetic immortality (a theme first suggested in lines 101–6). This return to aesthetic considerations is accompanied by an appeal to Henri for patronage (l. 395ff.), itself a natural preliminary to a further eulogy of the king (l. 401ff.) and to the offering of advice concerning evil counsellors, flatterers and slanderers (l. 429ff.), a theme lexically prepared as early as line 384 ('Les piés boiteus de la malice') and recalled as late as line 480 by the word 'envieus'. This idea is now continued (ll. 437–68) within the framework of an allusion to the calumny of Saint-Gelais and to the differences between good and bad poetry, a discussion prefigured by a previous reference to Ronsard's superiority over the *Grands Rhétoriqueurs* and other 'rimeurs' (ll. 361–8).

Further parallels and patterns of balance and repetition can be found throughout the ode and these provide a strong sense of organisation and unity. The early account of the cosmic functions of Peace (ll. 37–68) is echoed later in the poem (ll. 319–24), whilst the two balanced sections of the Francus legend correspond largely to the two central prophecies (ll. 101–50, 201–68) : a deliberate recall of the earlier prophecy at a later stage (ll. 269–74) is designed to contribute to the closely woven texture of the poem. The opening lines containing a discussion of humility, arrogance and reason (ll. 1–5) have a parallel in lines 441–50, and the passages devoted to the vulnerability and fragility of man similarly form a diptych of equal proportions (ll. 369–74, 387–90). The evocation of peace in terms of the passing of a storm and the advent of fine calm weather is introduced on three occasions (ll. 11–18, 305–10, 373–80) and the appeal for royal patronage is also arranged in triplicate (ll. 285–6, 395–400, 469–86). Again the theme of creation provides a unifying link, for the creation of the world from chaos anticipates both the creation of the French nation and monarchy by Francus and the discussion of poetic creation.

This sense of regularity and unity is most evident, however, in Ronsard's use of antithesis, a device operating throughout the ode at thematic, stylistic and structural levels. Such contrasting patterns include those relating to peace and war, birth/infancy and death, light and dark,[32] chaos and creation (ll. 37–68, 319–24), Troy and Greece (ll. 85ff., 117–18), the absence and presence of Montmorency at court (ll. 375–86), the fragility of man and the immortality of verse (ll. 101–6, 387ff., 466–8), good and bad poets (ll. 366–8, 437–68), loyal and dissembling advisers (ll. 349–50, 429ff.), just and evil kings (ll. 404–28), humility and arrogance (ll. 1–5, 441–50), storm and calm (ll. 11–18, 305–10, 373–80), and since many of these are mutually supportive they emphasise the finely textured nature of the poem.

A multitude of more localised antithetical items (cf. ll. 432–6, 459–60, 472–90) and other subtle structures of pairing and unifying exist within the ode. Henri is endowed with the 'double honneur' of humility and reason (ll. 1–10) and, like the wise man who tries to 'Doubler les dons que Dieu lui baille, / Et les vertus qu'il a des Cieus' (ll. 20–1), he has managed to ally 'Des biens & des vertus ensemble / . . . en un' (ll. 29–32),[33] so that his person (his 'vieille jeunesse', l. 411), his reign ('lacher & serrer les brides', l. 410) and his pattern of territorial conquest ('. . . sa conqueste / Es deus bords où le soleil / S'endort & fait son reveil, / Panchant & dressant sa teste': ll. 247–50) are all a perfect harmony of opposites. As a ruler Henri is described in fact as a reflection of a divine moral order of contrasting principles (ll. 441–50), and this order is exemplified on the one hand by Montmorency and associated mythological figures (ll. 351–60), and on the other by the fact 'Qu'un homme engressé de medire / Megrist à la fin malheureus' (ll. 455–6). In turn a lexical repetition ('contrebalance . . . contrepois . . . paisible contrainte' : ll. 50, 324, 359) clearly associates this moral balance with cosmic order, a parallel suggested earlier (ll. 69–86) by the two thrones given by God to

Peace and War and by the pattern 'de l'un . . . de l'autre' established throughout the antistrophe. Similarly the elemental harmony resulting from the creation of cosmos from chaos (ll. 37–68, 319–24) is illustrated later in the poem (ll. 329–36) by a passage in which water and heat are seen to counterbalance each other's excesses, and here too the thematic level is supported by the symmetrical structure of a tightly organised simile. Once again cosmic, moral and aesthetic aspects interlock and centre on common concerns.

Finally the ode is held in *paisible contrainte* by further patterns of imagery and lexis and, in addition to those already mentioned, those associated with love and sexual pantheism, the elements, sound, with human relationships (often hierarchical and of family and ancestral reference), and with fertility, abundance and growth are especially emphatic and poetically sustained throughout.[34] On occasions certain lexical recalls are chosen to draw parallels between separate contexts or different visions, and by doing so reinforce the structural unity of the ode: thus the word *fureur* evokes not only the wrath of Mars (l. 12) and the elemental fury of wind (l. 161) but also the prophetic ecstasy of Cassandra (ll. 95–8, 158), whereas the item *vagabond* (ll. 52, 290, 316) links once again cosmic and aesthetic preoccupations. Similarly the verb *compasser* (ll. 450, 462) relates moral and aesthetic aspects within this poem:[35] significantly the word *compas* is used elsewhere by Ronsard (VIII, 145) to associate cosmic and aesthetic principles. Thus in the field of aesthetics, as in the cosmic and social frameworks, the vision is consistent: change, abundance and variety are stabilised into balanced perfection, and this ode of 1550, like the *Discours* to Chauveau of nearly twenty years later, is an excellent illustration of a creative process which is a permanent feature of some of the best of Ronsard's longer poems.

NOTES TO CHAPTER TWO

1 *De rerum natura*, I, 215–64; 763–802; 1008–117; II, 67–79; 753–4; III, 519–20; 964–71. For the influence of Lucretius on Ronsard and for a fuller bibliography in this respect, see S. Fraisse, *L'Influence de Lucrèce en France au seizième siècle* (Paris, 1962), chaps. IV–V. Note also M. Morrison, 'Another book from Ronsard's library: a presentation copy of Lambin's Lucretius', BHR, XXV (1963), 561–6. For the Senecan influence, cf. *Ad Lucilium Epistulae*, XXXVI, 10–12; LXV, 24; LXXI, 12–16.

2 Lines 59–64 of the *Discours* reproduce, in a condensed form, the basic ideas and illustrations of *Metam.*, XV, 361–71, 375–8, 382–3, 389–90, whilst ll. 79–86 of the French poem are developed from ll. 385–8 of the Latin text. Even Ovid's technique of posing rhetorical questions (ll. 199–200, 'Quid? non . . . adspicis'; 362 and 382, 'nonne vides . . . ?') finds an echo in Ronsard (cf. l. 79), as Laumonier has demonstrated (XV, 156, n.2).

3 On the *translatio imperii*, see C. Trieber, 'Die Idee der vier Weltreiche', *Hermes*, XXVII (1892), 321–44; J. Ward Swain, 'The Theory of the four Monarchies',

Classical Philology, XXXV (1940), 1–21; F. Joukovsky, *La Gloire dans la poésie française et néolatine du XVIe siècle* (Geneva, 1969), Index Rerum: *Empires*. For the *ubi sunt?* theme, see J. W. Bright, 'The *ubi sunt* formula', *Modern Language Notes*, VIII (1893), cols. 187–8; E. Gilson, *Humanisme Médiéval et Renaissance dans les idées et les lettres* (Paris, 1932), pp. 9–38.

4   Lines 1895–6. For this legend concerning the Trojan origins of France, consult M. Klippel, *Die Darstellung der Fränkischen Trojanersage in Geschichtsschreibung und Dichtung vom Mittelalter bis zur Renaissance in Frankreich* (Marburg, 1936). For 'la conception cyclique de l'histoire', see A. Roubichou-Stretz, *La Vision de l'histoire dans l'œuvre de la Pléiade* (Paris, 1973), chapt. I.

5   Cf. Ronsard, XI, 23. Also Robert Garnier, whose tragedy *Porcie* was originally entitled: *Porcie, tragedie françoise ... representant les guerres civiles de Rome, propre pour y voir depeintes les calamités de ce temps*. On this equation, see Joukovsky, *La Gloire*, pp. 315–17; Roubichou-Stretz, chapt. VI.

6   Cf. also, *Physics*, III, iv, 203b18; III, viii, 208a8–10; *Metaphysics*, VIII (discussion of matter and form: see especially VIII, v, 1044b21–1045a6); XII, i–iii, 1069a18–1070a9; XII, vi, 1072a8–18. On the treatise *De Generatione*, see *Aristotle: On Coming-To-Be and Passing-Away*. Revised text with introduction and commentary by H. H. Joachim (Oxford, 1922), pp. xiii–xxxviii; and for Aristotle's conception of matter, form, change and cyclical regularity, see Solmsen, pp. 74–91, 118–35, 208–16, 295–8, 321–35, 378–89, 420–39.

7   For the Horatian influence, see Laumonier's notes to this poem. On Ronsard's debt to Ovid here, cf. ll. 5–8 of the French ode and *Metam.*, XV, ll. 178–85, 199–213; Ronsard, ll. 13–16, and Ovid, ll. 420–35; Ronsard, ll. 17–20, and Ovid, ll. 199–213; Ronsard, ll. 21–8, and Ovid, ll. 259–72.

8   Cf. III, 46; XIV, 194. On this theme, consult P. Renucci, *L'Aventure de l'humanisme européen au Moyen-Age* (Paris, 1953), chapter III; F. Joukovsky, *La Gloire*, pp. 41, 58ff., 149ff., 166–8, 214–18, 250–1. For the important work by Franco Simone in this respect, see Jean-Claude Margolin, 'Signification et fonction du concept de «translatio studii» dans la pensée et l'œuvre de Franco Simone', *Revue de Littérature Comparée*, LI (1977), 457–78.

9   Cf. Horace, *Odes*, II, X; III, xxix, 29–32; Pindar, *Pythian*, III, antistr. and ep. 3; *Isthmian*, V, ep. I; VII, antistr. and ep. 3.

10 For the Prometheus myth, see below pp. 148–9. On the Gigantomachy, consult F. Joukovsky, 'La guerre des dieux et des géants chez les poètes français du XVIe siècle (1500–1585)', *BHR*, XXIX (1967), 55–92. On Phaethon, Icarus and Bellerophon, see R. Vivier, *Frères du ciel: Quelques aventures poétiques d'Icare et de Phaéton* (Brussels, 1962), pp. 59–71; M. Eigeldinger, 'Le mythe d'Icare dans la poésie française du XVIe siècle', *CAIEF*, XXV (1973), 261–80; V. E. Graham, 'Fables of Flight in Ronsard's Poetry', in *Renaissance Studies in Honor of Isidore Silver* (ed. F. Brown), *Kentucky Romance Quarterly*, XXI, Supplement No. 2 (1974), 39–46.

11 For Ronsard's philosophical conception of Nature and for his developing pantheism, consult Busson, *Le Rationalisme*, pp. 364–5, 368–72, 374–5, 384–8; D. B. Wilson, *Ronsard, Poet of Nature*, chapt. III; I. Silver, 'Ronsard's Reflections on Cosmogony and Nature', sections VII and VIII.

12 Busson, pp. 230–3. For the origins and evolution of Nature's role, see E. R. Curtius, *European Literature and the Latin Middle Ages*. Translated from the German by W. R. Trask (London, 1953), pp. 106–27.

13 XVIII, 134. Cf. VIII, 250, var.; XVI, 355; XVII, 421; XVIII, 16. See also Guy de Tervarent, *Attributs et symboles dans l'art profane, 1450–1600* (Geneva, 1958–9), s.v. *Femme aux nombreuses mamelles*, II; and *Emblemata. Handbuch zur*

Sinnbildkunst des XVI. und XVII. Jahrhunderts. Herausgegeben von Arthur Henkel und Albrecht Schöne (Stuttgart, 1967), col. 1534.

14 XVIII, 253–4. Cf. VIII, 353–4. The comparison is Pindaric (*Nemean*, VI, antistr. I; XI, antistr. 3). Same idea, different image, in Ronsard, XVIII, 486.

15 Pindar, *Olympian*, II, ep. 1 and 2; VII, ep. 5; *Pythian*, III, antistr. and ep. 5; VIII, antistr. and ep. 5; *Nemean*, XI, antistr. and ep. 3; *Isthmian*, III, ep. 1; IV, str. 1; Horace, *Odes*, I, vii, 15–17; II, ix, 1–8; IV, vii, 9–12.

16 Developing at length a suggestion found in a pseudo-Anacreontic text (cf. *Anacreontea*, in volume II of *Elegy and Iambus*: LCL, 1931, pp. 49–51), the opening lines of an ode of 1555 (VI, 258) state the general principle of this mythology of change and give some idea of the extensive range of examples to be found in Ronsard's poetry. On metamorphosis as a theme and a literary device, see P. Brunel, *Le Mythe de la métamorphose* (Paris, 1974); G. Demerson, 'Poétiques de la métamorphose à la Renaissance', in *Poétique de la Renaissance et poétique du XXe siècle*, *Revue de Littérature Comparée*, LI (1977), 152–7.

17 From a wealth of references, see in particular IV, 122, s. CXXV; V, 139–40, s. CVIII; IX, 185; X, 129–32; X, 224–6; XII, 108–26. The starting point for this section is certain interesting pages of T. Cave, 'Mythes de l'abondance et de la privation chez Ronsard', *CAIEF*, XXV (1973), 247–60; and of I. D. McFarlane, 'Ronsard's poems to Jean Brinon', in *Renaissance Studies in Honor of Silver*, pp. 55–8. On the wider question of Ronsard's use of mythology and for a fuller bibliography in this respect, consult G. Demerson, *La Mythologie classique dans l'œuvre de la 'Pléiade'* (Geneva, 1972); T. Cave, 'Ronsard's mythological universe', in *Ronsard the Poet*, pp. 159–208.

18 For this combination of love, metamorphosis and mythological illustration (frequently Jupiter), see I, 35–9; II, 67–79; IV, 19–20, s. XVI; 23–4, s. XX; V, 109–10, s. XLI; VI, 258–9; VII, 256–7; X, 224–6; XV, 139–40.

19 *Metam.*, I, 548–52. See also, *Metam.*, II, 346–55; IX, 349–55; X, 488–502. For a study of the Daphne myth, see Yves F.-A. Giraud, *La Fable de Daphné* (Geneva, 1968).

20 Pausanias, *Description of Greece*, VII, xvii, 9–11; Catullus, LXIII; Ovid, *Fasti*, IV, 223–44; Arnobius, V, v, 7.

21 The same technique of describing the actual process of metamorphosis in realistic detail is evident in Baïf, II, 52–3; 180–1; 194; 316; Belleau, III, 40–1; 81–2; Tyard, pp. 205–6; 255–77 (*Douze fables de fleuves ou fontaines*).

22 M. Raymond, *Baroque et Renaissance poétique* (Paris, 1955); 'La Pléiade et le Maniérisme', in *Lumières de la Pléiade* (Paris, 1966), pp. 391–423; the introduction to his anthology *La Poésie française et le maniérisme*, prepared in collaboration with A. J. Steele (University of London Press and Geneva, Droz, 1971); I. D. McFarlane, 'Aspects of Ronsard's poetic vision', in *Ronsard the Poet*, pp. 24–34; O. de Mourgues, 'Ronsard's later poetry', *ibid.*, pp. 288–302.

23 X, 8–9. For the sources of this passage, see W. B. Cornelia, *The Classical Sources of the Nature References in Ronsard's Poetry* (Columbia Univ. Press, 1934), pp. 103–4, 116–17. Cf. similar imagery, vocabulary, stylistic and structural devices, III, 59; VIII, 120–1; IX, 134; XI, 134; 159–60; XIII, 269; XVI, 104; 211; XVII, 270–1, s. XXX; XVIII, 111. See pp. 53–9 for a more developed discussion of the aesthetic principles raised by this extract of 1559.

24 Cf. Ficino, *Commentary on Plato's 'Symposium'*, Speech V, chapt. 3; Louis Le Roy, *Le Sympose de Platon* (Paris, 1558), fols. 63v, 108r; Le Roy, *De la vicissitude ou variété des choses en l'univers* (Paris, 1576), fol. 5r; Tyard, *Le Premier Curieux*, in *The Universe of Pontus de Tyard*, p. 122. See other

references to an aesthetic based on Nature's variety in Ronsard, I, 32–3; 146; II, 95–6; III, 180; XVI, 332; 334; 340–1; 345.

25   II, 148–9. For this principle of *copia*, see T. Cave, 'Ronsard's mythological universe', in *Ronsard the Poet*, pp. 160–81; 'Copia and Cornucopia', in *French Renaissance Studies (1540–70)*, edited by P. Sharratt (Edinburgh Univ. Press, 1976), pp. 52–69. A book by Dr Cave (*The Cornucopian Text: Problems of Writing in the French Renaissance*) is to be published shortly by Oxford University Press, and its first chapter will discuss this notion of *copia* as defined by Erasmus and his contemporaries.

26   Cf. Louis Le Caron, *Les Dialogues* (Paris, 1566), fol. 138r; Le Roy, *Le Sympose de Platon*, fol. 108r; Tyard, *Le Premier Curieux*, in *The Universe of Pontus de Tyard*, p. 122. See also Pico della Mirandola's commentary on a love song of Benivieni in *Opere di G. Benivieni* (Venice, 1522), fols. 21v–22r.

27   VIII, 142. Cf. XI, 169; XVII, 334–5, s. LVI. On the cosmic and aesthetic implications of the circle in the verse of the Pléiade, consult G. Poulet, 'Poésie du cercle et de la sphère', *CAIEF*, X (1958), 44–57; *Les Métamorphoses du cercle* (Paris, 1961), chapt. 1; I. Silver, 'Ronsard's Reflections on the Heavens and Time', pp. 345–6, 354–5.

28   For details of the work by Raymond and Cave in this respect, see notes 22 and 25 to this chapter. See also the conclusions of a recent study of 'Le Baroque et la Pléiade' in André Baïche's *La Naissance du baroque français* (Toulouse, 1976), pp. 23–111. On these aspects of the visual arts, consult in particular John Shearman, *Mannerism* (Harmondsworth, Penguin Books, 1956); *Les Fêtes de la Renaissance*, ed. J. Jacquot, 2 vols. (Paris, 1956 and 1960); E. Panofsky, 'The iconography of the Galerie François Ier', *Gazette des Beaux-arts*, LII (September 1958), 113–77. A specific comparison between a mannerist painting and a poem of Ronsard is considered by R. A. Sayce, 'Ronsard and mannerism : the *Elegie à Janet*', *L'Esprit créateur*, VI (1966), 234–47.

29   Cf. ll. 29, 35, 36, 38, 84, 119–20, 162, 165, 214, 216–18, 219, 263–4, 339, 387–9, 411, 417, 456, 466–8, 480, 496.

30   Besides the supernatural element of the prophecies, see also ll. 187–200, 270–4, and the allusions to destiny structured throughout (ll. 7, 32, 104, 113, 149–50, 186, 195–200, 261, 283, 415–18, 487).

31   From a multitude of examples, see in particular ll. 15–18, 28, 37–68, 70–82, 89, 91–100, 106, 112, 122–50, 154, 165, 170–1, 173–4, 177, 187–94, 204, 209, 211, 219–37, 247–50, 257, 262, 270–2, 278, 280–6, 305–24, 337, 339, 343, 372–80, 384, 401–10, 430, 446–50, 451–3, 475, 480, 487–97. In many of these cases verbs of action are developed in patterns of main verb plus a series of infinitives and/or present participles.

32   Peace and war, ll. 11–18, 36, 75–106, 123–40, 225–8, 247, 251, 259–60, 265–7, 305–10 337–46, 373–80, 404–6, 491–7. Birth/childhood and death, ll. 10, 41–4, 64–5, 84, 89, 104, 115, 121, 137, 164, 174–8, 187–90, 201, 219–20, 225, 266, 354, 387–90, 418, 464–8, 496. Light and dark, ll. 6, 14, 17, 40–4, 57–60, 87, 91, 101, 160, 188, 190, 243–4, 248, 269, 272, 337, 339, 342, 363, 375–80, 389, 401, 412, 459–60, 485.

33   A similar idea of duality being unified is repeated in the final lines and provides a circular structure to the poem, for here Ronsard, speaking of Henri and his son, says that he will be 'le sonneur / De l'une & de l'autre gloire' (ll. 499–500). This pattern *de l'un . . . de l'autre* has a parallel in an earlier antistrophe (ll. 75–86).

34   Love and sexual pantheism, ll. 34, 49–50, 51–6, 65–8, 90, 107–10, 172–4, 315, 329–36, 344–6, 486. Elements, ll. 37–63, 74, 87, 91, 101, 105, 107–10, 122, 134, 144–6, 161–2, 194, 208–10, 278–80, 287–9, 308, 316, 318, 321–4, 331–6, 339,

342, 346, 401, 485. Sound, ll. 12–13, 80–2, 100, 143, 175, 195–6, 269, 393–4, 417, 429–36, 440, 454, 457–8, 465, 476–8, 499. Human relationships, ll. 7–10, 26–7, 84, 99, 136, 166, 179, 202, 205, 256, 279, 285, 331, 372, 419, 479, 485, 495. Fertility, abundance, growth, ll. 35, 36, 88, 106, 131, 147, 159, 207, 232, 265–7, 294, 297–300, 329–36, 365, 388, 412, 420–1, 455, 472, 484, 494, 498.

35 Other such lexical repetitions exist within the poem and serve a similar structural purpose: cf. *ventre* (ll. 42, 318); *enfanter* (ll. 43, 89, 266); *courber* (ll. 28, 61); *echine* (ll. 145, 319); *picquer* (ll. 80, 157); *nourriciere/nourriture* (ll. 334, 365); *grosses de/riche de* (ll. 88, 265; 159, 472–3, 498).

CHAPTER THREE

Ronsard and the concept of Fortune

THE PHILOSOPHICAL AND COSMOLOGICAL VISIONS

Before analysing Ronsard's conception of Fortune it is worth noting that he is aware of some of the various cosmic roles attributed to Chance in certain ancient philosophies. For example he briefly alludes on two occasions to the philosophical attitude of the Epicureans, who associated the general trend of human affairs and the conduct of the material world with Fortune, and he specifically does so in order to refute this 'erreur', and to express his fervent belief in a rational pattern to the universe: 'Le monde ne va pas, comme dit Epicure, / Par un cas fortuit, mais il va par raison' (x, 71, s. vi. Cf. xii, 280). Similarly in a sonnet of *Les Amours Diverses* of 1578, Ronsard, who was familiar with the Atomic theory of creation (iv, 40; 62, s. lx), refers in passing to the belief of the Atomists and Epicureans, who attributed the world's genesis to Chance: '... si Fortune ou Dieu ont fait cest Univers'.[1]

Although Ronsard may be aware of certain classical definitions of Fortune's role in the universe, it is difficult to form a precise view of his *own* philosophical or cosmic conception of Chance from the two long poems written specifically on the subject of Fortune, namely the *Priere a la Fortune* of 1555 (viii, 103–14) and the *Complainte contre Fortune* of 1559 (x, 16–38). Henri Busson has already concluded in his study of Ronsard's 'Etres Divins' that all that can be said with any certainty about Fortune's status from the *Priere* and the *Complainte* is that Ronsard recognises the power of Chance over the entire sublunar world and that he is 'au courant des dissertations qu'ont provoquées les deux chapitres (v–vi) du second livre de la *Physique* où Aristote étudie le rôle de la Fortune' (*Le Rationalisme*, p. 372).

Busson, however, produces no evidence at this point to substantiate his thesis, and one must look elsewhere than these two predominantly allegorical poems on Fortune for the clearest influence of the commentaries on the Aristotelian doctrine of *Tyche*.[2] Particularly relevant to this study of Ronsard is the way in which countless philosophers and theo-

logians had interpreted Aristotle's doctrine of *Tyche* in order to introduce the notions of Chance or Fortune into a Christian conception of the
universe. The argument of the Early Church Fathers, who adapted and
commented on the Aristotelian philosophy of *Tyche*, was that Fortune,
being a secondary cause or *causa per accidens*, could not possibly be in
control of the disposition of the world-system. Their conclusion was
that the prime cause, the first agent, of a rational universe, which is
based on a series of hidden logical causes, is to be identified with the
Christian God and that Fortune is merely an instrument of Divine
Providence.[3]

For the most emphatic Christian interpretation of the Aristotelian
philosophy of *Tyche* in the verse of Ronsard, one must turn not, as
Busson suggests, to the *Priere* and the *Complainte*, but rather to a long
opening passage of the *Discours a . . . Monseigneur le duc de Savoye* of
1559 (IX, 157–73):

> Vous Empereurs, vous Princes, & vous Roys,
> Vous qui tenez le peuple sous vos lois,
> Oyez icy de quelle providence
> Dieu regit tout par sa haulte prudence.
> Vous apprendrez, tant soyez vous appris,
> Puis vous aurez vous mesmes à mespris,
> Et cognoistrez par preuve manifeste
> Que tout se fait par le vouloir celeste,
> Qui seul va l'homme & haussant & baissant :
> Qui d'un berger feit un Roy trespuissant,
> Et un grand Roy, pour trop se mescognoistre,
> Entre les beufs aux champs le laissa paistre.
> C'est du grand Dieu le jugement treshault,
> C'est son advis, contre lequel ne fault
> Point murmurer : mais bien à bouche close
> Comme tresjuste approuver toute chose.
>   (ll. 1–16)

God has here usurped the functions—and lexical associations (*haussant & baissant*)—more generally reserved for Fortune, and it would be
difficult to imagine a more insistent or orthodox Christian interpretation of the goddess's assimilation to Divine Providence. Not only is the
passage based freely on a sacred text as Laumonier notes, but Ronsard
adds a religious tone to the lines by specifically referring to two biblical
figures—David and Nebuchadnezzar—who illustrate the concept of the
reversals of man's estate. What is also significant is that once again the
theme of human instability is expressed with a total absence of melancholy. The inconstancy of man's condition is seen to correspond to the
'haulte prudence', the 'jugement treshault', the rational purpose of God.

By submitting to providence, to the justice of a Superior Will, Ronsard is once again able to integrate man and his dilemmas with the more stable forces, with a divine universal law. It is this fusion which provides compensation for the poet and leads him to accept stoically the inevitable vicissitudes to which he is subjected.

In the following lines of this *Discours* Ronsard returns to the equity of God's prerogatives in terms of an evocative potter comparison, and, by discreet allusions to the wheel of Fortune (*pousse en bas, va tournant, léve, devale*), further emphasises the equation between Divine Providence and Fortune within a context advocating wholehearted acceptance of 'le vouloir celeste'. Laumonier has already demonstrated that this movement owes its imagery and general inspiration to the Epistle of Paul to the Romans 9.14–23, although it is likely that the potter reference in Psalm 2.9—the source for Ronsard's opening passage—suggested the text of St Paul's Epistle to the French poet. Furthermore the Christian adaptation of the Aristotelian doctrine of *Tyche* is here explicitly evoked by the use of Aristotelian terminology (*l'Agent, la cause*) and by the definition of God as the Unmoved Mover. At the same time this fragment is a further illustration of the aesthetic principles of diversity within unity, abundance within measure, discussed in the previous chapter, for although it has a single thematic centre and an organisation of stylistic and structural items (a series of rhetorical questions, the repeated *Qui* and *si* formulae, a balance of antithetical terms distributed throughout), nevertheless the elaborately developed potter image, the emphasis given to verbs of movement and action, the multiplicity of focal points and the shifting perspectives provided by the five rhetorical patterns all give these lines momentum and vitality and reveal a creative energy which is essentially centrifugal :

> Qui oseroit accuser un potier,
> De n'estre expert en l'art de son mestier,
> Pour avoir faict d'une masse semblable
> Un pot d'honneur, l'autre moins honorable?
> D'en faire un grand, l'autre plus estreci,
> Plomber celuy, et dorer cestuy ci,
> Ou les fesler, ou bien si bon luy semble,
> Quand ils sont faicts, les casser tous ensemble?
> Les pots sont siens, le seigneur il en est,
> Et de sa roüe il fait ce qu'il luy plaist.
> Qui voudroit donc accuser d'injustice
> Le Toutpuissant, comme autheur de malice,
> Si d'une masse il fait un Empereur,
> Et de la mesme un povre laboureur?
> S'il pousse en bas les Rois & leurs couronnes,
> Et s'il fait Rois les plus basses personnes?

S'il va tournant les honneurs comme il veult?
Il est l'Agent, c'est la cause qui peult,
Nous, ses subjects qui recevons la forme,
Bonne ou mauvaise, ainsi qu'il nous transforme.
Aucunesfois il nous léve aux estats,
Des haults estats il nous devale en bas,
Nous fait fleurir & flestrir en mesme heure,
Et changeant tout, sans changement demeure.

(IX, 158–9. Cf. IX, 169)

Closely linked to this concept of Fortune as Divine Providence is the notion of Fortune as Nemesis or Adrasteia, the goddess of retributive justice who performs a corrective and punitive function in the universe.[4] In classical philosophy and literature, Nemesis was a post-Homeric personification of the moral respect for law and order, a personification of the principle that wrong, excess and *hubris* should be punished. On the man who is too often blessed with good fortune Nemesis inflicts suffering and hardship so that he may learn humility, an idea based on the belief that the immortals were jealous of excessive and continuous human felicity and prosperity (cf. Tournier, pp. 45–91). Thus Nemesis was seen as an obstacle to the extravagant favours given to man by *Tyche* or *Fortuna*, and closely associated with this idea was the notion of her as a divinity of chastisement and vengeance who, like Justice (*Dike*), punished the guilty and the arrogant.

What is especially significant to this present study of Fortune as Nemesis is the way in which classical poets confused the personification of the moral idea and the philosophical concept of Nemesis with the functions, attributes and personality of those goddesses who most closely resembled her, among them Adrasteia, Nortia, and especially *Tyche* or *Fortuna*.[5] Medieval literature happily substituted Fortune for Nemesis, and even Boccaccio in his *Genealogia deorum* makes no mention of Nemesis as a goddess.

Similarly artistic representations of Nemesis, which had formerly given the goddess distinctive attributes of her own (cf. Tournier, pp. 110–19), gradually began to depict her with motifs more commonly attributed to Fortune, such as the rudder, wheel, wings and even the cornucopia. Certain illustrations in Jean Cousin's *Livre de Fortune* (1568) and the copper-plate engraving executed by Albrecht Dürer between 1500 and 1503 entitled *Nemesis* or *The Great Fortune* (*Das grosse Glück*), clearly show that at the beginning of the sixteenth century popular tradition tended to think of Nemesis and Fortune as having similar personalities and functions, if not as being one and the same goddess.[6] In Dürer's picture (plate 2, facing p. 72) the fusion is nearly complete, for Nemesis is depicted with the wings, forelock and ball commonly attributed to Fortune, whilst even those characteristics once peculiar to Nemesis alone, which Dürer includes—such as the bridle and the urn, in which she mixes man's fortunes—cannot be considered wholly distinctive, for these too had in turn been usurped by Fortune.[7]

In the poetry of Ronsard too Fortune is often closely related to Nemesis both as a personification and as a moral principle for order, as a chastiser of excess and *hubris*. Nemesis herself is rarely personified in a distinctive manner. Apart from a brief allusion in the *Hymne de la Justice*,

> Nemesis d'assez loin les suyvoit par derriere,
> Ayant le pied boiteux, & ne pouvant en l'air
> De ses ailles, si tost que les autres, voler
> (VIII, 67)

where 'le pied boiteux' is translated from Horace's 'pede Poena claudo' (*Odes*, III, ii, 32) and is meant to symbolise, in visual terms, the long delay which may elapse between the committed crime and the punishment of it, Nemesis is never given a detailed physical or mental description, never developed as a personality or as a goddess in her own right. She remains very much a personified moral and philosophical concept, whose status is associated, though not entirely fused, with that of Fortune or Divine Providence.

True to a commonplace literary tradition, Nemesis has a special role to play in Ronsard's love poetry, where she is often coupled with Fortune as a poetic conceit. Fortune is associated with the antithetical balance of favours given or denied by the lady and with the vicissitudes of the poet's love, whilst the function of Nemesis is to punish the loved one's arrogant disdain.[8]

Although rarely mentioned by name and rarely personified as an allegorical figure or divinity, nemesis is more frequently the philosophical and cosmic principle used by Ronsard to suggest some sort of superior justice, a rigid ethical hierarchy, which must be respected in the name of universal order. In this respect Fortune is not the pagan goddess of inconstancy, but the instrument through which the principle of nemesis is seen to work. Bad fortune and reversals of estate are sent as a punishment for excess or pride, and this adversity has a necessary and salutary effect in that it checks man's *hubris* and restores the balance and harmony of the world. Most important of all, the chastised offender serves as a moral example of the dangers of trespassing beyond the confines of the human condition:

> Quand l'homme est elevé aupres de ces grands Dieux,
> Il devient bien souvent superbe, audacieux,
> Et s'enflant tout le cueur d'arrogance & de gloire,

Mesprise les petits, & si ne veult plus croire
Qu'il soit homme sugect à supporter l'assault
De fortune, qui doit luy donner un beau sault.
Mais certes à la fin une horrible tempeste
De la fureur d'un Roy luy sacage la teste,
Et plus il se vouloit aux Princes egaler,
Et plus avec risée on le fait devaller,
Par la tourbe incognue, affin qu'il soit exemple
D'un orgueil foudroyé, à qui bien le contemple.

(x, 43–4)

Similarly in Ronsard's *Complainte contre Fortune* there is a clear suggestion that Fortune represents some punitive form of Divine Providence, since it is she who disciplines the poet's overweening ambition and his betrayal of the Muses, and is, ultimately, the instrument of his penitence and confession. This corrective and punitive concept of nemesis is again assimilated into the activities of Fortune in a passage of *La Salade* of 1569 (xv, 79–80), where, with the aid of a brief allusion to the divine potter image from St Paul and a reference to the Gigantomachy, Ronsard once more unites pagan and Christian visions and makes Fortune an agent of God. In both these texts Fortune is given the same moral significance as Nemesis, the goddess of retributive justice, whose function—that of punishing man's pride—she appears to have usurped early in literature.[9]

With the advent of the civil upheavals in France Fortune–Nemesis assumed a new cosmic role in the verse of Ronsard. In ancient mythology Nemesis had been associated with war through the legend concerning Helen's birth and the Trojan conflict.[10] Therefore the relationship between Fortune–Nemesis and war sent as a punishment for human *hubris*, which is developed as an important theme in the Pléiade's polemic poetry, is not without classical authority. In his *Panégyrique de la Renommée* (1579), for example, Ronsard searches his conscience for a possible cause for the civil religious disturbances and concludes that they are sent by Nemesis–Adrasteia as retribution for the sin of *hubris*. In the passage quoted below, which echoes the powerful rhetoric and the emotional intensity of the best political poems of 1562–3, Ronsard insists on the pride of the French people by emphatic lexical patterns (*superbes, grandeurs, la pompe & le fard, l'orgueil, arrogans, enflées, insolens, audace*), and by references to the crime of the Giants and to the mythological prototype of civil war,[11] and these lend a kind of historical truth and a universal authority to the ideas. By referring to 'David's people' in the final line of the extract, Ronsard creates a synthesis between pagan and Christian allusion and equates Nemesis with an avenging Christian Deity, for the chastisement of the civil war is compared by implication to the biblical punishments inflicted on sinful man by God:

> La Deesse ennemie aux testes trop superbes,
> Qui les grandeurs egale à la basseur des herbes,
> Qui dedaigne la pompe & le fard des humains,
> A chastié l'orgueil des François par leurs mains.
> Eux arrogans de voir leurs voiles trop enflees
> Du vent de la Fortune heureusement soufflees,
> D'abonder insolens en succez de bon heur,
> D'obscurcir leur voisins d'Empires & d'honneur,
> Geans contre le ciel, d'une audace trop grande
> Ne recognoissoient Dieu qui aux sceptres commande,
> Ains contre sa grandeur obstinant le sourcy
> Avoient contre sa main le courage endurcy:
> Quand la bonne Adrastie en vengeant telle injure
> Citez contre Citez de factions conjure,
> Fit le Soc & le Coutre en armes transformer,
> De leurs vaisseaux rompuz pava toute la mer,
> Les plaines de leurs ôs, renversa leurs murailles,
> Et mit leur propre glaive en leurs propres entrailles:
> Si que leur sang vingt ans aux meurtres a fourny,
> Et David ne vit onq son peuple si puny.
>
> (XVIII, 3; 1584 text)

THE ALLEGORICAL VISION

In spite of Ronsard's awareness of certain metaphysical attitudes and distinctions concerning Fortune's cosmic activities, he was probably more conscious of the literary rather than the purely philosophical tradition of the goddess. This fact is demonstrated by verses in Ronsard's *Complainte contre Fortune* in which the Muses stress the idea that the goddess Fortune owes her very existence and her deification specifically to poetry (x, 25). It is uncertain whether this is a direct allusion to the conflict between theologians and Christian philosophers, who tried unsuccessfully to annihilate Fortune's presence in the world-system, and the poets, who persistently introduced this pagan goddess into their poetry and ensured her survival,[12] but it does show that Ronsard was aware of the significance of Fortune in previous literature, and particularly in poetry. It should be noted at the outset that, whilst Ronsard effected a compromise between classical and Christian thought by assimilating Fortune into Divine Providence in his philosophic attitude, the *allegorical level* reveals a duality or a tension in his outlook for his conception of Fortune is uncomfortably close to the pagan goddess of chance and anarchy, whom Patch defines as: 'The capricious goddess, then, is what we shall mean by the "pagan Fortuna". She is in control of the universe, but she is quite arbitrary about it' (*SCS*, III, p. 147).

Description of Fortune: physical and mental

The origins of *Tyche–Fortuna* as a personification are complex and confused, but all scholars agree that at the time of the early Roman Empire Fortune had already become the goddess of chance, with the symbolic motifs and the mental and physical attributes which bear witness to her capricious nature.[13] Although the transitional period from paganism to Christianity showed continuing interest in the personification of Fortune, it was left to the medieval imagination to emphasise the essentially visual and external aspects of the goddess, to give a whole personality and character to Fortune, to describe her dwelling place, apparel, attributes, activities and cults with such detailed insistence that she at once transcends the purely symbolic level of allegory and becomes a living entity, a real presence in the world.

Ronsard in turn gives fairly detailed and graphic descriptions of Fortune on two occasions. In *La Promesse* of 1564, which is an allegorical statement of his ambitions and deceptions expressed by means of the medieval device of the *songe*, there appears a description of 'Dame Fortune'. Deaf to pleas, blind, or blindfolded, to the sight of the misery and misfortune she causes, mad and irrational in the treatment of her victims, Fortune is endowed with all the conventional physical and mental defects which heighten her irresponsibility and underline her inconstancy :

En pompe, devant elle, alloit Dame Fortune,
Qui sourde, aveugle estoit, & sans raison aucune :
Par le milieu du peuple à l'adventure alloit
Abbaissant & haulsant tous ceulx qu'elle voulloit,
Et folle, & variable, & pleine de malice,
Mesprisoit la vertu & cherissoit le vice.

(XIII, 7)

A similar portrayal had already appeared five years previously in the *Complainte contre Fortune*, in which Fortune's personality had been evoked by an enumeration of epithets commonly associated with her :

De fortune ennemie, inconstante & legere,
Sourde, muette, aveugle, ingrate & mensongere,
Sans foy, sans loy, sans lieu, vagante sans arrest,
A qui le vice agrée & la vertu desplaist,
Mechante, piperesse, abominable, infame,
Et digne (comme elle est) de l'habit d'une femme.[14]

Plate 1   *Fortuna et Sapienta*

Plate 2 Albrecht Dürer, *Nemesis*

Plate 3   Lorenzo Leonbruno, *Allegoria della Fortuna*

Although these descriptions are brief, Fortune nevertheless surpasses the empty symbolical personification of classical literature, for she is endowed with a vivid presence, with movement, with human status—the insistence on the woman comparison in the quotation from the *Complainte* underlines this human element[15]—with a whole mental and physical personality after the manner of the medieval tradition. She has a certain volition of her own, for not only has she likes and dislikes, ('A qui le vice agrée & la vertu desplaist'), but she chooses her victims carefully ('Abbaissant & haulsant tous ceulx qu'elle *voulloit*'), purposely refraining from buffetting lowly people, such as sailors who search for gold or poor workers and peasants (x, 18), deliberately attacking instead the powerful and the rich, the successful, the protected and the contented, the noble and the virtuous, as an example to the world of her own sovereign power. Thus although Fortune is capricious and is referred to as 'ceste aveugle sotte', 'sans loy', 'sans raison aucune', there is nevertheless definite method in her madness and more than a hint that she is not wantonly destructive or anarchic, for her victims are not chosen gratuitously and her fickleness has a determined end, in so far as it testifies to her omnipotence and serves as a public admonition (IX, 106; X, 17–18; 43–4).

Fortune's symbols

Inherently linked to this allegorical description of Fortune are those attributes which bear witness to her character and personality. The most important motif given to Fortune in both the classical and medieval traditions is the wheel, which was, at first, meant to symbolise her mobile and whimsical nature. Medieval art and literature, however, improvised on and developed the symbol of the wheel, adding motifs not contained in the classical tradition.[16] In classical art Fortune is not directly or personally associated with the wheel or with human affairs, and is not involved in turning or controlling the wheel herself. The wheel, like the ball, sphere, globe and wings, is merely an implied symbol of her variability, nothing more. Whilst it is true that in Roman literature there is 'a closer connection between the wheel and the fortunes of man . . . a vital relation between the wheel and human fortune' (Patch, *The Goddess Fortuna*, p. 150), it is left largely to the medieval tradition to emphasise and develop this aspect. In medieval literature and art Fortune is intimately associated with the wheel and is actually involved in turning it. The result of this important allegorical development is that the presence of Fortune becomes a living reality in the affairs of man rather than a nebulous symbolic force. The distinctive human element, the concrete realism, of the personification is underlined. Another result of this evolution of the wheel motif in medieval art and literature, is that the stress is as much on the *hostility* and *cruelty* of the goddess as on her mobility. The wheel ceases to be a pure symbol : it becomes a *weapon*, turning at Fortune's capricious will, elevating some to momentary wealth and fame, only to hurl them down again into the depths of poverty and misery as the wheel completes its circle.

Ronsard's frequent references to the wheel motif reveal signs of the development which this theme had undergone during the Middle Ages. In his verse Fortune is expressly involved in human affairs, for she herself actually turns the wheel,

> «La Fortune gouverne, & en tournant sa rouë
> «Rid de nostre conseil, & de nos faictz se jouë
> (IX, 117),

and, by doing so, she is the deliberate instrument of, among other activities, the vicissitudes of war and peace, and of the success and failure of military conquest :

> Bref vous [Henri II] estes le Roy qui plus avez esté
> En guerre & en discord, qui plus avez tenté
> Le hazard de Fortune, & comme sur sa rouë
> Des princes & des Roys, en s'en moquant, se jouë :
> Elle vous a montré que peuvent les combas :
> Aucunesfois en haut, aucunesfois en bas
> Elle vous a tourné : pour exemple, qu'au monde
> Un Roy, tant soit il grand, d'infortunes abonde.
> (IX, 106)

The figure of the goddess here clearly surpasses the limitations of mere symbolism and attains human shape and personality, for there is a direct association of the wheel and Fortune's hostile will—a common feature of Ronsard's treatment of this particular motif. Furthermore, in this extract, the victims of Fortune's malevolence are described as being situated ,on the wheel, as being attached to the rim, and this is a medieval subtlety foreign to classical art or literature.[17] In fact Ronsard develops this particular feature elsewhere with the help of yet another medieval refinement which had equated man's success and good fortune with his precise position at the top of the wheel, and his misery and misfortune with his place at the bottom or sides of the revolving circle (X, 5–6). It is within this context of the circular movement of the wheel, the 'retours inconstans' of Fortune and the reversals of estate that a multiplicity of contrasting lexical and structural items—many of them centred on verbs of action—find their natural place in Ronsard's verse : 'met du haut en bas' (X, 6); 'aux Princes egaler, / ... devaller' (X, 44); 'Aucunesfois en haut, aucunesfois en bas' (IX, 106); 'Tantost heureuse, & tantost malheureuse' (XV, 4); 'La Deesse ... / Qui les grandeurs egale à la basseur des herbes' (XVIII, 3); 'haussant & baissant: / ... d'un berger feit un Roy trespuissant' (IX, 157: cf. IX, 169; XIII, 7); 'Plomber celuy, et dorer cestuy ci; un Empereur ... un povre laboureur; les Rois ... les plus basses personnes; pousse en bas ... nous léve ... nous devale en bas; Bonne ou mauvaise; fleurir & flestrir' (IX, 158–9).

In *Les Estoilles* of 1575 Ronsard gives an interesting interpretation of the wheel motif and returns to this same idea of Fortune's victims actually being placed on the rim:

Bref les humaines creatures
Sont de Fortune le jouët:
De sus le rond de son rouët
Elle tourne noz avantures.

(XVII, 39)

Because of the fact that Ronsard has previously referred to the 'Parques filandieres' and to the inexorable force of Destiny, Laumonier has been tempted to see in this passage a fusion of the allegories of Fortune and the Fates: 'On représente plutôt la Fortune volant sur une roue; ici elle est assimilée à une fileuse, dévidant le fil de notre destinée sur un rouet' (*ibid.*, n. 2).

Whilst the first part of this statement is an oversimplification of the diverse artistic and literary interpretations of the wheel attribute, it is possible, as Laumonier states, that Ronsard has here equated Fortune's wheel with the spinning wheel due to an association of ideas and images. However, there is no literary precedent or artistic counterpart for such an interpretation in medieval or classical thought, although the possibility that Ronsard is here creating an original visual idea from a chance fusion of two allegories cannot entirely be ruled out.[18] However, it is altogether more likely that the clue to the visual idea in this passage lies rather in the image of the wheel of Fortune as a toy. The notion of Fortune playing with human beings like a toy is something of a commonplace in medieval art and literature.[19] Similarly Ronsard frequently describes man as a 'jouet de Fortune' and uses the verb *jouer* to evoke the sadistic pleasure and frivolity with which the goddess exalts and debases the human condition (VIII, 170–1; X, 333). In order to state this theme in visual terms, medieval and Renaissance artists had replaced the usual large wheel by a handwheel, which looked like a plaything or toy, and on which the figures of Fortune's victims revolved. One of the best-known illustrations of this motif of the handwheel is the picture of *Fortuna et Sapientia* which appeared in Charles de Bouelles, *Liber de Sapiente*, published in Paris in 1510.[20] This illustration (plate 1) shows a bindfolded Fortuna sitting on a globe ('Sedes Fortune rotunda') to denote her inconstancy, and holding in her left hand a small wheel on which four figures turn. Facing her is *Sapientia*, in a four-sided seat to symbolise her stability ('Sedes virtutis quadrata'), and holding a mirror in which her face is reflected. This illustration is also found on the title page of a French translation of Petrarch's *De remediis utriusque fortunae* published in Paris in 1523.[21]

It is possible that Ronsard had seen this illustration and is recalling it here in *Les Estoilles*, interpreting its visual motifs and its graphic symbolism in words. It is not only Ronsard's reference to Fortune's wheel as a toy and to the figures upon it which suggest this. What is of primary importance in suggesting a relationship between this illustration and Ronsard's poem is that the opposition of *Sapientia* and *Fortuna* in the drawing has a verbal counterpart in the French text, for the verses following those quoted above specifically refer to the power that the wise man—'le sage'—has over the stars and Fortune (XVII, 40).

Besides the wheel motif, the other commonplace symbols of Fortune appear in Ronsard's poetry, and nowhere more emphatically than in the following description of the *Priere a la Fortune* :

> Et si tu fais cela dont je te prye,
> Tu n'auras plus de boule sous tes piedz
> Comme devant, ny les deux yeux liez,
> La voile en main, ny au front la criniere,
> Ny ton roüet, ny des ælles derriere,
> Ny tout cela dont furent inventeurs
> En te peignant les vieux peintres menteurs,
> Pour demonstrer que tu n'es plus volage
> Comme tu fuz . . .
>
> (VIII, 114)

This essentially visual account would seem to suggest a debt to a more pictorial and plastic art than any literary or verbal tradition, an idea borne out by the fact that Ronsard himself attributes this stylised description to 'les vieux peintres menteurs'. Indeed all the features he specifies—the ball, the blindfold, the sail, the forelock of *Occasio–Fortuna*, the wheel and the wings—are recurrent motifs of medieval art, and some of them (the ball, wheel and wings) can be traced back to a strong figurative tradition beginning with early Roman representations.[22] However, on reading Ronsard's description of Fortune's traditional emblems, it is the copperplate engraving of Dürer, called *Nemesis* or *The Great Fortune*, which immediately comes to mind, the more so if we remember Dürer's extensive influence in France throughout the sixteenth century.[23] A comparison between Dürer's picture (plate 1) and Ronsard's poetic portrait reveals similarities in respect of the globe on which the goddess stands, the forelock and wings. Although these same characteristics are present in purely verbal accounts of Fortune, this passage of Ronsard would suggest that he makes use of both the medieval literary and artistic traditions in his allegorical conception of the goddess. Indeed it is certain that the whole evolution and development of Fortune—as well as of numerous other personifications—depends on a constant association and inter-influence of the two art forms.

Fortune's cults

An essential part of the allegorical personification of Fortune in classical and medieval literature and art was the emphasis placed on her cults and activities. These were those functions for which Fortune was specifically responsible and for which, once deified, she was worshipped. At the time of the Roman Empire there were a multitude of cults and *cognomina* associated with *Fortuna*, many of which continued into the medieval tradition.[24] In his own allegorical conception of Fortune, Ronsard does not develop extensively this particular aspect of the goddess's activities but assimilates this theme into a general evocation of her omnipotence. And yet he is clearly aware of the better known cults of Fortune, and especially of those which had found favour in the medieval tradition, for he refers to these—without, however, dwelling on them in detail— on several occasions.

Apart from the cult of the Fortune of Love, which has already been noted (above page 68), the activity which Ronsard develops most fully and refers to most frequently is that which associated Fortune with the vicissitudes of military conquest. Appropriately enough the two most emphatic expressions of the Fortune of War—a cult (*Fortuna Victrix*) much favoured in both classical and medieval traditions—appear in the *Franciade*, where *Victoire* is personified as the 'soeur de Fortune' and associated, among other activities, with the uncertain outcome of armed conquest (XVI, 195-7), and in the eulogistic section of the *Priere*, where the sight of Henri II and his princes in battle array against the Spanish forces provides the inspiration for an evocation of the goddess's omnipotence. On this occasion the historical example of Xerxes lends validity to the superstitious notion of Fortune and serves as an encouragement to the French troops.[25] Ronsard is also acquainted with the classical and medieval cults which had traditionally associated *Fortuna* with the sea (*Fortuna Redux*), with agriculture and horticulture and with commerce. For example, in the following passage of the *Priere*, which is constructed from reminiscences of Horace, Ammianus Marcellinus and Pliny the Elder, he apostrophises the inconstant and omnipotent goddess and briefly refers to her associations with the sea and with war. In addition this text is a perfect illustration of aesthetic principles already discussed. It is a single movement of inspiration contained within one lengthy sentence which gathers its momentum from repeated structural patterns (*qui ... et ... seule*) and from the related technique of accumulation: there is considerable embroidery around the central theme of Fortune's omnipotence. At the same time these patterns give the extract its firm organisation and its rhythmical measure, as indeed do the many antithetical formulae, a common stylistic feature of Ronsard's evocations of Fortune's activities. These aesthetic considerations of controlled energy, of *libre contrainte*, have a thematic parallel in the passage, for Fortune is described throughout as an example of the concepts of diversity within unity ('Es appellée en langages *divers*, / *Mais tout d'un sens*, royne de l'Univers') and of balanced duality (an idea expressed by structures of 'seule' plus lexical contrasts and by the final line, 'Et le fueillet des deux pages remplis'):

> O grand' Deesse, ô FORTUNE, qui tiens
> Entre tes mains les hommes & leurs biens,
> Dessus les champs qui conduitz les armées,
> Et sur la mer les galeres ramées,
> Qui t'esjouïs de n'avoir point de foy,
> Qui d'un potier fais, s'il te plaist, un roy,
> Et d'un grand roy fais un maistre d'escole,
> Qui de ton chef hurtes le haut du pole,
> Et de tes piedz la terre vas foulant
> Dessus un globe incessamment roulant,
> Qui n'euz jamais ny arrest ny demeure,
> Qui des humains à toute-heure-à-toute-heure
> Es appellée en langages divers,
> Mais tout d'un sens, royne de l'Univers,
> Qui seule es bonne & mauvaise nommée,
> Seule haye, & seule reclamée,
> Seule invoquée, & seule qui fais tout,
> Seule qui es commencement & bout
> De toute chose, à qui châcun refere
> Egualement son bien & sa misere:
> Et bref, qui tout en ce monde accomplis,
> Et le fueillet des deux pages remplis.[26]

Similarly on the other notable occasion when the poet emphasises the sovereignty of Fortune over the sublunar world, he develops the same passage from Horace's ode to Fortune (I, xxxv) and specifically mentions the cults which link her to navigation, agriculture, commerce and military success (x, 23–4).

The court of Fortune

In the *Complainte contre Fortune* there appears a lengthy allegorical description of Fortune's court and attendants, and it is here that the medieval inspiration, strong throughout the poem, is most clearly in evidence, for nowhere in the classics can such a detailed and visual account be found to serve as a model, whereas, as Professor Patch has shown (*The Goddess Fortuna*, pp. 123–46), medieval literature is full of such descriptions of Fortune's dwelling place, palace and retinue. In this passage too Ronsard's predilection for abundance and accumulation reappears, counterbalanced, as always, by devices of measure and structural organisation (the repeated *Là* pattern, the rigid division of the personifications into two opposing camps, the regular caesura breaks and balanced items within many of the lines—note especially the *Là plus qui* structure employed across the caesura partition and the definite article plus adjective plus noun formula echoed in each hemistich of certain lines):

Autour des ses coutés, cette grande Déesse
A mille serviteurs en une tourbe espesse,
Qui n'attendent, sinon de se voir appeller
De leur maistresse, à fin de promptement aller
A ses commandemens, pour au monde parfaire,
Comme Fortune veut, bonne ou mauvaise afaire.
Là se voit le depit, qui se ronge le cueur,
La pasle maladie, & la foible langueur :
Là se voit meinte nef contre un rocher cassée,
Et meinte grande armée à terre renversée :
Là sied le deconfort, qui se rompt les cheveux,
La flambante fureur, le courroux outrageux,
...
Là pesle-mesle aussi avecques les tristesses
Tiennent rang les plaisirs, la joye, & les lyesses,
Le credit, les faveurs . . .
Là se roulent autant de sortes de fortunes
Qu'on voit d'herbes es prez, ou d'estoilles aux cieux,
Ou de sablon aux bords d'un fleuve impetueux.

                                                  (x, 26–7)

Laumonier suggests that 'Cette fiction, ainsi que l'énumération suivante des serviteurs de la Fortune, est imitée d'Ovide, *Met.*, xi, 592 sqq., de Virgile, *En.*, vi, 273 sqq., et du *Roman de la Rose*' (*ibid.*, n. 2). However, apart from the briefest of reminiscences from Ovid and Virgil,[27] these Latin passages, and the descriptions of Fortune's domain in lines 5921–6118 of *Le Roman de la Rose*, reveal no evidence of textual contact and have little similarity beyond the general allegorical design and the technique of personification. A much closer and more rewarding textual comparison can be made with a description of Fortune's court and courtiers found in the *Pontificis Epistolarum Liber*, i, cviii, of Enea Silvio Piccolomini, Pope Pius II (1405–64):

Fortune herself was a tall matron of twofold appearance, her face now smiling, now terrifying ... On her right hand honour sat in command, and favour, splendour, joy, duty, feasting, laughter, wedded love, vigour, modesty, beauty, singing, drinking. And set no lower was fame, glory, victory, nobility, reverence, peace, happiness ... At her feet like maidservants or attendants stood riches, money, delights, allurements and pleasures with ears pricked up, ready to hear and obey whatever their mistress commanded (*stabant arrectis auribus, si quid iussisset hera auditurae facturaeque*) ... After this I turned to her left hand. There sat poverty, ignominy, derision, injustice, diseases, old age, tortures, prisons, hunger, grief, screaming, fear, shame, hatred, envy, despair, charity, war, plague, loneliness, scourgings, cares, and the names of a thousand misfortunes.[28]

Whilst the division of the personified attendants into good and evil categories is traditional in such descriptions, Ronsard's account may well owe a direct debt to this Latin passage. Not only is there a similarity between the two lists of allegorical figures and a parallel in the construction, general atmosphere and overall impression of the passages, but there may even be a direct textual reminiscence of the Latin 'Ad pedes ... stabant arrectis auribus, si quid iussisset hera auditurae facturaeque' in lines 2–5 of Ronsard's extract.

A painting by Lorenzo Leonbruno (plate 3, facing p. 73), which depicts the palace of Fortune (top centre) and her personified attendants —Ignorance, Envy, Hatred, Innocence, Repentence, Fraud, Calumny— may also hint at an artistic, as well as literary, tradition to which Ronsard could have turned for his visual and allegorical account of Fortune's court and courtiers.

THE HUMAN CONSEQUENCES OF FORTUNE

Originally *Tyche* and *Fortuna* had an exclusively favourable significance in classical literature and thought, but gradually the idea of bad fortune or reversals of chance became associated with the goddess as religious feeling weakened and the reliance on the favour of the gods was questioned. In Roman thought at the time of the Empire, *Fortuna* had usurped many of the activities and prerogatives formerly attributed to other divinities, and slowly the benevolent aspects associated with her had been partially replaced by notions of her fickleness and anarchy. It is this inconstancy and hostility of Fortune which the medieval tradition emphasised, largely from Boethius, narrowing down and simplifying the multifarious activities and the multitude of *cognomina* of classical thought in order to weave its own web of complexity around the goddess's unfavourable characteristics.

Although in Ronsard's poetry the favourable associations of Fortune are almost totally excluded, he is nevertheless aware of this area of the goddess's activities. The description of Fortune's court in the *Complainte* specifically includes good as well as evil attendants and elsewhere he allows that Fortune is 'Tantost heureuse, & tantost malheureuse' (XV, 4. Cf. VIII, 106; IX, 159; X, 24). In one instance, indeed, Ronsard even praises Fortune's 'divine clemence' for allowing Seigneur de Neufville, Seigneur de Villeroy, to be born as a moral and virtuous example in an age so full of vice and evil (XVIII, 40), but such an attitude is here merely a concession to the exaggerated sentiment of the eulogy. Moreover, Ronsard suggests that although Fortune is capable of giving good luck and favours after a misfortune, it is only as a further illustration of her inconstancy and cruelty (X, 73, s. VIII). Good fortune forms part of the goddess's evil technique for she and Destiny smile at man in order to lull him into a false sense of security so that they can the more cruelly mock and betray him (XV, 79–80). Indeed even when she allots favours it is typical of her capricious nature that she gives them to those who do not deserve them, and gives nothing to those who are worthy of such rewards (VII, 302).

Thus Ronsard tends to reject the favourable aspects of Fortune's activities, omitting those attributes—the rudder, ears of corn and corn of abundance—formerly associated with her benevolence in the classical tradition,[29] crystallising instead the goddess's original complexity on her inconstancy and omnipotence. Since reference has already been made to Fortune's omnipotence over the entire sublunar world in the discussion of her cosmic and philosophic roles, as well as in the section related to her cults and *cognomina*, it will suffice to mention in this respect those occasions on which Ronsard poetically expresses the inequality of the struggle between the sovereign strength of Fortune and his own puny weakness by certain evocative images and by a rich patterning of forceful verbs of action:

> Or ce monstre cruel, hydeux, & plein d'effroy
> Seulement nuit & jour ne se moque de moy,
> Mais, comme un grand Breton qui luitte d'artifice
> Contre un nain impuissant de corps & d'exercice
> M'a pressé contre terre, & m'a froissé le corps
> De ses bras ennemys qui dontent les plus fors.
> Aucunesfois le ventre, aucunefois la gorge
> Me serre tout ainsi qu'en la fumeuse forge
> Des ouvriers de Vulcan, la tenaille dedans
> Sa machoire de fer serre des cloux ardens;
> Et ne puis eschapper de sa grife cruelle.
>
>   (X, 18–19 : 1584–7 text)

Another image underlining man's fragile relationship to Fortune and to an apparently hostile universe is that which envisages the world as a stage, an immense theatre: human beings are the actors, and Fortune is the director of the chorus, the 'bon chorage', the controlling agent of 'la farce humaine'. In the following extract from an elegy of 1560 Ronsard's now familiar preference for a *discordia concors* of aesthetic principles is once more apparent, and the techniques of accumulation and balance, far from being mutually exclusive, are in fact translated by a common structural device (*l'un ... l'autre*) and stylistic (antithesis). Here too, as in a text from the *Priere a la Fortune* already discussed, this aesthetic concept of multiplicity within unity has a thematic counterpart in that the diversity of roles are acted out on a single enclosed stage under the direction of a single sovereign power :

> Tout ce qui est enclos soubz la voulte des cieux
> N'est sinon un theatre ouvert & spacieux,
> Auquel l'un deguisé, l'autre sans faux visage
> Joue sur l'eschafaut un divers personage,
> Où madame Fortune aux grandz & aux petitz
> Ainsi qu'un bon chorage apreste les habitz :
> Aucunefois Vertu en preste, sy Fortune,
> Qui fait jouer les jeux, ne luy est importune.
>   L'un joue avec l'habit d'un pompeux empereur,
> Et l'autre d'un soldat, l'autre d'un laboureur,
> Et l'autre d'un marchant : ainsi la farce humaine
> Au plaisir de Fortune au monde se demaine.
>   (x, 333)

Identical imagery and similar philosophical and aesthetic considerations appear again in a poem written as an epilogue to a theatrical performance at Fontainebleau in February 1564.[30] Here Fortune is the 'maitresse de la Scene' and 'Les cieux & les destins ... les grands spectateurs', but elsewhere Destiny is given a much more active role, working in conjunction with Fortune, enslaving man within the predestined mould of his particular destiny whilst the inconstant goddess plays with him at will (xviii, 37). In other contexts Fortune's omnipotence is associated with a philosophy of history and the principle of *translatio imperii*, as well as with political and moral advice offered to a ruling monarch (xi, 9–10; xii, 241–2, var.).

Inherently linked to these notions of the sovereignty and hostility of Fortune is the idea, common in both the classical and medieval traditions, of what Professor Patch has termed 'genuine tragedies';[31] that is those famous examples from history, mythology and contemporary life who have fallen from high to low estate and whose names illustrate the theme of Fortune's inconstancy and give authority, validity and universal significance to the otherwise superstitious nature of the allegory. The most widely read and influential anthology of the more famous of Fortune's victims was Boccaccio's *De Casibus Virorum Illustrium*, described by Patch as the 'development of the tragic theme (with examples) perfected to the highest degree', and a work which 'excited favourable comment and appreciation in its own time and had many translators and imitators'.

Whilst definitions of Fortune's reversals of estate take into account changes from low to high condition (IX, 158–9), in accordance with his insistence on Fortune's hostile nature, it is the tragic reversals which appeal to Ronsard's imagination, and it is this aspect which he constantly defines (X, 6; 27; 44; XIII, 68), and illustrated with mythological, biblical and historical names—Cadmus, Oedipus, Dionysius the Younger, Xerxes, Cyrus, Croesus, Hannibal and Nebuchadnezzar.[32]

However, as Ronsard states in his *Discours* to Prince Emmanuel-Philibert of 1559, there is no need to delve into ancient history for instances of the goddess's inconstancy, for contemporary life provides innumerable examples of tragedies (IX, 159). Elsewhere François Ier and his lineage serve as models for this idea (XVII, 83–4), whilst an elegy, composed on Mary Stuart's departure from France in August 1561, blames 'Dure Fortune, indontable & felonne' for the cruel circumstances which beset the life of this queen (XII, 194). These particular illustrations of the goddess's recent victims are obviously linked to Ronsard's circumstantial and panegyric poetry, for Fortune is a convenient device with which to pinpoint the instability of favour and the fragility of life at court,[33] and with which to draw attention to the injustice of a nobleman's temporary disgrace, to excuse his past mistakes and to eulogise on his (real or imaginary) virtues.

The contemporary example of Fortune's cruelty which appealed the most to Ronsard and which was poetically the most productive—and financially the most rewarding?—was that concerning the tragic fate of the Châtillon family. It is interesting to note that six of the principal poems which develop the themes of Fortune and the uncertainty of life are dedicated to Odet de Coligny, Cardinal de Châtillon.[34] Nor is it mere coincidence that, with the exception of the *Priere* of 1555, all these poems were published between the years 1559–60. These two factors would seem to point to some important circumstance for the composition of these six poems and for Ronsard's insistence on the tragic theme of Fortune at this stage. The answer is to be found in the history of the Châtillon family and particularly in the political and military vicissitudes of Odet's uncle, the *Connétable* Anne de Montmorency. Anne's political career was a series of reversals. Initially successful under François Ier, made *connétable* in 1538, Montmorency was disgraced in 1541 as a sympathiser of Diane de Poitiers in her fight against the Duchesse d'Etampe, who then dominated the king. Montmorency finally returned to favour on the accession of Henri II (April 1547), who immediately reinstated him to his offices and made him duke and peer (July 1551).[35]

More important than these political fluctuations, it was the military disaster of Saint-Quentin (27 August 1577) and the capture of Anne and his nephew, Gaspard de Coligny, which prompted Ronsard's momentary preoccupation with the Châtillon family as tragic illustrations of Fortune's inconstancy. It was Montmorency's release from captivity, as a result of a ransom and concessions made by Henri II in the treaty of Cateau-Cambrésis (1559), and his imminent return to France which occasioned Ronsard's *La Bienvenue de Monseigneur le Connestable* (IX, 117–23). In this circumstantial piece it is Fortune which provides the convenient excuse for France's military disasters and for the fluctuations of war and peace, since it is the same inconstant goddess who caused the French defeat at Saint-Quentin who now smiles on France and returns Montmorency to her (ll. 1–20).

In Ronsard's other poems addressed to Odet de Coligny on the subject of Fortune there are constant references to the tragic circumstances of Montmorency and his nephew (X, pp. 7, 9, 18, 31, 72–3), and when the poet comes to write the epitaph of Anne, who died at the battle of Saint-Denis in 1567, he alludes again to the duke's political and military vicissitudes but finds, on this occasion, some stoical comfort in the universal equity of Fortune's omnipotence and in the thought that such patterns of change are a natural and inevitable part of man's condition:

> François premier aux honneurs l'esleva,
> Où la Fortune inconstante esprouva,
> Tantost heureuse, & tantost malheureuse:
> Mais de son cœur la vertu genereuse
> Ne s'abaissa veincu' de la douleur,
> Prenant vigueur de son propre malheur.
> «L'home en naissant n'a du Ciel assurance
> «De voir sa vie en esgalle balance:
> «Il faut sentir de Fortune la main,
> «Tel est le sort de nostre genre humain.
> (xv, 4. Cf. xv, 7)

Faced with these examples of the tragic uncertainty of life and finding himself imprisoned in a theatre-world ruled by Destiny and Fortune, the Renaissance poet, like a host of classical and medieval writers before him, was obliged to search within himself for remedies and consolations which would nullify the power exercised over the human condition by the extralunar forces. In this respect Ronsard was helped by classical precept, for Ancient writers, sensitive to the inexplicable element in human life, attempted to achieve spiritual salvation and peace of mind by curbing Fortune's apparently over-riding influence on worldly affairs.

One method they adopted was to show fortitude and courage, to toughen body and soul, in face of adversity : others were to use reason, wisdom and prudence, or to devote one's life to the pursuit of virtue and philosophy. By such methods one could defeat Fortune : her power is not universal once a stand is taken against her and once one accepts that she has no control over man's mind and soul. It is a question of choosing the most effective weapons. Reason and constancy each has a value beyond Fortune's unreason and inconstancy; virtue and knowledge each has a significance outside her prerogatives, because, being herself evil and only interested in physical and worldly phenomena, she forfeits control over man's goodness, his spiritual devotion.

This was the philosophical reasoning which was adopted and evolved by the Stoics, whose aim it was to put themselves physically and mentally beyond the reach of Fortune. 'For what can possibly be above him who is above Fortune?', wrote Seneca, and it was especially this Latin writer who, together with Petrarch (De Remediis Utriusque Fortunae), popularised this idea of pagan remedies to Fortune.[36] This theme and its attendant philosophical reasoning became the subject of a vast cult in Latin, Italian and French literature and art.[37]

Although Ronsard questions the effectiveness of these traditional remedies on occasions (IX, 55; 117–18; X, 333), he much more frequently employs them as a means of annihilating the goddess's power, and advocates a pseudo-stoical attitude of patience, constancy and rational fortitude, based loosely on his reading of Seneca, Horace and Plutarch, in order to achieve spiritual consolation. Virtue—a rather vague, global concept which, in spite of humanist attempts to redefine it more strictly in terms of moral, spiritual and intellectual qualities, nevertheless still encompassed physical prowess and martial heroism in the sixteenth century[38]—is the remedy the most commonly adopted by Ronsard in his fight against Fortune. Since the goddess despises goodness and is attracted only to vice (X, 17; XIII, 7), and since she has no power over man's spiritual domain, virtue proves the most effective weapon against Fortune (X, 9). Virtue is the resistance offered by the house of Châtillon against the worst assaults of Fortune (X, 18; XV, 4), whilst in Ronsard's débat between Volupté and Vertu in La Vertu Amoureuse of 1560, the latter defines the stoic ideal of ataraxia and emphasises the notion that virtuous man, protected by 'philosophie' and reason, is impervious to the effects of change, time and Fortune :

Tous humains accidens il dedaigne & mesprise,
. . . & constant il se joue
De l'aveugle Fortune, & des tours de sa roue,
Il n'a jamais soucy du change des saisons,
Car tout envelopé d'immobiles raisons

S'enferme d'un rempart clos de philosophie,
Qui meprise le temps & Fortune defie.

(X, 346)

If 'the main trend of Renaissance thought conceives the relation of
these two forces (Virtue and Fortune) as an irreconcilable feud' (R.
Wittkower, 'Chance, Time and Virtue', p. 318), a less intransigent view
is taken by Ronsard when, in line with a minority humanist attitude, he
reconciles the two allegories. Virtue and Fortune are not always hostile
and must, writes Ronsard, be interdependent and complementary for
either force to be really effective:

Car la Vertu n'est que fable commune
S'elle n'est jointe à la bonne Fortune:
Et la Fortune heureuse ne peut rien
Si la Vertu ne luy sert de soutien.[39]

On other occasions Ronsard proposes the remedies of philosophy and
wisdom (II, 64; XII, 71; XIII, 157; XVIII, 102), whilst the Horatian ideal of
prudence and moderation (Odes, II, x), which results from the awareness
that the more successful one becomes and the higher one climbs the
more vulnerable one is to Fortune and the further it is to fall (X, 44; XIII,
73), was a concept which also appealed to Ronsard, sensitive as he was
throughout his career to the relationship between the forces of flux and
hubris. In his epitaph on Anne de Montmorency Ronsard specifically
congratulates the duke for having accepted with moderation both prosperity and adversity, and for not having fallen into the excesses of pride
and despair usually associated with good and bad fortune (XV, 7).
Similarly in Les Estoilles of 1575 he refers to the man who courts disaster
because he trespasses beyond the sublunar confines allotted to him, and
is unable to use moderation in his conduct of Fortune:

L'un sans peur de meschef
Bat d'un superbe chef
Le cercle de la Lune,
Qui tombe outrecuidé
Pour n'avoir bien guidé
Les brides de Fortune.

(XVII, 41)

Again the remedies of constancy, patience and fortitude are often opposed to Fortune, 'Et apren desormais avecques la constance / A mes-
priser Fortune & toute sa puissance' (IX, 123), and it is this stoical philosophy which, Ronsard states in 1563 and 1564 with the aid of the same

Horatian reminiscence, is the attitude best befitting the philosopher-poet and the one which conforms most closely to his own *naturel*.[40]

Finally, man's ability to reason, to seek causes and effects, is seen as a further safeguard against Fortune's domination and provides another element of spiritual comfort. It is human reason which attempts to define the motivating purpose behind the goddess's cruelty, and which seeks to console mankind by explaining Fortune's role in the world-scheme in terms of a necessary corrective and punitive morality and a just order administered by God. In the same way there are a number of philosophical arguments provided by man's reason, which are specifically designed as remedies to console victims of Fortune or to further justify the goddess's presence in the world. The first of these arguments, already seen in a passage from Ronsard's epitaph on Montmorency, emphasises the universal, the equitable nature of Fortune's rule. For Ronsard there is comfort in the knowledge that adversity is allotted equally to all mortals without exception, and that the vicissitudes of Fortune are an inevitable condition of man's status, regardless of wealth, rank or class.[41] Again there is solace in the idea, often expressed in stoical or consolatory writings, that bad fortune is necessary, and indeed spiritually beneficial, for it hardens and forms the character, teaches man virtues that would lie dormant in continual prosperity (V, 260; VIII, 224–5; XV, 4), and reveals those friends which are true by unmasking flatterers and dissemblers (X, 5–7).

Ronsard's treatment of the theme of Fortune thus reveals a duality of attitude which is best resolved by distinguishing between two visions, the philosophical and the allegorical. On the philosophical level Fortune is reconciled with a rational purpose, with Divine Providence, a reconciliation achieved both by a Christian interpretation of the Aristotelian doctrine of *Tyche* and by the identification of Fortune with Nemesis, whose principal function as a force for moral order and justice is to correct abuse and excess and to preserve the delicate equilibrium between microcosm and macrocosm. However, although Fortune is constantly endowed with punitive and moral functions which link her to the universal scheme, nevertheless her mental and physical characteristics, her attributes, cults, court and activities are described in such a way that she ceases to be a cosmic principle or an abstract symbolical force, and becomes a substantial personality, a humanised presence, closely identified with the pagan goddess of anarchy who so obsessed the medieval imagination. In his attitude to Fortune, as in his treatment of Change, Ronsard is drawn into a philosophical reflection on the position of man within the universe, and into a discussion both of the moral consequences of such a relationship and of the ways to remedy and transcend the limitations and inevitable sufferings imposed on man as a result of his frail condition. Much of Ronsard's philosophical, scientific and lyrical poetry is directly linked to his awareness of man's instability and mortality, and, viewed from this wider perspective, the antithesis of flux and stability provides a fertile and constant source of inspiration.

NOTES TO CHAPTER THREE

1 XVII, 316, s. XXXV. Same question posed by Seneca, *Epist.*, XVI, 5. For the role of Chance in the philosophy of Democritus and the Atomists, as well as in that of Epicurus, consult C. Bailey, *The Greek Atomists and Epicurus* (Oxford, 1928), pp. 139–43, 324–7. Cf. Aristotle's comment on the Atomists in *The Physics*, II, iv, 196a25ff. See also Lucretius, II, 216ff.; V, 416ff.

2 For Aristotle's conception of *Tyche*, see W. C. Greene, *Moira, Fate, Good and Evil in Greek Thought* (Cambridge, Harvard Univ. Press, 1944), chapt. X; Solmsen, pp. 102–17.

3 For the history of Fortune up to and including the medieval period, and for the compromise ultimately effected between Christianity and the pagan goddess, see H. R. Patch, 'The Tradition of the Goddess Fortuna in Roman Literature and in the Transitional Period', *Smith College Studies in Modern Languages*, III (1922), 131–77; 'The Tradition of the Goddess Fortuna in Medieval Philosophy and Literature', *ibid.*, pp. 179–235; 'Fortuna in Old French Literature', *Smith College Studies*, IV (1923), 1–45; *The Goddess Fortuna in Medieval Literature* (Cambridge, Harvard Univ. Press, 1927). Future references to these three articles by Patch will be denoted by the initials *SCS* and the volume and page numbers : reference to Patch's book will be denoted by the short title, *The Goddess Fortuna*. On this question, consult also A. Doren, 'Fortuna im Mittelalter und in der Renaissance', *Vorträge der Bibliothek Warburg*, I (1922–3), 71–144.

4 For the complex and confused evolution of Nemesis, first as a moral precept and much later as a divine personification, consult E. Tournier, *Némésis et la jalousie des Dieux* (Paris, 1863); C. V. Daremberg and E. Saglio (editors), *Dictionnaire des antiquités grecques et romaines* (5 vols., Paris, 1877–1919), s.v. *Némésis*; H. Posnansky, 'Nemesis und Adrastea', *Breslauer Philologische Abhandlungen*, V (1890), 1–184; D. M. Greene, 'The Identity of the Emblematic Nemesis', *Studies in the Renaissance*, X (1963), 25–43.

5 For *Tyche–Fortuna's* assimilation of other goddesses, including Nemesis, see Daremberg and Saglio, s.v. *Fortuna*, pp. 1265, 1272ff.; Posnansky, pp. 52–6; Tournier, pp. 99–110, 227–33, 277–82, 233–40, 246. The full extent of the identification between Nemesis and *Fortuna* in literature can best be seen by comparing the account of Adrasteia–Nemesis in Ammianus Marcellinus, XIV, xi, 25–6, with the descriptions of *Fortuna* by Pacuvius, quoted in the *Rhetorica ad Herennium*, II, xxiii, and by Horace, *Odes*, I, xxxiv, 12–16, and xxxv. The functions, physical descriptions and attributes of both goddesses are very similar.

6 *Le Livre de Fortune: recueil de deux cents dessins inédits de Jean Cousin*, publié par Ludovic Lalanne (Paris and London, 1883), plates XI, CXXIX, CXXXI, CLXXVII. On the Dürer engraving, its date of composition, literary source and full significance, see E. Panofsky, *Albrecht Dürer* (2 vols., London, 1948), vol. I, p. 8off.

7 Cf. J. Cousin, plates XV and XXXI; Patch, *The Goddess Fortuna*, pp. 82–3; Tervarent, s.v. *Mors avec les rênes*, II (Nemesis), III (Fortune).

8 XII, 221 (var.); XV, 87; XVII, 203–4, s. VIII; 328, s. XLVIII. On the traditional

association of Nemesis and love, consult Tournier, pp. 98, 108–9, 117–18, 267–77; Posnansky, pp. 6–23. According to Pausanias (*Description of Greece*, I, xxxiii, 7) the wings of Nemesis are borrowed from Eros. The appearance of Fortune in love poetry is commonplace (Patch, *The Goddess Fortuna*, pp. 90–8) and the coupling of Fortune and Love is frequent in the plastic arts too (cf. J. Cousin, plates LXVII, LXIX).

9 Ronsard, X, 25. Cf. same association of Fortune, reversals of estate, *hubris* and the ethical concept of nemesis in Ronsard, VI, 120–1; XVII, 91–2. For Fortune's assimilation of Nemesis' role as the punisher of *hubris*, see Patch, *SCS*, III, pp. 153, 210; *The Goddess Fortuna*, pp. 69–70; Cousin, *Livre de Fortune*, plate CXIX.

10 Daremberg and Saglio, s.v. *Némésis*, p. 53 and n. 6; Tournier, pp. 38, 106. Baïf refers to the union between Jupiter and Nemesis–Adrasteia which produced Helen (II, 134).

11 Lines 14–18 of the extract quoted clearly evoke the civil chaos of the Iron Age after the peace, stability and social harmony of the Age of Gold. Ronsard's main source is Ovid., *Metam.*, I. 89–150 (even the allusion to the Giants in l. 9 of the French extract may have been suggested by Ovid., *ibid.*, l. 151ff.). Cf. Virgil, *Georgics*, I, 125–46; *Ecl.*, IV, 18–45. Similar role given to Nemesis–Fortune in Baïf (II, 330–1; V, 30–1) and Belleau (I, 110–13).

12 Cf. Patch, *SCS*, III, chapters II–IV; *The Goddess Fortuna*, pp. 14–34. As Ronsard was aware from his translation of Juvenal, X, 365–6, for Pierre de la Ramée's *Dialectique* (Paris, 1555), p. 17, it is precisely man's ignorance of causes which makes him invent and deify Fortune as an explanation (Ronsard, X, 382).

13 Cf. Daremberg and Saglio, s.v. *Fortuna*; W. Warde Fowler, *Roman Ideas of Deity in the last century before the Christian Era* (London, 1914), pp. 61–80; H. V. Canter, 'Fortuna in Latin Poetry', *Studies in Philology*, XIX (1922), 64–82; Patch, *SCS*, III, chapter I and Appendix C. The power of Fortune at the time of the Empire is evoked by Pliny, *Nat. Hist.*, II, v, 22.

14 X, 17. For a compilation of the adjectives traditionally associated with Fortune, see Patch, *The Goddess Fortuna*, p. 38; J. B. Carter, *Epitheta Deorum quae apud Poetas Latinos leguntur* (Leipzig, 1902), s.v. *Fortuna*.

15 With reference to the famous anecdote concerning Charles Quint's remark that Fortune was a woman—an anecdote to which Ronsard himself alludes (V, 216, var.)—see Laumonier's note, VIII, 108. For this human presence of Fortune, cf. XVIII, 79.

16 For the history and evolution of Fortune's wheel, as well as for its artistic representations, consult Patch, *The Goddess Fortuna*, pp. 147–77; Doren, 'Fortuna im Mittelalter', *passim*; S. L. Galpin, 'Fortune's wheel in the *Roman de la Rose*', *PMLA*, XXIV (1909), 332–42; Cousin, *Livre de Fortune*, *passim*; Tervarent, s.v. *Roue*, I, II.

17 Cf. Patch, *The Goddess Fortuna*, pp. 155–60, 164ff., 176 and plates; Galpin, p. 333; Doren, figs. 5–8, 10–13, 15, 19.

18 Another factor that argues against Laumonier's interpretation is that *rouet* did not have the restricted sense in the sixteenth century that it now has. E. Huguet, *Dictionnaire de la langue française du seizième siècle* (7 vols., Paris, 1925–67), s.v. *Rouet* (vol. VI, p. 638), gives *rouet* as the equivalent of *roue* and quotes several examples of it referring to Fortune's wheel. Cf. Ronsard, VIII, 114.

19 Patch, *The Goddess Fortuna*, pp. 81–2; Cousin, plate XLV.

20 *Caroli Bovilli. Que hoc volumine continentur: Liber de intellectu . . . Liber de sapiente . . .* (Paris, 1510), fol. 116v. Cf. R. Brun, *Le Livre illustré en France au XVIe siècle* (Paris, 1930), p. 164 and plate V.

21   *Des Remedes de l'une et l'autre fortune prospere et adverse* (Paris, 1523). Reproduced and discussed by Doren, p. 143 and fig. 15. See also p. 144 and fig. 19.

22   For these attributes, see in particular Daremberg and Saglio, s.v. *Fortuna*, p. 1277; Cousin, *Livre de Fortune, passim*; Doren, pp. 134-6, and plates; Tervarent, s.v. *Boule*, I; *Sphère*, VII; *Bandeau sur les yeux*, II; *Voile*, I; *Ailes*, XIII. For the fusion of *Kairos–Occasio* with Fortune, see below pp. 118, 119.

23   E. Mâle, *L'art religieux de la fin du moyen âge en France*, 6th edn. (Paris, 1969), pp. 443-56.

24   Daremberg and Saglio, s.v. *Fortuna*, pp. 1268-76; J. B. Carter, 'The Cognomina of the Goddess *Fortuna*', *American Philological Association Transactions*, XXXI (1900), 60-8; Patch, *SCS*, III, pp. 144-5, 153-6, 174-5; *The Goddess Fortuna*, pp. 88-122.

25   VIII, 107-8. Cf. other references to the Fortune of War, IX, 106 (quoted above p. 74); XVI, 299-300; XVII, 72; XVIII, 123.

26   VIII, 106. For a fuller discussion of the sources and identities of these lines, see M. D. Quainton, 'Some classical references, sources and identities in Ronsard's *Prière à la Fortune*', *French Studies*, XXI (1967), 293-301. Cf. brief references to this cult of *Fortuna Redux* in the *Franciade* (XVI, 29-30; 105).

27   Cf. *Metam.*, XI, 613-15, and ll. 16-18 of the French extract; Virgil, *Aen.*, VI, 275 ('pallentes . . . Morbi') and Ronsard's 'la pasle maladie' (l. 8). Ovid's descriptions of the cave of Envy (*Metam.*, II, 76off.) and the house of Fama and the personified figures who flock there (XII, 39-63), have little in common with Ronsard's text beyond the general allegorical vision. For the more general question of Ronsard's debt to *Le Roman de la Rose*, and for its persistent favour in sixteenth-century France, consult H. Guy, 'Les sources françaises de Ronsard', *RHLF*, IX (1902), 237-46; H. Chamard, *Les Origines de la poésie française de la Renaissance* (Paris, 1920), chapt. III.

28   *Aeneae Sylvii Piccolominei senensis . . . opera quae extant omnia . . .* (Basle, 1551), pp. 613-16. The opening description of Fortune's rich palace and throne, and the central portion devoted to the throng of famous historical figures in attendance, have been omitted.

29   Daremberg and Saglio, s.v. *Fortuna*; Patch, *SCS*, III, pp. 144-5. These favourable symbols continue to appear, although infrequently, in the medieval tradition (see Patch, *The Goddess Fortuna*, pp. 120-1; Doren, p. 134; Tervarent, s.v. *Corne d'abondance*, V; *Gouvernail*, I).

30   XIII, 212-14. For this world-stage metaphor, consult E. R. Curtius, *European Literature*, pp. 138-44; J. Jacquot, ' "Le théâtre du monde" ', *Revue de Littérature Comparée*, XXXI (1957), 341-72.

31   *The Goddess Fortuna*, p. 68ff.; *SCS*, III, pp. 152-3, 166-8, 191-2, 196, 210-12.

32   III, 27-8 (and var.); VIII, 106; 108; IX, 158; X, 10. The tragedies of Cadmus (I, vi), Oedipus (I, vii), Dionysius (IV, iv), Xerxes (III, vi), Cyrus (III, xxi), Croesus (III, xx), and Hannibal (V, x) are all included in Boccaccio, *De Casibus Virorum Illustrium*.

33   It is worthwhile noting that a number of the references to Fortune's instability occur either in the poems originally written for the court verse of *Le Bocage Royal* of 1584, or in certain eulogistic pieces which ultimately found their way into this collection (e.g. IX, 157-73; XII, 241-2, var.; XIII, 68; 73; 158; XVII, 91-2; XVIII, 102).

34   The *Priere* (VIII, 103-14), the *Complainte* (X, 16-38), *La Bienvenue de Monseigneur le Connestable* (IX, 117-23), an elegy (X, 5-15) and a sonnet (X, 72-3) of the second book of *Meslanges*, and an elegy of the first collective edition of 1560 (X, 333-5).

35 F. Decrue de Stoutz, *Anne de Montmorency à la cour, aux armées et au conseil du roi François Ier* (Paris, 1885); *Anne, duc de Montmorency sous les rois Henri II, François II et Charles IX* (Paris, 1889).

36 Seneca, *De Brevitate Vitae*, v, 3 (*Moral Essays*, LCL, 1932, vol. II, p. 301). For Seneca the object of life is to escape from Fortune's sway as quickly as possible (*Epist.*, LXX, 13). In this escape virtue (*Epist.*, LXVI, 23; LXXIV, 1, 6, 7; XCVIII, 9) and philosophy (*Epist.*, XVI, 5; LXXXII, 5; *Ad Helviam Matrem De Consol.*, XVII, 5) were the sovereign remedies. Reason (*Epist.*, LXXIV, 19–21) and Fortitude (*Epist.*, IV, 6, 7; LI, 8; XCVI; XCVIII) could also prove effective against Fortune.

37 Patch, *SCS*, III, *passim*; *SCS*, IV, *passim*; *The Goddess Fortuna*, pp. 13–16, 20, 24–5, 42, 48, 83 and plates 2, 5; R. Wittkower, 'Patience and Chance', *JWCI*, I (1937–8), 171–7; 'Chance, Time and Virtue', *ibid.*, pp. 313–21 and plates 51c, 52a, 52b, 53a, 53b; Cousin, *Livre de Fortune*, plates LXXXIII, LXXXVII, XCI, XCIII, XCVII, CVII, CIX.

38 E. F. Rice, *The Renaissance Idea of Wisdom* (Cambridge, Harvard Univ. Press, 1958), pp. 149–207; F. Joukovsky, *La Gloire*, Index Rerum: *Vertu*.

39 XIII, 158. Cf. XVI, 329. Fortune and Virtue are sometimes seen in each other's company (VII, 71; XVIII, 150–2, ll. 2, 51, 59). On the Renaissance reconciliation of these two allegories, see Wittkower, pp. 316–18 and plates, and Cousin, *Le Livre de Fortune*, plates LXXXI, XCIX.

40 XII, 7; 69 (& var.). Cf. Horace, *Odes*, III, iii, 7–8. See also Ronsard, II, 169–70; 173; VI, 120–1; IX, 158; XIII, 248–9; XVI, 185.

41 See especially, VIII, 224–8 (cf. Plutarch, *Consol. ad Apollonium*, chapts. 8 and 9). See also, VI, 120–1; XVII, 84; 91–2.

CHAPTER FOUR

Ronsard and the concept of Time

THE MYTHOLOGICAL, ALLEGORICAL AND COSMOLOGICAL VISIONS

It is the myth of Cronos/Saturn and the early confusion between *chronos* (time) and Cronos the god which explains the complex evolution of the artistic and literary representations of Time,[1] and which, in turn, provides the French poet with certain allegorical and metaphorical features concerning the destructive nature of that force. Ronsard is fully conversant with the myth of Cronos as recounted by Hesiod (*Theogony*, l. 453ff.), Callimachus (*Hymn to Zeus*), Ovid (*Fasti*, IV, 197–214; V, 111–28) and later mythographers (Fulgentius and Hyginus), and he refers to its main elements on several occasions (VII, 38–9; XVI, 139–40). It is, however, in the *Franciade* that he gives his most visual description of 'Saturne, affamé de nature' :

> En cheveux blancs, de vieillesse agravé
> A la grand'faux, qui avoit la machoire
> Du sang des siens toute relante & noire.
> (XVI, 139)

Originally interpreted as an agricultural implement relating to his reign during the Age of Gold or as an instrument of castration, the attribute of Saturn's scythe or sickle became associated with the god of Time after the confusion of identities—'Some others say that Saturn is the god of those times which return like a sickle upon themselves' (Servius, *In Bucolica et Georgica Commentarii*, II, 406). This explains not only the traditional image, frequently found in the verse of Ronsard, of the 'grand Faucheur inexorable' laying waste all things terrestrial ('. . . la faulx du temps qui toute chose abbat': X, 105), but also the metaphorical embroidery around the idea of Time as a harvester. Besides the scythe, the only other symbol that Ronsard gives to Time in his rather cursory descriptions, is that of wings (XIII, 153), a traditional motif associated with *Kairos–Occasio* and not originally connected with the Saturn myth (Tervarent, s.v. *Ailes*, III; *Vieillard ailé*). The other motifs commonly attributed to Time/Saturn in Renaissance and Baroque art—an hourglass, a snake or dragon biting its own tail, a zodiac, clock and crutches[2]—receive no mention in the verse of Ronsard, apart from passing allusions to 'la deuscentiéme année / Queue à queue en soi retournée' and to 'en serpent retournée' (III, 11; IV, 147, s. CLIII). In these brief references to Time we are essentially in the presence of a formal personification, which has the value of a simple animate metaphor with very little visual substance.

Another metaphor originating from the myth of Saturn eating his children and from the iconographical tradition associated with the legend[3] is that which pictures Time devouring its own creations: 'Le temps nous fait, le temps mesme nous mange' (XVI, 330). Whilst such stylised expressions as 'Le Temps mangeard toute chose consomme', 'l'an qui tout mange' (I, 81; XV, 155) may suggest that the metaphor has lost its original associations with the Saturn legend, and is little more than a restatement of a commonplace found in well-known texts of Ovid (*Metam.*, XV, 234–6; *Ex Ponto*, IV, viii, 49–50), nevertheless a passage from the posthumously published elegy to Desportes (1587) clearly demonstrates that Ronsard is aware of the mythological derivation of the metaphor:

> Or l'ouvrage & l'ouvrier font un mesme voyage,
> Leur chemin est la Mort. Athenes & Carthage,
> Et Rome qui tenoit la hauteur des hauteurs,
> Sont poudre maintenant comme leurs fondateurs.
>   Pour ce les Grecs ont dit, que glout de faim extreme
> Saturne devoroit ses propres enfans mesme.
> Le general est ferme, & ne fait place au temps,
> Le particulier meurt presque au bout de cent ans.
>   (XVIII, 248–9)

Similarly an addition of 1587 to the *Tombeau de Marguerite de France* (1575) adapts a Pindaric metaphor concerning 'Time the father of all' (*Olympian*, II, ep. 1) in order to relate the vision of the destruction of time more emphatically to its original mythological source: 'Le temps est nostre pere, & le temps nous remange. / Un Saturne affamé, il faut luy obeïr' (XVII, 80: var.). On one occasion Ronsard distantly recalls both aspects of the Saturn myth—the scythe and the devouring metaphor—and fuses them in a manner which may well reveal a simultaneous debt to iconographical tradition as well as to the Hesiodic account of the castration of Uranus by Cronos: '. . . la faux dentee / Des ans, dont toute chose à la fin est domtée'.[4]

On the astrological level Saturn was considered the coldest and slowest of the planets and had always been associated with old age and death (Cf. Ronsard, VIII, 91; 250–1; XVIII, 338). From very early times artistic representations of Death had appropriated Saturn's scythe (Panofsky, pp. 76–7; Tervarent, s.v. *Faux*, I, II), and it was only natural that the fusion of Saturn and Time the Destroyer would lead to the assimilation of Time and Death : '... Time, having appropriated the qualities of the deadly, cannibalistic, scythe-brandishing Saturn, became more and more intimately related to Death' (Panofsky, p. 82). There is, naturally, evidence of this complex fusion of the personifications of Saturn, Time and Death in the poetry of Ronsard, not only in the manner in which his allegorical description of Death in the *Hymne de la Mort* appropriates the scythe attribute originally associated with Saturn/Time (VIII, 175. Cf. XII, 267; XIII, 184), but also in the way that the metaphors of harvesting and devouring are transferred on occasions from Saturn/Time to Death (V, 214; XIII, 184; XVII, 6; 124; XVIII, 290).

Distant echoes of the Saturn/Time confusion are heard again in Ronsard's *Hymne de l'Esté* (1563) where, in the context of an allegorical account of the birth of the four seasons from the 'adulterous' union of Nature and the Sun, Time is portrayed as the elderly, impotent husband of Nature. Although the framework of this fable is taken from Teofilo Folengo (*alias* Merlino Coccaio), *Macaronicae*, XIV, ll. 147–65, Ronsard's conception of Time surpasses the purely allegorical and attains cosmic proportions nowhere apparent in his source. Time, in Ronsard's account, has a cosmological function, that of the generation and preservation of the species, for it is from his marriage to Nature,

> ... que ce grand univers
> Fut peuplé tout soudain de nos enfans divers.
> Car tout cela qui vit, & qui habite au Monde
> Est yssu du plaisir de nostre amour fecunde.
>
> (XII, 37)

In accordance with his general tendency to integrate his personifications and allegories into his cosmology, Ronsard consistently attempts to incorporate his notion of Time as a force for creation and conservation into his complex vision of the universe. An ode of 1550 already associates Cronos/Time with generation and plenitude (I, 148), whilst in the *Ode a Michel de l'Hospital* (1552) Time participates in the act of human creation, but here his role is essentially passive, for although he places the spindles in a coffer and presents the finished 'fuzeau humain' to Jupiter, it is the *Parcae* who choose the individual spindle and allot the life span of thread (III, 154–5). Moreover, as certain lines of the *Hymne de la Justice* (1555) make clear, Time has no power over the destiny of man once it has been allotted (VIII, 64). In the *Hymne du Ciel* of the same year the constituent parts of time—the hours, days, months, years, seasons and centuries—are described as children of Heaven and contribute to a perfectly ordered cosmos (VIII, 148), in the same way as in the *Hymne de l'Eternité* (1556) Saturn—again clearly identified with temporal considerations—the *Heures* and *L'An* have their well-defined places in the extralunar hierarchy, and the regularity and sureness of their movements actively support the preservation and stability of the universe (VIII, 250–1).

More especially the *Heures* are singled out for certain specific cosmic functions. In Homer the *Horae* guard the gates of Olympus (*Iliad*, V, 749; VIII, 393): they open and close these by dispersing or condensing the clouds, thereby promoting the fertility of the earth by a prudent variety of weathers. In later mythology the *Horae* became identified with the seasons (Daremberg and Saglio, s.v. *Horae*), but although this confusion is still in evidence in the poetry of the Pléiade, Ronsard returns to the Homeric definition in his *Hymne des Astres* (VIII, 150–61). Here he explains how, at the genesis of the universe, the stars wandered aimlessly about the heavens, 'eparses, sans vertu' (ll. 19–24), and then, with the help of a beautiful image recalled from du Bellay, he describes how the *Heures*, as instruments of cosmic order, were accorded the task of collecting the stars together in the morning and releasing them in space with the evening moon (ll. 25–38. Cf. XIX, 111). In Ronsard's *Hymne de l'Esté* (XII, 40), on the other hand, the Hours are chambermaids in Sun's palace, a role probably suggested by Ovid (*Metam.*, II, 26 and 118).

In the same manner the allegory of Youth is introduced into Ronsard's cosmology, for although *Jeunesse* is equated with Hebe/Juventas, the goddess who married Hercules and who filled the cups of the gods with nectar before Ganymedes obtained this office (XII, 83; XV, 251–2), she clearly transcends the mythological and allegorical levels in Ronsard's verse and serves an important cosmic function beyond that allotted to her by tradition. In *Hercule Chrestien* (1555) the myth of Hercules' marriage to *Jeunesse* is given universal significance, for it symbolises Christ's resurrection and ascension and man's ultimate conquest of death (VIII, 222). It is, however, in the *Hymne de l'Eternité* of the following year that a detailed description of *Jeunesse* appears, which owes a debt both to iconographical representation and to the Marullus text which is the immediate source for Ronsard's passage:[5] this is accompanied by a definition of the goddess's cosmic role which has no counterpart in the neo-Latin model:

A ton dextre costé la Jeunesse se tient,
Jeunesse au chef crespu, dont la tresse luy vient
Flottant jusqu'aux talons par ondes non tondue,

Qui luy frappe le doz en filz d'or estendue :
Cette Jeunesse ayant le teint de roses franc,
D'une boucle d'azur ceinte de sur le flanc,
Dans un vase doré te donne de la dextre
A boire du nectar, afin de te faire estre
Tousjours saine & disposte, & afin que ton front
Ne soit jamais ridé comme les nostres sont.
De l'aultre main senestre, avec grande rudesse
Repoulse l'estomac de la triste Vieillesse,
Et la chasse du Ciel à coups de poing, afin
Que le Ciel ne vieillisse, & qu'il ne prenne fin.

(VIII, 248–9)

The goddess, therefore, preserves the heavens in eternal youth and the
conflict between *Jeunesse* and *Vieillesse* is yet another illustration of the
antithetical balance between flux and stability, life and death, peace and
discord, which characterises Ronsard's cosmic vision.

Although most of the subsequent references to *Jeunesse* are brief—
she is glimpsed alternately in the company of Flora and Bacchus (XII, 29;
63), and it was she, we learn, who built the palace of Spring and breast-
fed Love (XII, 58; XVII, 333, s. LIV)—there is a restatement of her cosmic
function in the *Hymne de l'Esté*, where Sun gives Nature the gift of 'la
Deesse Jouvence' in order that her regenerative power and her fertility
remain constant (XII, 42).

The same preoccupation with the cosmic significance of youth and
old age, fertility and sterility, preservation and destruction is seen in
Ronsard's anthropomorphic treatment of the Seasons in his four *hymnes*
of 1563. From his earliest odes Ronsard had always considered seasonal
change as evidence of a rhythmic order (I, 208–9; V, 165–7; VIII, 225),
but it is more precisely in these later *hymnes* that the allegories and
myths are constantly paralleled by cosmological interpretations which
introduce the seasons into a dynamic vision of time which embraces the
natural cycle of fecundity and generation. In the *Hymne du Printemps*
(XII, 27–34), Spring is not only associated with Love in the creation of
cosmos from chaos (ll. 1–4), but the coupling of Flora and Spring results
in the world's rejuvenation, in its return to a Golden Age state of fertile
auto-productivity (ll. 37–46). Again, by imprisoning Winter for nine
months, it is Spring who ensures the return to Earth of the fecundating
Sun (ll. 81–120). This association of Spring and plenitude is found in the
description of her palace (XII, 58–9), whilst the same sense of cosmic
preservation is demonstrated when eternal Spring is divided into the
other seasons, for on Juno's intervention the excessive heat of Summer
is tempered by rain, thereby saving the world from destruction by fire
(XII, 31).

The *Hymne de l'Esté* (XII, 35–45) too contrasts the senility and impotence of Time (ll. 21–58, 161–72) with the youthful vigour, ardour and fertility of Nature and Sun (ll. 79, 108, 152: cf. xii, 52–3), and this old ages versus youth opposition has a counterpart in a reference to the myth of Tithonus and Aurora (ll. 123–4). This relationship between Nature and Sun is paralleled in turn by the union of Ceres and Summer which is fundamental to the preservation of the world in a state of maturity and perfection (ll. 187–216). My role, says Ceres to Summer, described earlier as '. . . toujours en action, / Vigoreux, genereux, plain de perfection, / Ennemy de repos' (ll. 115–17; cf. xii, 60–1), is to

> . . . garder ce Monde, & lui donner puissance,
> Vertu, force, & pouvoir, lequel n'est qu'en enfance,
> Debile, sans effect, & sans maturité,
> Par faute de sentir nostre divinité.
> . . .
> Pleine de ta vertu, je feray mon devoir,
> De meurir les amours de la Terre infeconde,
> Et de rendre perfait l'imperfait de ce Monde.
>   A toy fils du Soleil est la perfection :
> Tu soustiens & nourris la generation,
> Car rien sans ta vertu au monde ne peut estre.
>   (ll. 189–92, 204–9)

The repetition of the word *vertu* and certain associated patterns (*ennemy de repos, vigoreux, force, puissance*), as well as the emphasis throughout on Ceres' mobility, energy and perfection, are not gratuitous, for they recall several cosmological texts discussed early in chapter one in which Ronsard defines the pantheistic role of the *Anima Mundi* in precisely the same terms. Identical lexical clusters reappear in the *Hymne de l'Autonne* (xii, 46–67) where Autumn is portrayed as immature, childish, feeble (ll. 95–104, 144–8), as 'seule à repos' (l. 115), 'Qui n'eut rien de vertu ny de puissance en elle' (xii, 40). Her sterility and lack of vitality are not only a denial of life, puberty and natural instinct (ll. 87–94), but they destroy the pattern of germination, growth, maturation begun by the other seasons: they are thus pernicious to man and nature alike (ll. 358–68). It is as a result of her fertilisation by Bacchus that Autumn becomes 'Maitresse du vaisseau que l'Abondance tient' (l. 447) and attains womanhood, thereby completing the natural rhythm of preservation by her abundance and fructification ('. . . de tous biens richement couronnée, / Des humains le grenier, le cellier, la planté' : ll. 454–5). A similar concern for preservation and order informs the *Hymne de l'Hyver* (xii, 68–86), for it is in the name of cosmic harmony and balanced perfection that Jupiter liberates and pardons Winter for siding with the Giants in their war against the gods ('. . . Hyver, je te delivre, / Afin qu'en amitié le monde puisse vivre' : ll. 371–2) and agrees to integrate his three-month reign into the natural design of the world, on the one condition that Winter undertakes never to interfere with the cycles of germination, growth and fertility (ll. 373–86). Once again a subtle use of lexis (*amitié* and, later in the poem, *heureuse concorde*: l. 388) suggestively situates us in those neo-Platonic passages, noted in the first chapter, where Ronsard considers all cosmic activity as a fragile balance between *Amitié* and *Discorde*.[6]

At the same time some recurrent themes and motifs of these seasonal *hymnes* suggest parallels with certain aesthetic principles which, it has been seen, are constantly defined and illustrated throughout Ronsard's poetry. What encourages such an association between thematic statements and poetic concerns are the lengthy opening sections of all but one of the *hymnes*, for these centre on the mission of the poet and the nature of poetry and give an aesthetic framework to the ensuing myths and allegories (XII, 35–6; 46–50; 68–72). For example, the idea that creation and abundance depend on moderating extremes and excess is found on several occasions in these poems (XII, 31; 32–3; 82–3), and such a notion echoes the aesthetic concepts of restraint and measure. The four seasons themselves—all born from a single source (XII, 31–2; 40–1) but with a variety of contrasting characteristics relating to their sex (male, female, hermaphrodite)—are a good illustration of the twin concepts of a balanced perfection of opposites and of diversity within unity. Similarly there is a constant thematic movement in each individual poem from discord and chaos to harmony, from imperfection to perfection, from sterility and stagnation to conception and activity, and such an arrangement of material clearly parallels the artistic process itself. These internal movements are reflected in the general structure of the four poems, for the *Hymne du Printemps* begins with the theme of creation from chaos (ll. 1–4) and the *Hymne de l'Hyver* concludes with the solitary, exiled Winter (ll. 99–102) reintegrated, after the discord of war, into the 'heureuse concorde' of family and seasonal activity. Moreover, the unfolding of the seasons, with its dynamism and momentum contained within the tight pattern of cyclic order and sequential dependence (autumn is described as 'part au Printemps, . . . part en l'Esté': XII, 67), is a perfect image of the aesthetic techniques of controlled energy, *libre contrainte* and 'la belle disposition de vers' with its 'elegante et parfaicte collocation & ordre des choses inventées' (XIV, 13–14). A detailed consideration of the *hymnes*, and especially those of *Esté*, *Autonne* and *Hyver*, would reveal that their structures obey these same aesthetic principles.

Thus Time and his personified component parts—the Hours, Youth, the Seasons—have important cosmic functions beyond the realm of allegory, and they actively participate in the stability and balanced perfection of the universe and in the preservation of natural cycles of generation and fertility. At the same time aesthetic preoccupations are never far from Ronsard's mind, and these are richly implanted in his cosmic and allegorical visions in a number of suggestive ways.

Ronsard in turn gives a cosmological explanation for the existence and nature of time beyond the allegorical account of the birth of the Seasons in the *Hymne de l'Esté* and the *Hymne du Printemps*, and, like Plato and Aristotle, he associates the measure of time with the movements of the heavenly bodies. The implications of Plato's definition of time as the 'movable image of Eternity' will be considered shortly : for the moment it suffices to note that Plato equates time with the birth of the universe and with the rotatory motion of the outer sphere of the heavens, the Prime Mover.[7] Aristotle's definition of time—'number of movement in respect of the before and after' (*Physics*, IV, x–xiv)—is related in turn with his conception of movement as the passage from latency to realisation, virtuality to action (*Physics*, III, i–iii; V–VIII): it is circular motion, and in particular the rotation of the Prime Mover, which serves as a measure of time in his definitions, for circular motion, the number of which is best known, is alone primary, regular, uniform and eternal.[8]

Thus when Ronsard, in his *Hymne du Ciel*—and again very briefly in the *Franciade* (XVI, 224)—attributes time to the circular movement of the heavenly vault and insists on the eternal regularity and uniformity of this motion, he clearly surpasses the brief references in his immediate source (Marullus, *De Caelo*, ll. 14–15; *Aeternitati*, ll. 16–17) and echoes the Greek definitions, and more particularly that of Aristotle :

> Toy comme fecond pere en abondance enfantes
> Les siecles, & des ans les suittes renaissantes :
> Les moys, & les saisons, les heures, & les jours,
> Ainsi que jouvenceaux jeunissent de ton cours,
> Frayant, sans nul repos, une orniere eternelle,
> Qui tousjours se retrace, & se refraye en elle.
> (VIII, 148)

More frequently in Ronsard's verse, it is the movement of the sun through the heavens and its position in the zodiac which provides the measure of time. In the following passage, as in the previous quotation and in other similar contexts (VIII, 158; XVII, 38–9), the relentless marking of time is evoked by a common visual image (*frayant . . . une orniere, se retrace; à grands pas, pied certain, mesme trace; bornes marquées; legers de pieds retournés*), by structural pairing (*Les siecles, & des ans les suittes . . . / Les moys, & les saisons, les heures, & les jours; Frayant . . . se retrace, & se refraye; passe & repasse; entre ou sort; refranchist . . . / Et nous refaict; son estre & son bout; Sortent & rentrent; De là . . . De là*) and by certain associated word groupings (*fecond, abondance, suittes renaissantes, eternelle, tousjours; tous egaulx, tant de fois, certain, mesme; tant de siecles, Tous les ans tant de moissons*):

Le Soleil vient dessous à grands pas tous egaulx,
Et l'An qui tant de fois tourne, passe & repasse,
Glissant d'un pied certain par une mesme trace.
Vive source de feu, qui nous fait les saisons,
Selon qu'il entre ou sort de ses douze maisons.

(VIII, 251, var.)

In both these texts Ronsard, like Aristotle,[9] uses the uniformity, regularity and perfection of circular movement to suggest the eternal nature of both the universe and of time itself. Elsewhere, it is the dynamic energy and self-perpetuating rapidity of the diurnal rotation of the heaven which is evoked, and, once again, the metaphor of footsteps (*tes pas, d'un pied, d'un pied de fer, courir*), the repeated doubling of structures (*que la vitesse . . . / Des Aigles, ny des ventz; viste & dispos; qui parfais . . . qui sans cesse retourne; d'un pied . . . d'un pied; jamais recreu . . . jamais ne sejourne; En volant . . . en l'espace . . . en paresse*) and patterning of lexical items (*vitesse/vistesse/viste; aislée/volant; egaller/egalle; venant/retourne/part/ne sejourne*) reappear as the now familiar stylistics of such passages:

O CIEL . . .
. . . qui roules si tost ta grand'boule esbranlée
Sur deux essieux fichez, que la vistesse aislée
Des Aigles, ny des ventz par l'air, ne sçauroient pas
En volant egaller le moindre de tes pas.
Seulement le penser de l'humaine sagesse,
Comme venant de toy egalle ta vitesse.
O CIEL viste & dispos, qui parfais ton grand Tour
D'un pied jamais recreu, en l'espace d'un jour,
Ainçois d'un pied de fer, qui sans cesse retourne
Au lieu duquel il part, & jamais ne sejourne,
Trainant tout avec soy, pour ne souffrir mourir
L'Univers en paresse à-faute de courir.

(VIII, 141–2)

Although the equation of the rapidity of mental activity with the speed of celestial movement may have been suggested by Seneca, *Ad Helviam De Consolatione*, VI, 6–8, the ultimate authority for the idea that the circular motion of the heaven is the swiftest of all movements is a passage from Aristotle, *De Caelo*:

Again, the revolution of the heaven is the measure of all motions, because it alone is continuous and unvarying and eternal, the measure in every class of things is the smallest member, and the shortest motion is the quickest, therefore the motion of the heaven must clearly be the quickest of all motions. But the shortest path of those which return upon their starting-point is represented by the circumference of a circle and the quickest motion is that along the shortest path. If therefore the heaven (a) revolves in a circle and (b) moves faster than anything else, it must be spherical.[10]

For Ronsard it is not only the circular motion of the *Prima Mobile* but also the spherical *form* of the universe which is evidence of its unity, perfection and eternity (VIII, 146, var.; 254), an idea which has its philosophical origins in Plato (*Timaeus*, 33B; 34B) and Aristotle (*De Caelo*, II, iii, 286a10–12; II, iv, 286b10–33). Again Ronsard's insistence on the all-embracing nature of the outer globe of the heaven (VIII, 146; 147; XVII, 334–5, s. LVI), and his rejection of the Lucretian idea of a plurality of worlds (*De rerum natura*, II, 1048ff.), also forms part of his definition of the circular unity and eternity of the world, and in this respect too he is close to the Platonic and Aristotelian hypothesis.[11]

If Ronsard, therefore, like Aristotle and Plato, associates time with the eternal uniformity and regularity of the heaven's circular motion and accepts the principle of a universe which has no end in time, which lasts the infinity of time, similarly his final position concerning the relationship between time and the creation of the universe will bring him closer to Aristotle. Although in 1555 (VIII, 145), 1563 (XI, 70; 105), and again in 1566 (XVIII, 327) he opts for creation *ex nihilo*—'ce grand Dieu qui bastit tout de rien'—and for the Mosaic conception of time, a variant of the 1584 edition of the *Hymne du Ciel*, 'Bref, te voyant si beau, je ne sçaurois penser / Que quatre ou cinq mille ans te puissent commencer',[12] clearly suggests that Ronsard is here adopting the Aristotelian belief in matter as eternal and uncreated, and is evoking a vision of the universe as a development dependent on time as infinite.

In its turn Plato's definition of time as the 'movable image of Eternity' will enable us to appreciate more clearly Ronsard's cosmological and metaphysical conception of eternity and to assess the distinctions he draws between time and eternity. Although Richelet repeatedly equates Eternity with God in his commentary on the *Hymne de l'Eternité*—and it must be admitted that Ronsard's use of the word elsewhere in his work seems to support such an identification (cf. VIII, 222)—more precisely the poet uses the figure of Eternity to personify the absolute, immutable essence and idea of God. From the outset of his *Hymne de l'Eternité* Ronsard refuses to consider eternity as an extension of time to infinity, but insists rather on the fundamental difference between eternity, immutable and unchanging, and time, periodic and inconstant in its cyclic return:

[Eternité] . . . qui jamais pour les ans ne se change,
Mais bien qui faict changer les siecles & les temps,
Les moys, & les saisons & les jours inconstans,
Sans jamais se muer, pour n'estre poinct sujecte,
Comme Royne & maistresse, à la loy qu'ell' a faicte.

(VIII, 246)

Towards the end of the poem Ronsard defines in more detail his opposition between time as periodic and mobile, and eternity as unchangeable and absolute essence, an eternal, global present, incomprehensible to man's imperfect vision with its limited human and temporal conceptions:

La grand trouppe des Dieux . . .
Quand elle parle à toy ne dict point il sera,
Il fut, ou telle chose ou telle se fera,
C'est à faire aux humains à dire telle chose:
Sans plus le temps present devant toy se repose
Et se sied à tes piedz : car tout le temps passé
Et celluy qui n'est pas encores advancé
Sont presens à ton œil, qui d'un seul clin regarde
Le passé, le present, & cestuy là qui tarde
A venir quant à nous, & non pas quant à toy,
Ny à ton œil qui voit tous les temps davant soy.

(ll. 105–16)

Although both these extracts owe a debt to certain *hymni* of Marullus (*Iovi Optimo Maximo*, ll. 46–9; *Aeternitati*, ll. 18, 26–8), and although the 1584–7 variants of the second extract bring Ronsard's lines textually closer to the neo-Latin model, rather than distancing them from it as Professor Silver suggests,[13] nevertheless the ultimate and principal authority for the French poet's distinction between time and eternity is to be found in the following passage of Plato, as the American scholar himself demonstrates:

. . . He planned to make a movable image of Eternity, and, as He set in order the Heaven, of that Eternity which abides in unity He made an eternal image, moving according to number, even that which we have named Time . . . 'Was' and 'Shall be' are generated forms of Time, although we apply them wrongly, without noticing, to Eternal Being. For we say that it 'is' or 'was' or 'will be', whereas, in truth of speech, 'is' alone is the appropriate term; 'was' and 'will be', on the other hand, are terms properly applicable to the Becoming which proceeds in Time, since both of these are motions; but it belongs not to that which is ever changeless in its uniformity to become either older or younger through time, nor ever to have become so, nor to be so now, nor to be about to be so hereafter . . .[14]

However, in the subsequent lines of his *hymne* Ronsard adds a theological and moral dimension to his metaphysical discussion, which is nowhere apparent in Plato or Marullus, when he considers the cause of this fundamental distinction between human time and eternity:

> Nous aultres journalliers, nous perdons la memoire
> Des temps qui sont passez, & si ne pouvons croire
> Ceux qui sont à venir, comme estans imperfaictz,
> Et d'une masse brute inutilement faictz,
> Aveuglez & perclus de la saincte lumiere,
> Que le peché perdit en nostre premier pere :
> Mais ferme tu retiens dedans ton souvenir
> Tout ce qui est passé, & ce qui doibt venir,
> Comme haulte Deesse eternelle, & perfaicte,
> Et non ainsy que nous de masse impure faicte.
>
> (ll. 117–26)

Cut off from the Eternal and from knowledge, man's limited, imperfect conception of time is the consequence of Adam's sin of *hubris*: forgetful of the past, ignorant of the future, man is condemned by his fall from grace to live in the ephemeral present, forever aspiring to the all-embracing, timeless vision of Eternity but forever unable to attain or even comprehend it.

This opposition between two temporal conceptions corresponds in turn to the antithesis between mortality and immortality, between the terrestrial world of 'peine & . . . soucy / . . . vieillesse & . . . mort' (VIII, 252) and the timeless, immutable extralunar world, 'Où les ans fermes demeurent' (III, 73), for the human and the divine operate within two totally different time systems:

> «Les dieux tout en un coup à leur age parviennent,
> «Les hommes par le temps en accroissance viennent :
> «Car ils sont immortels, les hommes d'icy bas
> «Des dieux enfans bastards croissent pour le trespas.
>
> (XII, 43, var : 1587)

In turn the relationship between time and *hubris* formulated in the *Hymne de l'Eternité*, is developed throughout Ronsard's verse as a fundamental aspect of his cosmology. In an earlier discussion of Ronsard's ode *A Anthoine Chasteigner* (1550) and of a passage from an *Epistre a Charles de Pisseleu* (1555), it has already been noted that change is the expression of a law of Nature and of time's motion, and that this law specifically retains man and human endeavour within the limits of imperfection and mortality in the name of cosmic order. An interesting restatement of this cosmic significance of time's movement is found in a passage from an *epistre* to Charles de Lorraine of 1556:

C'est peu de cas aussi de bastir jusque aux Cieulx,
Des Palais eslevez d'un front ambitieux,
Qui ne servent de rien que de pompeuse montre,
Qui ne peuvent durer (tant soient fortz) alencontre
De la fuitte du temps : . . .
. . . les Temps
D'eulx mesmes les feront dans le cours de cent ans
Renverser pied sur teste, & à la petitesse
Des champs egalleront leur superbe haultesse.

(VIII, 331–2)

Within the wider framework of the poem Ronsard employs the theme of time's motion to underline a moral and philosophical lesson on the subject of human *hubris*. The opening movements of the *epistre* (ll. 1–80) are concerned with the virtues of humility and modesty—qualities which Charles de Lorraine possesses ('Si n'estes vous pourtant ny superbe ny fier' : l. 41),—with an attack on the conceit of noblemen and courtiers, and with a statement concerning the vanity and misery of worldly honours. The passage quoted above is therefore both a commentary on, and an illustration of, the general ideas expressed in the preceding lines, and it pin-points, by a developed antithesis, the pathetic reality of worldly pomp and of conceited human aspirations. Moreover, the arrogance of man's endeavour is suggested by certain contrasting lexical patterns—*Cieulx*, *Palais eslevez*, *front ambitieux*, *pompeuse*, *fortz* and *peu de cas*, *servent de rien* (ll. 1–5); *teste*, *superbe haultesse* and *pied*, *petitesse* (ll. 8–9)—and also, more subtly, by comparing human pride to the sin of the Giants as recounted in Ovid, *Metamorphoses*, I, 152–3, for just as they 'essayed the very throne of heaven, piling huge mountains, one on another, clear up to the stars' (LCL, vol. I, p. 13), in the same way ambitious man constructs his 'Palais . . . d'un front ambitieux . . . jusque aux Cieulx', regions forbidden to the human condition by the ruling cosmic forces. Thus within this passage and within the context of the poem as a whole, the cosmological role of time is formulated and the condemnation of human *hubris* emphasised.

On the mythological level too Ronsard makes an association between the sin of *hubris* and the seasonal cycle of time. In his *Hymne de la Justice* (1555) Ronsard refers to the eternal spring which initially accompanied '. . . la pure innocence, / La creinte de mal faire & la simple bonté' of the Age of Gold (XIII, 102), and, in a speech in which the goddess Justice upbraids mankind and in which antithesis again figures strongly as a stylistic and structural device (*printemps/hyver*; *chaleureuses*, *halleront*, *flammes/frimatz*, *pluye*, *glace*, *froid*; *jeunesse/vieillesse*; past, present and future verb tenses), he specifically envisages the division of the year into seasons and the human consequences of time's motion as punishments for man's depravity during the Age of Iron:

Le printemps, qui souloit te rire tous les jours,
Se changeant en hyver, perdra son premier cours,
Et sera departy en vapeurs chaleureuses,
Qui halleront ton corps de flammes douloureuses,
En frimatz, & en pluye, & en glace, qui doit
Faire transir bientost ton pauvre corps de froid:
Ton chef deviendra blanc en la fleur de jeunesse,
Et jamais n'ateindras les bornes de vieillesse.

(VIII, 55: 1578–87 editions)

Whilst Ovid, and not Virgil (*Georgics*, II, 336–45), provides the details concerning the everlasting spring of the Age of Gold, he relates the partition of the seasons to the Age of Silver (*Metam.*, I, 107–8, 116–20). It is by transferring the Latin reference from its original context to the depravity of the Age of Iron in his own account, and by adding details concerning the loss of longevity from Hesiod, *Works and Days*, ll. 109–201, that Ronsard makes the seasonal round, the precocity of old age and the brevity of life-expectancy *direct consequences of man's evil*. This contamination and structuring of source material result in a dramatic contrast and an emphasis which are foreign to Ovid, Hesiod and the other possible sources of this myth. Moreover, by placing his reference in a religious context where Justice echoes the words of Jehovah expelling Adam and Eve from the Garden of Eden (cf. Laumonier's note, VIII, 54), he more emphatically relates his material to the Christian original sin.

These same preoccupations with *hubris* and with man's enslavement to time and old age are associated in other suggestive ways with Ronsard's numerous references to the Age of Gold myth. These nostalgic evocations, together with the equation Ronsard frequently draws between the depravity and barbarity of his own century and the Age of Iron,[15] are clearly in themselves expressions of a dissatisfaction with the present moment, of a desire to reverse or to escape from time into the past ('Helas! que n'ai-je esté vivant de ce temps là': IX, 23). More precisely the original Age of Gold is associated in Ronsard's mind not only with eternal spring and the absence of seasonal change, but with a conquest of time, with longevity, painless death and rejuvenation, ideas suggested to him in the *Bergerie* (1565: XIII, 102) by Hesiod and Sannazaro (*Arcadia*, song of Opico). Similarly his appeal to his friends to flee contemporary Europe and its Age of Iron in order to seek the Golden Age of *Les Isles Fortunées* (V, 175–91), is specifically voiced in terms of a liberation from illness, human fragility, time and death (ll. 149–60), whilst, in those pagan visions of an after-life in which Ronsard projects himself forward in time and equates the 'printens éternel' of the Elysian Fields with the idyllic existence of the Age of Gold, what primarily interests him about this future paradise is its defeat of death and the absence there of Fortune, Destiny and time:

> Et en toute saison avec Flore y souspire
> D'un souspir eternel le gracieus Zephire.
> Là, comme ici n'a lieu fortune ny destin,
> Et le soir comme ici ne court vers le matin,
> Le matin vers le soir . . .
>   Là, bienheureux Salel, ayant à la nature
> Payé ce que luy doit chacune creature,
> Tu vis franc de la mort . . .
>
> (VI, 34–5)

Reversal of time, anticipation of time; nostalgic evocations in the past, present and future. Ronsard creates his own temporal cycle centred on the Age of Gold myth, as if in an attempt to liberate himself from his subjection to time and mortality. Even his frequent use of the Virgilian theme of the return of the Age of Gold under a contemporary monarch, prince or patron forms part of the same obsession with reconstructing a cycle of time, and it is precisely this idea of *translatio* which enables him to escape from a vision of history and a conception of time which are associated with sin and with a linear regression from a state of moral and social perfection.[16]

TIME, MOVEMENT AND THE HUMAN CONDITION

It has already been seen that on the cosmological level the motion of time is associated with the rotation of the heavenly sphere, and that the relentless regularity and uniformity of this movement is evidence of the eternity of the universe and of time itself. In the same way an earlier discussion of an important passage from the *Epistre a Charles de Pisseleu* revealed that for Ronsard, as for Aristotle (Solmsen, pp. 144–59), the movement of time controls the cycles of generation in the sublunar world and that change is synonymous with preservation, fertility and continuity. This dynamic conception of time—allegorically restated in the seasonal *hymnes* of 1563—is never far away from Ronsard's mind and its implications for the human condition are frequently under review. The lesson of joyful submission to the fluctuating variety of time's motion and to Nature's prudent law which he had learnt from Horace and Seneca, and which he had advocated in the ode *A Anthoine Chasteigner* (1550), and again in the epistle to Pisseleu (1555), finds consistent expression in his work and is a fundamental aspect of his philosophy. It is this mixture of epicureanism and stoicism (so reminiscent of Horace) that is expressed again in the opening movement of an ode *A René D'Oradour* of 1550:

Le tens de toutes choses maistre,
Les saisons de l'an terminant,
Montre assés que rien ne peut estre
Longuement durable en son estre
Sans se changer incontinant.

Ores l'iver brunist les cieus,
D'un grand voile obscur emmuré,
Ores il soufle audacieus,
Ores froid, ores pluvieus,
En son inconstance assuré.

Puis quand il s'en fuit variable,
On revoit Zephyre ariver,
Amenant un ciel amiable,
Qui est beaucoup plus agreable
Apres qu'on a senti l'iver.

Quand un souci triste & hideus,
Oradour, te viendroit saisir,
Ne t'effraie d'un ni de deus,
Car le tens seul en depit d'eus,
Te rendra libre à ton plaisir.
                    (I, 208–9)

Besides the Pindaric metaphor concerning 'Time, the father of all', these lines are indebted mainly, according to Laumonier, to Horace, *Odes*, I, vii, 15–17; II, ix, 1–8; x, 15–18. However, certain important details of Ronsard's text are clearly foreign to his source and reveal an attitude of mind and a process of thought which are emphatically his own. Lines 3–5, for example, owe nothing to Horace and are a first statement of the principle, so poetically endorsed in the epistle to Pisseleu, that life and generation are dependent on time's movement and change. Behind the seasonal flux and in the bleakest of winter days Ronsard traces a stability and an order which comfort—'En son inconstance *assuré*'—an idea nowhere apparent in his model. Similarly the human condition is joyfully integrated into this natural pattern, for time is seen to be conducive to man's happiness: just as the rigour of winter is necessary to intensify by contrast the enjoyment of spring, so the passage of time heals the present sorrow and prepares a future of pleasure. The epicurean attitude, which is extensively developed in the remainder of the poem with the aid of further Horatian reminiscences, is therefore based on a philosophy of time which is Ronsard's significant addition to his source material. Very much the same reasoning, imagery and wholehearted resignation to the equity of time's motion ('Quant à la reste alon avec le tens / Heureusement contens': ll. 21–2) permeate the ode *A Gaspar D'Auvergne* of 1550 (II, 169–74), whilst another Horatian poem of the same year suggests that by conforming wisely to the natural pattern of time the lover ultimately receives his reward, for the same 'inexorable loi du tens' which ripens the grapes allots a season to everything and brings love to fruition (I, 218–19). Later texts of 1553 (V, 165–7), 1559 (IX, 54–5) and 1562 (XI, 60) return to similar Horatian imagery in order to integrate man into a natural order of time, change and opportunity.

This comforting philosophical reasoning, which equates human happiness and fulfilment with a prudent, opportunist submission to the rhythmic variety of time, does not, however, prevent Ronsard from being preoccupied throughout his work by the more commonplace and melancholy themes of time's flight, and especially by the irretrievable nature of time, the brevity and precariousness of life, and by the notion of Time the Destroyer: '... l'on sentait alors comme toujours, et avec une acuité peut-être encore accrue, le caractère précaire et fugitif de chaque moment vécu ... ce sentiment, qui est l'angoisse essentielle de l'homme,—de l'homme dans le temps ...'.[17] It is at such moments that the other side of the duality referred to earlier reappears, for in these contexts time's motion, the lack of *durée* and the rhythms of change in the world are seen not as essential factors of preservation and permanence, but as aspects of life's misery and insecurity:

> S'il y avoit au monde un estat de durée,
> Si quelque chose estoit en la terre asseurée,
> Ce seroit un plaisir de vivre longuement:
> Mais puis qu'on n'y voit rien qui ordinairement
> Ne se change, & rechange, & d'inconstance abonde,
> Ce n'est pas grand plaisir que de vivre en ce monde.
>
> (VIII, 172–3. Cf. X, 318–19)

Although the idea of time's motion is a literary and artistic commonplace, familiar to the Pléiade from many of their favourite classical, Italian and French authors, nevertheless to express the bald statement of the irreversible nature of time Ronsard (VIII, 105; XV, 233; XVI, 43) turns most frequently to the epigrammatic line of Virgil which had become something of an adage, *Sed fugit interea, fugit inreparabile tempus* (*Georgics*, III, 284), and which Seneca quotes (*Epist.*, CVIII, 24–7), together with another Virgilian passage on the same theme (*Georgics*, III, 66–8), in the context of a lengthy commentary on time's flight.

It is rather in the choice of images and metaphors which the French poet uses to evoke the rapidity of time's motion and to give the Virgilian statement visual and concrete reference, that one may hope to find poetic emphasis and variety, if not originality, for here too the temptation is strong to repeat certain traditional formulae. Apart from variations on the metaphor of time's flight, which is so commonplace as to defy the allocation of precise sources, it is the equally conventional comparison of flowing water which finds frequent favour with the poet, often via the intermediary of Ovid, *Metamorphoses*, xv, 179–85.[18] Other images used to embroider the basic Virgilian line include the flight of an arrow (III, 33; XII, 276; XVI, 185, var.), retreating footsteps (III, 105), and this simile found in an elegy to Charles IX of 1575:

L'age vole tousjours sans espoir de retour,
Et comme hors des dents la parolle sortie
Ne retourne jamais apres qu'elle est partie,
Ainsi l'age de l'homme apres qu'il est passé,
Ne retourne jamais quand il nous a laissé.

(XVII, 50)

In the same way, although statements concerning life's brevity and fragility exist in bald isolation often reminiscent of maxims, it is much more common for them to be complemented by poetic images, similes and contrasting lexical patterns which juxtapose life and death with suggestive and dramatic concision. A good number of these images are used to focus attention on the Pindaric definition of men as 'creatures of a day' (*Pythian*, VIII, ep. 5), and Ronsard recalls Pindar and translates the Greek ἐπάμεροι as 'les hommes journaliers' on several occasions (I, 89; V, 259–60; VII, 60). Thus in these lines from his *A un sien ami fasché de suivre la court* (1550) the comparison of night and day is adapted either from Horace, as Laumonier suggests, or from Ovid (*Metam.*, xv, 186–7) and is suggestively condensed in a tight uncommented association of ideas—the brevity of life as the equivalence of a day, the finality of death, the darkness of the tomb:

Mais pour vie si breve
Faut-il tant qu'on se greve
D'amasser & d'avoir?
Matin le jour se leve
Pour mourir sus le soir.

(II, 195)

Elsewhere, notes Laumonier, it is the movement of Pindar ('Creatures of a day, what is anyone? what is he not? Man is but a dream of a shadow': LCL, 1924, p. 269), coupled with a biblical comparison from Psalms 102.15, which provide Ronsard with these lines from the *Ode de la Paix* (1550) where once again antithesis figures strongly:

Et qu'esse que des mortels?
Si au matin ils fleurissent
Le soir ils ne sont plus tels,
Pareils aus champs qui fenissent.
(III, 28–9)

Although in other contexts Ronsard remains faithful to Pindar alone for both the idea and the simile ('Et l'homme ne vit qu'un jour / Fuiant comme un songe ou fumée' : II, 121), or else employs the metaphor of smoke and flame to equate the brevity of man's life with the measure of a day ('. . . l'homme n'est que fumée / Qu'un petit traict de feu tient un jour allumée' : X, 368), by far the most frequent image in this respect remains that of the rose. In his *De rosis nascentibus*, Ausonius had limited the duration of the rose to the equivalence of a day in lines of balanced inevitability : 'one day brings forth and the same day ends . . . As long as is one day, so long is the life of the rose' (ll. 40, 43 : LCL, 1961, vol. II, p. 279). These lines find many echoes in the verse of Ronsard (II, 181; V, 196; XV, 205) and the rose, as symbol of the brevity of life, youth and beauty, often supports an epicurean plea—a theme which will be studied in detail later. Ronsard extends the image of diurnal brevity, commonly associated with the rose, to the 'Soucy du jardin' and, by insisting heavily on Ausonius's technique of antithetical balance, achieves a vision in which life and death become synonymous :

. . . ton chef florissant,
Qui toute fleur au temps d'Hyver surpasse,
Que l'Aube engendre & qu'une nuit efface,
Te voyant naistre aussy tost que fanir,
Soir & matin fay le moy souvenir
Que nostre vie aux fleurettes resemble,
Qui presque vit & presque meurt ensemble.
(XV, 176)

Similarly it is to the poetic realism of nature imagery that Ronsard turns in his sepulchral verse in order to evoke more poignantly the youthfulness of the deceased, and here too classical reminiscences are heard. Man is snatched away in his prime before even the fullness of his brief life is accomplished in the same way as *young birds* are seized from their nests by cruel shepherds (XV, 297–8; 301–2 : cf. Virgil, *Georgics*, IV, 511–15); or as *April flowers* or an *unripened cornfield* are crushed by a sudden storm or harvested prematurely (XV, 298; XVII, 6 : cf. Virgil, *Georgics*, I, 311–33); or as the *green leaves* of spring and summer are torn from trees by autumnal winds (Homer);[19] or as the *mature vigour* of an oak tree is sapped by parasitic ivy (XVIII, 413).

Ronsard's preoccupation with the irreversible nature of time and with the brevity and precariousness of life crystallises itself in turn on an antithesis between youth and old age, an opposition given its most detailed and graphic statement in an *Ode a Christofle de Choiseul* of 1555:

> Non, ce n'est moi qui veut or
> Vivre autant que fist Nestor :
> Quel plaisir, quelle liesse
> Reçoit l'home en sa vieillesse,
> Eust-il mile talens d'or?
>
> L'home vieil ne peut marcher,
> N'ouyr, ne voir, ni mâcher,
> C'est une idole enfumée
> Au coin d'une cheminée
> Qui ne fait plus que cracher.
>
> Il est toujours en couroux,
> Bacus ne lui est plus doux,
> Ni de Venus l'acointance,
> En lieu de mener la dance,
> Il tremblote des genoux.
>
> Si quelque force ont mes vœus,
> Ecoutés, Dieux, je ne veus
> Atendre qu'une mort lente
> Me conduise à Rhadamante
> Avecques des blancs cheveus.
>
> Aussi je ne veus mourir,
> Ores que je puis courir,
> Ouir, parler, boire, rire,
> Dancer, jouer de la lyre
> Et de plesirs me nourir.
> . . .
> Car je vis : & c'est grand bien
> De vivre, & de vivre bien.
>   (VI, 192–3)

Whilst the first four stanzas are borrowed from a fragment of Mimnermus quoted in Stobaeus, *Florilegium*, LXIII, 16,[20] and from other pieces conserved in section CXVII (*Vituperium Senectutis*) of the same anthology,[21] a comparison of the French and Greek texts reveals that Ronsard takes little beyond the general theme of the censure of old age. To this general statement he adds a realistic description of senility, nowhere apparent in the Greek texts, and by doing so provides a commentary on his sensualist repulsion for the inactivity and physical deterioration of old age. It is worth noting that here, as elsewhere in his work (VI, 198–9; VII, 102), he transfers to old age some of the descriptive emphasis and sense of horror for physical decrepitude that he generally denies to his evocations of the human body in death. Similarly the hymn to life which follows has no equivalent in any of the Greek passages, and it is by creating this antithesis that Ronsard at once reinforces his stricture of senility, and draws a dramatic distinction between the physical processes of youth and the cessation of pleasure and sensual activity which accompanies old age.

This same love of youth and antipathy for old age are consistently and forcefully expressed throughout Ronsard's entire poetic career. Already in 1553 and again in 1554 two texts (v, 192–3; vi, 102–3) had prefigured the themes of the ode to Choiseul, whilst a poem of the *Meslanges* (vi, 198–9) and the ode *Ma douce jouvance est passée* of 1555 (vii, 102–3) define old age once more as the absence of pleasure and activity, and on these last two occasions Ronsard significantly adds a realistic description of the physical decrepitude of senility to the pseudo-Anacreontic texts which are the essential sources. In the *Hymne de l'Eternité* (1555), and again in the *Hymne de l'Esté* (1563), the antithesis between youth and old age is given allegorical and cosmological significance (above, pp. 94–7), whilst a minor variant of the 1567 edition of a poem originally published in 1565, is a subtle but revealing commentary on the poet's attitude to senility (xiii, 184, ll. 35–40: var.).

Ronsard's final statements of 1580–5 strike a more personal note and reveal his distress at his advancing years ('. . . je porte en l'ame une amere tristesse, / Dequoy mon pied s'avance aux faubourgs de vieillesse': xviii, 42. Cf. xviii, 119), and his dismay at the inactivity, torpor and physical debility of his own old age ('. . . ma lente vieillesse / M'engourdisse en un lict enervé de paresse': xviii, 265–6). A poem of *Les Derniers Vers* (1586) states the poet's position unambiguously for the last time: 'Le vray tresor de l'homme est la verte jeunesse, / Le reste de nos ans ne sont que des hivers.' With the wisdom of hindsight, and with the aid of a Senecan text (*Epist.*, LVIII, 29–30), he now rejects a hedonist attitude and advises not the abusive excess of pleasure, which prematurely ages (cf. xvii, 333, s. LIV), not the pseudo-Anacreontic philosophy he had advocated in 1555 ('. . . le vieil homme doit, ou jamais, recevoir / Ses plaisirs, dautant plus qu'il voit sa mort prochaine': vi, 199), but the preservation of the tender flower of youth by moderation and reasoned restraint (xviii, 176).

It is the preoccupation with youth and pleasure and this personal antipathy for old age, with its deterioration of the senses and its loss of activity, which rejuvenates in turn certain commonplace amatory themes. If one's mind understandably turns to the frequent and beautiful expressions of the *carpe diem* and *carpe florem* appeals, which will be discussed more fully later, one should not forget those statements *outside of the epicurean formula* when Ronsard's sensual love of youth transforms the banality of both the idea and the imagery, and, by a delicate choice of antithetical word groups, makes the verse vibrate with a suggestive eroticism:

> J'aime un bouton vermeil entre-esclos au matin,
> Non la rose du soir, qui au Soleil se lâche:
> J'aime un corps de jeunesse en son printemps fleury:
> J'aime une jeune bouche, un baiser enfantin
> Encore non souillé d'une rude moustache,
> Et qui n'a point senty le poil blanc d'un mary.
>
> (XVII, 326, S. XLV)

Neither should those occasions in his later collections of amatory poetry be forgotten where some of the most poignant sonnets are inspired by his awareness of the pathetic discrepancy which exists between his love and his advanced years (XVII, 255, S. X; 316, S. XXXVI), a discrepancy which he desperately tries to justify by mythological example and Petrarchist imagery,

> Soit qu'un sage amoureux, ou soit qu'un sot me lise,
> Il ne doit s'esbahir, voyant mon chef grison,
> Si je chante d'amour: volontiers le tison
> Cache un germe de feu sous une cendre grise.
> Le bois verd à grand peine en le soufflant s'attise,
> Le sec sans le soufler brusle en toute saison.
> La Lune se gaigna d'une blanche toison,
> Et son vieillard Thiton l'Aurore ne mesprise,[22]

and by frequent reference to the annual slough of the serpent and to the Medea/Aeson fable with their associations of rejuvenation (XVII, 263, S. XXI; 268, S. XXVI; 313, S. XXXII).

In the same way the erotic consequences of Ronsard's obsession with youth and old age should not obscure the poet's concern for the passage of time in areas other than the amatory, and especially in that of creative activity. It is in an *Elegie au Seigneur L'Huillier* of 1560—'ore que je suis vieulx' writes Ronsard, aged thirty-five (X, 296)—that one first finds the idea that the ardour and enthusiasm necessary for poetic inspiration are dependent on youth, and that when the early years disappear the poet is left without creative force or energy (X, 293–5). That this idea is not merely the expression of momentary anger at the rich rewards offered by patrons to less able poetasters, but seems to represent a genuine preoccupation for the aging Ronsard, is demonstrated by its reappearance in a sonnet of the same collection (X, 336), in *La Lyre* of 1569 (XV, 16–17) and again in the *Preface sur la Franciade* (1587): 'Car en ... imitation de la nature consiste toute l'ame de la Poesie Heroïque, laquelle n'est qu'un enthousiasme & fureur d'un jeune cerveau. Celuy qui devient vieil, matté d'un sang refroidy, peut bien dire à dieu aux Graces et aux Muses' (XVI, 345).

Yet despite this constant censure of senility and this obsession with youth, there is evidence here too of the duality referred to in the introduction, for a more reasoned attempt is made in Ronsard's later collections to reconcile himself to his condition and to submit to old age and the passage of time in the name of Nature's law. In a poem published in 1575 (XVII, 50–3) as a reply to verses addressed to him by the youthful Charles IX, Ronsard adapts the commonplace arguments and consolatory tone of the *laus senectutis* of classical literature—and of Cicero, *De Senectute* in particular[23]—in order to demonstrate how the equity and 'meure sagesse' of Nature have ensured that each period of life has its compensations, pleasures and comforts ('Si la jeunesse est bonne, aussi est la vieillesse'). Ronsard resigns himself thus to 'le cours / De Nature' and to the universal rhythm of time after the manner of consolatory literature:

> Voyés au mois de May sur l'espine la rose,
> Au matin un bouton, à vespre elle est esclose,
> Sur le soir elle meurt: ô belle fleur, ainsi
> Un jour est ta naissance & ton trespas aussi.
> Si villes, si cités de marbres estoffees,
> Si Empires, si Roys, si superbes Trophees
> Vieillissent, je puis bien en imitant le cours
> De Nature descroistre & voir vieillir mes jours.[24]

Whilst this text to Charles IX is perhaps something of a defensive literary exercise after the manner of the *laus senectutis* and the consolatory epistle, nevertheless a poem written in 1580 or 1581 strikes the same note of resignation: here Ronsard bids farewell to the pleasures of youth without sadness, as one who has tasted them all and is reconciled to wearing the 'habit convenable au temps & à mon âge' (XVIII, 37). Even as late as the 1587 collection an effort is made to face up to the reality of old age and to submit to it without hypocrisy. In the first of two sonnets, where antithesis is once again the predominant stylistic, it is a mutual reconciliation to 'la loy de la nature' and an honest acceptance of the physical consequences of old age which are seen to rejuvenate the aged lovers and to transform them from ugliness to beauty:

> Vous estes deja vieille, & je le suis aussi.
> Joignon nostre vieillesse & l'accollon ensemble,
> Et faison d'un hyver qui de froidure tremble
> (Autant que nous pourrons) un printemps adouci.
> Un homme n'est point vieil s'il ne le croit ainsi:
> Vieillard n'est qui ne veut: qui ne veut, il assemble

Une nouvelle trame à sa vieille : & ressemble
Un serpent rajeuni quand l'an retourne ici.
   Ostez moy de ce fard l'impudente encrousture,
On ne sçauroit tromper la loy de la nature,
Ny derider un front condamné du miroir,
   Ni durcir un tetin desja pendant & flasque.
Le Temps de vostre face arrachera le masque,
Et deviendray un Cygne en lieu d'un Corbeau noir.

                    (XVIII, 221)

However, the tone, it must be conceded, is pathetic and the desperate attempt at self-conviction has limits—('Autant que nous pourrons')—which the ironic commentary of the following sonnet clearly underlines. Here, in a brutal, realistic vision of death comparatively rare in his verse, Ronsard expresses the essential stupidity of man's loyal service to female beauty, doomed ultimately to old age, corruption and the worms, and silently justifies his lifelong epicurean philosophy of love (XVIII, 222).

Reference has already been made to the fact that on a cosmological level time is seen by Ronsard as a constructive and creative force in that it controls, through Nature, the dynamic cycles of generation and fecundity in the world and ensures the preservation and progress of both spiritual and physical forces. On the more mundane level a commonplace of classical literature had envisaged the passage of time as beneficial in so far as it is the great revealer, an essential agent of progress and discovery, an aid to justice and truth. I have demonstrated elsewhere in an article[25] the literary and artistic tradition for this constructive vision of time, and have suggested that the Pléiade's treatment of this theme does not constitute a sustained philosophical or moral attitude, but is rather the expression of proverbial usage which in no way poetically revitalises the commonplace. As with his treatment of the human consequences of Fortune, Ronsard is on the whole not attracted to the favourable aspects of time and prefers to crystallise his attention on its destructive qualities. This he does consistently and emphatically throughout his collections, assimilating the literary and artistic commonplace of Time the Destroyer into either brief general statements reminiscent on occasions of maxims or sentences ('La rose à la parfin devient un grate-cu, / Et tout, avecq' le tems, par le tems est vaincu': x, 228), or, more poetically, into a global vision of utter desolation designed to evoke the omnipotence of 'l'inexorable loi du tens' over all human endeavour :

   . . . tout ce qui est né devoit finir en rien,
Et que Rome à la fin, son marbre et son porfyre,
Sa hauteur, sa grandeur, & bref tout son empire

Par la charge des ans deviendroit un tombeau,
Sur lequel le pasteur conduiroit son troupeau.

(x, 105)

The hardest of precious stones, medals, palaces, castles, the pyramids, towns, monarchies and their splendours, empires and even the spiritual institution of the Church—nothing is sacred from 'l'aage qui tout brise', 'le Temps qui tout change & destruit'.[26] Nothing escapes the gluttonous appetite or the scythe of Saturn/Time. The superlative *tout* and an impressive variety of active verbs are applied to Time throughout the poetry of Ronsard (*donter, mettre bas, mettre par terre, vaincre, renverser, manger, ronger, dévorer, consommer, précipiter, briser, user, trébucher, casser, détruire, atterrir, se faire maistre, réduire en rien, avoir commandement sur, dévaler*), and these are designed to emphasise the omnipotent, aggressive and physical nature of Time and to lend personified values to the vision of complete devastation.

THE REMEDY : THE EPICUREAN ATTITUDE

The full extent of Ronsard's preoccupation with the passage of time and the brevity and fragility of life is best measured by the consistency and emphasis of the epicurean attitude in his verse. However, scholars in the past have inevitably focused attention on the popular *carpe diem* and *carpe florem* themes, and this concentration of interest, whilst it has revealed the sources, originality and poetic beauty of such appeals, has tended to obscure the full diversity of the French poet's epicurean position—a diversity which, it will be seen, embraces allegorical and philosophical statements as well as the pseudo-Anacreontic and Horatian erotico-bacchic pleas.

The epicurean allegory: Time as Kairos–Occasio

Ronsard's *Livret de Folastries* of 1553 contains the following epigram *De Posidippe. Sur l'Image du Tems* :

Qui, & d'où est l'ouvrier? Du Mans. Son nom? le Conte.
Et mais toy qui es tu? le Tems qui tout surmonte.
Pourquoy sur les ergos vas tu toujours coulant?
Pour montrer que je suis incessemment roulant.
Pourquoy te sont les piedz ornez de doubles aisles?
Affin de m'en voler comme vent desus elles.
Pourquoy va ta main dextre un rasoüer touchant?
Pour montrer que je suis plus agu qu'un trenchant.
Pourquoy dessus les yeux voltige ta criniere?
Pour estre pris davant & non par le derriere.
Et pourquoy chauve? affin de ne me voir hapé,

Si des le premier coup je ne suis atrapé.
Tel peint au naturel le Conte me decueuvre,
Et pour toy sur ton huys a mis ce beau chef d'euvre.

(v, 90–1)

The French translation fairly faithfully renders the original Greek
text, except that Ronsard modernises his translation and makes it more
accessible to the contemporary reader by replacing Lysippus by Nicolas
Denisot (1515–1559), a painter and poet, who took as an anagram the
name of the Conte d'Alsinois:

Who, whence is thy maker? Sicyon. His name is what? Lysippus. What art
thou? Kairos, the all-subduer. Why doest thou stand on the tips of thy toes?
I turn forever. Why hast thou double wings on either foot? I fly carried by
the wind. In thy right hand why carriest thou a razor? To men a sign that
quicker than any edge I am. But thy hair, why is it over the eye? In order to
be grasped, forsooth, by him that meets me. The back of thy head, why is it
bald? Because he, whom I have once rushed by with winged feet, will never
grasp me afterwards, though he desire it. Why did the artist fashion thee? For
thy sake, o stranger, he placed this warning lesson into the doorway.[27]

The statue of *Kairos* by Lysippus personifies the idea of the fleeting
opportunity which has to be seized before it is irrevocably lost, or, as
Panofsky describes it, the 'brief, decisive moment which marks a turn-
ing-point in the life of human beings or in the development of the
universe'.[28] This statue has been lost, but there remain descriptions of it
by Posidippus and by Callistratus, who had seen the statue and who,
unlike Posidippus, does not mention the attribute of the razor (LCL,
1931, pp. 395–9).

Other references to the allegory, together with fairly detailed descriptions of *Kairos*, or *Occasio* as the Romans called it, can be found in a
famous distich of Cato, II, 26, in the Latin fables of Phaedrus (Book v,
no. 8, entitled *Tempus*), in epigram XII of Ausonius (*In Simulacrum
Occasionis et Poenitentiae*), in a Greek eclogue of Humerius, a contemporary of Ausonius, in a passage of Poliziano contained in a *rispetti* beginning 'O trionfante sopra ogni altra bella', and also in a lengthy dis-
sertation on the expression *nosce tempus* in Erasmus, *Adagia*, who, in
addition to his own commentary, quotes the epigram of Ausonius, and
that of Posidippus, which he also translates into Latin distichs. Again in
the Lyons edition (1551) of Andrea Alciati's much published *Emblemata*,
which was the standard for many subsequent editions, there appears an
emblem depicting a nude female figure with the motifs of *Kairos–
Occasio*. This emblem is accompanied by a Latin version of Posidippus's
epigram on the Lysippian *Kairos*.

This allegorical conception of *Kairos–Occasio* continued in iconography and literature up until the Renaissance as a male or female nude with the familiar attributes of wings at the shoulders and heels, a pair of scales balanced on a shaving knife or razor and the proverbial fore-lock by which the otherwise bald-headed figure could be seized. How-ever, after the eleventh century the distinctive characteristics of *Kairos–Occasio* became confused with those of the goddess Fortune, who so obsessed the medieval imagination.[29] Although it is likely that Ronsard was aware of the majority of these descriptions of *Kairos*, his own trans-lation of the Greek epigram shows no apparent contamination of any of these other texts, as I have demonstrated elsewhere ('Ronsard's . . . Con-ceptions of Time', pp. 14–17).

It is as an allegorical statement concerning the irreversible passage of time and the epicurean theme of seizing the immediate present, that *Kairos–Occasio* appears on several instances in the French poet's verse. Ronsard, who briefly introduces *Occasio* into his cosmology as a servant of the stars (VIII, 154), tends to substitute Time for *Occasio*,

> Les ans legers s'enfuient.

> Le tens bien peu durable
> Tout chauve par derriere,
> Demeure inexorable
> Si franchist sa cariere

> (II, 196–7)

and this confusion was widespread and arose early in literature (R. Wittkower, 'Chance, Time and Virtue', p. 313). Besides such direct refer-ences there are a number of oblique allusions to the gesture of holding the proverbial forelock of *Kairos–Occasio* in the hand—the allegorical equivalent of the idea of utilising the immediate present before it can escape. Such statements as

> Le Temps s'enfuit, le Temps qu'on ne r'attrappe
> Quand une fois des mains il nous echappe,

and

> Nous ne tenons en nostre main
> Le futur ni le lendemain,

and

> «Et ne faut que l'homme humain
> «S'asseure de nulle chose,
> Si ja ne la tient enclose
> Etroitement dans la main,[30]

whilst divorced from specific reference to *Kairos–Occasio*, nevertheless have their distant origin in this allegory. There is also evidence in Ronsard's verse of the confusion between *Occasio* and Fortune which had arisen during the Middle Ages:

> ... ce bany sans cueur et sans esprit,
> Qui n'a sceu prendre aux cheveux la fortune!
> (XVI, 238)

The philosophical reasoning: the role of Seneca

In a sonnet of Ronsard's third collective edition of his works (1571), there appears an interesting discussion of the nature of time and an expression of the essential philosophical reasoning behind the poet's numerous epicurean statements:

> Trois temps, Seigneurs, icy bas ont naissance,
> Le temps passé, le present, le futur:
> Quand au futur, il nous est trop obscur,
> Car il n'est pas en nostre connaissance.
> Quand au passé, il fuit sans esperance
> De retourner pour faire un lendemain,
> Et ne revient jamais en nostre main:
> Le seul present est en nostre puissance.
> Doncques, Seigneurs, jouissons du present,
> Incontinent il deviendroit absent:
> Baigne ma couppe, emplis moy ce grand verre:
> Pendant que l'heure en donne le loisir
> Avecq' le vin, l'Amour & le plaisir
> Charmons le temps, les soucis & la guerre.
> (XV, 344)

The inspiration for this metaphysical discussion of the three phases of time would appear to be Seneca, *De Brevitate Vitae*, x, 2–6:

Life is divided into three periods—that which has been, that which is, that which will be. Of these the present time is short, the future is doubtful, the past is certain. For the last is the one over which Fortune has lost control, is the one which cannot be brought back under any man's power.

> (*Moral Essays*, LCL, 1932, vol. II, p. 317)

A comparison of the French and Latin texts reveals a significant difference in reasoning and philosophical conclusion, for although Seneca and Ronsard are in agreement concerning the uncertain nature of future time, the latter inter-changes his attitude with his source on the question of past and present time. For Seneca the past is certain since it is removed from the dominion of Fortune, the Stoics' arch-enemy; it is also sacred and intact if one's conscience is clear (*ibid.*, x, 2–4). Present time, on the other hand, is so brief and ephemeral that it is intangible and almost non-existent (*ibid.*, x, 4–6). Ronsard, on the contrary, attributes his model's analysis of present time to the past (ll. 5–7) with the aid of a reminiscence of two passages of Virgil—one of which Seneca himself quotes and discusses in this same treatise[31]—and a distant allusion to the allegory of Time as *Kairos–Occasio*. In the same way he relates Seneca's reasoning concerning the certainty of past time to present time in typically epicurean fashion. The conclusion of Ronsard's tercets is therefore dependent on this reversed attitude to past and present time, for if Seneca uses his arguments to advocate a moral of stoical consolation, the French poet interprets his material in the erotic–bacchic spirit of pseudo-Anacreon, *The Greek Anthology* and Horace. Man's greatest victory over time and his imprisonment in the fleeting present lies in the active utilisation of every instant. Such a conclusion is all the more noteworthy here for it results not from an amatory or festive context, but from a specifically philosophical analysis of time and, moreover, is dependent on a fundamental inversion of his source material.

Elsewhere in his writings—and especially in the *De Brevitate Vitae*—Seneca makes a fervent plea for the active and conscious use of present time, and for the thrifty and positive employment of every day as a means of giving life its full value. However, Seneca's epicurean reasoning has an emphatically moral and philosophical dimension in that it is not a pseudo-Anacreontic or Horatian call to erotico–bacchic pleasures, but rather an urgent appeal for a life of intellectual awareness, mental activity, virtue and contemplative wisdom. Textual echoes of this Senecan attitude are clearly heard in the verse of Baïf, and especially in *Les Mimes*.[32]

A consequence of this emphasis on the conscious exploitation of present time in Seneca is the idea that life should be measured by its quality and not by its quantity; that a brief, intense life of virtue, wisdom and noble deeds is preferable to a long, undistinguished existence of obscurity and inactivity. This reasoning, found in Aristotle and Plutarch,[33] is developed as a fundamental argument in the writings of Seneca, where it appears not only in the moral essays ('Undertake to estimate him by his virtues, not by his years, and you will see he lived long enough'), but in his *Ad Lucilium Epistulae* ('the wise man . . . always reflects concerning the quality, and not the quantity, of his life').[34] Ronsard, who puts forward as a general principle the idea that '. . . toute excellence ici ne vit long temps' (XVII, 136), has recourse to this Senecan attitude in his *Tombeau de Charles IX* (1574):

> Bien qu'il meure en jeunesse, il a beaucoup vescu.
>   Si sa Royauté fut de peu d'age suyvie,
> L'age ne sert de rien, les gestes font la vie.

Alexandre à trante ans vesquit plus que ne font
Ceux qui ont la vieillesse & les rides au front :
Peu nous servent des ans les courses retournées :
Les vertus nous font l'age, & non pas les années.

(XVII, 5–6. Cf. VIII, 259)

The popular refrain: carpe diem and carpe florem

Certain scholarly studies have already established the major sources and the literary tradition of Ronsard's *carpe diem* and *carpe florem* themes, and have assessed the nature and extent of his originality and poetic superiority in these respects.[35] Indeed, as has already been suggested, the concentration of attention on the popular *carpe diem* theme has tended to obscure certain other features of Ronsard's epicurean position, and this is why this present study has centred on the neglected allegorical and philosophical statements and on the contribution of Seneca, rather than on the much-studied vulgar refrain. However, in spite of the critical material on this subject, there has been an understandable tendency to focus attention on the most beautiful expressions of this theme and on the anthology pieces in particular—*Mignonne, allon voir*, and *Quand vous serez bien vieille*.[36] It is for this reason that a catalogue of Ronsard's principal *carpe diem* and *carpe florem* statements is given below in a note,[37] so that the reader can appreciate the consistency and emphasis of the epicurean refrain, and can also assess the full extent of the poet's obsession with the passage of time and the fragility of life which are the essential factors leading to its formulation.

If less well known examples of this epicurean theme are chosen in the following pages, it is in order to illustrate dimensions of Ronsard's attitude which are frequently neglected and to show that the poetic quality of such statements is spread more widely than often supposed. For example, although the general idea of the following sonnet from the *Continuation des Amours* (1555) may be suggested by an epigram from *The Greek Anthology* or from Marullus (both texts are quoted by Laumonier in his edition), Ronsard's originality is clearly evident in the way that the final epicurean plea is richly supported throughout by a poetic meditation on the destructive nature of time :

Je vous envoye un bouquet de ma main
Que j'ai ourdy de ces fleurs epanies :
Qui ne les eust à ce vespre cuillies,
Flaques à terre elles cherroient demain.
   Cela vous soit un exemple certain
Que voz beautés, bien qu'elles soient fleuries,
En peu de tems cherront toutes flétries,
Et periront, comme ces fleurs, soudain.
   Le tems s'en va, le tems s'en va, ma Dame :

Las! le tems non, mais nous nous en allons,
Et tost serons estendus sous la lame :
  Et des amours desquelles nous parlons,
Quand serons morts n'en sera plus nouvelle :
Pour-ce aimés moi, ce pendant qu'estes belle.

(VII, 152–3)

The emphatic use of certain word patterns (*vespre, demain, en peu de tems, soudain, tems, tost, quand, ce pendant*), the manner in which these lexical items increase in number as the poem progresses, and the restless movement throughout between present, past, conditional and future verb tenses (a movement repeated in the opening quatrain of *Quand vous serez bien vieille*, where the future tense is replaced by the present and then by the past in an attempt to seize poetically the passage of time: XVII, 265–6): these techniques create a global vision of time within which man and nature are engulfed. Similarly the important rhyming words of the octet (*epanies, cuillies, demain; fleuries, flétries, soudain*) are not only instrumental in creating the fusion between the flowers and the girl's beauty, but they also plot the destructive course of time and the movement from life to death. In this respect the important lexical item *soudain* of line 8 is foregrounded by the inversion and by the syllabic division of the line (4/4/2). We are thus prepared for lines 9–10 where the inevitable onrush of time is evoked by the monotonous succession of monosyllables, by the rhythmical structure of line 9 (4/4/2) and by the triple repetition of *le tems* and the verb *s'en aller*. Line 10, with its syllabic count (1/3/6), its foregrounded *Las!* and its emphatic contradiction *non*, brings an apparently spontaneous discovery that time, although fleeting, is stable in its infinity and that it is man alone who is transient. Ronsard's sonnet has other poetic virtues— for example the alliance of sound and sense in lines 2–4, where a pattern of high 'i' sounds (*ourdy, epanies, Qui, cuillies*) falls away like the flowers themselves to the low 'a' values of *Flaques à* (a word stressed at the head of the line and lexically reinforced throughout the poem by similar clusters: *cherroient, cherront, estendus*)—but its beauty lies essentially in its emphatic and dense use of lexical, structural and stylistic items to evoke the relentless passage of time.

In the same way a rarely quoted passage from the *Ode à Monsieur de Verdun* of 1565 not only demonstrates the consummate artistry with which Ronsard transposes multiple Horatian texts to form an original and poetic commentary on fleeting time, old age and impending death, but also reveals yet another dimension of his epicurean attitude which is often overlooked:

  Sois gaillard, dispost & joyeux,
Ny convoyteux ny soucieux

Des choses qui nous rongent l'ame :
Fuis toutes sortes de douleurs,
Et ne prens soucy des malheurs
Qui sont preditz par Nostredame.
    Ne romps ton tranquille repos
Pour Papaux ny pour Huguenotz,
Des deux amy ny adversaire,
Croyant que Dieu pere tresdoux
(Qui n'est partial comme nous)
Sçait ce qui nous est necessaire.
    N'ayes soucy du lendemain,
Mais serrant le temps en la main
Vy joyeusement la journée
Et l'heure en laquelle seras :
Et que sçais si tu verras
L'autre lumiere retournée?
    Couche toy à l'ombre d'un bois,
Ou pres d'un rivage, où la voix
D'une fonteine jazeresse
Tressaulte, & tandis que tes ans
Sont encore & vers & plaisans,
Par le jeu trompe la vieillesse.
    Car incontinent nous mourons,
Et bien loing banis nous irons
Dedans une nasselle obscure,
Où plus de rien ne nous souvient,
Et d'où jamais on ne revient,
Car ainsi l'a voulu Nature.
            (XIII, 260–1)

Whilst the basic framework for Ronsard's lines is provided by Horace, *Odes*, II, xi, there is also evidence of a dense assimilation of numerous other Horatian texts.[38] Yet in spite of this absorption of Latin material, Ronsard demonstrates his independence of his model by taking little beyond the general spirit and theme, and by interpreting his arguments within a contemporary and national context (references to Nostradamus and the civil conflict). It is clearly to Horace, however, that Ronsard is indebted for the manner in which he reconciles his epicureanism with his Christian belief in the first half of the extract quoted. In frequent texts Horace had effected a fusion between an epicurean philosophy of life and the religious significance of *hubris* found in Pindar,[39] for—so his argument went—since the future is in the hands of the gods and denied to man, only the present with remembrance of past pleasures can ensure human happiness. Ronsard too adopts this reasoning here—as he had already done at greater length in an ode of 1550 (II, 169–74)—and submits himself to the equity and assurance of the Divine Will in order, firstly, to release his mind from anxiety concerning the future and concerning externals beyond his control, and, secondly, to immerse himself wholeheartedly in the present, which employed actively and intensely —'*serrant* le temps en la main'—alone compensates for the passage of time and the limited perspective imposed on the human condition as a result of original sin. This submission to a Divine Order is reinforced further by the poet's acceptance of a natural law of mortality, for the resigned tone of the line 'Car ainsi l'a voulu Nature' is Ronsard's personal and significant commentary on a further Horatian borrowing on the theme of death's omnipotence and finality (*Odes*, ii, iii, 21–8).

A more detailed analysis of these stanzas will reveal that their poetic techniques and stylistic features are in many respects typical of those used elsewhere in similar epicurean contexts. Antithetical lexical patterns are built up to suggest anxiety, misery and suffering on the one hand (*convoyteux, soucieux, rongent, douleurs, soucy, malheurs, soucy*) and joy and carefree gaiety on the other (*gaillard, dispost, joyeux, tranquille repos, joyeusement, vers & plaisans*), and this contrasting scheme is not only supported by other word patterns throughout these lines (*lumiere, ombre, obscure; pres de, bien loing; vers, vieillesse*), but it is emphasised on the structural level by a series of negative and affirmative verbs, many of them imperatives (*Sois . . . ny . . . ny; fuis; ne prens; ne romps . . . ny . . . ny; N'ayes; vy; couche; trompe; nous mourons; irons; ne souvient; ne revient*). Throughout there is also an opposition established between present and future verb tenses (plus the past tense of the final line), and this underlines the poem's wide temporal perspective, a perspective evoked by strong word clusters centred on the concepts of time and death (*lendemain, le temps, journée, heure, tandis que, ans, encore, vieillesse, mourons, nasselle obscure, jamais*). If death is associated with a series of extreme and superlative statements (*bien loing, plus de rien, d'où jamais*) and with ideas of eternal exile, darkness and enclosure (*dedans*), the epicurean plea proper is placed within a natural setting near water which, by contrast, has suggestive connections with life, movement (*tressaulte*), sound (*voix, jazeresse*), youth, colour (*vers*), liberty (*jeu*) and protection (*à l'ombre*). A study of other epicurean refrains reveals a similar global vision of time and identical contrasting patterns, and although the details of the natural setting may vary— elsewhere for example references are made to wine, love, dancing, singing, flowers, fruit, evergreen vegetation, birds, perfume, rustic divinities —its associations with life remain constant and emphatic.

In the same way a rewarding study can be made of the variants in later editions of certain *carpe diem* refrains, for these revisions of old age will reveal an increased note of urgency and desperation in the epicurean appeal and a heightened awareness of the mobility of time and of the proximity of death.[40] An erotico–bacchic plea of 1555 is a good illustration of this process, for the original exhortation,

Qu'on m'ombrage le chef de vigne, & de l'hierre,
Les bras, & tout le col, qu'on enfleure la terre
De roses, & de lis, & que dessus le jonc
  On me caille du lait rougi de mainte fraise :
É n'esse pas bien fait ? or sus, commençon donq,
Et chasson loin de nous tout soing & tout malaise
                                     (VII, 131)

is recast in the 1578–87 editions as follows :

Apporte ces bouquets que tu m'avois cueillis,
Ces roses, ces œillets, ce josmin & ces lis :
Attache une couronne à l'entour de ma teste.
  Gaignon ce jour icy, trompon nostre trespas :
Peut estre que demain nous ne reboirons pas.
S'attendre au lendemain n'est pas une chose preste.
                (1584–7 : ... n'est pas chose trop preste.)

The epicurean aspect and the evocation of human fragility are thus rendered much more insistent by the addition of contrasting verb tenses (past, present and future) and by the introduction of time and death lexis (*jour, trespas, demain, lendemain, preste*). The natural setting of 1555, with its variety of associations with life and plenitude (wine, evergreen plants, flowers, milk, fruit), is focused uniquely on flowers in the later version, and this detail, together with the reference to *bouquets* and *cueillis*, situate us more suggestively within the *carpe florem* context of the 1555 sonnet *Je vous envoye un bouquet* analysed above. Moreover, the addition of the crown symbolism has rich associations with poetic immortality and with the problem of how to transcend time and human fragility (see below, p. 195).
    A more complex pattern of revision is evident in a free adaptation of a pseudo-Anacreontic text of 1555 (VI, 198–9 : cf. *Anacreontea*, p. 27, no. 7). Lines 1–16 of this ode were only minimally revised over the years, but the final verse containing the epicurean statement underwent systematic modification before attaining its final emphatic form of 1587. In the *editio princeps* lines 17–20 are rather loose, repetitive and prosaic, with several redundant phrases, weak and passive verbs (*voir, recevoir*), little descriptive realism and a vision of death veiled by a poetic fiction :

Mais puis que tu me dis que j'irai bien tost voir
Charon, tu m'en devrois dautant plus estre humaine,
Car le vieil homme doit, ou jamais, recevoir
Ses plaisirs, dautant plus qu'il voit sa mort prochaine.

In the 1560–84 editions Ronsard corrects lines 17–18 by introducing a slightly more active verb (*avoir*) and by replacing the classical reference by the more realistic word *tombeau* : 'Mais puis que le tombeau me doit bien tost avoir, / Certes tu me devrois d'autant plus estre humaine.' This increasing emphasis on visual realism and on the awareness of human mortality is further strengthened in the 1578–84 variants of line 20 with its lexical reference to time and with the introduction of the verb *sentir* : 'Ses plaisirs, mesme au temps qu'il sent la mort prochaine.'

The definitive version of this stanza appeared in the posthumous 1587 edition in a completely modified form :

> Mais puis que mon corps doit sous la terre moisir
> Bien tost, & que Pluton victime le veut prendre,
> Plus il me faut haster de ravir le plaisir,
> D'autant plus que ma vie est proche de sa cendre.

Not only does Ronsard progressively distance his lines from his pseudo-Anacreontic source, but in this final version he condenses his ideas into a taut and dense poetic unity. He adds a whole new physical dimension to human mortality (*corps, sous la terre moisir, victime, cendre*) and underlines the process of bodily decay and the urgency of the epicurean plea (*doit, il me faut*) by strong active verbs (*moisir, prendre, haster de ravir*). He reintroduces a classical fiction within this context of increased urgency and physical realism, and retains the time aspect and the idea of death's proximity by lexical reference (*Bien tost, proche*) and by juxtaposing and balancing the antithesis *vie/cendre* in stressed positions (the caesura and the end rhyme).

A similar process is evident in the variants of other epicurean pleas (cf. I, 216; VI, 104), and these revisions not only give the reader an insight into the poetic artistry of the mature Ronsard, but they have a psychological value in that they reveal his personal preoccupations as he nears the grave.

This present study has sought to demonstrate that in Ronsard's poetry, time is an important consideration, encompassing a diversity of attitudes and conceptions—mythological, allegorical, cosmological, philosophical —and that it is not merely a notion which resulted in a poetic rejuvenation of the lyrical commonplaces concerning 'la fuite du temps' and the familiar epicurean themes. Although this latter interpretation has received the constant attention of the majority of scholars in the past, it fails to do justice to the scope and plenitude of Ronsard's treatment of temporal themes. For Ronsard's conception of time is frequently linked to a philosophical and quasi-scientific definition of the universe, and to a discussion of man's relation to the world of which he is a small but necessary factor. If, on the more commonplace level, the obsession with the irreversible motion and destructive nature of time, the fragility and brevity of life and the cleavage between human duration and eternity finds its natural and instinctive remedy in the epicurean refrain—itself a complex and diverse attitude involving allegorical and philosophical statements as well as the popular *carpe diem* appeal—on the cosmological level Ronsard achieves consolation by fusing man with an equitable universal order (alternately of divine or natural origin), which is dependent on time's movement and cyclic change for its preservation and dynamism. Human happiness and wisdom are seen to reside in a submission to the rhythmic variety of time and in a stoical acceptance of man's inevitable transience in the name of cosmic harmony.

NOTES TO CHAPTER FOUR

1 Cf. Daremberg and Saglio, s.v. *Saturnus*; E. Panofsky, *Studies in Iconology* (New York, 1962), chapt. III; A. Greifenhagen, 'Zum Saturnglauben der Renaissance', *Die Antike*, XI (1935), 67–84. The original confusion is discussed by Cicero, *De Natura Deorum*, II, 64. This section owes a considerable debt to Professor I. Silver's article 'Ronsard's Reflections on the Heavens and Time'.

2 Panofsky, p. 71 and plates; Tervarent, s.v. *Béquilles*; *Horloge*, II; *Sablier*, I, VI; *Serpent en forme de cercle*, II.

3 Panofsky, figs. 45–7, 56, 60; Tervarent, s.v. *Homme dévorant un enfant*.

4 XVIII, 59. Ronsard's expression 'faux dentee' is a direct reminiscence of Hesiod, *Theogony*, 179–180 ('long sickle with jagged teeth'). For this idea in artistic representations, cf. Panofsky, fig. 48.

5 Marullus, *Hymni*, I, V, *Aeternitati*, ll. 6–9. For representations in iconography and emblematic literature, see *Emblemata. Handbuch zur Sinnbildkunst*, s.v. *Juventas* (cols. 1535–6). Cf. Cesare Ripa, *Iconologia* (Padua, 1611), pp. 197–8. See also G. Lafeuille, pp. 46–53.

6 See above pp. 15–16. Identical lexical items appear in social contexts (above, p. 23 and note 42). On Ronsard's seasonal *hymnes*, see in particular D. Stone Jnr., *Ronsard's Sonnet Cycles* (Yale Univ. Press, 1966), pp. 107–20; M. C. Smith, 'The Hidden Meaning of Ronsard's Hymne de l'Hyver', in *Renaissance Studies in Honor of Silver*, pp. 85–97.

7 Cf. *Timaeus*, 34A; 37C–39E. For Plato's conception of time, consult J. F. Callahan, *Four Views of Time in Ancient Philosophy* (Cambridge, Harvard Univ. Press, 1948), pp. 4–37.

8 Cf. *Physics*, IV, xiv, 223a29–223b23; VIII, viii–ix; *De Caelo*, I, ii, 269a20–30; II, iii, 286a10–12; iv, 287a24–30; vi, 288a15–289a10. On Aristotle and time, see Solmsen, pp. 144–59; Callahan, pp. 38–87.

9 *De Caelo*, II, iii, 286a10–12; II, vi, 288a22–7. Cf. pseudo-Aristotle, *De Mundo*, II, 391b17–19.

10 *On the Heavens*, LCL, 1939, pp. 159–61. Cf. *De Caelo*, I, iii, 270b20–4; II, vi, 288a22–5; *De Mundo*, II, 392a5–8; Pliny, *Nat. Hist.*, II, iii. Cf. Silver, 'Ronsard's Reflections on the Heavens and Time', p. 350; and the notes in Ronsard, VIII, 141; XIX, 109.

11 Cf. *Timaeus*, 30D–31A; 32D–33D; *De Caelo*, I, vii, 275b5–12; I, viii–ix, 276a18–279b3; *Metaphysics*, XII, viii, 1074a32–9.

12   VIII, 149, var. Cf. Busson, *Le Rationalisme*, pp. 374–5; Silver, 'Ronsard's Reflections on Cosmogony and Nature', pp. 225–6. For a different interpretation of these lines, see A. Stegmann, 'L'inspiration Platonicienne dans les *Hymnes de Ronsard*', *Revue des Sciences Humaines*, Fasc. 122–3 (1966), 204–5.

13   Cf. Ronsard, ll. 105–7 (var.), and Marullus, *Aeternitati*, ll. 18, 20–21. Silver is clearly wrong to state that Ronsard's debt to Marullus largely disappears in the variants ('Ronsard's Reflections on the Heavens and Time', p. 364 and n. 148).

14   *Timaeus*, 37D–38A (LCL, 1929, pp. 75–7). Cf. Plotinus, *Ennead*, III, 7; Petrarch, *Trionfo dell'Eternitá*, ll. 64–9. See also Lafeuille, pp. 41, 57–9.

15   Cf. IX, 23–4; XII, 186; XIII, 103–4; XVII, 408–9.

16   For this theme of the return of the Age of Gold, see in particular VI, 201–2; VIII, 65–72; XIII, 58–9; 105–10. Cf. Virgil, *Eclogues*, IV; *Aeneid*, VI, 791–7. For the associated vision of history, consult A. Roubichou-Stretz, chapt. IV.

17   G. Poulet, *Etudes sur le temps humain* (Edinburgh Univ. Press, 1949), p. 15.

18   Time's flight: II, 83; XII, 276; XIII, 153. Water metaphor: II, 107; VI, 103–4; VIII, 178; 358.

19   Source is *Iliad*, VI, 145–9; XXI, 464–6. As Laumonier states, both passages are quoted by Plutarch, *Consolatio ad Apollonium*, chapt. 6, and paraphrased by Simonides of Ceos in a fragment preserved in Stobaeus, *Florilegium*, XCVIII, 29. Cf. Ronsard, V, 192; VIII, 170; XI, 64; XVIII, 437; 504. The edition of the *Florilegium* used throughout this study is *Dicta Poetarum quae apud Io. Stobaeum exstant* (Paris, Buon, 1623). Whilst the numbering of the sections in this edition differs slightly from the sixteenth century editions by Gesner and Oporinus available to Ronsard, the contents of individual sections are identical.

20   English translation in *Elegy and Iambus* (2 vols., LCL, 1931), vol. I, pp. 89–91.

21   See in particular fragments of Mimnermus nos. 1, 34, 35 (English translations in *Elegy and Iambus*, vol. I, pp. 91–93). Also fragment no. 9 by Menander (English translation, LCL, 1921, p. 495). Sources noted by Laumonier, *loc. cit.*

22   XVII, 247–8, s. I. Cf. Petrarch, *Rime*, s. CCLXXI, 'L'ardente nodo ov'io fui d'ora in ora', first tercet. See also, Ronsard, XVII, 208, s. XIV; 339–40, s. IV.

23   Source suggested by Laumonier. Cf. also Seneca, *Epist.*, XII; LVIII, 31–6; Stobaeus, *Florilegium*, CXVI.

24   XVII, 50–1. In addition to the sources proposed by Laumonier in his notes, cf. Seneca, *Ad Polybium De Consol.*, I, i–iv; *Epist.*, LXXI, 12–16. Further comforting arguments familiar to the *genre* of the *consolatio* are voiced in the following lines of Ronsard's poem: here he opposes the brevity of life with the infinite compass of eternity in order to preach a lesson of resignation to human mortality and time's passage (cf. Lucretius, III, 1090–4; Plutarch, *Consol. ad Apollonium*, chapters 17 and 31; Cicero, *Tusculanarum Disputationum*, I, xxxix, 94; Seneca, *Ad Lucilium Epistulae*, XLIX, 3; LXXIV, 10; XCIX, 10; *Ad Marciam De Consol.*, XXI, 1–2).

25   M. D. Quainton, 'Ronsard's Philosophical and Cosmological Conceptions of Time', *French Studies*, XXIII (1969), 12–14.

26   Cf. Ronsard, I, 162; II, 63; 89; V, 166; VII, 78–9; VIII, 331–2; XI, 139; XIV, 114; XV, 154–5; XVI, 42; XVIII, 411.

27   This epigram is quoted in Greek and translated by J. E. Matzke, 'On the Source of the Italian and English Idioms meaning "To Take Time by the Forelock"', *PMLA*, VIII (1893), 314–15. See also, G. L. Kittredge, 'To Take Time by the Forelock', *Modern Language Notes*, VIII, (1893), 230–5; K. Pietsch, 'On the Source of the Italian and English Idioms meaning "To Take Time by the Forelock"', *Modern Language Notes*, VIII (1893), 235–8. A translation of the

Greek epigram can also be read in *The Greek Anthology* (5 vols., LCL, 1915–18), vol. V, p. 325, no. 275.

28 *Studies in Iconology*, p. 71. For the Greek and Roman conception of *Kairos–Occasio* and for representations of the figure, see Daremberg and Saglio, s.v. *Kairos*; A. Greifenhagen, 'Zum Saturnglauben der Renaissance', figs. 2–4.

29 On this confusion, see H. R. Patch, *The Goddess Fortuna*, pp. 115–17; A. Doren, 'Fortuna im Mittelalter', pp. 135–6 and fig. 16; Tervarent, s.v. *Corne d'abondance*, V, VI; *Mèche de cheveux flottant à l'avant du front*, I–III; *Rasoir*; *Roue*, I, II; *Sphère*, VII.

30 VIII, 105; VI, 174; 211–12. Cf. II, 171; XIII, 260; XV, 344.

31 Virgil, *Georgics*, III, 66–7 and 284. Seneca discusses the first passage in his *De Brevitate Vitae*, IX, 2–5. For other aspects of Seneca's role in the humanistic evaluation of time, consult R. Glasser, *Time in French Life and Thought*. Translated by C. G. Pearson (Manchester Univ. Press, 1972), pp. 198–201, 209, 211–12.

32 Baïf, V, 205–10 (a paraphrase of *De Brev. Vitae*, I, 1 – III, 4). See also, maxims at V, 117–18; 120–1; 127; 130; 136. Cf. Seneca, *Epist.*, I; XV, 4; XXXII, 2–4; XLV, 12–13; XLIX, and especially 5 and 10; LXI, 1; XCIV, 27; CI; CXVII, 32; *De Tranquillitate Animi*, III, 8.

33 *Nicomachean Ethics*, III, vi, 1115a32–5; ix, 1117b7–15; IV, iii, 1124b6–9; *Consolatio ad Apollonium*, chapt. 17. Cf. I. Silver, 'Ronsard's Reflections on the Heavens and Time', p. 362.

34 *Ad Marciam de Consolatione*, XXIV, 1 (*Moral Essays*, LCL, vol. II, p. 85); *Epist.*, LXX, 4–5 (LCL, 1930, vol. II, p. 59). Cf. *De Brevitate Vitae*, VII, 10; *De Tranquillitate Animi*, III, 8; *Epist.*, XLIX, 10; LXXVII, 20; LXXXV, 22–3; XCIII (this entire epistle is devoted to this subject).

35 See P. Laumonier, *Ronsard poète lyrique*, 2nd edn. (Paris, 1923), pp. 560–634; and H. Weber, *La Création poétique*, vol. I, pp. 333–56, together with their bibliographical references (in particular articles by Guy, Parturier, Thomas). The literary tradition includes Theocritus, XXIII; XXVII, 8–11; XXIX, 25ff.; XXX, 11–23; Tibullus, I, i, 69ff.; viii, 41–8; Propertius, III, XXV, 11–18; Ovid, *Ars Amatoria*, II, 113ff.; III, 59–80; Horace, *Odes*, I, iv; xi; xxv; II, iii; xi; IV, x; xii; Catullus, V; Ausonius, *De rosis nascentibus*; Secundus, *Elegiae*, I, v, 39ff.; II, viii, 69ff.

36 V, 196–7; XVII, 265–6. Cf. Laumonier, pp. 581–91; Weber, I, pp. 345–8; F. Desonay, *Ronsard, poète de l'amour*, vol. I, pp. 164–7, and vol. III, pp. 337–8; D. Stone, *Ronsard's Sonnet Cycles*, pp. 3–13; L. Spitzer, 'Sonnets pour Hélène, Livre II, 43', in *Interpretationen zur Geschichte der französischen Lyrik* (Heidelberg, 1961), pp. 20–4; W. Blechmann, 'Imitatio creatrix bei Ronsard. (Zum Sonnett "Quand vous serez bien vieille")', *Zeitschrift für französische Sprache und Literatur*, LXXIII (1963), 1–16.

37 Vol. I, 189–91; 207–8; 208–11; 215–16; vol. II, 33–5; 127–8; 196–8; vol. V, 79–80; 196–7; 231; vol. VI, 71–2; 102–3; 103–4; 105–7; 172–4; 174–6; 191–4; 198–9; 219–20; 243–4; vol. VII, 130–1, s. XIII; 152–3, s. XXXV; 189–90; 195–6; vol. X, 96–7, s. XII; vol. XII, 169–70; 276; vol. XIII, 260–1; vol. XIV, 151; vol. XV, 121; 176; 195, s. II; 204; 219; 220–1; 233; vol. XVII, 224, s. XXXV; 264, s. XXII; 265–6, s. XXIV; 267–8, s. XXVI; 313–14, s. XXXIII; 319, s. XL; 370–3; 381–2; vol. XVIII, 119.

38 In addition to the sources suggested by Laumonier, see also *Odes*, II, iii, 1–16; II, vii, 17–28; xvi, 25–7; III, viii, 25–8; *Satires*, II, vi, 93–7; *Epistles*, I, iv, 13–14. Laumonier's reference p. 260, n. 3, should read Horace, I, 9, and not I, 8.

39 Cf. *Olympian*, II, antistr. 2; XII, antistr. 1; *Pythian*, III, antistr. 3; *Nemean*, VI, str. 1; XI, ep. 3.

40   On the more general question of Ronsard's variants, see especially L. Terreaux, *Ronsard correcteur de ses œuvres. Les variantes des Odes et des deux premiers livres des Amours* (Geneva, 1968), and its bibliographical references. For a good definition of the controversy between those scholars who defend the thesis that Ronsard's revisions are generally an improvement on the original text, and those who extol the poetic superiority of the *editio princeps*, see I. Silver, 'Deux points de vue sur Ronsard "Aristarque de ses œuvres" ', *RHLF*, LVIII (1958), 1–15.

CHAPTER FIVE

Ronsard's philosophical and cosmological visions of death

Whilst Ronsard's view of death may not have the nightmarish insistence and the macabre obsession associated with the medieval and baroque imaginations,[1] it is still an ever-present preoccupation of his inspiration and an integral and important aspect of his vision of a mutable world and of man's place in it. Indeed it is crucial not to oversimplify Ronsard's attitude on the sole testimony of such anthology pieces as his *Comme on voit sur la branche* (XVII, 125), for his conception of death—'dont l'horreur espouvante un chacun' (XVIII, 134)—has many facets and is often expressed in his verse by means of a systematic and sometimes painful struggle to transcend and escape his mortal condition. Neither is it wise to look for a clear-cut and convenient evolution of attitude in Ronsard's work, for what will be found is a rich mosaic of different visions of death in no way resolved by chronological reference. In the final analysis, amidst the abundance of material and the diversity of attitudes, an authentic voice will be heard, a dominant note, and it is this which will direct this study and guide its conclusions.

It has already been shown that, as a philosophical concept, death is inherently associated with a transformist theory of matter, with the reduction to, and preservation of, elemental substance through the continual change of forms. Relating this definition of death more particularly to the human condition, it will be seen that man also conforms to the same transformist pattern and that Ronsard will explore, with the help of Lucretius—but with the prudent reservations of Christian orthodoxy—the human consequences of this doctrine. For Ronsard, as for Lucretius, human death is essentially the dissolution of the body's material components and a return to its first elements, but unlike the Latin author for whom the mind and soul were composed of atoms and therefore mortal (III, 417–869), Ronsard makes an orthodox Christian–Platonic distinction between mind and matter.[2] In this way Ronsard integrates the human condition into the natural cycles of matter operat-

ing within the universe, for corruption is seen as the necessary preliminary to rebirth, and the preservation of the species (matter) is effected
through the death of individuals (form). In the following extract these
ideas may have been suggested by Plutarch, *Consolatio ad Apollonium*,
chapters 6, 10 and 16, although the French lines are also textually close
to the materialistic ideas and tone of certain Lucretian passages (I, 263–
4; III, 964–71):

> L'homme n'est que misere, & doit mourir expres
> A fin que par sa mort un autre vive apres,
> L'un meurt, l'autre revit, & tousjours la naissance
> Par la corruption engendre une autre essence.
>
> (X, 319, var.)

The same aspects are found in poems of 1571, 1578 and 1584 (XV,
318; XVII, 383; XVIII, 157), but it was much earlier, in the *Hymne de la
Mort* of 1555, that Ronsard had made his most emphatic and poetic
attempt to assimilate the balanced corruption and generation pattern of
the human species into a cosmic vision of enduring matter and changing
forms:

> Car naissans nous mourons, telle est la destinée
> Des corps sujectz à toy, qui tiens tout, qui prens tout,
> Qui n'as en ton pouvoir certaine fin, ne bout,
> Et ne fust de Venus l'âme generative,
> Qui tes fautes repare, & rend la forme vive,
> Le monde periroit: mais son germe en refait
> Autant de son costé, que ton dard en deffait.
> Que ta puissance (ô MORT) est grande & admirable!
> Rien au monde par toy ne se dit pardurable,
> Mais tout ainsi que l'onde à-val des ruisseaux fuit
> Le pressant coulement de l'autre qui la suit,
> Ainsi le temps se coulle, & le present faict place
> Au futur importun qui les tallons luy trace:
> Ce qui fut se refaict, tout coulle comme une eau,
> Et rien dessous le Ciel ne se void de nouveau:
> Mais la forme se change en une autre nouvelle,
> Et ce changement là, VIVRE au monde s'appelle,
> Et MOURIR, quand la forme en une autre s'en va.
> Ainsi, avec Venus la Nature trouva
> Moyen de r'animer par longs & divers changes,
> La matiere restant, tout cela que tu manges:
> Mais nostre ame immortelle est tousjours en un lieu,
> Au change non sujette, assise aupres de DIEU,
> Citoyenne à-jamais de la ville ætherée
> Qu'elle avoit si long temps en ce corps desirée.
>
> (VIII, 177–8)

This idea of a balance of opposing forces of corruption and preservation may be inspired from those chapters of Plutarch's *Consolatio ad Apollonium* recently mentioned, for this is a major source of the French *hymne*.[3] However, textual similarity is slight and is restricted to the basic idea of the world as a continual pattern of destruction and generation. Ronsard's double reference to Venus (significantly absent in Plutarch) would suggest that in this particular instance he is not primarily recalling this Greek text, but rather certain passages of Lucretius which define the procreative and preservative role of Venus in a world balanced between creation and corruption:

Besides, if time consuming all the material utterly destroys whatever by lapse of years it removes, whence does Venus restore living creatures to the light of life each after its kind, or when they are restored whence does the wonder-working earth nourish them and make them grow, providing food for each after its kind?[4]

Although Lucretius mentions the destructive nature of time, the central image of passing time and flowing water is clearly inspired by Ovid, *Metamorphoses*, xv, 178–85. The generalised definition of life and death in terms of the change and renewal of matter is borrowed from these texts of Ovid, Lucretius and Seneca which have been quoted in respect of the *Discours* to Chauveau (above pp. 31–2), whilst the first hemistich of the French extract is an echo of Manilius, *Astronomica*, IV, 16. Not only does Ronsard assimilate and arrange his multiple borrowings to a poetic purpose, not only does he add his own prudent Christian commentary to his transformist vision as is his wont, but he gives a personal emphasis and structure to the material which reveal a state of mind characteristic of his attitude to the question of flux. Throughout the passage, and in two separate movements, the notions of human transience and the omnipotence of death are paralleled and cancelled out by the philosophical concept of cyclic regeneration. In turn this whole central movement is bracketed by the two passages emphasising the preservation of the species and the eternity of matter. In this way the development on death does not evoke any sadness on the part of the reader, for the arguments, the construction of the passage and the tone of breathless admiration, as Ronsard moves from the individual human plane to the harmony of the wider cosmic pattern, are all designed to comfort and to establish man's fusion with a universal order.

Whilst Ronsard refers to the regenerative functions of Venus in a sonnet of the *Bocage* of 1554,[5], and again in the *Hymne de l'Eternité* (1556: VIII, 251–2) and *La Paix* (1559: IX, 111–12), elsewhere it is rather the Platonic Eros who is associated with the preservation of the species, a role which complements his functions as creator, organiser and binding knot of the universe. Plato and the neo-Platonists distinguished between two Erotes : Aphrodite Urania (the celestial Venus) represented ideal love, and was associated with the birth of Venus from the seminal fluid after the castration of Uranus, whilst Aphrodite Pandemos (the popular Venus), born from the union of Zeus and Dione, presided over procreation.[6] In a *Cartel* of 1569 Ronsard draws the distinction between the two Erotes and refers to the procreative role of the popular Eros— 'Pere germeux de naissance', as he is called elsewhere (XVI, 142)—in the following terms :

> . . . l'Amour aucteur de noz naissances
> Terrestre & bas, qui nostre humanité
> Rend presque egalle à la divinité,
> De pere en filz concevant noz semblables
> Pour reparer les siecles perdurables.
>
> (XV, 115. Cf. XV, 101; XVII, 62)

It is, in fact, his materialistic tendencies and the reliance on Lucretius noted above, which in turn explain Ronsard's philosophical sensualism concerning life and death. This sensualism expresses itself, as will be seen, in an over-riding concern for the destiny of the body in death as opposed to that of the soul : it also provides the key to a duality in Ronsard's vision. On the most obvious and instinctive level death causes dismay and regret, for it entails the termination of sensation, pleasure and beauty, and it periodically focuses attention on physical decomposition and dislocation. Although prefigured in earlier poems,[7] by far the most macabre and visually realistic of Ronsard's references to bodily corruption is found in his description of du Bellay's ghost in an elegy of 1560 :

> . . . have & descharné, planté sur de grands os.
> Ses costes, sa carcasse, & l'espine du dos
> Estoyent veufves de chair, & sa diserte bouche,
> . . . fut sans langue & sans dens,
> Et ses yeux, . . .
> Estoyent sans blanc, sans noir, sans clarté ny prunelles,
> Et sa teste, qui fut le Caballin coupeau,
> Avoit le nez retraict, sans cheveux, & sans peau,
> Point de forme d'oreille, & la creuse ouverture
> De son ventre n'estoit que vers & pourriture.
>
> (X, 366–7)

The picturesque detail, the adjectival emphasis, the body lexis and the repetitive *sans* pattern make this the most poetically compelling of Ronsard's descriptions. In turn this account clearly anticipates some of

Ronsard's evocations of physical emaciation and decay found in later collections, and especially that of sonnet I of *Les Derniers Vers*, where the lexical item *decharné* is echoed from earlier references and poetically reinforced by repetition:

> Je n'ay plus que les os, un Schelette je semble,
> Decharné, denervé, demusclé, depoulpé,
> Que le trait de la mort sans pardon a frappé,
> Je n'ose voir mes bras que de peur je ne tremble.
> . . .
> Mon corps s'en va descendre où tout se desassemble.[8]

What obsesses the sensualist in Ronsard is the lack of corporeal substance and weight in death; the fact that one is 'privé de sens, de veines, & d'arteres', a mere 'semblance veine, / Sans corps', a 'vain hoste du sepulchre', a 'vain fardeau', 'Sans chair, sans sang, sans os, sans mouvement / . . . Ombres gresles, & vaines, / . . . sans muscles & sans veines, / Foibles, sans poix, debiles', and that death gives a poor exchange for life: 'Pour le vray le faux . . . / Et pour le corps seulement l'ombre'.[9] However, the decomposition of the body does not signify total destruction or absence for Ronsard: indeed, as Marc Bensimon has declared, Ronsard cannot bear to reduce the body to nothing and contemplate a void.[10] He is always at pains to emphasise what persists after death, be it the nebulous outline of the classical 'ombre', 'un petit je ne sai quoi', 'poudre', 'fantaume sans os', 'cendre & l'oubly', 'premiers Elemens', 'cendres & . . . os', 'reliques en paix'.[11]

The other dimension of the duality referred to above—what one might term the rational level—leads Ronsard to explore the various consequences of a philosophical sensualism and to construct a theory, based on a definition of death as the absence of physical and mental pain, which is designed for the most part to comfort. It is in the *Hymne de la Mort* that we first find a sensualist argument used to reject the medieval vision of death and to give consolation:

> Beaucoup ne sçachans point qu'ilz sont enfans de Dieu,
> Pleurent avant partir, & s'atristent au lieu
> De chanter hautement le Pëan de victoire,
> Et pensent que la MORT soit quelque beste noire,
> Qui les viendra manger, & que dix mille vers
> Rongeront de leurs cors les ôs tous descouvers,
> Et leur test, qui sera, dans un lieu solitaire,
> L'effroyable ornement d'un ombreux cimetiere :
> Chetif, apres la mort le corps ne sent plus rien,
> En vain tu es paoureux, il ne sent mal ny bien
> Non plus qu'il faisoit lors que le germe à ton pere
> N'avoit enflé de toy le ventre de ta mere.
>
> (VIII, 167–8)

This equation of death with a pre-natal state must be seen as another example of Ronsard's preoccupation with the cyclic processes of life which he traces beyond flux and which constantly comfort him. Here, as elsewhere in the *hymne*, death is familiarised and robbed of its horrific associations by integrating it into a natural rhythm of life, birth and conception. This statement echoes images of fertility and conception first mentioned in lines 64–6 of the *hymne*, although on the lexical level there are already suggestions in lines 31, 47, 58 and 60. In turn this passage prepares the widening perspective of the poem's conclusion, with its cosmic vision of the regenerative role of Nature and Venus and with the introduction of the preservation of the species into the transformist pattern of the world.

Whilst the association of death with a pre-natal state is something of a classical commonplace, in the context of this *hymne* the principal model for this idea according to Laumonier is Plutarch, *Consolatio ad Apollonium*, chapter 15. However, besides the influence of Plutarch in these lines there is also a contamination of reminiscences from Lucretius. For example, whilst the macabre fantasy and the poetic evocation of the gothic vision of death clearly reveal Ronsard's own originality, nevertheless the choice of imagery, the tone of scornful rationalism and the development of the arguments owe a debt to Lucretius, III, 870–5:

Accordingly when you see a man resenting his fate, that after death he must either rot with his body laid in the tomb, or perish by fire, or the jaws of wild beasts, you may know that he rings false, and that deep in his heart is some hidden sting, although himself he deny the belief in any sensation after death.
(LCL, p. 231)

Similarly, although the poetic density and the suggestive realism with which Ronsard associates conception, generation and death is his own masterly contribution, the borrowings from Plutarch are again complemented by an assimilation of certain lines of Lucretius (III, 830–44, 972–3). Ronsard's attitude is clearly close in spirit and tone to the sensualistic materialism of Lucretius: like the Latin poet Ronsard's conception of death centres on the absence of sensation, and the repetition of the verb *sentir* is a common feature of both texts (cf. Lucretius, III, ll. 832, 841, 843, 861, 875, 883). In the following lines of the French *hymne* (ll. 109–14), in which the names of the Trojan heroes are used to illustrate and authenticate this definition of death as an insentient state, the emphasis is again achieved by a repetition of the same verb.

Two odes of the *Nouvelle Continuation des Amours* (1556) provide a more philosophically sustained discussion of certain sensualist arguments and reveal a more substantial debt to Lucretius and his master, Epicurus. The first ode begins with a stanza evoking the finality of death in Lucretian terms and then continues:

Incontinent que l'homme est mort,
Pour jamais, ou long temps, il dort
Au creux d'une tombe enfoüye,
Sans plus parler, ouyr, ne voir :
Hé, quel bien scauroit on avoir
En perdant les yeux, & l'ouye!
　　Or' l'ame, selon le bienfait
Qu'hostesse du corps elle a fait,
Monte au ciel, sa maison natalle :
Mais le corps, nourriture à vers,
Dissoulz de venes & de nerfz
N'est plus qu'une ombre sepulcralle.
　　Il n'a plus esprit, ny raison,
Emboiture, ne liaison,
Artere, poux, ny vene tendre,
Cheveil ne teste ne luy tient,
Et qui plus est, ne luy souvient
D'avoir jadis aymé Cassandre.
　　　　　　　　(VII, 281–2)

These verses are a complex and dense assimilation of ideas from diverse passages of Lucretius and from certain maxims and epistles of Epicurus quoted in Diogenes Laertius, *Lives and Opinions of Eminent Philosophers*, Book x, *Epicurus*. In spite of its commonplaceness, in this context of multiple Lucretian reminiscences the euphemistic association of death and sleep (ll. 1–3 of extract) is probably suggested by *De rerum natura*, III, 904–30: in which case Ronsard's *pour jamais* may well translate 'Yes, as you now lie in death's quiet sleep, so you will be *for all time that is to come* (sic eris aevi / quod superest) removed from all distressing pains' (III, 904–5: LCL, p. 233), and the reservation *ou longtemps* may refer obliquely to the theory of regeneration of matter as mentioned by Lucretius a few pages later (III, 964–71). The following lines of the French poem, which equate life's sovereign good with the pleasures of the senses, recall the famous saying of Epicurus reported by Athanaeus (*Deipnosophistae*, VII, 278F; 280A–B; XII, 546E), Cicero (*Tusculanarum Disputationum*, III, xviii, 41) and Diogenes Laertius: 'I know not how to conceive the good, apart from the pleasures of taste, sexual pleasures, the pleasures of sound and the pleasures of beautiful form.'[12] In the same way the inference that sensation determines the existence of a body and the definition of death as an end to feeling are ideas found in Epicurus and Lucretius.[13]

The hasty, conventional reference to the soul (ll. 7–9 of the French extract) is totally submerged in a predominantly sensualist consideration of the body's dissolution—as will be a later allusion in line 30 of the ode—and is little more than a concession to religious orthodoxy. This brief digression on the destiny of the soul was probably suggested to Ronsard by the arrangement of Lucretius's material as well as by a prudent wish to reject the atheism of his source on this delicate point. In the Latin account Lucretius follows his description of death as an insentient state (III, 830–42) with a short aside devoted to the supposition that the soul does feel after death (ll. 843–6). Having rejected this hypothesis, he returns to his materialistic considerations of the effect of death on the body. The development of Ronsard's verse is identical, for after his cursory reference to the soul he also returns (ll. 10–16 of the extract) to a vision of the dissolution of the body's material components —an evocation he also borrows from certain passages of Lucretius.[14] In the next two lines (17–18) Ronsard continues to develop his sensualist arguments in exactly the same manner as Lucretius does in his analysis of death in Book III of the *De rerum natura*. For Ronsard death is not merely the end of physical desire, but it is also the cessation of mental pleasure since after death there is no remembrance of past delights, no recollection of love. The thought that death signifies the loss of memory is borrowed from Lucretius, III, 847–61, whilst Ronsard's exclamation *Qui plus est* refers to the Epicurean belief that mental pleasure is more important than physical pleasure (Diogenes Laertius, X, 137): thus the loss of the former is held of greater account than the loss of the latter.

In the remaining verses of this ode Ronsard draws the philosophic conclusions and considers the more immediate human implications of his sensualist account of death:

> «Le mort ne desire plus rien :
> Donc ce pendant que j'ay le bien
> De desirer vif, je demande
> D'estre tousjours sain & dispos :
> Puis, quand je n'auray que les os,
> La reste à Dieu je recommande.
>   Homere est mort, Anacreon,
> Pindare, Hesiode, & Bion,
> Et plus n'ont soucy de s'enquerre
> Du bien & du mal qu'on dit d'eulx :
> Ainsin apres un siecle ou deux
> Plus ne sentiray rien soubz terre.
>   «Mais dequoy sert le desirer
> «Sinon pour l'homme martirer !
> «Le desir n'est rien que martire,
> «Car content n'est le desireux,
> «Et l'homme mort est bienheureux :
> «Heureux qui plus rien ne desire.

As Paul Laumonier has already remarked (*RPL*, pp. 563–4), these stanzas represent a dialogue between two opposing attitudes to death.

The attitude expressed in the first verse of the extract is essentially pseudo-Anacreontic: it constitutes a defence of life and a whole-hearted acceptance of those desires and passions which compensate for human mortality and make life enjoyable. Death is evil because it terminates desire and encroaches on the pleasures of life. The contrary opinion, that of Lucretius, is voiced in the final stanza. This states that desire is an evil and that death, by terminating the grief that man's craving causes, is a good which should be welcomed. This conclusion is the ultimate logical consequence of the Epicurean belief that human happiness resides in the absence of pain, fear and passion.[15] Of these two attitudes to life and death it is the pseudo-Anacreontic one which most frequently found favour with Ronsard : however, on this occasion, the French poet adopts the arguments of his principal source, Lucretius, and his debt to the Latin writer is so extensive that he is drawn into making a statement which is foreign to his character and philosophy. However, his conclusion should not be seen as pessimistic, for in the context of the Lucretian reasoning Ronsard's final argument—although untypical of his attitude —is presented as a consolation : 'l'homme mort est bienheureux'. His aim, like that of Lucretius (III, 37–40), is to reveal the fallacious nature of certain philosophical attitudes, to allay the terror of death by rational argument, and to investigate, with the help of his source, the implications of a sensualist position.

Lucretius's influence is seen in the whole arrangement and development of the internal debate. In the long discussion devoted to death in Book III of the *De rerum natura*, Lucretius himself, in a series of inner monologues, considers and roundly rejects the pseudo-Anacreontic attitude to death :

This also is the way among men, when they have laid themselves down at table and hold goblets in their hands and shade their brows with garlands, that they often say from their hearts 'Short enjoyment is given to poor mankind; soon it will be gone, and *none will ever be able* to recall it'. As if after death their chief trouble will be to be miserably parched with thirst and burning drought, or a craving possess them for some other thing! 'No longer now will your happy home give you welcome, no longer will your best of wives and sweet children race to win the first kisses, and thrill your heart to its depths with sweetness. You will no longer be able to live in prosperity, and to protect your own. Poor man, poor man!' they say, 'one fatal day has robbed you of all these prizes of life.' But they do not go on to add 'No longer withal does any craving possess you for these things.' If they could see this clearly in mind and so conform their speech, they would free themselves from great fear and anguish of mind.[16]

Whilst the above lines provided the essential arguments and the format of Ronsard's dialogue on death, as well as the repeated 'ne ... plus rien' structure ('iam ... neque; iam iam non ... neque ... nec; nec ... iam'), he may well have complemented his ideas with other passages from Lucretius and pseudo-Anacreon. Line 1 of the extract is probably a direct reminiscence of a pseudo-Anacreontic text as Laumonier suggests, although it should be noted that this idea is also present in the Latin passage quoted above. Similarly, in the stanza centred on the Lucretian attitude to death, the idea that desire torments life and the consoling thought that death puts an end to man's craving may be recollections of diverse passages of Lucretius.[17] Even the construction of the exclamative statement of lines 13–14 of the French extract would appear to recall the following rhetorical question of Lucretius: 'Besides, what is this great and evil lust of life that drives us to be agitated amidst doubt and peril?' (ll. 1076–7: LCL, p. 245).

Moreover Ronsard's verse on the mortality of poets is developed from a reminiscence of Lucretius. In the Latin discussion of death there is an enumeration of those famous kings, warriors, sages, poets and philosophers who had already died, and the reader is exhorted to find comfort in the universal equality of death's omnipotence (III, 1024–45). In this enumeration Lucretius mentions Homer ('add the brotherhood of Helicon, whose one and only king, Homer, has been laid to rest in the same sleep with all the others': ll. 1037–8, LCL, p. 243), and Ronsard develops this idea, which he expresses on several occasions throughout his work, with his own examples. Here this theme is used both as a restatement of the sensualist principle that death is the absence of feeling, and as an implied argument against the value of poetic immortality—a notion which will be more fully developed in an elegy to Desportes of 1587 (below, pp. 141–3). Within this context of multiple Lucretian recollections, this last idea may have been suggested to Ronsard by De rerum natura, III, 78, which points to the vanity of immortality as a remedy against the fear of death.

The same extensive debt to Lucretius and an identical sensualist interpretation of death are evident in the following poem of the collection (VII, 283–4), which is essentially a development of the comparison between death and sleep briefly referred to in the previous ode. Such sensualist considerations are not simply confined to the collections of 1555–6, when Ronsard was preoccupied with moral and philosophical attitudes of death for the Hymne de la Mort. Two pieces of the posthumously published 1587 edition echo these odes of 1556 and form, as it were, a second diptych. It is in a sonnet entitled Dialogue de l'Autheur & du Mondain that Ronsard adopts the same debate technique and the 'ne ... plus' structure he had used in the final verses of his ode of 1556, and reproduces parallel Lucretian arguments to reach almost identical conclusions:

Est-ce tant que la Mort : est-ce si grand malheur
Que le vulgaire croit? Comme l'heure premiere
Nous faict naistre sans peine, ainsi l'heure derniere
Qui acheve la trame, arrive sans douleur.

Mais tu ne seras plus? Et puis : quand la paleur
Qui blesmist nostre corps sans chaleur ne lumiere
Nous perd le sentiment! quand la main filandiere
Nous oste le desir perdans nostre chaleur!

Tu ne mangeras plus? Je n'auray plus envie
De boire ne manger, c'est le corps qui sa vie
Par la viande allonge, & par refection :

L'esprit n'en a besoin. Venus qui nous appelle
Aux plaisirs te fuira? Je n'auray soucy d'elle.
«Qui ne desire plus, n'a plus d'affection.

(XVIII, 218–19)

Surprisingly there is no essential difference between the vision of 1556 and that of old age, for as in the earlier ode the author's philosophical sensualism is designed to console. Death is described as the painless termination of sensation and desire and, as in the *Hymne de la Mort*, it is equated with the natural cycle of life and birth. Even the reference to the absence of food, drink and pleasure should be seen as a comforting reply to a complaint he had made in two poems of 1555 (VI, 174; 209). However, Ronsard does correct his original vision slightly and, almost as if in answer to his earlier poem, departs from the more extreme consequences of Lucretius's attitude. Desire is no longer termed an evil or a 'martire'; the deceased is no longer envied because he is beyond mental craving. What is left is a bald statement of fact concerning death, with a certain desperation in the attempt at self-conviction, perhaps, but nevertheless with a reasoned acceptance of the inevitable, devoid of anguish.

The elegy *A Philippes des-Portes Chartrain* of 1587 can be seen as the final statement of Ronsard's philosophy of death : its long opening passage is an assimilation of classical ideas which Ronsard fashions into a reflection on the essential differences between life and death :

Nous devons à la Mort & nous & nos ouvrages :
Nous mourrons les premiers, le long reply des âges
En roulant engloutist nos œuvres à la fin :
Ainsi le veut Nature & le puissant Destin.

Dieu seul est eternel : de l'homme elementaire
Ne reste apres la mort ny veine ny artere :
Qui pis est, il ne sent, il ne raisonne plus,
Locatif descharné d'un vieil tombeau reclus.

C'est un extreme abus, une extreme folie
De croire que la Mort soit cause de la vie :
. . .

L'une est sans mouvement, & l'autre nous remue,
Qui la forme de l'ame en vigueur continue,
Nous fait ouyr & voir, juger, imaginer,
Discourir du present, le futur deviner.
　　Les morts ne sont heureux, d'autant que l'ame vive
Du mouvement principe en eux n'est plus active.
L'heur vient de la vertu, la vertu d'action :
Le mort privé du faire est sans perfection.
　　L'heur de l'ame, est de Dieu contempler la lumière :
La contemplation de la cause premiere
Est sa seule action : contemplant elle agist :
Mais au contemplement l'heur de l'homme ne gist.
　　Il gist à l'œuvre seul, impossible à la cendre
De ceux que la Mort faict soubs les ombres descendre.
... Ainsi le froid giron
De la tombe assoupist tous les sens de nature,
Qui sont deuz à la terre & à la pourriture.

(XVIII, 247–9)

The theme of death's omnipotence over man and human endeavour
is Horatian (*Ars Poetica*, 1. 63), and the materialistic dissolution of the
'homme elementaire' and the sensualist, physical distinctions between
life and death are Epicurean and Lucretian. The whole passage is in fact
a poetic development of a maxim of Epicurus reported by Diogenes
Laertius, X, 136 : '... joy and delight are seen to consist in motion and
activity' (LCL, vol. II, p. 661), and of certain passages of Aristotle.[18] At
the same time certain lines can be seen as a commentary on, and a
revision of, ideas expressed in his 1556 ode analysed above. 'Qui pis est'
of line 7 specifically recalls a construction of the earlier ode ('Et qui plus
est' : VII, 282), but whereas the absence of feeling had provided consolation in 1556, in the elegy to Desportes it is seen as a principal cause of
regret and a major distinction between life and death. Similarly the
hemistich 'Les morts ne sont heureux' echoes and negates the line '»Et
l'homme mort est bienheureux' of the 1556 ode (VII, 283). The tone is
darker : consolatory attitudes are avoided or rejected and the result is a
brutal reality, an antithesis, which philosophical argument and Christian vision cannot bridge. For it is in the same context that Ronsard
roundly rejects the Christian-Platonic notion that happiness resides in
the soul's contemplation of God. In this passage, where religious inspiration is reduced to a stylised minimum, he shows little enthusiasm for a
soul which is passive and which does not have the perfection of movement or action ('Car que sert la contemplation sans l'action ?': XVIII, 459–
60). Human happiness for Ronsard, as for Epicurus and Aristotle, lies
essentially in the active involvement in the processes of life and the

functions of the body, and not in the mystical and nebulous spiritualism of Christian–Platonic theory.

This reasoning explains Ronsard's epicurean attitude to poetic immortality which is expressed in the remainder of this elegy; for whilst the rejection of immortality—and indeed the sombre tone of the whole poem—may to some extent be a result of the aging Ronsard's eclipse by Desportes,[19] nevertheless the logical consequence of his definitions of life and death, and the inevitable outcome of this enthusiasm for action and feeling, naturally coincide in a desire to enjoy the present fruits of his fame rather than to await the intangible and uncertain rewards of posterity. Although this is an idea which Ronsard had several times formulated in the past (v, 245–6; vi, 44; vii, 308; x, 343–4), he had never developed it at such length or expressed it with such an emphatically sensualist vocabulary (ll. 37–88). Once again a line ('«L'homme qui ne sent plus, n'a besoin de loüange') seems designed as a deliberate piece of self-quoting, for it recalls a stanza of the 1556 ode studied above (vii, 283, ll. 31–6) and thereby strengthens the impression that these two poems, separated by more than thirty years, act as the extremities of a framework within which Ronsard situates his sensualist discussions of death.

Although certain critics have stressed the pessimism of this posthumous elegy,[20] it should be emphasised that Ronsard's sensualist conception of death very rarely leads him to the conclusions of the poem to Desportes or to the sombre vision evoked by his principal model, Lucretius (cf. Fraisse, pp. 117–18). Similarly the pessimism of the elegy to Desportes is not total or definitive[21] and could be partially circumstantial in that it may have its source in a momentary mood of envy and pique. This isolated expression, however emphatic, should not conceal the fact that, although Ronsard modified the details of his vision over the period 1555–87, nevertheless his philosophical sensualism is generally designed to allay fears and give consolation. Again, in relation to the number of references to death in his work, his materialism only rarely gives rise to visually detailed and macabre descriptions of physical decomposition or to anguished and tortured accounts of death's horror. Frequently, moreover, his sensualist conception of death is complemented and reinforced by an accompanying attachment to life, in such a way that the vision of death provides the necessary impetus, the most emphatic argument for an epicurean exhortation to find compensation for human mortality within the context of physical existence (cf. x, 97, s. xii).

Whilst a detailed discussion of Ronsard's conception of the nature and origin of the soul does not fall within the central areas of this study, the question of the *destiny* of the soul after death is of importance, although clearly secondary and relative, to the poet. It has already been noted that, as a sensualist, Ronsard is more concerned to explore the bodily implications of death, and that he is not impressed by a soul whose only function after death lies in passive contemplation of the Divinity, and whose only pleasure is metaphysical. Indeed it is due to his love of active and dynamic forces that Ronsard's conception of the soul becomes perverted by unorthodox pantheistic overtones in some of his later verse,[22] and that he rejects Platonic dualism either for a theory which gives the body supremacy over the soul (XVII, 213, S. XX; 229, S. XLI; 230, S. XLII), or for a conception, not unlike that of Lucretius, which is based on the interdependence of an active, sentient body and a receptive soul ('la connexion, enlassement, societé, participation et union des deux').[23] Similarly he is antipathetic to the Platonic theory of reminiscence and is a sensualist in that he believes, like Aristotle and Lucretius (Book IV), in the theory of the *tabula rasa* and in the acquisition of knowledge via the senses.[24]

In spite of this Ronsard never questions the immortality of the soul or the belief in an after-life and, on at least one occasion, his attitude is the direct result of a fideist position (V, 257). Similarly, as has been shown, he is constantly at pains to temper the more extreme materialism of his pagan sources (and of Lucretius in particular),[25] and to accompany his sensualistic preoccupations with prudent Christian references to the soul, however brief, formal and stylised these allusions might be. Even in the context of the unorthodox pantheism of *Le Chat*, where Ronsard pictures the human soul as an emanation from the Universal Soul which penetrates the body, the immortality of the soul is assured even though it loses all personality and individuality in death (XV, 39–40).

The most orthodox and poetic statement of Ronsard's religious convictions concerning the immortality of the soul is contained in the *Hymne de la Mort*, where Christian and pagan inspiration interweave to preach a lesson of consolation. Here Ronsard specifically rejects the horrific picture of death associated with the pagan and medieval imaginations (VIII, 167; 172), in favour of a Christian vision of Heaven as a refuge after a life of vanity and suffering—a theme to which he returns in his *Epitaphe de Loyse de Mailly* of the same collection (VIII, 230–1)—and categorically affirms the immortality of the soul by tracing man's victory over death to Christ's sacrifice on the cross.[26] However the beauty of the *Hymne de la Mort* should not obscure the fact that this poem remains to a large extent both a mock encomium and a literary exercise in the tradition of the *consolatio*, and that the attitudes expressed in it run counter to some of Ronsard's fundamental and consistent beliefs. Like the Shade of Achilles (*Odyssey*, XI, 488–91) Ronsard more commonly demonstrates a profound attachment to life (VI, 192–3; XIV, 119), and the idea that earthly existence is a preparation for death

and Heaven and a redemption for sin, is extremely rare in his work and
totally foreign to his character. Moreover the references to the soul's
immortality, other than those in the *Hymne de la Mort*, tend to be brief
and stylised, whilst Margaret de Schweinitz has already remarked on the
surprising lack of prominence given to Christian elements in Ronsard's
epitaphs.[27] Even the tone of his *A son ame* of *Les Derniers Vers* (1586:
XVIII, 182) is one of light-hearted *badinage*, a tone which, however,
contrasts sharply with the apparent religious conviction of a sonnet of
the same collection:

> Heureux qui ne fut onc, plus heureux qui retourne
> En rien comme il estoit, plus heureux qui sejourne
> D'homme fait nouvel ange aupres de Jesuchrist,
>   Laissant pourrir ça bas sa despouille de boüe
> Dont le sort, la fortune, & le destin se joüe,
> Franc des liens du corps pour n'estre qu'un esprit.
>
> (XVIII, 181, S. VI)

Whilst, therefore, the soul's immortality and the thought of Christ's
redemption comfort the poet on those relatively few moments of emphatic Christian reflection (cf. XVIII, 328–9), rather more central to
Ronsard's preoccupations are those occasions on which he attempts to
fit the destiny of the soul into the cyclic regenerative processes which so
obsessed him. In this respect a sonnet of the 1578 edition lamenting the
death of Charles IX is revealing. In the first quatrain Ronsard uses the
biblical image of the rotting corn seed to illustrate once again the scheme
of corruption and renewal which is so fundamental to his materialistic
vision. In the remainder of the poem, moreover, these transformist precepts are given a Christian justification, for Christ's (and subsequently
man's) resurrection is seen as yet another example of this regenerative
process (XVII, 383–4. Cf. XV, 155). Similarly Ronsard's interest in the
Pythagorean–Platonic doctrine of metempsychosis[28] is an expression of
this same desire to integrate the destiny of the soul into eternal cycles.
It is true that Ronsard tempers his curiosity for the theory of reincarna-
tion with prudent Christian reservations, employing the hypothetical
si (II, 65), restricting the Ovidian account in *Metamorphoses*, XV, to
exclude the soul or periodically rejecting the doctrine in the name of
religious principles (VIII, 176–7; XV, 157; XVIII, 251). And yet the number
of references made to metempsychosis throughout his poetic career
(alternately borrowed from Ovid and Virgil)[29] is itself significant, and
clearly demonstrates a fascination for—if not a belief in—the theory of
transmigration of souls: '. . . ces espris jadis hostes des mors, / Qui
plains d'oubly revont en nouveaux corps' (XVI, 186). Indeed it is left to
Amadis Jamyn in his *Argumens des quatre premiers livres de la
Franciade* (quoted by Laumonier, XVI, 17–18) to excuse Hyante's

lengthy exposition of the doctrine in the *Franciade* with its detailed account of the purification of the soul and the process whereby '... les esprits qui sont sortis de hors / De leurs vieux corps, r'entrent en nouveaux corps' (XVI, 283). In comparison with Baïf, du Bellay, Jodelle and Tyard, who each mention the Pythagorean theory of metempsychosis on an isolated occasion,[30] Ronsard's consistent curiosity and protestations seem perilously close to a temptation.

In the same way Ronsard's evocation of an after-life is not emphatically Christian, for, apart from a few exceptions (III, 73–5; VIII, 176–7), references to the sort of existence the soul leads in Heaven are brief, unconvincing and confused.[31] Indeed even in the context of the Christian–Platonism of the *Hymne de la Mort*, 'Ronsard is careful to use a mythological rather than a theological concept of heaven'.[32] He is uncertain whether the soul goes *là-haut* to Heaven or *là-bas* to the classical Elysian Fields (III, 85; V, 255–6; VIII, 236; XVII, 122), but more frequently he favours the latter, for the most developed descriptions of an after-life in his work are all in the pagan manner. Modelling his vision on Homer, Virgil, Ovid and Tibullus,[33] Ronsard finds consolation in the fact that in the Elysian Fields and Myrtle Grove the senses are fully gratified and pleasure reigns supreme. Ronsard's after-life is clearly not in the Christian mode and is essentially a poetic fiction, a sensualist's paradise, a pagan extension of the Golden Age of earthly existence where all is beauty, eternal spring, love and youth, and where former friends, classical poets and lovers are reunited in a setting in which time and death are finally abolished.[34]

Ronsard, in fact, further idealises the Virgilian account, for he deliberately contradicts the idea that suffering follows the lovers into death (*Aeneid*, VI, 440–4),

> Entre les amoureus,
> Et comme eus sans souci,
> Nous i vivrons aussi
> > (I, 251)

and he extends this idea to include all the dead (VI, 35; XIV, 118, and Laumonier's note 4). Again, unlike Virgil, who places the Myrtle Grove in the Mourning Fields ('Lugentes Campi'), Ronsard prefers to follow Tibullus, I, iii, and Secundus, *Basia*, II, and situate it within the Elysian Fields proper. In such an idyllic context death is never visualised as a rupture, but as a continuation of life's pleasures and activities:

> Ains comme freres vivent,
> Et morts encore suivent
> Les métiers qu'ils avoient
> > Quand ils vivoient
> > > (II, 102)

as well as of its emotional processes:

L'amitié des parens regne encore icy bas,
Vivant je l'ay sentie, & apres le trespas.
(x, 144)

Neither does death entail separation:

En mesme an, & mesme heure,
Et en mesme saison,
Irons voir la demeure
De la palle maison
(I, 250)

and Ronsard's appeal to the departed Chasteigner equates life and death under the sign of friendship:

Garde moi place aupres de ton idole,
Afin que méme place ensemble nous aions,
Et vifs & mors ensemble nous soions.
(v, 250)

Indeed death in the Elysian Fields is often depicted as an improvement on life: witness the epitaph to Hugues Salel,

Tu vis franc de la mort, & du cruel soucy
Tu te moques là bas, qui nous tormente ici:
Et moi chetif, je vy!
(VI, 35)

or again an elegy of 1564, where Death the leveller is seen to unite the lovers by correcting the social inequality which had separated them in life (XII, 222–3).

The reason for man's mortality is a question which periodically interested Ronsard and, in an ode to Guy Peccate of 1550, he finds the answer in the framework of pagan and Christian theology. The poem's opening meditation on the omnipotence and equality of death—heavily condensed from diverse Horatian texts[35]—is followed by two stanzas in which the fates of Phaethon and Bellerophon are used to preach a lesson of moderation and to comment on the dangers of *hubris*. These ideas are not present in the immediate texts Ronsard has been adapting but are developed from a dense assimilation of additional Horatian and Pindaric passages.[36] The next four verses are similarly borrowed from a variety of Horatian texts and are devoted to Ronsard's hopes of immortality and to the graphic description of a recent fever. This 'fievre grosse' (ll. 49–54) provides the personal inspiration for the preceding reflections on death and, within the double context of the brevity of life in the sixteenth century and of Ronsard's obsession with illness and physical decrepitude, it furnishes the reader with a brief but revealing insight into the anxieties of a poet and his age. Ronsard then returns to the relationship between *hubris* and death with reference to the myth of Prometheus, and it is yet another passage of Horace which is the immediate source here, together with distant echoes of Hesiod:

A bon droit Promethée
Pour sa fraude inventée
Endure un torment tel,
Qu'un aigle sur la roche
Lui ronge d'un bec croche
Son poumon immortel.

Depuis qu'il eut robée
La flamme prohibée
Pour les Dieus dépiter,
Les bandes inconnues
Des fievres sont venues
Parmi nous habiter.

Et la mort dépiteuse
Au paravant boiteuse
Legere gallopa :
D'ailes mal ordonnées
Aus hommes non données
Dedale l'air coupa.
        (ll. 67–84)

Laumonier (*RPL*, pp. 359–60) has remarked on the fact that these verses—and the final two stanzas of the poem, which refer to Pandora, the end of the Age of Gold, Astraea's flight to Heaven, the resulting depravity of mankind and the wrath of Zeus—seem designed as a separate ode having little relation with the first eleven stanzas. The poem, however, although constructed on aesthetic principles of *copia* and diversity, is tightly interwoven as a unity by certain associative ideas and recurrent themes,[37] and the transition from the discussion of death to the moral significance of the Prometheus myth[38] is prepared by the reference to man's *hubris* and insatiable curiosity (ll. 31–42). The thematic coherence of the ode lies in the constant association of death and *hubris*, which is itself dependent on the complex interweaving of multiple classical passages to form a unified argument and an original emphasis. Death, evil, illness and suffering for Ronsard are not only the direct result of man's primal sin, but *hubris*—typified here by Prometheus, Daedalus, Phaethon and Bellerophon—is seen as a constant threat to the order and hierarchy of the universe. Ronsard's plea for moderation is designed to encourage man to accept the limitations of his mortality and not to trespass beyond the allotted bounds of his fragility. Death—like Change, Time, Destiny and Fortune—is designed to ensure cosmic harmony in so far as it determines a hierarchy based on man's subservience to the gods, for, as Ronsard writes elsewhere, death is the only thing which prevents man from being perfect and divine (VIII, 61; XIII, 182).

This association of *hubris*, the Prometheus–Pandora myth and the mortality and suffering of the human condition not only reappears in an ode of the same collection (II, 182), but it is frequently found in the subsequent poetry of Ronsard. It occurs again in the *Ode sur les miseres des hommes* of 1553 (V, 192–6), but here the legend is interpreted with an additional episode recounted in Nicander, *Theriaka*, ll. 343–59, in which Zeus gives men fire and the gift of eternal youth as a reward for having denounced the sin of Prometheus to him. The same relation between the Prometheus myth and human fragility—but a different interpretation of the episode found in Nicander—appears in the *Hymne de la Mort*, where the context of the *consolatio* explains why here the reward given to men is Death herself (VIII, 175). Prometheus, human misery and mortality are linked again in an elegy to Henri III written late in 1574 (XVII, 91–2), and in the same way Ronsard's several maledictions against Prometheus, whose theft of fire is directly related to the Iron Age and to the invention of instruments of war, are part of his preoccupation with the Prometheus–Pandora myth as illustrative of destruction, death and *hubris* (I, 152–4; V, 168–70; VIII, 50–9; IX, 22–4).

The Renaissance contribution to the development of the Prometheus–Pandora myth was, as Raymond Trousson has demonstrated,[39] to assimilate the pagan archetype with the Christian original sin of Adam and Eve, and it is only to be expected that Ronsard, for whom pagan and Christian mythology were closely correlated, should make this equation. He does so in his most famous example of pagan–Christian syncretism, the *Hercule Chrestien* (1555), where the liberation of Prometheus by Hercules is seen as a counterpart to the redemption of Adam (VIII, 217). A more emphatic interpretation of death as a consequence of Adam's fall from grace is found in the *Hymne de l'Eternité* of the following year: in a passage already commented on,[40] the original sin of *hubris* is described in neo-Platonic terms as stifling man in the limitations and imperfections of bodily matter and depriving him of spiritual light. At the same time a pathetic contrast is drawn between mortal man's limited conception of time and the global, timeless vision of Eternity which is forever present.

One of the most important aspects of Ronsard's philosophical and cosmological visions of death is the question of the destruction of the world, but unlike du Bellay (*Les Antiquitez*, s. IX; XXII) and Baïf (II, 5; 29; IV, 228), he follows Aristotle and the Averroists in emphasising the immortality of the universe. He does so, as has already been noted, by tracing the fragile and complex mechanism of the cosmos to a pattern of harmonised opposing forces, symbolised by the allegory of Peace and Discord and expressed through the eternal transformation of matter.[41] He also pictures the flux of the world orchestrated into unity and stability by a whole series of natural and divine universal laws, and sees the delicate balance of the world assured by a dynamic cohesive pantheism and by numerous allegorical forces whose cosmic functions embrace order and preservation. Yet again the spherical form of the world system and the circular movement of the Heaven are further testimonies to the eternity of the universe. Ronsard's scientific verse is full of references to the immortality of the world. There is, on the other hand, only one explicit mention of the destruction of the world in Ronsard's work, and that is in *Le Tombeau du feu Roy Tres-Chrestien Charles IX* (1574) where the following lines are almost certainly inspired by Seneca:

> Toy, fille d'Empereur, espouse de ce Roy,
> Au milieu de tes pleurs, patiente, reçoy
> La consolation de la misere humaine,
> C'est qu'à la fin la mort toutes choses emmeine:
> Et que mesme le ciel, qui fait mourir les Rois,
> Et perir un chacun, perira quelquefois.[42]

Although there may also be a verbal and structural reminiscence of *Les Antiquitez* (s. III, 7; IX, 14) in these lines, the tone is totally different from the profound despair of du Bellay, for Ronsard, like Seneca, uses the omnipotence of death to fuse man once again with the cosmos in an equitable and common law, and to preach a conclusion of stoical consolation. It is likely, moreover, that this single allusion to the destruction of the world is occasioned here by circumstance—be it the demands of the eulogistic conceit or the appearance and extinction of the star Tycho Brahé which momentarily seems to have worried Ronsard.[43] Whatever the cause, this idea certainly does not conform to Ronsard's cosmic vision.

NOTES TO CHAPTER FIVE

1 For the changing attitude to death in medieval, Renaissance and baroque literature and for a fuller bibliography, see E. Dubruck, *The Theme of Death in French Poetry of the Middle Ages and the Renaissance* (The Hague, 1964).

2 XVIII, 122. See also XV, 39–40; XVIII, 46. Cf. Lucretius, I, 54–61; 215–16; 248–9; 262–4; Diogenes Laertius, *Epicurus*, X, 139.

3 A. H. Krappe, 'Pierre de Ronsard's *Hymne de la Mort* and Plutarch's *Consolatio ad Apollonium*', *Modern Language Review*, XVII (1922), 150–6.

4 Lucretius, I, 225–9 (LCL, 1959, p. 19). Cf. I, 4–5; 19–20; II, 173–4. For Lucretius's vision of the world as a balanced conflict between creation and destruction, cf. II, 569ff. For Laumonier's contribution to the establishment of sources for this passage, see his notes, *loc. cit.*

5 VI, 53–4, s. IX. Cf. IV, 42, s. XXIX; X, 282.

6 Cf. Plato, *Symposium*, 180–5; Stobaeus, *Florilegium*, LXIII; Ficino, *Commentary on Plato's 'Symposium'*, Speech II, chapt. VII.

7 VII, 209; 219; VI, 282; VIII, 167; X, 97, s. XII.

8 XVIII, 176–7. Cf. VI, 104 (ll. 10–12, var.); XV, 89; 220–1 (ll. 13–14, var.); XVIII, 222; 248; 249.

9 VIII, 343; X, 97, s. XII; 310; XIV, 117; XVII, 118; XVIII, 218, s. LXXVI.

10 'Ronsard et la Mort', *Modern Language Review*, LVII (1962), 186. Cf. an interesting variant in a sonnet to Cassandre (IV, 50, s. XLVII). In 1552 l. 12 refers to the dead body as follows : 'Sans sentiment *vostre rien* est heureux'. In subsequent editions (1553–87) this line reads : 'Sans sentiment *leur repos* est heureus'.

11 XIV, 117; V, 241; VII, 284; XVII, 266, s. XXIV; X, 80, s. XIV; XVIII, 122; XV, 306; XVII, 388.

12 X, 6. *Diogenes Laertius: Lives of Eminent Philosophers* (2 vols., LCL, 1925): vol. II, p. 535. For the work already done by Laumonier on establishing the sources of this ode, see the notes in his edition and *RPL*, pp. 563–4.

13 Diogenes Laertius, X, 39 and 139; Lucretius, I, 422–3; II, 904–6; 944–51; III, 214–15; 830–911.

14 II, 904–6; III, 870–1. Cf. a maxim of Epicurus in Diogenes Laertius, X, 139 (vol. II, p. 665).

15 Cf. Epicurus in Diog. Laertius, X, 11; 131–2; 139(3); and Lucretius, II, 10–21.

16 Lines 912–18, 894–903. I have followed the rearranged line order proposed by Postgate and adopted by W. H. D. Rouse in his translation (LCL, 1959, pp. 231–3).

17 III, 957–60; 995–1010; 1053–70; 1082–4; V, 1120–35; 1430–5. Cf. Epicurus, maxims 26, 29–30, in Diog. Laertius, X, 148–9.

18 *Nicomachean Ethics*, I, X, 1100a10–14. Cf. I. Silver, 'Ronsard's Ethical Thought', *BHR*, XXIV (1962), 368–9.

19 On the mutual antipathy between the two poets, see C. Faisant, 'Les relations de Ronsard et de Desportes', *BHR*, XXVIII (1966), 323–53. On the inter-influence in the work of the two poets, consult M. Morrison, 'Ronsard et Desportes', *ibid.*, pp. 294–322.

20 M. Bensimon, 'Ronsard et la Mort', p. 193; I. Silver, 'Ronsard's Ethical Thought', p. 369.

21 Cf. I. Silver's remarks, XVIII, p. LVII.

22 Cf. *Le Chat* (1569) in particular (XV, 39–47). See also on this question, Busson, pp. 379–88; Weber, vol. I, pp. 44–9. Contrast the interpretation of M. Bensimon, 'Ronsard et la Mort', pp. 188–92.

23 XVIII, 473. Cf. Lucretius, III, 845–6: '. . . the welding and wedding together of

body and spirit exist compacted into one whole' (LCL, p. 229). See also III,
331–6; 350–8; 548–72; 788–9.

24   II, 15–16; XVII, 213, s. XX; 229, s. XLI; 230, s. XLII. Guy de Brués also makes
Ronsard reject the Platonic theory of reminiscence in his *Dialogues* (1557):
see *The Dialogues of Guy de Brués* (Paris, 1557). Critical edition by P. P.
Morphos (Baltimore, 1953), pp. 39, 112, 115, 126. Morphos argues (pp. 71–3)
that Brués authentically represents the philosophical opinions of his inter-
locutors, a viewpoint not universally shared by scholars.

25   On occasions Ronsard couples his affirmation of religious orthodoxy with an
attack on the Epicurean sect and their materialism: cf. VI, 40–1; X, 368
(ll. 93–6, var.).

26   For the principal Christian elements of Ronsard's *hymne*, see ll. 45, 67–9, 97,
115–40, 191–206, 255–8, 288–308, 333–6. For the motif of Christ conqueror of
death and liberator of humanity, see also V, 257–8; VIII, 221; X, 321; XVIII,
179, s. V.

27   *Les Epitaphes de Ronsard* (Paris, 1925), pp. 82–3. Typical of the formal brevity
of Ronsard's references are VIII, 149; 161; X, 313; XV, 306; 402.

28   Cf. Plato, *The Republic*, X, 617D–21D; *Phaedo*, 79–82B; *Phaedrus*, 248–9;
Timaeus, 41D–42D; 90E–2C; Ficino, *Theologiae Platonicae*, XVIII, viii. On this
question, see H. S. Long, *A Study of the Doctrine of Metempsychosis in Greece
from Pythagoras to Plato* (Princeton Univ. Press, 1948).

29   A full catalogue of Ronsard's references reads: II, 65 (cf. Virgil, *Aeneid*, VI,
748–51); V, 132, s. XCVI; VIII, 176–7; XIV, 119; XV, 157 (cf. Ovid, *Metam.*, XV,
158–9, 165–75, 456–62); XVI, 186; 283–9 (cf. *Aeneid*, VI, 719–51). Cf. XVIII, 251,
n. 3. Brués, *Dialogues* (1557), makes Ronsard reject metempsychosis in his
dialogue with Baïf (ed. Morphos, p. 142).

30   Baïf, I, 185 (2); du Bellay, III, 136; Jodelle, II, 323; Tyard, p. 20.

31   Cf. I, 236; V, 248; X, 143; XV, 222; XVII, 12. Typical of Ronsard's confusion
over the nature of the soul in Christian contexts, is his uncertainty about
whether it can hear or feel after death. Affirmative statements (VII, 308; VIII,
168) are categorically refuted (X, 312–13). His confusion is seen in the frequent
use of the hypothetical *si* (VI, 23; XVIII, 288).

32   A. H. T. Levi, 'The role of neoplatonism in Ronsard's poetic imagination', in
Ronsard the Poet, p. 143.

33   Homer, *Odyssey*, IV, 563–8; Virgil, *Aeneid*, VI, 440ff., and 637ff.; Ovid,
Amores, III, ix, 60–7; Tibullus, I, iii, 55–66. Sources established by Laumonier
in relation to passages quoted in the following note.

34   Cf. I, 250–1; II, 101–3; V, 250; VI, 28–9; 34–5; XII, 221–3; 269–70; XIV, 117–19;
XVII, 236–8.

35   II, 107–9. For the influence of Horace, see Laumonier's notes.

36   In addition to the Horatian sources noted by Laumonier, see also Pindar,
Nemean, XI, antistr. and ep. 3; *Isthmian*, VII, antistr. and ep. 3.

37   Ronsard's illness recalls to him Horace's near fatal accident recounted in
Odes, II, xiii, and he models his next lines (55–66) on this poem. The word
fievre in Ronsard's totally original lines 49–54 evokes a reminiscence of
Horace, *Odes*, I, iii, 30–1 ('. . . wasting disease and a new throng of fevers
(*febrium*) fell upon the earth': LCL, p. 15), and this ode becomes one of the
principal sources of ll. 67–96 of the French text. Similarly the example of
Prometheus may have been suggested to Ronsard by Horace, *Odes*, II, xiii,
which he adapts in ll. 55–66, for there is a reference to the suffering of
Prometheus in the Latin ode: this in turn may have recalled the more
developed reference in Horace, *Odes*, I, iii, the inspiration for much of l. 67ff.
of Ronsard's poem.

38 For Ronsard's treatment of the Prometheus legend, consult R. Trousson, 'Le mythe de Prométhée et de Pandore chez Ronsard', *Bulletin de l'Association Guillaume Budé*, IVe série, no. 1 (1961), 351–9.

39 *Le Thème de Prométhée dans la littérature européenne* (2 vols., Geneva, 1964), vol. I, pp. 95, 123–4.

40 VIII, 253–4 (discussed above, pp. 102–3). The variants of ll. 119–20 of the 1587 edition ('... comme naiz imparfaits, / Encroustez d'une argille & d'un limon espais') reveal the same pagan-Christian syncretism at work, for the vocabulary clearly associates Adam with Prometheus in the context of Ronsard's other references to the creation of man (V, 168; XV, 310; 371; XVII, 92). The detail of the above variant comes from Ovid, *Metam.*, I, 82–3.

41 Brués puts the following words into Ronsard's mouth: 'Aristote donques, pensant à l'eternité du monde, il a veu ceste emerveillable vertu et puissance de nature, engendrant d'une et mesme matière, par continuelles corruptions, grande diversité de choses' (*Dialogues*, ed. Morphos, p. 130).

42 XVII, 9. Cf. Seneca, *Ad Marciam De Consol.*, XXVI, 6; *Ad Polybium De Consol.*, I, 1–4.

43 Ronsard refers to the Tycho Brahé earlier in the same poem (ll. 31–4) and its appearance seems to have been the basic inspiration behind *Les Estoilles* of 1575 (XVII, pp. V–VI; 37–8). Cf. XVIII, 39.

CHAPTER SIX

The commonplace themes of death

Helas cruel Pluton . . . ta sale obscure
  Reçoit de tout cartier
Tout ce qui est au monde, & . . . de la Nature
  Tu es seul heritier.
          (VII, 95)

This bald, general statement of the omnipotence of death, distantly remembered from Horace (*Odes*, I, iv, 13–17), provides, as it were, the
starting point from which Ronsard will embroider a whole series of
themes and attitudes—often literary and artistic commonplaces of
classical and national traditions—centred on man's awareness of his
mortality and on his attempts to come to terms with, escape from or
transcend his condition.

Death is the great leveller for it comes to all men alike, and this
theme, much favoured by Ronsard throughout his work, is often assimilated from texts of Pindar and Horace,[1] and is frequently expressed, as
in their verse, by a series of antithetical examples designed to suggest
universality—'povres . . . Princes; Achile . . . Thersite; le sage . . . le fol,
jeunes . . . vieus, pauvres . . . fils des Dieus, le laboureur . . . un enpereur'.[2]
However, in spite of the faint echoes of Horace and Pindar remaining in
an ode of 1555, Ronsard manages to transcend the literary commonplace by expressing the antithesis between the 'chetif laboureur' and the
'Empereur' in terms of their tools and clothing, and, although the latter
idea may have its distant source in a text of Pindar (*Nemean*, XI, ep. I),
the realistic and specialised vocabulary is Ronsard's picturesque contribution:

  Courage, coupeur de terre!
Ces grans foudres de la guerre
Non plus que toi n'iront pas,
Armés d'un plastron, là bas,

Comme ils alloient aus batailles :
Autant leur vaudront leurs mailles,
Leurs lances, & leur estoq,
Comme à toi vaudra ton soc.
   Car le juge Rhadamante
Asseuré ne s'espovante
Non plus de voir un harnois
Là bas, qu'un levier de bois,
Ou voir une souquenie,
Qu'une cape bien garnie,
Ou qu'un riche acoutrement
D'un Roi mort pompeusement.

(VII, 103–4)

Similarly in *La Salade* (1569) Ronsard succeeds in injecting poetic life
into this well-worn theme by the image of the chess game, and here
even distant reminiscences of Pindar and Horace have disappeared,
leaving only the general similarity of idea. Here too, as in the ode of
1555 where the equality of death was designed to give the labourer
comfort and courage in the context of a universal law, Ronsard adds his
own personal commentary to the commonplace by advocating resignation to the equity of 'la loy de la bonne Nature' :

Les pauvres sotz dignes de tous mechefz
Ne sçavent pas que c'est un jeu d'eschetz
Que nostre courte & miserable vie,
Et qu'aussy tost que la Mort l'a ravie
Dedans le sac somes mis à la fois
Tous pesle mesle, & Laboureurs & Rois,
Valetz, Seigneurs en mesme sepulture.
Telle est la loy de la bonne Nature,
Et de la Terre, en son ventre qui prend
De fosse egalle & le Pauvre & le Grand.

(XV, 81–2)

Another aspect of this theme is the illustration of the statement of
death's universality by a list of her famous victims, referred to either by
name or by category. This idea comes from the *genre* of the consolatory
treatise, the abbreviated form of which is the letter of condolence, and
it is essentially from Plutarch, *Consolatio ad Apollonium*, chapters 9
and 15, that Ronsard draws his inspiration for this theme, and its accompanying exhortation to resignation, in a passage from the *Hymne de la
Mort* (VIII, 167). An equally important source noted by Laumonier here
is the enumeration of the famous victims of death's implacable rule
found in Lucretius, III, 1024–45, where the tone is also designed to allay
fears and to console. Ronsard's most developed treatment of this theme

appears in the *Epitafe de Jan Martin* (1553: V, 252–5): here Horatian echoes are complemented by this Lucretian passage and, like Lucretius (ll. 1027, 1036, 1039–44, 1029–35, 1037–8 respectively), Ronsard's catalogue includes kings, sages, philosophers, sailors, warriors and poets (ll. 10–46). It has already been noted (above, pp. 138–40, 143) how Lucretius's allusion to the mortality of poets, and his specific mention of Homer, particularly preoccupied Ronsard, and led him, on isolated occasions of discouragement, either to question momentarily the value of poetic immortality or to develop an epicurean attitude to fame.

The goddess Death is not only omnipotent but she is inexorable, and her final decree cannot be postponed, avoided or revoked. That wealth, beauty, prowess, eloquence, family, virtue and nobility are no defence against an inevitable death is an idea either overtly expressed or implicit in several texts of Pindar and Horace.[3] Ronsard improvises freely and extensively around this theme, especially in the context of his sepulchral verse where it is a convenient motif to eulogise the deceased and family, and he adds countless virtues to the list of ineffectual weapons against death without, however, rejuvenating the commonplace. Piety, eloquence, martial courage, intellectual prowess, virtue, youth, the lamentations of France, his mother and wife could not save Charles IX (XVII, 4; 6), any more than wealth, bribes of money, nobility, heritage and powerful relations could save Louise de Mailly (VIII, 229–30). Prayers, beauty and gold are all equally ineffectual (II, 108; VI, 260–1; VIII, 205; XVII, 118–19) for the implacable goddess is sightless, deaf and has a rock where her heart should be (XV, 302). Youth too is no guarantee against her for she is impervious to the suffering she causes, and although she would have enough victims if she took only the aged, she is unwilling, writes Ronsard, to let the young

> D'achever doucement le cours jusqu'à la fin,
> Sans couper leur moisson avant qu'elle fust meure :
> Mais contre *sa* rigueur personne ne s'asseure.
> Ainsi les fleurs d'Avril par l'orage du temps
> Meurent dedans la prée au milieu du printemps.
>
> (XVII, 6. Cf. XIII, 184)

As well as being unavoidable, death is also final and irrevocable, and this commonplace is often developed from Horatian texts in Ronsard's work, as in the ode *A Gaspar D'Auvergne* of 1550,[4] which is one of many early poems entirely devoted to a meditation on human mortality. Closely associated with these ideas is the theme of the diversity of death's attacks. This notion, found briefly in Pindar and Horace,[5] is more especially developed by Seneca who adds a list of examples to their general statements (*Epist.*, LXVI, 42–3), and it is this idea of an illustrated

catalogue of death's diversity which appeals to Ronsard in his frequent
expressions of this theme and which imparts to his verse those
characteristic qualities of rhythmical energy and momentum :

> Aussi bien en fuiant la mort vous assaudroit,
> Et dedans vos maisons mourir il vous faudroit,
> De caterre, ou de fievre, ou par l'ire segrette
> D'un proces mal vuidé, ou d'une vieille debte,
> De peste, ou de poison, ou d'un autre mechef
> Qui tousjours poursuit l'homme & luy pend sur le chef.
> (IX, 10. Cf. II, 181; V, 194–5; VIII, 224–5; XV, 161–2)

The diversity and unexpected nature of death render life uncertain,
and it is this fear of death, this constant penetration of death into life,
together with man's ambition which is completely disproportionate to
his fragility, which are the principal causes of human suffering—ideas
heavily condensed from texts of Lucretius (III, 37–40; 978–1023) in the
following extract from an elegy to Robert de la Haye of 1560. Present
too in these lines are familiar stylistic and structural patterns of accumulation and balanced pairing (De tous les animaux le plus lourd animal;
d'infortune & de mal; endure en vivant ... endure mort; Et celle de ...
& celle de; ou par ... Ou par; Et plus un ... & plus l'autre), and these
are instrumental in giving the verse its movement and measure, its
customary libre contrainte :

> De tous les animaux le plus lourd animal,
> C'est l'homme, le subject d'infortune & de mal,
> Qui endure en vivant la peine que Tantale
> Là bas endure mort dedans l'onde infernalle,
> Et celle de Sisyphe, & celle d'Ixion :
> Il porte son enfer, ou par ambition,
> Ou par crainte de mort qui toujours le tourmente,
> Et plus un mal finit & plus l'autre s'augmente.
> (X, 316–17)

Ronsard is not only preoccupied with life's uncertainty (cf. I, 115; II,
182–3; VI, 103–4; VII, 195–6), but also, as has already been noted in the
discussion on time, with its brevity and fragility—a fragility symbolised,
according to a classical commonplace, by the birth of man, tearful,
naked and without armour, unlike all other animals who are born with
protective clothing and in-built weapons.[6] The ultimate and cruellest
paradox of the human condition is, as Ronsard states in the Epitaphe de
feu Monseigneur D'Annebault (1565), that God should have created man
near-divine in respect of his soul and reason and yet so frail and vulner-

able physically (XIII, 182–3). The explanation for this, as has been shown above, lies in the fact that human mortality is specifically designed to control man's *hubris* and to stop him impinging on the divine preroga-tives in the name of cosmic order, but in this epitaph Ronsard is more interested in pin-pointing the dilemma than in seeking philosophical justification for it. This was not the case, however, in a passage published two years earlier in the *Remonstrance au Peuple de France*, for here Ronsard prefigures certain lexical clusters which were to appear in the epitaph of 1565 ('. . . si petites veines, / Si petitz nerfs, peaux si foibles & vaines'), and gives one of his most eloquent expressions of the dis-crepancy between man's physical weakness and his intellectual arro-gance. Once again certain aesthetic principles, defined and discussed throughout this study, are evident in these lines from the *Remonstrance*, for their dynamism and *copia*, as well as their structural firmness and rhythmical measure, can be traced to common origins—the pattern of three opening and closing questions, the rhetorical device of anaphora (the repeated *Qui* formula), the twinning of lexical and syntactic features (*ces petits animaux . . . Ces petits animaux; creves & consommes; qu'on appelle . . . Que . . . Nomment; les doctes Romains, & les doctes Gregois; ou par songe ou par nue; entrepreneurs, & discoureurs; longue dispute & curieux propos; imposteur & menteur; puniras tu . . . Tiendras tu; Le Seigneur des larrons, & le Dieu de querelle?*) and the balancing of rhymes at the end of the line and, internally, at the caesura break (*animaux, peaux, animaux, eaux*):

> Ne vois tu pas [God] du ciel ces petits animaux
> Lesquels ne sont vestus que de petites peaux,
> Ces petits animaux qu'on appelle les hommes,
> Et comme bulles d'eaux tu creves & consommes?
> Que les doctes Romains, & les doctes Gregois,
> Nomment songe, fumée, & fueillage des bois?
> Qui n'ont jamais icy la vérité cogneue,
> Que je ne sçay comment ou par songe ou par nue?
>   Et toutesfois, Seigneur, ils font les empeschez,
> Comme si tes segretz ne leur estoient cachez,
> Braves entrepreneurs, & discoureurs des choses
> Qui aux entendemens de tous hommes sont closes,
> Qui par longue dispute & curieux propos
> Ne te laissent jouyr du bien de ton repos,
> Qui de tes sacremens effacent la memoire,
> Qui disputent en vain de cela qu'il faut croire,
> Qui font trouver ton Fils imposteur & menteur.
> Ne les puniras tu, souverain createur?
> Tiendras tu leur party? Veux tu que lon t'appelle
> Le Seigneur des larrons, & le Dieu de querelle?
>   (XI, 64–5)

Man is thus reduced to his animal nudity, his essential physical fragility, by lexical repetition (*petits*), by a series of traditional images of human transience and by discreet allusions to specific ancient texts.[7] At the same time Ronsard rejuvenates the commonplace by ironically contrasting man's significance with the concept of *hubris*, with human conceit and curiosity, for man is forever trying to trespass intellectually beyond the limits imposed on his condition, forever troubling the sacred peace of God by seeking secrets denied to him. Here, as in later passages of the *Remonstrance* (ll. 143–78), Ronsard develops his antithesis between man's weakness and his boundless intellectual aspirations into a condemnation of presumption in matters of theological debate, and anticipates Montaigne's *Apologie de Raymond Sebond* in his fideist conclusion, his evocation of the inability of human reason to comprehend God and His divine mysteries, and in his adherence to the stability of traditional beliefs as opposed to the disorder of new ideas.[8]

A totally different insight into the anxieties of Ronsard and his age within the context of human fragility is afforded by a study of his attitude to illness. It has already been noted that one of Ronsard's most emphatic meditations on the significance of death was inspired by a personal illness (above, p 148), and a closer analysis of the references to man's frailty and suffering reveals that illness is one of his constant obsessions, as one might expect in an age when life expectancy was short and famine and plague not infrequent (cf. II, 184–6; VI, 10). One has only to consider the medical case-history of Ronsard,[9] the numerous allusions to the therapeutic value of poetry as a distraction in time of illness (XV, 59–60; 177; 185), and the frequent prayers addressed to the god of medicine, Phoebus Apollo (I, 154–9; II, 40–3; XVII, 54–60), to gauge the degree of personal preoccupation with illness, even allowing for literary convention.[10] Similarly illness is constantly associated with precocious old age, physical decrepitude, human mortality and misery (VII, 102–3; VIII, 224–6; X, 310; XV, 161–2; XVII, 78; XVIII, 175), and definitions of 'the happy life' often include mentions of good health ('Le meilleur bien que l'homme puisse avoir / C'est l'esprit sain, le corps sain, la jeunesse': XV, 342). Ronsard's visions of Paradise (the Blessed Isles, the Elysian Fields, the Christian Heaven and the Age of Gold) all insist on the absence of illness (III, 75; V, 184–5; VIII, 55; 176), whilst the personified *Maladie* lives in the Underworld with the poet's other enemies, Discord, 'Vieillesse, Ennuy ... & Soucy' (XIV, 117). Indeed Ronsard's grotesque and detailed description of 'la vieille Maladie' in the *Hymne de l'Autonne*, and the accompanying enumeration of illnesses, diseases and symptoms (XII, 55–6), clearly reveal an obsession with 'la maladie extreme fleau de l'ame' (XVIII, 175) that is real and non-literary. Again the frequency of metaphors and imagery which link cosmic, social and aesthetic ideas with physical illness, deformity and feverish

delirium,[11] is itself significant in the work of a poet who 'demande /
D'estre tousjours sain & dispos' (VII, 282) and who admits that he would
'trop mieux soudainement mourir / Que tant languir sans espoir de
guarir' (XV, 59).

Specific and direct statements reveal that for Ronsard illness is almost
synonymous with death ('Lors vient la maladie, & bien souvent la mort':
IX, 113), an equation partially explained by the fact that both have their
common origin in Prometheus's sin of *hubris* (II, 111–12; 182; V, 195–6).
A more contemporary and personal note, if one remembers the serious
illness of 1540 which left Ronsard's hearing severely impaired (VI, 69),
is struck in an ode of 1550 when the poet expresses grave doubts about
the efficacy of medicine to prolong life (II, 183), and this idea that the
human body can scarcely withstand illness, being '. . . si foible & tendre
/ Qu'à peine se peut il d'une fievre deffendre' (VI, 114), will be more
emphatically expressed in the 1584 variants of an ode Ronsard first published over thirty years earlier. Here the equation between illness and
death is all the more significant in that the poet departs from his source
(Horace, *Odes*, I, ix) at this juncture to make this personal statement:

> Pauvre abusé, ne sçais-tu pas
> Qu'il ne faut qu'une maladie
> Pour te mener bien tost là bas,
> D'où jamais ne revient le pas?
> Quelque chose qu'ici lon die,
> Ce n'est qu'horreur que le trespas.
>   (I, 216: var.)

An equally revealing text in this respect is an ode to Simon Nicolas of
1578. The horror caused by the memory of Nicolas's recent fever would
seem to evoke a recollection of Ronsard's own serious illness of 1567–9
(to which the poet makes frequent allusion in his collections of 1569),
and this in turn inspires a change of tone from the light-hearted epicurean opening movements to a serious, more personal discussion of the
debilitating effects of illness. Here, as elsewhere in his verse—'teste
toute élourdie' (VII, 102); 'impotent & perclus, / Fascheux, hargneux,
ayant l'ame estourdie / Et tout le corps de longue maladie' (XIV, 144);
'impotent & deffait' (XIV, 166); 'la maladie . . . / Refroidist ses jarrets, &
empesche sa course' (XVIII, 122)—a common core of obsessions appear,
for what concerns the sensualist in Ronsard about illness and old age is
that they prefigure death with their physical and mental lethargy, their
gradual ebbing away of the vital forces of movement, warmth and light-
ness. This concern is further emphasised by a subtle variant, for *surprend*
of line 6 of the following quotation becomes *matte* in the posthumous
1587 edition, and on several other occasions—'languir vieus au lit,

mattés de maladie' (v, 214); 'Les hommes maladis, ou mattés de vieillesse' (VII, 126, s. IX); 'vieil, matté d'un sang refroidy' (XVI, 345)—this same verb is used to link illness and old age with inactivity, lassitude and coldness:

> Quand ta fiévre, dont la memoire
> Me fait encores frissonner,
> Ne t'auroit apprins qu'à bien boire,
> Tu ne la dois abandonner.
> . . .
> Non seulement la maladie
> Qui nous surprend par ses efforts,
> Ne rend nostre masse estourdie,
> Enervant les forces du corps :
>   Mais elle trouble, la cruelle,
> Nostre esprit qui nous vient des cieux :
> Il n'y a part qui ne chancelle,
> Quand les hommes deviennent vieux.
>   Puis la mort vient, la vieille escarse.
>   (XVII, 372–3. Cf. VI, 107; X, 310)

However, in spite of the fragility of man ('. . . un vaisseau de terre entourné de foiblesse'[12]), he continues to behave as if he were immortal, and he wastes his brief life by misusing it and exposing himself to death and danger for the futile purpose usually of amassing material wealth or worldly favour. Horace had expressed this idea forcibly and had used this theme either to advocate a philosophy of moderation and internal contentment or an epicurean attitude to money, for, so the argument went, since gold cannot prolong man's years and a worthless heir will soon dissipate the riches amassed at another's cost and danger, wealth should be enjoyed.[13] In his turn Ronsard improvises on these arguments (VIII, 196–7; 202–5; X, 45), and, on another occasion, he contaminates multiple Horatian texts to compose an ode *Contre les Avaricieus et ceus qui prochains de la mort batissent* (I, 183–8).

Ronsard's preoccupation with these commonplace themes ultimately lead to the conclusion that life and death are synonymous, an equation resulting from the constant encroachment of death into life and from the awareness that the brevity and fragility of life juxtapose birth and death so dramatically : '. . . nostre vie aux fleurettes resemble, / Qui presque vit & presque meurt ensemble' (XV, 176). This equation of birth and death is a commonplace of classical literature, but it is especially associated with the consolatory reasoning of Seneca.[14] Similarly a line of Manilius, *Astronomica*, IV, 16 ('Nascentes morimur, finisque ab origine pendet') had juxtaposed birth and death with epigrammatic concision, and had expressed the idea with such brevity and sententious force that the single reference simultaneously evokes an antithesis and a comparison and has the energy and universal application of a maxim. Although this line of Manilius finds frequent favour in Ronsard's work,[15] it is, however, to Seneca that Ronsard is indebted for the interpretation and tone of the final movement of *La Salade* (1569) addressed to Amadis Jamyn:

> Laisse moy vivre au moins jusqu'à la fin
> Tout à mon aise, & ne sois triste Augure
> Soit à ma vie ou à ma mort future,
> Car tu ne peux, ny moy, pour tout secours
> Faire plus longs ou plus petis mes jours:
> Il faut charger la barque Stygieuse:
> «La barque, c'est la Biere sommeilleuse,
> «Faite en bateau: le naistre est le trepas:
> «Sans naistre icy l'home ne mourroit pas:
> «Fol qui d'ailleurs autre bien se propose,
> «Naissance & mort est une mesme chose.
>
> (xv, 84)

The treatment of the theme here is in many ways typical of Ronsard's general attitude to death. There is no real sense of despair manifested, and even the evocation of death is rendered by the classical euphemism of a comparison with sleep. Instead the implacable law of death is greeted with equanimity and becomes the inspiration to ignore the uncertain future and to 'vivre . . . jusqu'à la fin / Tout à mon aise'. The reasoning and the tone, which is at the same time one of stoical resignation and epicurean anticipation, and which has certain affinities with the 'stoïcisme joyeux' of Rabelais, is clearly borrowed from the *genre* of the *consolatio* and, more especially, from Seneca who, on frequent occasions, points to the equation of life and death and emphasises the consolation which accompanies the omnipotence and equality of death. The textual similarity between Ronsard's 'Fol qui d'ailleurs' and the Latin structure of the following passage may suggest a direct borrowing:

He says that *it is as foolish* (Is ait tam stultum esse) to fear death as to fear old age; for death follows old age precisely as old age follows youth. He who does not wish to die cannot have wished to live. For life is granted to us with the reservation that we shall die; to this end our path leads. Therefore, *how foolish it is to fear it* (Quam ideo timere dementis est), since men simply await that which is sure, but fear only that which is uncertain! Death has its fixed rule—equitable and unavoidable. Who can complain when he is governed by terms which include everyone? The chief part of equity, however, is equality.[16]

These passages of Seneca, which exhort man to seek solace in the resigned submission to the universal equity and naturalness of death, provide the key to a constant attitude of Ronsard. Although the abundance and consistency of references to the commonplace themes of death demonstrate that he is preoccupied throughout his career with the significance and consequences of human mortality, and although Professor Silver (Introduction, XVIII, pp. XLVII–LVII) has drawn attention to the more pessimistic note of several of the variants and new poems of the 1584 and 1587 collective editions—a note which finds its natural culmination in the sombre *Derniers Vers*—nevertheless this Senecan attitude of calm resignation to death's equality is consistently and emphatically expressed throughout Ronsard's verse, and is a fundamental aspect of his philosophy. It is first found in the *Epitafe de Jehan de Ronsard* of 1554 (VI, 44) and a year later it reappears in two texts (VII, 103–4; VIII, 167). The same attitude is expressed again in 1560 in the *Epitaphe d'André Blondet* (X, 310–12), where Ronsard envisages human mortality as part of a divine pattern, an expression of 'la volunté saincte', to which man must unquestioningly submit. Consolation in the universality of death appears again in an *Ode à Monsieur de Verdun* (1565: XIII, 261), in the *Epitaphe de Courte* (1567: XIV, 113) and in 1569 it is a central theme of *La Salade* (above, pp. 155, 162).

With old age and the approach of his own death this Senecan attitude of resigned acceptance does not disappear. It is not only that Ronsard never suppresses any of the above references in his variants of the 1578, 1584 and 1587 collective editions, but this idea finds fresh and consistent expression in his later collections. It occurs again in *Le Tombeau de Charles IX* (1574: XVII, 9), and in an addition to the 1578–87 editions of *Le Tombeau de Marguerite de France* (1575): 'Conforte toy grand Roy, la sentence est donnee / Que la mort est la fin de toute essence nee' (XVII, 76: var.). Whilst other variants of the 1578 edition emphasise the same naturalness of death's law (VI, 50, s. VI, l. 14, var.; VI, 151, l. 56, var.), and whilst certain lines of a piece written in 1580 accept the rhythm of life and death as part of a natural pattern (XVIII, 411), the most significant—because the most personal—appearance of this Senecan attitude during these later years is found in a dedicatory elegy published in 1584, but written from internal evidence in 1580 or 1581 when Ronsard was fifty-six (XVIII, 36–43). Here the tone is one of sombre lassitude and the themes of old age, sublunar flux and the omnipotence of Fortune and Destiny find poignant and personal expression (ll. 1–26, 69–70, 103–4). It is, then, within the context of world weariness and civil, religious upheaval (ll. 49–80) that Ronsard equates birth and death and stoically accepts the universal law of Nature:

J'ay couru mon flambeau sans me donner esmoy,
Le baillant à quelcun s'il recourt apres moy :

Il ne fault s'en fascher, c'est la Loy de nature,
Où s'engage en naissant chacune creature.

(ll. 27–30)

Other new poems and variants of the 1584 edition return to the same
idea of a natural law of death (VI, 82, var.; XVIII, 46).

This integration of death into a universal law of God and Nature explains in turn certain recurrent themes which are designed to console
man by creating links of sympathy between human mortality and the
natural and divine worlds. For Ronsard celestial and natural presages
are an expression of the Divine Will and reveal the workings of Providence, if man can learn to decipher the signs (VIII, 59; XVIII, 34–5; 168).
Thus the presages which announce human death are manifestations of
divine pity: they are, as Rémy Belleau says, 'divins augures' which
herald 'les palles frayeurs d'une image de mort' (II, 258–60). This idea is
a commonplace of classical literature and is associated especially with
the death of Caesar.[17] As such these portents are similar to those natural
disorders and celestial apparitions which precede and accompany
national disasters (war, civil strife, famine, plague), and which Ronsard
sees as further examples of the sympathetic intervention of the divine
into human affairs (V, 176–7; IX, 108–9; X, 358–9; XI, 24–5; XVIII, 39–40;
165–8). Ronsard, more particularly, has a predilection for the prophetic
nature of certain animals, and in Le Chat (1569), under the influence of
Cardano, he constructs a general theory of presages which explains how
God has given powers of foresight to animals and plants because they
are in direct contact with the Universal Soul (XV, 41–7). Thus, remem-
bering Homer, he explains how Achilles' death was predicted by his
horse (XV, 146), whilst an eclogue of 1565 adapts passages of Virgil or
Sannazaro in order to evoke the portentous behaviour of sheep prior to
the death of Henri II.[18] Not content with prophesying death, the natural
and divine worlds echo human mourning with their own lamentations
and demonstrations of sympathy. Adapting a commonplace idea of
Greek, Latin, neo-Latin and French literature,[19] Ronsard describes the
dirges of Nature and the complete upheaval of the natural order which
accompany human death, and, in the eclogue of 1565 recently mentioned, it is Virgil and Sannazaro who again provide the French poet
with certain details which he characteristically fashions into a catalogue
of controlled movement:

Toutes choses ça bas pleuroient en desconfort:
Le Soleil s'enfuït pour ne voir telle mort,
Et d'un crespe rouillé cacha sa teste blonde,
Abhominant la terre en vices si feconde.
Les Nymphes l'ont gemy d'une piteuse voix,

> Les Antres l'ont pleuré, les rochers & les bois.
> Vous le sçavez, forests, qui vistes es bocages
> Les loups mesme le plaindre, & les lions sauvages.[20]

Later in this eclogue Ronsard repeats the gesture found in Virgil and Sannazaro of engraving the bark of a tree (XIII, 99), and the symbolism of this action—namely to associate grief with the eternal cycles of Nature in order to ensure the survival of memory over death—is explained in the same poem.[21] It is by making Nature a confidante, by obliging her to participate in the tragedy of human death, that Ronsard makes sure that the memory of Henri II survives unchanging and ever-fresh :

> Nous ferons en ton nom des autels tous les ans,
> ... dançant main à main nous ferons aux forests
> Aprendre tes honneurs, afin que ta loüange,
> Redite tous les ans, par les ans ne se change,
> Plus forte que la mort, mais fleurisse en tout temps
> Par ces grandes forests comme fleurs au printemps.
>
> (XIII, 101)

Again Nature celebrates the victory of memory over time and death and participates in the apotheosis of the deceased into a god (XIII, 100). The cycle of Angelot's speech in this pastoral poem of 1565 thus moves from portents of death, natural upheaval and mourning to aspects of survival, spring renewal, immortality and deification.

The fact that the divine world too not only participates in the lamentations but plays an active role in the ceremony is significant, for as in classical sepulchral literature[22] the presence of various divinities at the funeral is a consolation for Ronsard, since it is at the same time a testimony to their sympathetic interest in human activity and an assurance of the deceased's immortality. In the opening movements of an elegy on the death of Chasteigner (1553) the mourners include a suitably funereal Cupid ('... son arc ronpu, & sa torche sans feu : / ... il vole tout morne, & d'une main courbée / Comme il noircît sa poitrine plonbée !'), as well as 'le Jeu, & les Muses pleurantes', 'les trois Graces errantes', and 'Venus sans confort / Toute pleureuse' (V, 244–5). Elsewhere the favourite participants in the funeral ceremony and mourning are the local rustic divinities (nymphs, dryads) who are incarnations of natural forces, and, especially if the deceased is a poet, the Muses, Graces and Cupid (VIII, 231; 234–6; XII, 122–4; XV, 223; 296).

If Ronsard can find compensation for death by introducing man into the context of a universal law and by fusing human mortality with the natural and divine worlds, the opposite and complementary attitude will also be seen to prevail. It is on those occasions when the poet suddenly sees man as isolated from the natural and divine cycles of the universe and not integrated into the wider and more durable cosmic pattern, that he is dramatically made aware of man's essential fragility and injects fresh life and vision into the themes of death and human misery.

Although subject to change, and although an endless source of illustrations and images of flux in Ronsard's verse, Nature herself is permanent beyond her mutability, whereas man passes away forever. This opposition between ephemeral man and eternal Nature first occurs in Ronsard's poetry in an ode of 1550 (I, 189) via a rather literal translation of Catullus, V, 4–6, and it makes its final appearance in an epitaph of 1571, where the following poignant question, although imitated indirectly from Moschus, *Lament for Bion*, ll. 99–104, is expressed more directly through the lyrical movement of a passage from Clément Marot:

> D'où vient cela que les herbes qui croissent
> Parmy les prez remeurent & renaissent,
> Et quand l'homme est souz le tombeau reclus
> Il va là bas & ne retourne plus?[23]

Between these two dates this opposition occurs often and is most in evidence in the years 1553–5. It is found in an ode *A la Fonteine Bélerie* (1553: V, 241–2), where the perpetual and rhythmical fluidity of the stream contrasts with the abrupt finality of the poet's death, and again in a love poem of 1554 (VI, 71–2), in which the antithesis between the renewed beauty of spring flowers and the irrecoverable beauty of the girl is adapted from the text of Moschus, and introduces a realistic description of old age and the accompanying epicurean exhortation. The same contrast between mortal man and eternal Nature makes a further appearance in the opening movement of an *Ode a Christofle de Choiseul* (1555: VI, 191), but it is in the ode *Quand je suis vint ou trente mois* (1555) that this opposition—stripped of all classical reminiscences—receives its most original, lyrical and technically perfect expression.[24] Although the poet appears to envy Nature her permanence in lines 1–30 of the ode, the final stanza introduces a surprising and epigrammatic conclusion which will alleviate the melancholy and redress the balance in favour of animate but mortal man:

> Si esse que je ne voudrois
> Avoir esté ni roc, ni bois,
> Antre, ni onde, pour defendre
> Mon cors contre l'age emplumé,
> Car ainsi dur, je n'eusse aimé
> Toi qui m'as fait vieillir, Cassandre.

Human fragility finds its compensation then within the context of the senses: 'Un rocher n'aime point, un Chesne ny la mer : / Mais le propre sujet des hommes c'est aimer' (xvii, 159. Cf. xii, 264–5), and Ronsard is unwilling to exchange mortality for an eternal life if he is to be inanimate. He accepts the consequences of a sentient being—old age, illness, death—if he can enjoy the attendant pleasures. He is not only consistent in seeking human fulfilment within the limitations of man's mortality, as his repeated epicurean pleas and rejections of neo-Platonic spiritualism demonstrate, but when, aged fifty-six, the time comes to take leave of '. . . les vers & les amours, / Et de prendre congé du plus beau de mes jours' (xviii, 37), he makes a desperate attempt to do so without regret (above p. 114) and to remain faithful to the lesson learnt in this ode of 1555.

This isolation of transient man from the eternal natural cycles of animal and vegetable life appears briefly in a sonnet of 1565 (xiii, 249), and it is a central theme once more of the *Epitaphe de feu Monseigneur D'Annebault* of the same collection. It is after an opening movement devoted to the opposition between man's physical frailty and the immortality of his soul and reason that the following passage occurs :

> Cruel destin! qui nos aages derobes :
> Quand les serpens ont desvestu leurs robes,
> Avec la peau ilz despouillent leurs ans.
> Quand au printemps les jours doux & plaisans
> Sont retournés, en mille & mille sortes
> On voit sortir les fleurs qui sembloient mortes :
> Les boys couppez reverdissent plus beaux,
> Mais quand la Parque a fillé nos fuseaux,
> Sans plus jouir du sejour de ce monde
> L'homme là bas s'en va boyre de l'onde
> Du froid oubly, qui sans esgard ny choys
> Perd en ses eaux les bergers & les Rois.
>
> (xiii, 183–4)

Unlike the ode *Quand je suis vint ou trente mois* the sources here are more in evidence, although, as is his custom in his mature years, Ronsard is inclined to borrow the general themes rather than precise textual details. The antithesis between mortal man and the returning spring flowers is again taken from Moschus; the reference to the rejuvenation of snakes is probably remembered here, Laumonier suggests, from Tibullus and Ovid, although this idea is explained by a detail of the Prometheus myth as recounted by Nicander.[25] The image of the 'bois couppez' is adapted from Horace,[26] whilst the commonplace concerning the equality and omnipotence of death is Pindaric and Horatian. In spite of the principles of *copia* and diversity at work here in the rapid accumulation of classical allusions and images, nevertheless poetic control and organisation—as well as originality—remain predominant. These are evident in the way Ronsard skilfully fuses his reminiscences into a tight series of illustrations which reaches a climax at the pivot of the antithesis ('... reverdissent *plus beaux*'), evokes durability within a pattern of change and isolates the human condition within the final despair of its own mortality by repeating across the contrast a major structure (*Quand ... Quand ... Mais quand*), twin items of balanced pairing (*doux & plaisans, mille & mille; sans esgard ny choys, les bergers & les Rois*), a lexical echo ('*plus* beaux ... sans *plus*') and alternating past and present verb tenses.

If this opposition between ephemeral man and the eternal cycles of Nature periodically sharpens Ronsard's awareness of human mortality, the gulf separating man from the wider cosmic structure suffices, on isolated occasions, to heighten even further his frailty and sense of insecurity. It has already been noted that the division of the universe into sublunar and extralunar worlds is part of Ronsard's vision of a harmonious cosmos based on the delicate balance of opposing forces, and that the barrier of the moon is designed by Nature to thwart man's *hubris* and to retain him in his prescribed place in the world system (see above p. 16). On the whole Ronsard is willing to accept that man, although the centre of creation, must submit to this hierarchical pattern in the name of cosmic order, and he is content to integrate man into the complex mechanism of the universe by establishing, on all possible occasions and at all levels, a fusion between microcosm and macrocosm, and by relating the human condition to a series of equitable natural and divine laws.

However, although this determination to create links of sympathy between microcosm and macrocosm is central to Ronsard's scientific and poetic vision, there are isolated moments in his verse where human fragility is specifically expressed in terms of man's alienation from the cosmic pattern. In Ronsard's verse this is not a mere re-writing of the classical statement concerning the differences between mortal man and the immortal gods—although this commonplace does appear in his verse, and may conceivably be a distant point of departure for his own conception of man's insignificance in the world system.[27] Another point of departure for this antithesis between mortal man and the eternal heavenly forces is found in certain passages of Horace and Catullus which Ronsard adapts in an ode of 1555 addressed to Christofle de Choiseul (VI, 191). But these 'sources' are nothing more than faint suggestions of the theme as it appears in Ronsard's scientific verse, and have very little to do with the cosmic canvas of his conception, which is, rather, an original and poetic interpretation of the Aristotelian distinction between the immortality and stability of the astral region and the fragility and inconstancy of the sublunar world of man.

This antithesis is a constant *leit-motiv* of Ronsard's scientific verse (III, 75; VIII, 145–6; 160; XVII, 42), but it receives its most poetically sustained and emphatic expression in the *Hymne de l'Eternité*. Eternity, it has been seen, represents the immutable essence of God, the force—at once transcendental and immanent—which ensures the harmony of the universe through intermediary cosmic powers (Destiny and Nature) and divine personified virtues of Providence (*Puissance* and *Vertu*). This definition of Eternity's cosmic role gives way to a long movement devoted to a contrast between the self-regenerating, immortal goddess and mortal man, whose life is full of anxiety and grief and who desperately preserves the species in the face of death's relentless omnipotence. Present once again in this passage are certain words (*nourris, sein, force, membres, ame, vie, vive vertu, puissance*) which clearly recall the sexual pantheism of poems discussed early in chapter one:

> O grande Eternité, merveilleux sont tes faictz!
> Tu nourris l'univers en eternelle paix,
> D'un lien aimantin les siecles tu attaches,
> Et dessoubz ton grand sein tout ce monde tu caches,
> Luy donnant vie & force, aultrement il n'auroit
> Membres, ame, ne vie, & confuz periroit :
> Mais ta vive vertu le conserve en son estre
> Tousjours entier & sain sans amoindrir ne croistre.
> Tu n'as pas les humains favorisez ainsy,
> Que tu as heritez de peine & de soucy,
> De vieillesse & de mort, qui est leur vray partage,
> Faisant bien peu de cas de tout nostre lignage,
> Qui ne peult conserver sa generation
> Sinon par le succés de reparation,
> A laquelle Venus incite la Nature
> Par plaisir mutuel de chaque creature
> A garder son espece, & tousjours restaurer
> Sa race qui ne peut eternelle durer :
> Mais toy sans restaurer ton estre & ton essence,
> Vivant tu te soustiens de ta propre puissance,
> Sans rien craindre la mort, car le cruel trespas
> Ne regne point au Ciel comme il regne icy bas,
> Le lieu de son empire, où maling il exerce
> Par mille estranges mortz sa malice diverse,
> N'ayant non plus d'esgard aux Princes qu'aux Bouviers,
> Pesle mesle egallant les sceptres aux leviers.
>
> (VIII, 251–2)

The concluding commonplace recalls a lesson learnt from Pindar and Horace, and the reference to the preservation of the species through

Venus owes a debt to Lucretius (cf. VIII, 252, notes 3 and 4; XIX, 115), but Ronsard's originality manifests itself in the way he welds his general reminiscences together to express an antithesis between man and Eternity nowhere apparent in these classical texts. It is true that certain lines of Marullus (*Hymni*, I, V, *Aeternitati*, ll. 21–5) have distantly suggested the opposition, but the French text develops these brief statements at length and in a totally personal manner, and, in a movement of rhetorical firmness and measured beauty, rejuvenates the commonplace theme of human mortality. This is not to say that the characteristic features of abundance and diversity are absent from these lines: on the contrary, aspects of accumulation and multiplicity are evident in the *tu plus* main verb pattern repeated throughout, whilst the single, complex sentence of lines 9–26 of the extract is a perfect illustration of sustained momentum and organic growth. However, these aspects are contained within an overall structure and unity. The major opposition between Eternity and man is constructed on two minor antithetical movements (ll. 1–8 and 19–22 contrasting with ll. 9–18 and 22–6), and the three focal points of these opposing blocks are underlined by a common formula (*Tu . . . Tu n'as pas . . . Mais toy*: ll. 2, 9, 19). In turn the major contrast is supported throughout not only by antithetical patterns of lexis but by affirmative and negative verbs: these stylistic devices are most evident in line 22, where the pivot of the contrast between the previous lines devoted to Eternity and the subsequent lines relating to man, comes at the caesura break and is expressed by the items *Ne regne point . . . il regne* and *Ciel . . . icy bas*. Other structural, stylistic and lexical patterns are found throughout—the use of present participles and infinitives, the *sans* formula, the frequent and familiar appearance of balanced pairing (*vie & force, entier & sain, de peine & de soucy* and so on)—and these reinforce the unity, measure and rhetorical firmness of the passage. This antithesis between man and Eternity, so poetically expressed in the above extract, has already been prefigured earlier in the *hymne* in short passages (cf. ll. 6–10, 23–6, 47–8), and it becomes all the more central to Ronsard's vision in the following lengthy movement, for it is here that he opposes extralunar and sublunar conceptions of time, and sees temporal definitions and distinctions as human inventions resulting from man's mortality and physical imperfection.

This opposition between the sublunar and extralunar worlds does not present Ronsard with a tragic impasse, however, but in turn can be seen as the starting-point for a discussion on the means of transcending the fragility of the human condition, of liberating the immortal soul or the mind from the restrictions of the imperfect, mortal body and of elevating it to the stability of divine contemplation. This release and ascension of the soul and this momentary victory over human mortality take place within the context of life itself, and are achieved by a series of mystical neo-Platonic arguments: it is to these that we now turn.

NOTES TO CHAPTER SIX

1 Pindar, *Nemean*, VII, ep. 1 and antistr. 2; XI, ep. 1; Horace, *Odes*, I, iv, 13–14; xxviii, 7–20; II, iii, 21–5; xiv, 9–12; xviii, 32–4; III, i, 14–16.

2 II, 108–9; V, 255. Cf. V, 214; VII, 58–9; X, 14; XIV, 113; XVII, 84.

3 Pindar, *Nemean*, XI, ep. 1; Horace, *Odes*, I, iv, 13–17; xxiv; II, iii, 21–8; xviii; IV, vii, 21–8. Cf. Lucretius, II, 37–8; Virgil, *Georgics*, IV, 469–470; Propertius, III, xviii, 20–8; Stobaeus, *Florilegium*, CXIX.

4 II, 182. Cf. III, 194; VII, 103; XIII, 261.

5 Pindar, *Isthmian*, VII, antistr. 3; Horace, *Odes*, I, xxviii, 15–20; II, xiv, 13–20. Cf. *The Greek Anthology*, vol. II, p. 333, no. 621; Statius, *Silvae*, II, i, 209–19.

6 Ronsard, VIII, 173; 188; IX, 21; X, 318. Cf. Pliny, *Nat. Hist.*, VII, i, 2; Lucretius, V, 222–34; Seneca, *Ad Marciam De Consol.*, XI, 3–4; *The Greek Anthology*, vol. IV, p. 47, no. 84.

7 For the symbol of the 'bulles d'eaux' and the proverbial nature of the idea 'Est homo bulla', see H. W. Janson, 'The Putto with the Death's Head', *The Art Bulletin*, XIX (1937), 446–7 and fig. 21; Tervarent, s.v. *Bulle*. The source of the 'songe' image is Pindar, *Pythian*, VIII, ep. 5. Cf. Job 20.8. The symbols of 'songe' and 'fumée' are frequent in Ronsard (II, 121; XIII, 213; 257; XVII, 139). For the image of the 'fueillage des bois', see above p. 110.

8 *Remonstrance*, ll. 41–56, 85–90. Cf. F. S. Brown, 'Interrelations between the political ideas of Ronsard and Montaigne', *Romanic Review*, LXVI (1965), 241–7.

9 For Ronsard's serious illnesses of 1540 and 1567–9, see P. Champion, *Ronsard et son temps* (Paris, 1925), pp. 31–2, 400, 405ff.

10 Although the allusions to illness in Ronsard's love poetry have been ignored, on occasions the references clearly transcend the level of a *concetto* and relate to personal experience (cf. XII, 284; XV, 168).

11 III, 24; VIII, 249; IX, 112–13; XIV, 10, 13; XV, 159–60; XVI, 4; 334; 337–8; 343.

12 XVII, 175. For the image, cf. Epist. of Paul to Romans 9.21–3; Psalms 2.9; 30.13; Job 10.9; Seneca, *Ad Marciam De Consol.*, XI, 3. See also, Tervarent, s.v. *Pot cassé*; *Vase brisé*; and P. J. Vinken, 'Some Observations on the Symbolism of The Broken Pot in Art and Literature', *The American Imago*, XV (1958), 149–74.

13 *Odes*, II, iii, 17–24; xiv, 21–8; xviii, 15–40; III, xxiv, 61–2; IV, vii, 17–20; *Epist.*, II, ii, 175ff. Cf. Seneca, *Epist.*, CI.

14 *Ad Marciam De Consol.*, X, 5; *Ad Polybium De Consol.*, XI, 2–4; *Epist.*, xxx, 10–11; XCIX, 8–9; *Troades*, ll. 371–408; *Hercules Furens*, l. 874. Cf. Plutarch, *Consol. ad Apoll.*, chapt. 28; *The Greek Anthology*, vol. II, p. 183, no. 339; Horace, *Odes*, I, xxviii, 6. For the iconographical traditions, see H. W. Janson, 'The Putto with the Death's Head', *passim* and figs. 10, 15, 17–24, 26–30.

15 VIII, 177; X, 312; XV, 302; 307; XVI, 295; XVII, 386. For this Latin line in the visual arts, see Janson, pp. 438–9 and fig. 30.

16 *Epist.*, xxx, 10–11 (LCL, 1925, vol. I, p. 217). Cf. *Epist.*, LXXVII, 12–13; XCIX, 8–9; CVII, 6; *Ad Polybium De Consol.*, I, 1–4; XI, 2–3; *Ad Marciam De Consol.*, XXVI, 6.

17 Cf. Plutarch, *Lives*, *Caesar*, LXIX, 3–7; Virgil, *Georgics*, I, 464–88; Ovid, *Metam.*, XV, 779–98; Lucan, *Pharsalia*, I, 522ff.

18 XIII, 97. Cf. Virgil, *Eclogues*, V, 25–6; X, 16–17; Sannazaro, *L'Arcadie … mise d'Italien en Françoys, par Jehan Martin* (Paris, 1544), fol. 31v.

19 Cf. Theocritus, I, *Thyrsis*, l. 71ff.; Moschus, *Lament for Bion*, ll. 1–49; Bion, *Lament for Adonis*, ll. 32–9; *The Greek Anthology*, vol. II, p. 9, no. 10; p. 223, no. 412; Virgil, *Ecl.*, V, 20–44; Ovid, *Metam.*, XI, 44–53; Sannazaro, *Arcadia*, fols. 29v and 31v; Clément Marot, *Eglogue sur le Trespas de ma Dame Loyse de Savoye*, ll. 97–128.

20 XIII, 97–8. Cf. Virgil, *Ecl.*, V, 20–1, 27–8; X, 13–15; *Georgics*, I, 466–8, 485–6; Sannazaro, *Arcadia*, fol. 31v. Similar expressions of Nature's sympathy in Ronsard, XII, 121; XV, 300–1; XVII, 83.

21 XIII, 110. Cf. Virgil, *Ecl.*, V, 13–15; X, 53–4; Sannazaro, *Arcadia*, fol. 27v. Similar gesture in Ronsard, IX, 183; X, 63; XII, 101; 104.

22 Pindar, *Isthmian*, VIII, str. 6; Theocritus, I, *Thyrsis*, l. 76ff.; Moschus, *Lament for Bion*, l. 25ff.; *The Greek Anthology*, vol. II, Book VII, nos. 8, 10, 218, 412, 593, 612; Virgil, *Ecl.*, V, 20–21; 35; Ovid, *Metam.*, XI, 49; *Amores*, III, ix, 7; Sannazaro, *Arcadia*, fols. 30r, 31v. Cf. Marot, *Eglogue sur le Trespas de Loyse de Savoye*, ll. 133–55.

23 XV, 298. Cf. Marot, *Eglogue sur le Trespas de Loyse de Savoye*, ll. 177–80 (text quoted by Laumonier, *loc. cit.*, n. 2). A translation of the Moschus poem can be read in *The Greek Bucolic Poets* (LCL, 1960), p. 453. On this theme, see I. Silver, 'Ronsard's Reflections on Cosmogony and Nature', pp. 232–3.

24 VII, 98–9. For commentaries on this ode, see Laumonier, *RPL*, pp. 463–4; F. Desonay, 'A propos de deux Odes de Ronsard', *Flambeau*, XXXII (1949), 178–82; Marcel Raymond, *Baroque et Renaissance poétique*, pp. 128–31.

25 Nicander, *Theriaka*, ll. 343–59. Ronsard had a copy of Nicander in his library: cf. P. Laumonier, 'Sur la Bibliotheque de Ronsard', *Revue du Seizième Siècle*, XIV (1927), 328–33. The idea of the rejuvenation of snakes is a classical commonplace (cf. Lucretius, IV, 60–1; Ovid, *Metam.*, IX, 266–7; Statius, *Thebaid*, IV, 95–8; Virgil, *Georgics*, III, 437; *Aeneid*, II, 469–75): it appears often in Ronsard's verse (II, 71; XVI, 198; 358; XVII, 268, s. XXVI).

26 *Odes*, IV, iv, 57–60. Cf. Ronsard, XVI, 349. There is also biblical (Job 14.7–9) and iconographical authority (see Tervarent, s.v. *Tronc brisé dont une branche reverdit*) for this idea.

27 Cf. I, 89; II, 121; VIII, 125; X, 308–9; XV, 318; XVIII, 46. Cf. Homer, *Iliad*, XXIV, 522ff. (quoted in Plutarch, *Consol. ad Apoll.*, chapt. 7); Pindar, *Nemean*, VI, str. 1; Lucretius, II, 646–51.

CHAPTER SEVEN

Means of transcending and escaping death

INTELLECTUAL ACTIVITY, KNOWLEDGE AND POETIC 'MADNESS'

Neo-Platonic arguments, as exposed by Marsilio Ficino—and as popularised in Italy by Pietro Bembo, Castiglione and Leone Ebreo, and in France by Antoine Héroët, Marguerite de Navarre and Pontus de Tyard—pictured the soul as fallen and imprisoned, discordant and dissonant, in the imperfect matter of the body.[1] Their spiritual dualism enabled the neo-Platonists to talk of releasing the soul from the corrupting restraints of the passions and senses, of harmonising its discordance and of elevating it to the Ideal World and God through four progressive stages of intellectual and spiritual perfection: Nature, Opinion, Reason and the Angelic Mind. This ascent to Unity, divine contemplation and perfect knowledge is in turn achieved by a progressive hierarchy of four kinds of 'fury' or 'madness': poetic (inherently linked to music), bacchic (related to mysteries and religious secrets), prophetic and erotic.[2]

Similarly neo-Platonic theory stresses particularly the importance of reason and knowledge in liberating man from his passions, and of elevating him to God after complete intellectual domination over the terrestrial regions and matter.[3] In this respect the humanist ideal of encyclopedic knowledge and the neo-Platonic belief in intellectual perfectionment are synthesised, providing a natural parallel to the ideas of human excellence and progress expressed so emphatically in Giannozzo Manetti's *De Dignitate et Excellentia Hominis* (1452), and more especially in Pico della Mirandola, *De Hominis Dignitate* (1486)[4] and Charles de Bouelles, *De Sapiente* (1510).[5] Through his knowledge man occupies an almost divine place in the world pattern—'Finally whatever the earth may be like, Man is its Lord. He is assuredly God on earth', writes Ficino (*Theologiae Platonicae*, XVI, 6)—comprehending and commanding all things earthly by his supreme will and intellect.[6] His soul, perfected by knowledge and harmonised by intellectual contemplation, returns unified to its former abode.

The whole movement of neo-Platonic theory is, therefore, from chaos to order, flux to stability, mortality to immortality, and it is by emphasising what is divine and eternal in man (the soul, reason, intellect), and by ignoring what is imperfect and changeable (the senses, the body), that such reasoning enables him to transcend the physical limitations of his ephemeral condition.

It is within this movement to 'intégrer l'encyclopédie aristotélicienne assimilée par le Moyen âge, à l'élan vers la beauté divine qui caractérise le néo-platonisme' (H. Weber, I, p. 33), that Ronsard adheres to the ideal of universal knowledge as a means of transcending human mortality and of releasing the soul from the stifling prison of bodily matter into which it fell after the original sin of *hubris* (VIII, 168; 253; XVIII, 471–2). True to the belief in human perfectibility voiced by Pico della Mirandola and others, Ronsard depicts man in the full realisation of his intellectual capabilities in all domains. Sensitive to man's position at the centre of the universe, Ronsard is conscious that the miracle of the world was accomplished for the pleasure of man as king of creation and that as such he is equal to the divine and angelic powers (VIII, 61–2; 209). Confident of man's god-like presence, Ronsard enumerates the aids which Nature daily dispenses to him, whilst at the same time demonstrating how man realises his full potential and attains mastery over the physical world by his own efforts, by technical, scientific and industrial knowledge, discoveries and inventions, divination and magic (VIII, 155–8). It is this vast knowledge which Ronsard enthusiastically praises in a hymn to Ancient Greece of 1565 (XIII, 137–8), and it is this same intellectual crown which, obeying the law of *translatio studii*, he now sees as having passed to France (II, 63; III, 46; XIII, 113, var.).

In his *Hymne de la Philosophie* (1555: VIII, 87–96), and again in shortened versions in his *Hymne de l'Hyver* (1563: XII, 70–1) and the *Panegyrique de la Renommée* (1579: XVIII, 10–12), Ronsard proposes nothing less than a comprehensive review of the whole of artistic, scientific and technical knowledge available to man, and, at the same time, describes his own programme as philosopher-poet. This encyclopedic knowledge is what men '... pouvoient, sans estre Dieux, comprendre' (VIII, 97), because Philosophy, the synthesis of all arts and sciences in the sixteenth century, enables man to transcend the mortality of his condition, attain perfectibility, dominate the physical world and '... l'elevant par esprit jusqu'aux Cieux, / Le fais repaistre à la table des Dieux' (VIII, 102, var.), where he finally reaches communion with God and the extralunar world, ordinarily beyond human comprehension:

> Elle, voyant qu'à l'homme estoit nyé
> D'aller au Ciel, disposte, a delié
> Loing, hors du corps, nostre Ame emprisonnée,

Et par esprit aux astres l'a menée,
Car en dressant de nostre Ame les yeux,
Haute, s'attache aux merveilles des Cieux,
Vaguant par tout, & sans estre lassée
Tout l'Univers discourt en sa pensée,
Et seulle peut des astres s'alïer
Osant de DIEU la nature espïer.[7]

In a note to his commentary on the 1609 edition, Richelet explains
that this passage 'est imité, voire traduit du livre du *Monde*, chap. I, de
quelque auteur que soit ce livre', and Laumonier reproduces a French
translation of the corresponding lines from the paraphrase of this
pseudo-Aristotelian treatise by Apuleius (VIII, 87, n. 2). At the same time,
it has been noted, the ideas of human excellence and the elevation of
the soul to God through universal knowledge are notions familiar to
Ronsard from multiple neo-Platonic sources. The wide currency of these
ideas at the time is clearly attested by Louis Le Roy's commentary on
Plato's *Symposium* (1558), and, more specifically, by a passage of
Manilius, *Astronomica*, which du Bellay translated for Le Roy's work
and which provides a close parallel with Ronsard's attitude in the *Hymne
de la Philosophie*:

Nature desormais ne nous est plus cachée,
Toute, en tout, & par tout nous l'avons recherchée :
Nous jouyssons du monde, ainsi que l'ayant pris,
Nous avons en esprit nostre pere compris,
Comme estans une part de l'essence divine,
Et retournons au ciel qui est nostre origine.
Qui doubte ce grand Dieu en noz cœurs sejourner?
L'ame venir du ciel, & au ciel retourner?[8]

Similarly, in an elegy of 1559 Ronsard describes the liberation of the
soul and its elevation to the heavens during sleep, and then proceeds to
enumerate at length the many areas of knowledge communicated to
man during his dreams after the soul's return to the body (X, 103-4. Cf.
I, 145-6; VIII, 126). It is this 'science honorable', this 'savoir venerable',
which is an important aspect of Ronsard's conception of *vertu* and
poetry and which, at the same time, equates man with God.[9] It is at such
moments of enthusiasm for the transcendental power of knowledge that
Ronsard, echoing Ficino's 'Man is assuredly God on earth', will write in
1560: '... rien plus sainct que l'homme au monde ne peut naistre' (X,
321. Cf. VIII, 213; XV, 47) or similarly in 1567:

L'homme est vrayement divin, savant, ingenieux,
Et sur tous animaux le plus semblable aux Dieux.
Parfaict en son divers
                    (XV, 372)

and again in 1584: '«Celuy est presque Dieu qui cognoist toutes choses' (XVIII, 34).

Within this neo-Platonic aim to surpass human mortality through intellectual perfection, the poet occupies an enviable position for he in particular has access to this encyclopedic knowledge. According to Plato, *Phaedrus* and *Ion*, and multiple neo-Platonic commentaries,[10] poetic 'madness' harmonises the dissonant soul—a function originally attributed to music in Plato—and awakens the mind to knowledge.[11] Whilst the poetic 'madness' is only the first of four progressive 'madnesses' in neo-Platonic doctrine, Ronsard tends to ignore the subtle distinctions of this mystical hierarchy and attribute all the virtues of the subsequent stages to the divinely inspired poet (I, 144–5; III, 139; XIV, 4–5). Thus the true poet, like the legendary Orpheus[12] and Eumolpus, is an intermediary between God and man, a priest, sibyl and prophet, the interpreter of the mysteries of Nature and the heavens, and it is this knowledge which will ultimately lead to his conquest over the physical world and his mortality, and to the elevation of the soul to divine contemplation. These ideas, which are an essential aspect of the musical humanism of Baïf and Tyard,[13] are consistently and emphatically expressed in their poetic context in Ronsard's work: they are found in an early ode to du Bellay (1550: I, 144–7), in the Pindaric ode *A Michel de l'Hospital* (1552: III, 138–46) and in the opening movements of the *Hymne des Astres* (1555: VIII, 150) and the *Hymne de l'Eternité* (1556: VIII, 246). They occur again in an elegy to Jacques Grévin (1561: XIV, 196–7), in certain lines of the *Responce aux injures & calomnies* (1563: XI, 121), in a passage from the *Hymne de l'Autonne* of the same year, where Ronsard's love of accumulation and balanced twinning is once again illustrated

> . . . une fureur d'esprit,
> . . . un don de Poësie,
> Que Dieu n'a concedé qu'à l'esprit agité
> Des poignans aiguillons de sa divinité.
>   Quand l'homme en est touché, il devient un prophete,
> Il predit toute chose avant qu'elle soit faite,
> Il cognoist la nature, & les secrets des cieux,
> Et d'un esprit boüillant s'esleve entre les Dieux.
> Il cognoist la vertu des herbes & des pierres,
> Il enferme les vents, il charme les tonnerres,
> Sciences que le peuple admire, & ne scait pas
> Que Dieu les va donnant aux hommes d'icy-bas,
> Quand ils ont de l'humain les ames separées
>   (XII, 46–7)

as well as in the *Art Poëtique François* (1565: XIV, 4–5), *La Lyre* (1569: XV, 17–22), and an elegy of 1584 (XVIII, 120–1). Thus poetry is an en-

cyclopedia of all human knowledge, and the poet has access to all intellectual experience: 'tantost il est Philosophe, tantost Medecin,
Arboriste, Anatomiste, & Jurisconsulte' (XVI, 336. Cf. I, 146; XIV, 10; XVI,
340).

Although Ronsard may occasionally, and for a variety of reasons,
reject poetic immortality,[14] he never questions divine 'madness' as a
means of acquiring knowledge and of transcending human mortality:
this is a domain of intellectual activity which remains beyond censure
or qualification. Nevertheless, whilst his abandonment is neither total
nor definitive, on isolated occasions, and more particularly within the
context of the worsening religious conflict, Ronsard will momentarily
question certain other aspects of the neo-Platonic ideal of human perfectibility and spiritual elevation through knowledge, and will seriously
cast doubts on the wisdom of reason and intellectual activity to seek to
contemplate the Divinity and discover his mysteries. Ronsard's reservations concerning this ideal date from 1560 and are largely explained by
reference to his preoccupation with the concept of *hubris* as an element
of social and cosmic instability. Certain passages from *La Vertu Amoureuse* (X, 342–3) and the *Elegie à Robert de la Haye* of 1560 parody neo-
Platonic lexis, and show that man's ceaseless search for knowledge and
his attempt to transcend his mortality and equate himself with God
through the intellect, are clearly associated in Ronsard's mind with presumption. At the same time the following extract from the *Elegie* demonstrates yet again the poet's preference for certain stylistic and
structural features—here illustrated by his use of repeated infinitives,
often linked by the *et vouloir* formula, to produce the effect of a catalogue; the structure *Car si nous congnoissions . . . Si nous cognoissions,*
which firmly holds together the long, complex second sentence; the constant pairing of items by the emphatic *et* pattern within many of the
lines; certain echoing word groups (*toutes choses . . . toutes choses . . .
les choses; la nature . . . nostre nature; veoir . . . eslongnés de nos yeux;*
the series of *toutes* and *tout*)—and these give the verse its characteristic *libre contrainte,* its simultaneous movement and measure, diversity
and cohesion:

> Que sert (dit Salomon) toutes choses entendre,
> Rechercher la nature & la vouloir comprendre,
> Mourir dessus un livre, & vouloir tout scavoir,
> Vouloir parler de tout, & toutes choses veoir,
> Et vouloir nostre esprit par estude contraindre
> A monter jusqu'au ciel où il ne peut atteindre?
> Tout n'est que vanité & pure vanité :
> Tel desir est bourreau de nostre humanité,
> Car si nous congnoissions nous & nostre nature,

Et que nous sommes faicts d'une matiere impure,

. . .

Si nous cognoissions bien que nous n'avons point d'esles
Pour voller au sejour des choses supernelles,
Nous ne serions jamais songneux ni curieux
D'apprendre les secrets eslongnés de nos yeux :
Ains contans de la terre, & des traces humaines,
Vivrions, sans affecter les choses si hautaines.

(x, 318. Cf. xv, 310–11)

Although Ronsard had been sensitive to the association of *hubris* and knowledge in earlier collections (II, 109–10; 170; V, 86; 253; VIII, 220), these more developed and emphatic statements of 1560 must be read in conjunction with those passages from the *Remonstrance au peuple de France* (1563 : XI, 64–5; 71–2), in which Ronsard attacks the intellectual arrogance of theological debate, demonstrates the inability of human reason to understand God's mysteries and redefines the legitimate provinces open to human enquiry so as to include natural and physical phenomena but to exempt the divine. Clearly Ronsard's censure of the doctrine of intellectual elevation is not so much an attack on knowledge *per se*[15] as a criticism of the arrogance of theological discussion, with its attendant reformist innovations, schism and social disorder. It is surely within the context of the religious and political chaos in France that one can best understand why Ronsard subordinates the intellectual to the moral virtues in his speech delivered at the *Académie du Palais* in 1576 (XVIII, 451–60).

Similarly it is the restrictions that Ronsard imposes on the ideal of human perfectibility through knowledge, his sensitivity to *hubris* and his fideism concerning religious matters which provide the essential framework for the more general dissatisfaction with human reason which manifests itself tentatively in 1559 (x, 34), and which a year later dominates the *Epitafe d'André Blondet* (x, 309–10) and the *Elegie à Robert de la Haye* (x, 315–17. Cf. XIV, 182–3). Again it is this same suspicion of reason and of man's ambitious search for knowledge which in part explains Ronsard's nostalgic preoccupation with the Age of Gold and his sympathy—reminiscent of that of Rousseau—for the primitive ignorance, innocence and happiness of the noble savage which is so forcibly and extensively expressed in the *Complainte contre Fortune* of 1559 (x, 33–5. Cf. XVIII, 458). This sympathy for the noble savage is based on a realisation that knowledge and ambition are perversions of man's natural ignorance and goodness, and that the divisive and discordant influence of civilisation, with its concepts of property and possessions, its legal system and government, and its progressively technical and industrial society, is a direct consequence of Prometheus's original sin of *hubris*.

Thus the religious situation in France in 1559–60, his sensitivity to the association of knowledge and *hubris* and his awareness that theological discussion threatened to impinge on the divine prerogatives, all resulted in certain reservations concerning the ideal of encyclopedic knowledge in the verse of Ronsard. These reservations, however, were restricted essentially to theological enquiry, were short-lived[16] and were, perhaps, to a certain degree circumstantial, official and tactical in inspiration. Having redefined his limits of intellectual curiosity to exclude divine mysteries, Ronsard continues to subscribe to the doctrine of human perfectibility and poetic 'madness' as valid means of transcending mortality and of elevating the soul to perfect knowledge and to God.

MEANS OF TRANSCENDING DEATH BY LOVE

It has already been noted in the brief *exposé* of neo-Platonism that the conquest of mortality and the ascent of the soul to unity and divine communion are achieved by four progressive 'furies', the last of which is Love. For Ficino and his disciples, human love is a process of mutual spiritual perfectionment and is the means by which the soul transcends the limitations of bodily imperfection, and finally returns to the divine light, its former abode.[17] Although Ronsard is conversant with the subtleties of the mystical theory, on the whole he chooses not to make the distinction between the four 'furies', but prefers to assimilate the erotic 'madness' (the last stage) into the poetic (the first), either specifically (IV, 30–1, s. XXVII) or in a general association of knowledge, inspiration, ardour and creative energy (IV, 141, s. CXLVI; V, 130–1, s. XCV; XVII, 308, s. XXV).

Whilst elements of this transcendental conception of love can be found in the work of practically every member of the Pléiade, extreme caution must be exercised when considering how fundamental neo-Platonism is to the essential vision of individual poets and to what extent it can be said to offer them any sort of consolation or salvation for human mortality. It is important to decide how much credence they themselves attach to the conquest of love over human transience, how consistently and emphatically they adhere to the mystical doctrines, and to what degree their neo-Platonism is the expression of their authentic voice or simply a concession to contemporary fashion or literary convention.

The evidence of Ronsard's antagonism towards neo-Platonic love doctrines is conclusive and well documented.[18] However, a chronological

study of his Platonistic statements and a close analysis of certain recurrent ideas and associated word patterns will reveal an interesting
dimension to his antipathy and a significant evolution of attitude and
emphasis. Without exception Ronsard's neo-Platonic pronouncements
in the *Amours de Cassandre* express the idea that spiritual love perfects,
activates and elevates the lethargic and heavy matter of the body :

> Ainsi mon tout erroit seditieux
>> Dans le giron de ma lourde matiere,
>> Sans art, sans forme, & sans figure entiere,
>> Alors qu'Amour le perça de ses yeulx.
> Il arondit de mes affections
>> Les petitz corps en leurs perfections,
>> Il anima mes pensers de sa flamme.
> Il me donna la vie, & le pouvoyr,
>> Et de son branle il fit d'ordre mouvoyr
>> Les pas suyviz du globe de mon ame.
>
> (IV, 45, S. XLII)

This insistence on love as a creative energy, as a life-giving force, is
evoked here, as elsewhere in the Platonistic sonnets of the collection, by
repeated word clusters, many of them active verbs, centred on items of
light, birth, warmth ('. . . le desir me r'allume les feux, / Qui languis-
soyent desoubz la morte braize' : s. CXLVI) and movement (s. LXII; LXXII;
CXXX; CXXXIX). Sonnet CLXXIV progresses in an ascending spiral from
concepts of inactivity and death (*lentement otieux*) to ideas of light
(*l'esclair, divine flamme*), movement (*vol, esleve, aisla, vola, epoin-
conné*), warmth (*enflamme*) and ultimate activity (*d'otieux actif je me
suis fait*), whilst sonnet XCV of the 1553 edition (V, 130–1) similarly
turns from associations of death and lethargy ('Morne de cors, & plus
morne d'espris / Je me trainoi' dans une masse morte') to those of
activity, with its lexical repetition of *faire* in the sestet.

This conception of spiritual love as an animating energy is essentially
restricted to the *Amours* of 1552–3, although it makes a brief reappearance in 1569 in Ronsard's two *apparently* most unambiguous and emphatic neo-Platonic statements—the speech of *Amour* in the *Discours
d'un amoureux deseperé* (XV, 97–102) and the *Cartel fait promtement
contre l'amour mondain* (XV, 110–14). However, it would be unwise to
attach too much value to these two pieces, for they are not only obvious
literary exercises devoid of conviction but they contain within themselves the seeds of their own negation and self-parody.[19]

What is most significant is that the neo-Platonic themes of the *Sonets
pour Helene* of 1578 (Book I, s. IV, XIX, XLV; Book II, s. XI, XXXVI), besides
being concessions to literary fashion and to the lady of the moment, are
also vastly different in tone and treatment from those of the *Amours de*

Cassandre. Most of the Platonistic sonnets of the 1578 collection deal with aesthetic considerations in that they describe Hélène as a paragon of moral and physical perfection, a reflection of the Ideal Beauty. Gone are the references to the soul activating the body, apart from a single brief allusion (XVII, 256, s. XI). Gone too are statements of the transcendental value of spiritual love and the related idea of the soul's ascension to the Ideal World—an idea parodied in an earlier poem of 1578 (XVII, 147–8) and rejected in the *Ode au Roy Charles luy donnant un Leon Hebrieu* of 1575 (XVII, 61–2), where Ronsard distinguishes between the two Erotes and expresses a preference for the earthly, popular Aphrodite Pandemos.

Complementing this change of emphasis in his Platonistic vision there is a reversal of attitude compared with that of 1552–3, for the mystical idealism of neo-Platonic love doctrine is now associated with death, with a betrayal of life's activity, with deception and vanity. For Ronsard life is always described in terms of movement, energy and action (see especially, XVIII, 248), whilst death, seen as a negation of these values, is linked to items of lethargy and inactivity. More precisely, certain lines which are contemporaneous with the Hélène collection equate death with deception, illusion, lack of substance and reality:

La mort soudaine m'a deceu :
Pour le vray le faux j'ay receu,
Et pour le corps seulement l'ombre.[20]

This idea of deception, the 'vray/faux' antithesis and their associations with death, reappear in the *Sonets pour Helene* within the context of Ronsard's several attacks on the etheral love philosophy of the neo-Platonists :

Bien que l'esprit humain s'enfle par la doctrine
De Platon, qui le chante influxion des cieux,
Si est-ce sans le corps qu'il seroit ocieux,
Et auroit beau vanter sa celeste origine.
    Par les sens l'ame voit, ell'oyt, ell' imagine,
Ell' a ses actions du corps officieux :
L'esprit incorporé devient ingenieux,
La matiere le rend plus parfait & plus digne.
    Or' vous aimez l'esprit, & sans discretion
Vous dites que des corps les amours sont pollues.
Tel dire n'est sinon qu'imagination,
    Qui embrasse le faux pour les choses cognues :
Et c'est renouveller la fable d'Ixion,
Qui se paissoit de vent, & n'aimoit que des nues.
                              (Book I, s. XLI)

Contrary to the 1552–3 statements, the perfecting and energising power is now given to the body, for without the active physical aspect the soul would be 'dead' (*ocieux*). Similarly line 12 and the subsequent myth not only contradict an earlier and more spiritual interpretation of the same fable (XVII, 182, Madrigal 1), but clearly link the idealism of neo-Platonism with death within the context of the 'vray/faux' definition quoted above.

The following sonnet XLII also evokes the primacy of the body over the soul, as do other poems of 1578 (XVII, 190, s. XII; 213, s. XX), and equates neo-Platonism with death and deception by the use of lexical emphasis (*vent, songe, feintise, sottise, vanité, discours fantastiq'*) and the reappearance of the 'vray/faux' pattern ('Je n'aime point le faux, j'aime la verité'). Yet another sonnet (Book II, s. XXV: cf. XV, 216) attacks the concept of honour— a cardinal feature of neo-Platonic love doctrine —by employing an identical vocabulary of betrayal and deception (*imposture, faussement, resveurs, trompez, faites injure, pipe, faux, ombre, sotte, vaine, sots*) before reaching the now familiar conclusion: 'Je ne veux pour le faux tromper la chose vraye'. Identical word clusters to those found in the Hélène collection reoccur in the sonnet, first published in 1609, in which Ronsard pours scorn on Leone Ebreo and calls his love philosophy 'fabuleux . . . fiction: / Faux, trompeur, mensonger, pleine de fraude & d'astuce' (XVIII, 314, s. LXIII). Texts of 1565 (XIII, 261), 1569—'Par le plaisir faut *tromper* le trespas' (XV, 221)—and a variant of 1578—'Gaignon ce jour icy, *trompon* nostre trespas' (VII, 131, s. XIII, var.)—add yet another poetic dimension to Ronsard's epicurean pleas by suggesting that he had decided to fight the deception of death with its own weapons. These considerations even extend into other areas of Ronsard's periodic criticisms of Plato, for although the Greek philosopher remains one of his favourite authors (XVII, 316, s. XXXVI, var.; XVIII, 33), and although it is essentially the intangible and illusory love doctrines of the neo-Platonists he attacks, he will nevertheless question certain areas of Plato's thought where there is a discrepancy between teaching and practice, and where the abstract theory remains *oysive* since it is not translated into practical action (VIII, 171; XIV, 186; XVII, 248, s. I).

Thus Ronsard's early flirtation with neo-Platonic love doctrine, his change of emphasis and vision, and his forthright rejections of 1578 all point to a consistent preoccupation with concepts of activity and lethargy, life and death (and its associated pattern of deception: 'faux/ vray'). It is not surprising that Ronsard looks to less ethereal and mystical ways by which love survives death. Whilst we shall soon find ourselves on the fringe of those numerous Petrarchist *concetti* which link love and death, and whilst it is doubtful whether these can be said to offer any real consolation to the poet in his attempt to perpetuate or surpass his mortality, nevertheless a number of these motifs do constitute a philosophy of memory in so far as the very strength of the passion experienced is seen to ensure its survival beyond death. To express the binding intensity of the union of love in an elegy of 1567, Ronsard has recourse to the image of the vine enlacing the tree—a traditional motif of Latin, neo-Latin and Italian verse, much favoured in turn by the Pléiade :

> ... j'ay le cœur lié
> Au vostre ainsi qu'une vigne se lie
> Quand de ses bras aux ormeaux se marie,
> Lien qui peut, tant il est dur & fort,
> Rompre les mains du tombeau de la mort.[21]

A variation of this theme is the idea, found originally in Propertius and adapted by Petrarch, that love engraves itself so deeply on the poet-lover's heart or mind that it survives passing time and death.[22] In the more sensual contexts of his kiss poems, the image of the enlacing of the tree by ivy or the vine and the conceit of the *baiser à l'italienne*, with its motifs of death, resurrection and exchange of souls, combine to suggest the intensity of the embrace and the perpetual nature of the kiss : these in turn are seen to survive death in the idyllic perpetuation of earthly existence which constitutes Ronsard's vision of the Elysian Fields (I, 248–51; XVII, 235–6). For Ronsard it is this same passion which perpetuates love beyond death by recalling the deceased in a vivid nocturnal dream which defies time ('Aussi vivante, & aussi belle / Comme elle estoit le premier jour': XVII, 130), whilst elsewhere the mutual intensity and the close marriage of souls in love survive death as an example of perfection for future generations (X, 242–3).

Another aspect of this same power of passion which found particular favour with Ronsard was the motif, borrowed from Ovid, of the lover inhaling the last breath of the beloved in a desperate attempt to assimilate the remains of the soul into his own body and thus to perpetuate the union beyond death :

> Icy pleuroit ta mere, icy pleuroit ta femme,
> Qui tristes ramassoient le reste de ton ame.
> Errant dessus ta bouche, & les yeux te fermoient,
> Te regardoient passer, & à longs traicts humoient
> Ta vie et ton esprit, maugré la mort voysine
> Pour, en lieu d'un tombeau, les mettre en leur poitrine.[23]

Elsewhere it is the depth of suffering associated with both love and death which sharpens memory and ensures survival (XV, 295–302; XVII, 127–31), whilst for Ronsard the best chance of perpetuating the memory of love beyond the tomb and of transcending death lies, as always, in integrating the suffering of the dying lover into the eternal cycles of nature:

Vous ruisseaux, vous rochers, vous antres solitaires,
Vous chesnes, heritiers du silence des bois,
Entendez les souspirs de ma derniere vois,
Et de mon testament soyez presents notaires.
  Soyez de mon mal-heur fideles secretaires,
Gravez le en vostre escorce, afin que tous les mois
Il croisse comme vous : ce pendant je m'en vois
Là bas privé de sens, de veines, & d'arteres.
(XVIII, 218, S. LXXVI)

Perhaps more personal and unexpected is the unwillingness of Ronsard to interpret the Orpheus–Eurydice myth as a symbol of the conquest of love over death. Nowhere do we find the legend used, as in Scève (*Délie*, CCCCXLV), to affirm the immortality of a virtuous love : instead Ronsard denies the validity of the myth as a statement of love's victory over death either by inference or by explicit reference.[24] Indeed one of Ronsard's final allusions to Orpheus, made significantly in the same year (1578) as one of his most categorical refutations of the symbolic value of the myth, emphasises him as a figure of inconstancy in love and insists heavily on the successful consolation he found for the loss of Eurydice in the arms of Calaïs (XVII, 322).

This rejection of the conventional significance of the Orpheus–Eurydice story enables us to appreciate the full value and complexity of Ronsard's epicureanism, for as Eva Kushner has remarked : '. . . Orphée bravant la mort pour son amour n'a plus aucune place dans une poésie où l'amour est si fortement lié à la vie terrestre et au pathétique de l'instant . . . Rien de moins orphique que cette conception d'un amour sans immortalité, amour exactement lié à la durée . . .'.[25] Ronsard may allow love's conquest over mortality through the intensity of memory —although his interpretation of the Orpheus myth and his description of the conduct of Venus after the death of Adonis suggest that the survival may well be brief (XII, 125–6; XVII, 322)—but elsewhere he categorically denies that love is any guarantee against death (XVII, 122; 138), and more generally prefers to make a clear distinction between life and death in matters of love (VII, 126, s. IX; XII, 276). As a sensualist and realist he is suspicious of mystical conceptions of love's immortality, preferring instead what is active, tangible and present. Since 'Apres la mort on ne voit rien qui plaise' (XV, 195, s. II); since death is essentially the termination of sensation, pleasure and beauty, it must also mean the absence of love ('Amour ne sçauroit vivre entre les morts d'enfer': x, 97, s. XII).

To waste life and deny love is therefore to anticipate death in time, to condemn oneself to a living death—'. . . & mesmes notre vie / Est une mort, si de toy [i.e. love] n'est suivie' (XVI, 143). It is another example of the constant penetration of death into life: 'Vivre sans volupté c'est vivre sous la terre' (XVII, 319, s. XL. Cf. VII, 124, s. VII). The act of love is thus a small but concrete victory over time and mortality ('Gaignon ce jour icy, trompon nostre trespas': VII, 131, s. XIII, var.). It is not surprising, therefore, to find that all obstacles to love are invariably associated with death. In the following sonnet of 1569, which has close affinities with certain lines of a poem of 1564 (XII, 264–5), the lady's frigidity parallels the coldness of the tomb, for she is described as a death force in terms normally reserved for the goddess Death ('En lieu d'un cœur tu portes un rocher', 'Farouche, fiere . . . fiere en cruauté': cf. XII, 266–7; XV, 302). Her disdain is a denial of life, activity, warmth (*languir froide*) and her *jeune sang*, and her absence of passion and feeling withers the poet (*desecher*), thereby echoing descriptions of death elsewhere ('un squelette seiché', XVIII, 222; 'mort & seq', XVIII, 413) and prefiguring the insentient *cendre* of the corpse in line 14 of this sonnet. It is in the context of this complex and poetic interweaving of antithetical forces and affirmative and negative verbs that the epicurean plea, developed freely from an erotic epigram of Asclepiades, achieves its ultimate conviction:

Douce beauté meurdriere de ma vie,
En lieu d'un cœur tu portes un rocher:
Tu me fais vif languir & desecher,
Passionné d'une amoureuse envie.
    Le jeune sang qui d'aymer te convie,
N'a peu de toy la froideur arracher,
Farouche, fiere, & qui n'as rien plus cher
Que languir froide, & n'estre point servie;
    Aprens à vivre, ô fiere en cruauté,
Ne garde point à Pluton ta beauté,
Quelque peu d'aise en aimant il faut prendre,
    Il faut tromper doucement le trespas,
Car aussi bien sous la terre là bas
Sans rien sentir le corps n'est plus que cendre.[26]

It was with an artistic feeling for the architecture of the 1584 edition that Ronsard followed this sonnet, transferred to the *Amours de Cassandre* in 1578, with the ode *Quand au temple nous serons* (1554: VI, 218–20), for this ode develops identical themes and motifs by contaminating the same Greek epigram with passages from Secundus, *Elegiae*, I, v (cf. Laumonier, *RPL*, pp. 527–30). Here Cassandre's coldness is seen in terms of religious asceticism in the three wholly original opening stanzas, and her nun-like refusal of life and pleasure is associated with deception and described as a prefiguration of the enclosed tomb ('Pourquoi ... / Contrefais-tu la nonnain / Dedans un cloistre enfermée?'). This in turn provides the essential inspiration for the epicurean plea and for the simultaneous vision of beauty and ugliness, life and death, present and future time—an antithetical symmetry already established in the first two stanzas of the ode, with the contrasting behaviour of the lovers in church and in bed, and supported throughout by patterns of negative and affirmative verbs. A year later (1555) Ronsard associates other obstacles to love—chastity (VI, 213) and fidelity (VII, 126, s. IX; 142–3, s. XXV)—with ideas of death, coldness, illness, old age and inactivity.

This present section has fallen from the mystical heights of Christian-Platonism to Ronsard's several confrontations with Pluto and to his epicurean rejection of the immortality of love and of all obstacles to immediate pleasure (asceticism, chastity, fidelity). Paradoxically, both attitudes have a common starting point, centre on identical preoccupations (death/life, lethargy/activity, 'faux/vray') and result from a similar wish to transcend, perpetuate or escape human mortality by love.

MEANS OF TRANSCENDING DEATH BY POETRY: POETIC IMMORTALITY

Reference has already been made to certain aspects of the immortality of the written word. It has been shown that for Ronsard poetic 'madness' is the means by which the poet transcends his mortality and the sublunar world of flux, elevates his soul to God and pure knowledge and performs his social function as prophet and interpreter of the divine mysteries. Similarly Ronsard's philosophy of history is frequently linked to the principles of *translatio imperii* and *translatio studii*, the latter being based on the preservation and transference of the collective glory —the cultural and spiritual heritage—of a race or nation. Again Ronsard's interpretation of human metamorphosis as a victory over time and death is often associated with the transcendental values of the creative mind, and of the immortality of poetry in particular.

The Pléiade's conception of poetic immortality is complex, and of the several critics who have devoted studies to this aspect it is Françoise Joukovsky who has placed the theme of *gloire* (both collective and individual) in its social and historical context, traced its evolution from the *Rhétoriqueurs* to d'Aubigné, and clearly demonstrated that the originality of Ronsard and his friends is not so much in respect of themes, motifs or symbols, which they had largely inherited from classical and national traditions, but rather in respect of tone, emphasis and poetic expression.[27]

The aim of this present section is not to duplicate previous research and to catalogue those numerous occasions on which Ronsard returns to the theme of poetry's conquest over transience,[28] but rather to concentrate on the manner in which poetic immortality is invariably described in his verse not as an abstract or general concept, but as an animate and animating power, a dynamic and concrete force for preservation. The confrontation between poetic immortality and the forces of destruction is seen in terms of an active continuing struggle, which is a microcosm of the wider cosmic pattern of flux and stability. A study of Ronsard's variants relevant to poetic fame demonstrates how his modifications, although only slight when considered individually, collectively point to a common aim, which is to emphasise and dramatise the antithesis between preservation and corruption. Sometimes in correcting his *editio princeps* and achieving his definitive version, Ronsard creates a confrontation between transience and immortality where originally there had been no such contrast.[29] On other occasions an implied opposition is rendered explicit in a variant by the introduction of a particular force of mutability,[30] or else one element of instability is substituted for another in order to clarify and strengthen the sense (II, 125, ll. 16–18, var.). Again a second aspect of transience may be added to stress an already existing antithesis more forcibly (xv, 38, ll. 463–8, var.).

The same active and concrete nature of this conflict between death and poetic fame is expressed in a complex and dense series of antithetical images, metaphors, symbols and motifs which are present throughout the entire corpus of Ronsard's work. On one side of the confrontation, and within a general tendency towards personification and allegory, death is often described as an active and aggressive force—'la mort boiteuse te suit . . . te menasse', 'la mort qui talonne vos pas'.[31] Death is seen alternately as stalking her prey (VII, 102), extending her hand over her victims (II, 108), welcoming her guests (VII, 103), striking with weapons (XVIII, 177, s. I). Verbs such as *ravir, abattre, accabler, couper, trancher, dévorer* are used to evoke the vivid nature of death's attack, and 'la Mort mangetout' is said to have a ravenous appetite (II, 109; V, 214). She is heartless and unfeeling, without human senses—she is deaf and blind—or blood (VIII, 175; XII, 266–7). Because death entails the absence of sensation and substance ('. . . de nous il ne reste, / . . . que la cendre & l'oubly': x, 80, s. XIV), it is associated essentially with a denial of the very needs and qualities of a living organism. Death is at once seen as the negation of light and sun: '. . . plus il ne verra la plaisante lumiere / De nostre beau soleil', 'banis . . . / Dedans une nasselle obscure', 'Noir, sombre & froid, que le Soleil evite', 'ma lumiere / Du tout estainte en une nuit derniere', 'le cercueil tenebreux, / . . . la Parque noire' (VII, 94; XIII, 261; XIV, 117; XV, 225; 373); the absence of warmth :

> . . . quand la paleur
> Qui blesmist nostre corps sans chaleur ne lumiere
> Nous perd le sentiment! quand la main filandiere
> Nous oste le desir perdans nostre chaleur!
> (XVIII, 219, S. LXXVII)

of colour :

> . . . tout à l'entour la mort pale y demeure,
> Toujours un peuple gresle autour d'un lac y pleure
> Ayant la peau brulée, & les cheveux cendreux,
> Le visage plombé, les yeux mornes & creux
> (VI, 209)

and of freedom of movement, for death is invariably referred to in terms suggesting claustrophobia and oppressive weight, 'Rhadamante a là bas / La main & la bouche pesante', 'tombeau pressant leur memoire',

> Des elements confus les accablantes sommes
> De tout animal né vont le corps oppressant,
> De moment en moment changeant & perissant,
> (VI, 196; XIII, 258; XVIII, 46)

enclosure, imprisonment,

> . . . la sepulture
> Presse soubz mesme closture
> Le corps, la vie, & le nom
> (III, 80)

and asphyxiation : '. . . si fort en ses neuds l'entortille & le serre / Qu'à la fin, mort & seq, trebuche contre Terre' (XVIII, 413). Using the same lexis of imprisonment and claustrophobia, the corpse is pictured alternately 'Dans la tumbe, / Sejour aveugle & reclus', 'Au creux d'une tombe enfoüye', 'dedans la fange noire / De Styx', 'Plongez au plus profond de l'onde / Du Styx' (III, 194; VII, 282; IX, 34; XIII, 258), or ready to be swallowed,

> . . . jusqu'au fond
> De la gorge la plus profonde
> De ce ventre le plus profond.
> (III, 130).

The verbs *engloutir, serrer, enserrer, enfermer, enclore, enfouir, ensevelir, enfondrer* are frequently used to evoke the same atmosphere of stifling enclosure.

In the same way death is described as withered, parched and sere ('Un squelette seiché': XVIII, 222). It is also a denial of activity (XVIII, 248) and, like old age, has its own vocabulary of inaction and lethargy, *oubli* and torpor—'fosse inutile', 'oublieus tumbeau', 'tombeau paresseux', 'languiroit d'oubly' (I, 228; II, 88; XIII, 72; XVII, 285, s. XLIX). Favourite word patterns include *languir, oisif, oyseux, debile, otieux, faillir, assoupir, sans force, sans vigueur, sans mouvement*. This evocation of absence in death, this oblivion, void, immobility of the tomb is paralleled by its total silence ('le silence endormi', 'l'envieus silence': I, 99; II, 151), a silence which is at once imprisoning and stifling—'Et une oblivieuse nue / Les tient sous un silence etrains' (I, 142)—cold, dark and heavy:

> ... du faix d'une tombe pesante,
> Dont la froideur aux hommes ne produit
> Que le Sommeil, le Silence, & la Nuit.
>
> (XIV, 119)

Contrasted on all levels with this evocation of death, either in the wider context of the poet's work or else, more particularly, within the same passage or movement, is the dynamic vision of poetic fame. The darkness of the tomb and forgetfulness is flooded with the light of immortality, the light of growth and fecundity. This comparison of fame with light can be found in Pindar and Horace and is a commonplace of Italian, neo-Latin and French poetry (Joukovsky, pp. 347–64): it finds special favour with the Pléiade, who take infinite pleasure in emphasising the brightness of immortality by multiplying their terms with dazzling luminosity. In 1555 Ronsard, for whom the sun is invariably a source of energy and fertility (XI, 66–7; XII, 52–3), promises Henri II that in his *Franciade* the king's '... vertus y luiront évidantes, / Comme luisent au ciel les étoilles ardantes' (VII, 33), in the same way as he had posed the following rhetorical question to François de Carnavalet in 1550:

> Quelle louange premiere
> T'ardera par l'univers,
> Flamboiant en la lumiere
> Que degorgeront mes vers?
>
> (I, 92)

Equally persistent is the way in which this metaphor is developed within the framework of an antithesis with the obscurity of death. In this

stanza from an ode to du Bellay the antithesis between light and darkness is densely supported by other contrasting patterns (*puissance/
Languist; n'est apparante/se montrer*) :

> La vertu qui n'a connoissance
> Combien la Muse a de puissance
> Languist en tenebreus sejour,
> Et en vain elle est soupirante
> Que sa clarté n'est apparante
> Pour se montrer aus rais du jour.
>
> (II, 36. Cf. I, 142; XIII, 61–2; 258)

Similarly the imprisonment, immobility and claustrophobia associated with the tomb are contrasted with the freedom of movement, the
Horatian metamorphosis of the poet into a swan and the soaring flight
of fame ('Tousjours tousjours, sans que jamais je meure / Je voleray
Cygne par l'Univers'[32]). This metaphor of flight, found frequently in
classical literature,[33] enables the poet to transcend the sublunar world
of flux and corruption, and to penetrate the celestial regions of im-
mutability and eternity :

> O BAÏF, la plume pronte
> Vouloir monter jusqu'aus dieus,
> D'un vol qui le ciel surmonte
> Trompe l'enfer odieus.
>
> (I, 131. Cf. I, 161; III, 54–5; XIII, 257)

In Ronsard's *Tombeau de Marguerite de Valois* (1551) the poet opposes
the stifling imprisonment of

> Ceulx qui meurent sans renom :
> Et desquelz la sepulture
> Presse soubz mesme closture
> Le corps, la vie, & le nom

with Marguerite's flight of release and freedom,

> Mais toi, dont la renommée
> Porte d'une aile animée
> Par le monde tes valeurs.
>
> (III, 80)

Poets '. . . se sont mis au dos des ailes / Pour voler eternellement' (I, 120),
and it is precisely this distinction between inaction and soaring movement, between death and life, which Ronsard sees as the essential difference between painting and poetry and as the reason for the latter's pre-
excellence :

Je n'ai pas les mains apprises
Au métier muet de ceus,
Qui font une image assise
Sus des piliers paresseus.

Ma painture n'est pas mue
Mais vive, & par l'univers
Guindée en l'air se remue
De sus l'engin de mes vers.
(II, 148–9)

It is within the same dynamic evocation of movement and flight that Ronsard adopts the Pindaric metaphor[34] of the poet as an archer:

La carriere du tens use
Les palais laborieus,
Non les trais victorieus
Venans de l'arc de ma muse.
(I, 162)

He boasts of having 'sous l'esselle un carquois / Gros de fleches nompareilles' (I, 73), and he assures Henri II that he will be

Le saint Harpeur de ta gloire,
Et l'archer de ta memoire
Pour la tirer dans les cieus.
(I, 62. Cf. II, 37)

Another aspect of this opposition to the immobility and torpor of death is the forceful vocabulary of action and aggressive movement associated with poetic immortality. Expressions such as 'resuscitez du tombeau paresseux', 'deterré … tirant leurs noms de l'obly', 'arracher vifs les hommes du tumbeau', 'arraché … des griffes de la mort … forceant le trespas' abound in the poetry of Ronsard (I, 234; XIII, 72; 258; XVIII, 61), and, together with numerous other verbs of action[35] and the tendency to multiply and accumulate images and metaphors, these underline the visual and dynamic nature of the struggle for survival:

Apres la mort un grand Roy n'est plus rien,
S'il n'est chanté d'une Muse animée,
Qui du tombeau ravist sa renommée,
Ne souffrant point qu'ainsi qu'un bucheron
Il aille boire aux rives d'Acheron:
Mais desrobant du trespas ses beaux gestes
D'homme l'envoye au nombre des celestes,
Et fait flamber son nom comme un Soleil.
(XIII, 61–2)

In the same way the tools of the poet are described as having qualities of action and life ('ancre qui combat', 'audacieuse encre', 'plume pronte', 'plume animée': I, 131; 140; V, 265; X, 105). Even memory, fame and poetry are endowed with movement and described as 'vagabonde' (II, 89; III, 55) or 'animée / Par le labeur de mes dois' (I, 92): the style of poetry itself has a strength and energy which contrast with the inaction and lethargy of death:

> Certes le fort & puissant stile
> Des Poëtes bien écrivans,
> Du creus de la fosse inutile
> Les a deterrés tous vivans.
> (I, 228)

If death is envisaged essentially as a denial of the needs of a living organism, poetic immortality is constantly evoked in terms of growth, as in Pindar and Horace,[36] and introduces the poet into the eternal natural cycles of fertility and germination. Everywhere fame is associated with a vocabulary (vif, animer, foisonner, fleurir, florir, semer) suggesting life and fecundity. Poetry is specifically qualified with the epithet faconde or fertile (I, 98; 180; III, 141; X, 23), and the poetic task is often evoked by a similar lexis of fertility.[37] Like Pindar (Nemean, I, antistr. 1; Isthmian, VI, antistr. 1) Ronsard pictures his fame sown as a seed, scattered all over France ('. . . la renommée / De tous costez en la France semée': XV, 17), Europe and the world (II, 89; XV, 24). Fame—often associated with warmth and heat ('Brulés de gloire & d'ardeur'; 'l'ardeur de leur faconde'; 'D'une flame divine allumer les esprits': I, 22; 145; XVIII, 91)— is watered by the 'large pluie feconde' of the Muses (I, 180): it germinates and grows as a plant, moving like a living organism to fill any empty space (III, 34), strengthening in a process which is at the same time accumulative and rejuvenating,

> Pour n'estre jamais finissant,
> Mais d'aage en aage verdissant
> Surmonter la mort & le change.
> (XIII, 258)

As in this extract certain repetitive formulae are designed to evoke fame's ever-strengthening pattern of growth and continuity,

> . . . c'est une richesse
> Qui par le tans ne s'use pas,
> Mais contre le tans elle dure,
> Et de siecle en siecle plus dure
> Ne donne point aus vers d'apas.
> (I, 140, var.)

Ronsard, ever-ready to link man's destiny with the more durable natural forces, introduces poetic fame into the cycles of human fertility, conception,

> Grossi-toi ma Muse Françoise,
> Et enfante un vers resonant,
> > (I, 236: cf. II, 121; VII, 115, var.)

and parenthood,

> Pourtant souvenez vous qu'*orfelins* de renom
> Diomede fust mort, Achille, Agamemnom,
> Sans la Muse d'Homere heureusement fertile
> > (XVII, 338, s. II)

as well as of seasonal fecundity,

> ... Troie est encor florissante
> Comme un beau printens, en renom.
> > (II, 176–7)

Glory, however, is considered to be superior to 'une fleur du renouveau' in so much as its growth is continual and it does not die to be reborn, 'Car tous les jours elle foisonne / En fruict qui n'a point son égal' (VI, 8), whilst the eternal flowers which mark the tomb bear witness to the fertilising power of fame: '... toujours renommés / Demeurent leurs tonbeaus de mile fleurs semés' (V, 213). Ronsard adds a whole poetic dimension of fertility and abundance to the lines of Horace which are his source ('On and on shall I grow, ever fresh with the glory of after time': *Odes*, III, xxx, 7–8: LCL, p. 279) when he visualises his fame absorbed into his native region, 'Eternizant les champs où je demeure / De mon renom engressés & couvers' (II, 153). On another occasion he achieves a Mallarmean density of suggestive associations when he accumulates his images and evokes the germination and maturation of the poet's 'vers doctes':

> Par eus la Parque est devancée,
> Ils ardent l'eternelle nuit,
> Tousjours fleurissans par le fruit
> Que la Muse ente en leur pensée.
> > (I, 112)

The freshness of Homer's presence is a living example of this fertilising process—'la Muse d'Homere heureusement fertile'—and in Ronsard's verse his fecundity is often seen in terms of light (XVII, 422) or as a spring which refreshes and inspires future generations :

> ... Homere,
> De qui, comme un ruisseau, d'âge en âge vivant
> La Muse va tousjours les Poetes abbruvant.
> (VIII, 181)

In another text Ronsard adapts an Ovidian reminiscence (*Amores*, III, ix, 25–6) and makes a proud declaration of his own 'plenitude' and 'fertile veine', which is clearly designed to equate him with Homer :

> ... car de ma plenitude
> Vous estes tous remplis ...
> Vous estes mes ruisseaux, je suis vostre fonteine,
> Et plus vous m'espuisés, plus ma fertile veine
> Repoussant le sablon, jette une source d'eaux
> D'un surjon eternel pour vous autres ruisseaux.
> (XI, 168–9)

For Ronsard, as for Pindar (*Nemean*, VII, ep. 3) and Horace (*Odes*, I, xx, 5–8; IV, ii, 5–24), water plays an important role in this symbolism of fertility and in the association of immortality with eternal natural cycles. Reference has already been made to the fact that Ronsard sees water as a generative principle, and if he relates fame so consistently to 'fontaines vives' and local rivers, it is not only because the *noise* of the running water has associations with poetic immortality as we shall soon discover, but because water is a symbol of life and movement, continuity and fecundity :

> Loir, dont le cours heureus distille
> Au sein d'un païs si fertile,
>   Fai bruire mon renom
>   D'un grand son en tes rives,
>   Qui se doivent voir vives
>   Par l'honneur de mon nom.[38]

Water symbolism is also frequently employed to evoke poetic purification and inspiration, as well as to differentiate between good and bad writers (III, 144–5; XII, 48–9; XV, 19–20). Similarly, in a vision of classical pantheism, Ronsard pictures the rivers and streams peopled by numerous rustic divinities (nymphs, sprites, 'belles Naiades / Oreades, & Dryades') and frequented by the Muses (I, 203–4; II, 129–30; V, 240) : thus by associating his fame with local waterways in this manner it is placed under the aegis of the natural and divine worlds. The stress on the local and 'paternal' context of the poet's immortality (I, 204; II, 105) is not gratuitous, for it contrasts with a lexis of exile and banishment frequently associated with death (I, 225; XIII, 261). In the final stanzas of an ode to Jacques Bouju of 1550, Ronsard evokes the widening perspective and gathering momentum of his fame as it flows from the Loire to the sea and then showers over the entire world like a fertilising, refreshing rain :

> Et le tournant en son onde
> Le rura dedans la mer,
> Affin que le vent au monde
> Le puisse par tout semer.
> (II, 89)

Similarly the commonplace motif of the poet's evergreen crown is not only a symbol of victory and eternity because of the aesthetic perfection of its unending circular form, but it also introduces the poet once more into the durable and fertile rhythms of natural vegetation. It is, appropriately, the 'Lorier sacré en tout temps verdissant' (XII, 36) which accompanies the victorious consecration of Ronsard and terminates the *Quatre premiers livres des Odes* (II, 153), whilst a later text not only demonstrates the poet's predilection for structural and lexical patterns which accumulate and catalogue (*ciel . . . mer . . . terre . . . le Soleil . . . La Lune*; the repetition of *couronne, rond, tout*; alternating affirmative and negative verbs), but it gives the symbolism of the crown its cosmic significance by equating him with the eternal, heavenly bodies :

> C'est pourquoy sur le front la couronne je porte,
> Qui ne craint de l'hyver la saison tant soit morte,
> Et pource toute ronde elle entourne mon front,
> Car rien n'est excellent au monde s'il n'est rond :
> Le grand ciel est tout rond, la mer est toute ronde,
> Et la terre en rondeur se couronne de l'onde,
> D'une couronne d'or le Soleil est orné,
> La Lune a tout le front de rayons couronné.
> (XI, 169)

It is within this wider context that one must interpret the recurrent evocations of the dance of the Nymphs, the Graces and the Muses, for its circular form is not only symbolical of the durability and perfection of poetry, but it is also to be associated with cosmic roundness and with the workings of a natural, cyclic order.[39]

Yet again certain metaphors and images found originally in Pindar, which link the poet and his task to bees and honey, are also designed to associate poetry, and the immortality it bestows, with a symbolism of natural fecundity.[40] An extension of this idea are those many images involving sugar, nectar and sweet, refreshing dew (I, 61; 175; III, 166).

Another aspect of this dynamic antithesis is the way in which the fluidity of transience and the insubstantial aspect of death—the absence and void—are contrasted with a symbolism and lexis of material strength, concrete presence and endurance used to evoke poetic immortality. Poetry is referred to as 'le plus de ma puissance', 'le fort & puissant stile', 'un stile endurci / Contre le trait des ans' (I, 228; V, 251; XI, 60), whilst the poet writes 'D'une plume de fer sur un papier d'acier' (XI, 35) so that '. . . les beaux vers toujours demeurent / S'endurcissans contre les ans' (III, 33). The written word is engraved 'par vives lettres d'airain', 'plus dur contre les ans que marbre ny qu'airain', 'plus dur qu'en fer, qu'en cuyvre ou qu'en metal' (III, 90; IV, 4; XVII, 418). The verbs *graver, engraver, empreindre* abound and there is a tendency to multiply terms in order to establish the durability of fame: 'Il me faudroit une aimantine main / La voix de bronze, une plume d'airain' (XV, 377, var.). Poetry, however, is considered superior to metals because

> . . . le savoir de la Muse
> . . . jamais rouillé ne s'use,
> Et maugré les ans refuse
> De donner place à la mort.
>   (VII, 79. Cf. p. 140, s. XXII)

Like many classical poets before him[41] Ronsard considers the poem as a spiritual monument and he sees himself as an architect and builder, constructing a fame 'Dessus les piliers de memoire / Maugré la carriere des ans' (I, 141). Ronsard, distantly echoing a Pindaric metaphor (*Nemean*, VIII, ep. 3), boasts that

> . . . nul mieus que moi, par ses vers
> Ne bâtist dedans l'univers
> Les colonnes d'une memoire
>   (II, 83)

and, using Pindaric masonry yet again (*Olympian*, VI, str. I), builds a poem-monument to Henri II:

> Je te veil bâtir une ode,
> La maçonnant à la mode
> De tes palais honnorés,
> Qui voulontiers ont l'entrée
> De grands marbres acoutrée
> Et de haus piliers dorés,
> . . .

Sur deus Termes de memoire
J'engraverai ta victoire.
(I, 167–8. Cf. I, 92; 99)

Ronsard's most poetic edifice, *A sa Muse* (II, 152–3), is an original and personal adaptation of Horace's *Exegi monumentum* (*Odes*, III, xxx), and here he richly juxtaposes images of flight, fertility, sound and vegetation within a proud declaration of survival ('Sous le tumbeau tout Ronsard n'ira pas / Restant de lui la part qui est meilleure') which culminates in a vision of divine consecration.[42] In the same way the *tombeau* as a *genre* is at once a monument in the literary and architectural sense, with its particular and complex symbolism of endurance, as Françoise Joukovsky has demonstrated (*La Gloire*, pp. 404–17).

Finally, within this extended contrast between death and poetic fame, the silence of the tomb and the sleep of death and forgetfulness are broken by the diverse sounds of immortality—the noise of rivers associated with the poet's glory, the trumpet of the goddess *Renommée*, the musical instruments of the poets, for, as Ronsard remarks,

Jamais la Muse ne soufre
Qu'un silence soumeillant
En ses tenebres engoufre
Les faits d'un homme vaillant.[43]

Ronsard contrasts the music of his 'luc Vandomois' with 'le silence endormi' in an ode to François de Carnavalet (1550), and he evokes the strains of its glory filling the entire world:

Le bruit de sa corde animée
Fredonnant ton los evident,
Fera parler ta renommée
De l'un jusque à l'autre Occident.
(I, 99–100)

My

... lirique faconde
...
Aveq' les flutes meslée
Chassera l'oubli de toi
(I, 98)

Ronsard informs Carnavalet, and Catherine de Médicis receives the same assurance: 'Ton nom bruiant en mes vers / Couvrira tout l'univers' (I, 69–70). It is in the *Hymne de Charles Cardinal de Lorraine* (1559), how-

ever, that Ronsard most poetically evokes the stillness and silence of the
tomb which only the voice of the poet can disturb: I will noise abroad
Charles's 'millier de vertus', says Ronsard,

> ... à ceus du futur age,
> Afin ... qu'aprés le trépas
> Son nom dedans l'oubli ne se perde là bas,
> Et l'araigne pendante à bien filer experte
> Ne devide ses retz sus sa tombe deserte.
>
> (IX, 35)

The tendency to accumulate symbols and metaphors which characterises Ronsard's treatment of this theme, and which aims to emphasise the
dynamic and visual nature of immortality, reappears in a sonnet to
Hélène where sonority is allied to architectural terms in order to stress
the immortalising power of Homer (and by extension of Ronsard himself): 'Mais son nom, qui a fait tant de bouches parler, / Luyt sert contre
la Mort de pilliers & de termes' (XVII, 285, s. XLIX). It is this association
of sound and immortality which explains why Ronsard describes virtue
that is unrecorded by poetry as *muete* and *sans langue* (I, 98; II, 150).

This dynamic, active, fecundating power of immortality acts as a
shield and armour throughout life (II, 32), and as a protective shroud in
death (XV, 11): it ultimately awards the poet, and whatever is recorded
by the written word, a second life which has the quality of being more
vital and intense than their physical existence: '... vifs hors du tombeau de la mort les delivre, / Et mieus qu'en leur vivant les fait encore
vivre' (VI, 39). This idea of a 'second life' has rich associations throughout Ronsard's work and forms yet another branch of the antithesis between poetry and death. In an ode of 1554 dealing with the fragility of
life and the finality of death, Ronsard echoes a passage of Bion and voices
the desire to be born twice (VI, 113–14). It is by defeating the finality of
death that fame offers him this possibility ('Un homme apres sa mort
peut racheter sa vie': X, 81, s. XVI), for although Charon refuses to re-
cross the Styx in spite of gold and entreaty (I, 187; II, 128; VIII, 205),
poetry 'plustost que l'or peut donner, / Maugré la mort, un second vivre'
(VI, 261). In the following lines from an elegy to Jean de Morel of 1556
the emphasis is not on 'la depite mort' and death's finality, but on a
vocabulary of action, life and fertility ('vive renommée', the movement
of flight, 'semera') and especially on the visual metaphor of 'la barque
des vers' which cheats Charon and recrosses the river Styx:

> ... ce livre un jour se formera
> En vive renommée, & vollant semera
> Tes honneurs par le Monde, & ceulx dont ton espose

Sa pudique maison divinement dispose,
Et ne vouldra souffrir que la depite mort
Emporte avec le corps voz noms oultre le bord
Qu'on ne peult repasser, si ce n'est par la barque
Des vers, qui font oultrage à la cruelle Parque.

(VII, 229)

Similarly the Orpheus/Eurydice myth, as recounted in Ovid and Virgil
and as interpreted by Ronsard (VI, 24–7; XII, 135–42), has associations
with the magical enchantment of poetry, its conquest over death and
the idea of Pluto allotting a second life. Ronsard's treatment of the resurrection of Hippolytus by Aesculapius, son of Apollo the god of poetry
and medicine, has identical associations (I, 156–7; cf. Virgil, *Aeneid*, VII,
765–73). For Ronsard an aspect of the Apollonian and Orphic nature of
poetry is that it can breathe life into the inanimate ('. . . flatés de sa vois /
Tiroit, racine & tout, les rochiers & les bois?': VI, 24), charm the Underworld ('. . . enchante / L'Enfer au silence endormi': I, 99, var.) and, by
its curative and magical qualities ('les vertueux miracles / Des vers
medecins enchantez'), resurrect from the dead ('fouler l'Enfer odieux':
III, 139).

Thus the poet envisages his apotheosis and deification as a triumph
over the Underworld forces of darkness, sterility, aridity, silence and
immobility, and it is by the fertile activity of the creative mind—the
'vers laborieus', the 'art industrieux', the 'laborieuse industrie' (II, 188;
VIII, 293; XVI, 336)—that he receives a second life and penetrates the
divine world:

La Muse l'enfer defie,
Seule nous éleve aus cieus
Seule nous beatifie
Ennombrés aus rengs des Dieus.[44]

However, it is not only the poet who attains divine status and who
participates in celestial activity, for Ronsard promises the heavens to
whoever 'se peut faire ami / Du luc Vandomois' (I, 99), an honour accorded in turn to the beauty of Cassandre (II, 188), to Pierre de Paschal
(I, 161–2) and, in lines which yet again illustrate the tendency to accumulate metaphor and symbolism, to Henri II: 'Lors cultivant un terroir
si fertile, / Jusques au ciel le fruit pourra monter' (I, 179).

A revealing and typically Ronsardian interpretation of this interpene-
tration of the divine and human worlds is found in the opening movement of an ode to Jean du Bellay of 1550:

Dedans ce grand monde où nous sommes
Enclos generallement,

Il n'i a tant seulement
Qu'un genre des dieus, & des hommes.

Eus, & nous n'avons mere qu'une,
    Tous par elle nous vivons,
    Et pour heritage avons
Cette grand' lumiere commune.

L'esprit de nous qui tout avise,
    Des Dieus compaignons nous rend.
    Sans plus un seul different
Nostre genre & le leur divise.

La vie aus dieus n'est consumée,
    Immortel est leur sejour,
    Et l'homme ne vit qu'un jour
Fuiant comme un songe ou fumée.

Mais celui qui aquiert la grace
    D'un bien heureus écrivant,
    De mortel se fait vivant,
Et au ranc des celestes passe.

Comme toi, que la muse apprise
    De ton Macrin a chanté,
    Et t'a un los enfanté
Qui la fuite des ans mesprise.

Elle a perpétué ta gloire
    La logeant là haut aus cieus,
    Et a fait egalle aus dieus
L'eternité de ta memoire.
                    (II, 120–1)

The development and ideas of lines 1–16 are, notes Laumonier, a free
paraphrase of Pindar, *Nemean*, vi, strophe 1:

One is the race of men, one is the race of gods, and from one mother do we
both derive our breath; yet a power that is wholly sundered parteth us, in
that the one is naught, while for the other the brazen heaven endureth as an
abode unshaken for evermore. Albeit, we mortals have some likeness, either
in might of mind or at least in our nature, to the immortals, although we
know not by what course, whether by day, no nor yet in the night watches,
fate hath ordained that we should run.

                                        (LCL, p. 369)

A comparison of the Greek and French texts reveals that the tone,
emphasis and underlying sentiment are vastly different in spite of Ronsard's obvious debt. In Pindar there is a notable humility and deference
based on an awareness of man's transience: even the similarities be-

tween the divine and human worlds are apologetically expressed and qualified, as if through fear of *hubris*, and the strophe ends on the idea of man's ignorance of his fate which is designed to set limitations to human knowledge. In the Ronsard poem on the other hand the stress is clearly laid on the several similarities between the gods and man, for not only does Ronsard follow Pindar in evoking the common mother, Gaia or Earth, and the spiritual likeness of mortals and immortals, but whereas the Greek poet opposes ephemeral man with the permanence of the 'brazen heavens', Ronsard, on the contrary, underlines yet another point of resemblance in that both have 'Cette gran' lumiere commune'. He also, significantly, suppresses the Pindaric reference to man's ignorance of his divinely ordered fate. What is contrast in Pindar is comparison in Ronsard. Even the opposition of lines 13–16, which are contaminated from two further Pindaric texts (*Pythian*, VIII, ep. 5; *Isthmian*, III, ep. 1), is used to introduce the developed reference to poetic fame and to point to the special relationship existing between the poet and the celestial powers. The focus moves from the basic antithesis and humility of the Pindaric text to the emphatic development of lines 16–28, which express the poet's unique penetration into the divine regions, and similarly to the remaining lines of the poem (ll. 29–40) which stress the poet's exclusive position in the world, where even kings and princes must honour his presence.

A similar interpretation can be seen if we compare the divine consecration of Ronsard in *A sa Muse*,

Sus donque Muse emporte au ciel la gloire
Que j'ai gaignée annonçant la victoire
Dont à bon droit je me voi jouissant,
Et de ton fils consacre la memoire
Serrant son front d'un laurier verdissant
                                                    (II, 153)

with the Horatian text (*Odes*, III, xxx, 14–16) which is its immediate source, 'Accept the proud honour won by thy merits, Melpomene, and graciously crown my locks with Delphic bays' (LCL, p. 279). The tone of the Latin is one of appeal and request, and Horace acknowledges that his immortality has been won by the merits of Melpomene to whom he humbly dedicates his 'proud honour'. The French equivalent is of a totally different nature, for not only does Ronsard *command* the Muse, but he claims the victory as a personal and well-deserved one (*j'ai gaignée, à bon droit*). The respect and humility of Horace are replaced by Ronsard's jubilant battle hymn, by a confident assertion of his own merit.

When, in 1584, Ronsard returns to one of his last definitions of the poetic mission, he demonstrates that he has remained remarkably faithful to the belief that 'the activity of the creative mind is its sole assurance of immortality, of its participation in divinity at the intersection of the human and celestial horizons' (I. Silver, 'Ronsard's Ethical Thought', p. 374). In the following passage not only are many of Ronsard's favourite ideas densely suggested—the conquest of fame over death, the divine nature of inspiration, the social and moral role of the poet, the theme of *odi profanum*, the poet's aspirations to divinity—but apparent once more is the characteristic technique of imparting movement and order to his verse by multiplying structures (the use of infinitives in every line, the repetition of the *et* pattern) :

Nostre mestier estoit d'honorer les grands Rois,
De rendre venerable & le peuple & les lois,
Faire que la vertu du monde fust aimée,
Et forcer le trespas par longue renommée :
D'une flame divine allumer les esprits,
Avoir d'un cueur hautain le vulgaire à mespris,
Ne priser que l'honneur & la gloire cherchée,
Et tousjours dans le ciel avoir l'ame attachée.

(XVIII, 91)

MEANS OF ESCAPING DEATH: THE CLASSICAL, EUPHEMISTIC VISION

If Ronsard consistently seeks to transcend human mortality, he also endeavours to escape his fragile condition by a number of traditional euphemistic techniques which are specifically designed to divert or distance the mind from the cruel presence of death. These euphemistic devices entail either the substitution of an unreal vision—generally a poetic fiction—for the brutal reality of death, or the substitution of a familiar and natural vision for a strange and horrific one.

One such euphemistic comparison is that which describes death in terms of sleep. There is nothing more commonplace or central to man's psychological needs than this association of sleep and death, as Edgar Morin has remarked (*L'Homme et la mort dans l'histoire*, Paris, 1957, p. 115). Homer describes Death and Sleep as brothers and twins, the off-spring of Night,[45] and Virgil in turn writes 'consanguineus Leti Sopor' (*Aeneid*, VI, 278). Greek artistic representations of Hypnos and Thanatos are remarkably similar.[46] Classical, neo-Latin and Italian literature is likewise full of references to the consanguinity of the two states, and although Ronsard on rare occasions denies the brotherhood (II, 123), much more frequently he repeats the Homeric and Virgilian formulae faithfully, recalling not only the close relationship between Death and Sleep, but also the metaphor of 'un dormir de fer', 'un somme ferré', 'Somme aux liens de fer', which has its immediate source in Virgil's 'ferreus urget somnus' (*Aeneid*, x, 745) and its more distant origin in Homer, *Iliad*, xi, 241, where death is described as a 'brazen sleep'.[47] It is, Ronsard explains, because of the brotherhood of Sleep ('fils de la Nuit & de Lethe oublieux': vii, 199) and Death that the latter has contracted 'De jamais n'outrager les hommes endormis' (viii, 176). This consanguinity extends into Ronsard's allegorical descriptions of Sleep and Death, for certain features are common to both personifications in his verse.[48]

Sometimes this comparison is developed as a sustained philosophical argument in Ronsard's work. Reference has already been made to the way he imitates Lucretius in two odes of 1556 and introduces this association into his comforting philosophical sensualism (above, pp. 136–40). These statements can in fact be considered as counterparts to an *Odelette au Somme* published in the *Bocage* of 1554 (vi, 109), where he had upbraided Sleep—'Le vrai simulacre des mors' (cf. Homer, *Odyssey*, xiii, 80)—because, like death, it robs the body of its life force, memory, action and ability to think. In another philosophical context he adapts a passage of Ficino and describes sleep as death due to the nocturnal voyage of the soul to heaven in search of knowledge and divine communion (x, 103).

More frequently, however, the comparison is expressed not as a philosophical argument, but as a euphemistic device which familiarises the horror and strangeness of death ('la mort sommeilleuse esteignoit ton flambeau': xii, 262, var.). The corpse is described as someone 'Qui ne ressemble un mort, mais un homme endormy, / Qu'encores le sommeil ne commence qu'à poindre' (xii, 123): it is buried 'pour prendre son sommeil', and in turn crosses Lethe not in 'la barque Stygieuse' (cf. Virgil, *Georgics*, iv, 506: 'Stygia . . . cumba') but in 'la Biere sommeilleuse' (xv, 84; xviii, 160). As if the bald comparison with sleep is insufficient consolation in itself, adjectives are multiplied and structures balanced to emphasise its peacefulness and sweetness: '. . . en paisible & sommeilleux repos / Puissent dormir ses cendres & ses os' (xv, 306). In turn sleep is often described in terms reminiscent of death, for inertia (*lassés, oysive*), heaviness (*pressés*), enclosure (*fermée, enfermés, basse*) and darkness (*nuit*) are common to both states:

> Il estoit nuit fermée, & les hommes lassés
> Dessus la plume oysive avoient les yeux pressés,
> Enfermés du sommeil, que la basse riviere
> De Styx fait distiller de sur notre paupiere.
> (xii, 114. Cf. xii, 81; xv, 333)

Another euphemistic association links death to various aspects of nature symbolism, and especially to plants and flowers. The corpse, for example, is described as a flower, wilted by rainstorm, heat or wind. This image is found in Homer, Virgil and Ovid, and Ronsard is indebted to an assimilation of their texts for the following account of the death of the Dauphin François (10 August 1536) :

> . . . au lict mort je le veisse,
> Non comme un homme mort, mais comme un endormy,
> Ou comme un beau bouton qui se panche à demy,
> Languissant en Avril, alors que la tempeste,
> Jalouse de son teinct, luy aggrave la teste,
> Et, luy chargeant le col, le fanist contre-bas,
> Ensemble prenant vie avecques le trespas.
> Je vey son corps ouvrir, osant mes yeux repaistre
> Des poulmons & du cœur & du sang de mon maistre.
> Tel sembloit Adonis sur la place estendu,
> Apres que tout son sang du corps fut respandu.[49]

The principal source is Ovid's account of the death of Hyacinthus in *Metamorphoses*, x, 190–5. This text in turn recalls to Ronsard the description of the death of Adonis, his transformation into an anemone and the evocation of the fragility of that flower found in lines 735–9 of the same Ovidian chapter: all he retains of the account, however, is the suggestive symbolism of the reference. Ovid makes no mention in either passage of the rainstorm which causes the destruction of the flower, and Ronsard may well have adopted this detail from Homer (*Iliad*, VIII, 306–8) or Virgil (*Aeneid*, IX, 435–7; XI, 67–71). Ronsard's total debt, however, does not extend beyond the flower image, and his originality is clearly apparent in the way he emphasises the peaceful and natural tone of the passage. He not only associates the flower symbolism with youthful beauty (*beau bouton*) and with the euphemistic equation of death and sleep, but he suggests regeneration and life beyond death—'prenant vie avecques le trespas'. This consoling idea is continued into the following lines which describe the autopsy : any horror is alleviated by the classical reference to Adonis and by the suggestion of the metamorphosis into a flower and of the natural cycle of rebirth.

Elsewhere—and nowhere more poetically than in the admirable *Comme on voit sur la branche*[50]—it is the shortness of the life of the rose which is specifically chosen to evoke the youth and beauty of the deceased. Here in this famous sonnet of 1578 freshness, perfume and colour linger long after the brief allusion to death has passed, and the pagan symbols of birth and fertility ('Ce vase plein de laict, ce panier plein de fleurs') and the beauty which survives, equate life and death within a natural cycle which renders the latter of no account ('. . . vif, & mort, ton corps ne soit que roses').

Again the same youthful beauty of the deceased may be evoked by the image of spring flowers, 'Ainsi les fleurs d'Avril par l'orage du temps / Meurent dedans la prée au milieu du printemps' (XVII, 6); of the unopened bud ravished before it can flower and bear fruit,

> . . . ainsi le vent destruict
> L'ante quand elle est preste à porter un bon fruict.
> . . .
> Jamais le mois d'Avril ne veit si belle fleur
> (XVII, 71)

or by a juxtaposition of birth, growth and death in a rapid, embracing vision of life's fragility: 'Qui de beauté, de grace & de lustre resemble / Au liz qui naist, fleurist & se meurt tout ensemble' (XVII, 65). Invariably the horror of death is familiarised, and what emerges from the antithetical lexical patterns is the natural image of beauty and the promise of rebirth and rejuvenation:

> . . . la fleur languissant pour un temps,
> Qui plus gaillarde aparoist au printemps,
> Par son declin prenant force & croissance,
> Et de sa mort une longue naissance.
> (XV, 20)

A variant of the 1584 edition of Ronsard's Le Narssis, originally published in 1554, draws the philosophical lesson of this flower symbolism by formulating a natural law of order and necessity which embraces the duration of flowers, trees and man alike (VI, 82, var.).

Another euphemistic technique, often involving flower symbolism, is for the poet to multiply several images of natural phenomena—or to develop a single image at length—in such a way that the theme is obscured by a stylistic emphasis, and attention is diverted from the idea expressed to the means of expression, from the reality to the appearance. An example of this technique of copia—as well as of Ronsard's love of strong, measured structures (Comme . . . Ou . . . Ou comme)—is found in his Discours Amoureux de Genevre (1564), where the motif of the wilting flower is accompanied by additional images (melting snow and wax) taken either directly from Ovid or via the intermediary of Marullus:

> De jour en jour coulant sa force s'écouloit,
> Sa premiere beauté sans grace s'en alloit,
> Comme une jeune fleur sur la branche seichée,
> Ou la neige d'hyver des pieds humains touchée,
> Que le chaut incertain distile peu à peu,
> Ou comme fait la cire à la chaleur du feu.[51]

Similarly flowers and evergreen branches placed on the tomb are not only symbols of a natural cycle of regeneration, but, since Ronsard insists on this being an annual affair (III, 85; XIII, 193), this pagan rite of 'spargite flores', which Christianity assimilated in its turn, bears witness to survival by memory. This motif—a commonplace of the sepulchral epigrams of *The Greek Anthology* and of Latin and neo-Latin funeral poetry, but relatively rare in French verse before 1549[52]—frequently finds favour with Ronsard, although he may, on isolated occasions, react rather unconvincingly against the paganism of the ritual (V, 257–8). Sometimes the gesture is recalled directly from *The Greek Anthology* or from Virgil or Marullus;[53] but more generally it is an assimilated commonplace which the French poet introduces into the concluding movement of his epitaphs in order to evoke the victory of memory and to leave a final impression of beauty, life, abundance:

> Or toy, passant, qui viendras par icy
> Verse un Printemps de roses espoissy
> Sur ce tombeau, & verse meintes branches
> De beaux Lauriers & vertes Esparvanches,
> Puis tous les ans raconte à ton enfant
> «Qu'un beau mourir rend l'homme triomphant,
> Dontant la mort . . .
> > (XIII, 193–4)

The completion of the natural cycle is symbolised in turn by the flowers which spring from the tomb. Although Ronsard borrows this idea faithfully from the neo-Latin poet Jean Cotta and employs it as a rather precious conceit on two occasions (VI, 270–1; XVII, 126), and in spite of the fact that it is also used in the context of the burlesque epitaph (VI, 20–1), nevertheless this notion does correspond to a serious view of regeneration. For Ronsard the body returns to universal Mother Earth, '. . . ce corps que la terre / Mere commune en ceste tombe enserre' (XV, 223, var.), in a vision reminiscent of Lucretius: '. . . wherefore she [the earth] has with reason obtained the name of mother. For that which once came from earth, to earth returns back again' (II, 998–1000: LCL, p. 157). Since Mother Earth is invariably associated in Ronsard's work with conception, fecundity and productivity,

> . . . la Terre, heureuse part du monde,
> Mere benigne, à gros tetins fœconde,
> Au large sein . . .
> > (XV, 40)

the germination and growth of flowers from the body bear testimony to a rebirth in the context of a fusion of natural and human metaphor, of

mythology and sexual pantheism.[54] As in *The Greek Anthology*, evergreen plants—or flowers which complete the full seasonal round ('Le
safran en hyver, les roses au printemps, / En esté les œillets': x, 144) and
parallel the everlasting specimens of the Elysian Fields ('D'autres plus
belles fleurs, qui ne meurent jamais': xiii, 100)—appear on the grave,[55]
and these are visual reminders both of a victory over death and forgetfulness and of man's absorption into the eternal natural cycles of the world.

Other aspects of Ronsard's descriptions of the tomb also euphemisti-
cally render death in familiar and natural terms, and integrate the deceased into his native soil—paternal and fertile (ii, 104–5)—and into the
eternal rhythm of nature. Within the idyllic rustic setting as depicted
in *De l'election de son sepulcre* (ii, 97–103) and *Aux cendres de
Marguerite de Valois* (iii, 79–85), attention is focused exclusively on the
vitality, colour, sound and movement of nature—the 'ruisseau murmur-
ant', 'eau non endormie', 'ondes . . . vagabondes'; the abundance of evergreen plants and grass; the everlasting manna, refreshing dew and honey;
the speeches, music and dancing of the visiting *pasteurs*, Muses and rustic
divinities. Densely interwoven with this vision, and operating on several
suggestive levels, is the idea of the protective embrace of Nature in
death. The tomb is secure from animals (*Aux cendres*, ll. 70–2), shaded
from the wilting sun (*Election*, ll. 29–40; *Aux cendres*, ll. 69, 91–3, 99)
and protected on an 'isle verte' by surrounding water and by mystical
number symbolism:

> Tous les ans soit recouverte
>   De gazons sa tumbe verte,
>   Et qu'un ruisseau murmurant
>   Neuf fois recourbant ses undes
>   De neuf torces vagabondes
>   Son sepulchre aille emmurant.[56]

Considering that in death the deceased returns to his birthplace and to
Mother Earth, some lexical items of protective human embrace suggest
a return to the womb (*Election*, ll. 18–24, 35), an idea reinforced in
certain stanzas by a movement from death to birth and by associations
with foetal sleep:

> ICY LA ROYNE SOMMEILLE
> . . .
> LA PLUS BELLE FLEUR D'ESLITE
> QU'ONQUE L'AURORE ENFANTA.
>   (*Aux cendres*, ll. 43–8)

This equation of death and a foetal state is strengthened by the use of
the word *giron* in *De l'election de son sepulcre* (l. 24) to evoke the liquid
embrace of the river Braie, for elsewhere in Ronsard's work this word

has associations with the woman's 'lap' (IV, 23, s. XX, var.) and, within a cosmic perspective, with sexual pantheism (IX, 33: quoted above, p. 14). These related ideas of death, Mother Earth, protection and the womb are suggested in *La Salade* of 1569 ('. . . la Terre, en son ventre qui prend / De fosse egalle & le Pauvre & le Grand': XV, 82 and var.), and they reappear in 1578 in Ronsard's appeal

> . . . que la terre
> D'un *mol giron* enserre
> Ces reliques en paix.
>   (XVII, 388)

The choice of a resting place and the linking of death and flowers—and especially the theme of *spargite flores*—can also be seen as aspects of a general substitution of a classical vision for a contemporary one, the euphemistic replacement of a brutal reality by a comforting poetic fiction. This classical vision assumes a number of other forms: it includes the evocation of the funeral ceremony itself, with the ritual libations, annual offerings of life symbols and diverse sepulchral formulae. As in classical sepulchral verse, Ronsard offers the deceased libations of milk, honey, fresh wine and, recalling Virgil and Horace, the sacrificial 'sang d'un blanc aignelet'.[57] He assembles the Muses and rustic deities around the tomb (III, 81–2), places the traditional eulogy, prayers and appeals in the mouth of the *passant*, the visiting shepherds or the manes themselves (II, 99–101), echoing in turn Horace ('Trois fois couvre moi de terre'), the Latin funeral inscription *sit tibi terra levis* ('Que la terre soit legere / A mes ôs') and *The Greek Anthology*:

> Les roses & les lis puissent tomber du ciel
> A jamais sur ce marbre: & les mouches à miel
> Puissent à tout jamais y faire leur menage.[58]

After Homer and Virgil, Ronsard repeats the pagan gesture of cutting his hair as a vow, instigates annual funeral games and festivities and erects an altar in honour of the deceased's manes.[59] He ensures the survival of the deceased's name in nature by inscribing an epitaph on the bark of a tree planted for the occasion or on the evergreen grass of the tomb.[60] The whole evocation is peaceful, idyllic and removed from reality.

The same euphemistic tendency can be seen in the frequent allusions to death in terms of the classical *Parcae*. Although the individual references are uniformly brief, a composite picture emerges which covers, with a certain amount of internal contradiction and uncertain definition, the lineage of the Fates—'D'Erebe & de la Nuit nées'—their activities of spinning and cutting the life-thread, their attributes ('dur cizeau', 'fuseaux d'airain', 'fatale quenouille', 'le filet & la trame') and their individual identities and functions.[61] The vision, however, is never horrific: this is not only due to the brevity of the individual allusions, but also to a tendency to describe the activities of the 'Parques filandieres' (XVII, 39) in bald and stylised formulae and to avoid realistic detail or descriptive emphasis. The pattern *trancher la trame*—with slight variations—is commonplace, and the adjective *cruelle* is so consistently applied to the Fates that it loses its emotive power. Even the longer and more visual account of the activity and attributes of the Three Sisters in Ronsard's *Ode a Michel de L'Hospital* (III, 153–6) is scarcely designed to cause fear or disgust, for it is developed within the framework of a eulogy of Hospital—'JE RETORDS LA PLUS BELLE VIE / QUE JAMAIS TORDIRENT MES DOIGS', remarks Clotho—and the *Parcae* are associated throughout not with death but with birth. Significantly the only word which suggests repulsion in these pages—*hideument* (l. 632)—is replaced in the 1567–87 editions by *tristement*.

In the same way Ronsard's two poems of 1584 entitled *Les Parques* are genethliacons modelled, notes Laumonier, on Navagero, and these present the Three Sisters presiding over birth and predicting glorious futures for Henri III and his favourite *mignon*, the Duc d'Epernon, respectively (XVIII, 150–3; 234–7). The presentation is in no way frightening, for the emphasis is clearly on the eulogy rather than on descriptive detail: on the contrary, the *Parcae*, in the respectable company of Virtue and Good Fortune on one occasion, dance around the cot, kiss the infant, breastfeed him, perfume the bed and strew it with flowers (XVIII, 150; 153; 235; 237). Nearly 20 years earlier (1565: XIII, 107–10) Ronsard had assembled the *Parcae* round the cradle of Charles IX, whilst the same year the Fates preside again at the birth of Lord Dudley, favourite of Queen Elizabeth, in order to create a miracle of perfection (XIII, 64–5).

Very much the same euphemistic process is found in Ronsard's evocation of the pagan Underworld. It has already been established that the poet's vision of an after-life centres almost invariably on lengthy descriptions of the idyllic Elysian Fields or of the Myrtle Grove of the lovers (above, pp. 146–7). This is not to say that frequent references to Hades do not occur: however, even when he reconstructs the various aspects of the Underworld with the help of assimilated details from the most famous classical accounts in Homer, Virgil and Ovid, the allusions are generally cursory and little more than a catalogue of suggestive names without commentary or descriptive emphasis (cf. I, 187; II, 127–8; VII, 95; XII, 75–6; 275; XVIII, 267). Moreover, the poetic fiction is so strong that the vision is distanced from contemporary reality by this classical veneer, and is without horror. There are rare exceptions when the mythological reference extends rather than alleviates fear because it is purposely designed to emphasise the alien and the horrific. One such occasion occurs, not surprisingly, in a sonnet of *Les Derniers Vers* where the agony and fear of approaching death is associated with a nightmarish vision of the Furies: here, in spite of its brevity, the dense classical reference is suggestively integrated into the verse—the balanced structures (*nuicts de . . . nuicts filles de . . . seurs de . . . Serpentes de; & fureur des fureurs; N'aprochez de . . . ou bien tournez*) already anticipate the patterns employed later in the sonnet (ll. 8–11) to describe the poet's painful twisting and turning—and it is this poetic use of myth which is essential to the evocation of the panic accompanying a momentary foretaste of the unknown:

> Meschantes nuicts d'hyver, nuicts filles de Cocyte
> Que la terre engendra d'Encelade les seurs,
> Serpentes d'Alecton, & fureur des fureurs,
> N'aprochez de mon lict, ou bien tournez plus vitte.
>
> (XVIII, 177, S. II)

Similarly, in the same way as it is relatively rare—given the multiplicity of references to death in the verse of Ronsard—for him to insist on the physical decomposition of the body in the tomb, so too the evocation of the insubstantial body in the Underworld is practically never rendered in visual or horrifying detail. He prefers instead to describe the lack of corporal substance in stylised terms reminiscent of Ovid's 'the shades bloodless, without body and bone' (*Metam.*, IV, 443: LCL, vol. I, p. 209): '. . . sans muscles & sans veines, / Sans sang, sans nerfz . . .' (XV, 89. Cf. XVIII, 126; 218, S. LXXVI), or to evoke the shadows of Tartarus by a series of Virgilian, Horatian and Ovidian periphrases ('gresle bande', 'debile troupeau', 'trope legere', 'Ombres gresles, & vaines, / . . . Foibles, sans poix, debiles', 'leger fardeau').[62] Or again he eschews horrific detail by describing the manes either by the use of the Homeric term εἴδωλον (*idole* or *image*) or by comparisons, borrowed from Homer and Virgil, which associate the spirits with natural and familiar phenomena (birds, gnats, crickets, bees).[63] The macabre and realistic account of du Bellay's 'vaine idole' in Ronsard's *Elegie a Loïs des Masures* (1560: X, 366–7) remains exceptional in its descriptive detail and its medieval atmosphere, and it contrasts notably with the lack of picturesque realism in an earlier prosopopoeia (VI, 40–3), where the ghost of Ronsard's father appears simply as '. . . une image / Gresle, sans ôs' (ll. 9–10). Even in the elegy to des Masures, however, du Bellay's ghost is familiarised by comparisons with birds and insects (X, 367) and the poem ends on an evocation of the Elysian Fields which helps to dissipate the horror of the repulsive vision.

Significantly—and contrary to Ronsard's general tendency towards descriptive realism and ornate textures—even the longer accounts of

Hades contain comparatively little visual detail. One would look in vain (even, interestingly enough, in the *Franciade*)[64] for the graphic equivalent of Virgil's realistic and frightening description of the descent of Aeneas into Tartarus, although, inevitably, this account remains one of the French poet's principal sources for reminiscences. Of Ronsard's more developed evocations of the Underworld, two (VI, 26–7; XII, 135–9. Cf. XV, 298–9) paraphrase the Ovidian and Virgilian accounts of the descent of Orpheus into Hades to retrieve Eurydice: on both occasions Ronsard avoids visual and horrific detail for the narrative account, and emphasises the request of Orpheus and the manner in which the infernal powers are charmed and mollified. The Underworld is tamed and humanised, sympathetic to man's sorrow and responsive to the beauty of poetry and music.

Very much the same picture emerges from Ronsard's longest evocation of Hades—his *Prosopopée de Beaumont levrier du Roy, & de Charon* of 1567 (XIV, 114–19)—for here the tone is kept uniformly light: the epitaph swiftly becomes a eulogy of Charles IX (l. 28ff.); Beaumont's body is, as in life, 'un si beau corps' (ll. 11–12) and his mind is still actively involved in the processes of the living (ll. 19–22). Charon shows Beaumont kindness ('Sans rien payer entre dans ce bateau': l. 41), and Cerberus comes to heel, '. . . aussi tost que la taille il eut veüe / De ce levrier, le flatta de la queüe (ll. 59–60). The poem ends with a lengthy vision of the Elysian Fields (ll. 89–130) which finally equates life and death, for here Beaumont rediscovers his faithful dog Courte, '. . . là bas comme icy sans pareille' (l. 100), and passes his days 'sans travail & sans peine' hunting '. . . tout ainsi / Comme il faisoit quand il estoit icy (ll. 117–18). Once again death is seen not as a rupture but as a natural extension of life's activity and pleasure.

Ronsard's other references to the Underworld include a passage in the *Hymne de la Mort* (VIII, 172) where the poet christianises a Lucretian passage in order to reject the pagan vision; a rapid enumeration of the major aspects of Hades in the *Hymne de la Philosophie* (VIII, 92–3), where knowledge is designed to enable the philosopher to live '. . . bien-heureux & content, / Sans craindre rien' (ll. 326–7); and a *mascarade* of 1571 in which Charles IX is disguised as Hercules, conqueror of Pluto and Cerberus and liberator of mankind (XV, 355–6). In Ronsard's brief allusions, as in his more developed accounts, the classical vision of the *Parcae* and the Underworld avoids the descriptive for the narrative, the horrific for the euphemistic, the realistic for the poetic fiction.

'In the writing of Ronsard life is continually more absorbing than death', remarks D. B. Wilson, and elsewhere he makes a similar observation: 'when Ronsard writes about death, he writes about life'.[65] This general movement from death to life which has been noted during the course of this study, is seen yet again in Ronsard's interest in the biographical and historical epitaph: in such epitaphs the emphasis rapidly switches from associations of death to a detailed reconstruction of the deceased's lineage, glorious feats and virtues, and provides, as it were, a lasting and living monument to the survival of memory.[66] It is within the context of the same technique of diverting attention from death to life that Ronsard employs the epitaph on occasions either to eulogise a living person associated with the deceased or to direct interest on to his own personal problems (VI, 35–6; XIV, 114–19).

However true Dr Wilson's statement is as a general conclusion, it should not blind us to the complexity and diversity of Ronsard's vision of death or to his lasting preoccupation with human mortality. His conception of death is rendered all the more complex and elusive by the abundance of material and by the absence of any clear-cut evolution of attitude or simple chronological development, for what we are given is a rich mosaic of diverse attitudes and visions, and these do not follow consecutively but exist simultaneously. However, within this bewildering richness of material an authentic voice is sounded, and it is this which has dictated our analysis and conclusions. In Ronsard's work the dominant note is one of optimism and life, for a constant effort is made to overcome the fear of death, to transcend or escape human mortality, to rationalise death, to explain it as a moral, cosmic and philosophical necessity, and not to see it as an absurd accident which negates the value or purpose of existence.

Ronsard finds compensation for man's fragility by various methods: he fuses man with the materialistic, transformist cycles of the world, with an ordered pattern of individual death (form) and preservation of the species (matter); he stoically accepts human mortality as an inevitable part of the harmonious functioning of the cosmic mechanism and finds comfort in a Senecan resignation to a natural law of universal equality and necessity. He constructs a sensualist philosophy centred on the absence of physical and mental pain which is designed to console, associates man's death with the eternal forces of the natural and divine worlds, and contemplates an after-life in the Elysian Fields which is essentially a sensualist's paradise and a continuation of the halcyon days and active processes of earthly existence. Antipathetic to the soul's passive metaphysical communion with the Divine, he demonstrates a serious interest in the doctrine of metempsychosis for it is a further assurance of man's survival in an eternal cyclic process.

At the same time he transcends human mortality by the intensity of creative and intellectual activity—by knowledge and poetry—surmounting momentary doubts, crises and moods of pessimism, redefining the limits of mental enquiry to accommodate his sensitivity to the concept of *hubris*, accepting his immortality—poetically expressed by a dense series of antithetical images and symbols—and his ultimate divinisation as a just reward and adequate compensation. On the other hand his rejection of the Orpheus/Eurydice myth as a symbol of the conquest of love over death, and his generally ambivalent attitude to the transcendental value of love, are utterly consistent with his antipathy for the nebulous mysticism of neo-Platonism and his predilection for the concrete present of an epicurean position. If needs be he can escape the presence of death by a classical euphemistic vision which diverts or distances the mind and substitutes poetic fictions and natural, familiar images for the brutal reality of death.

Ronsard, ever-reluctant to commit himself to the finality and solitude of death, never visualises death as a void, as *le néant*, and only rarely as decomposition. It is true that isolated examples of what Marcel Raymond calls a *maniérisme noir*[67] can be found periodically in Ronsard's verse, and that these represent one half of a duality or tension in his perception of reality as defined in the introduction (above, p. 5), but this macabre evocation of death occupies a relatively minor place in his inspiration. Whilst it is necessary to note such a perspective as one of his many attitudes to death and to acknowledge the poetic quality of such a vision—nowhere more evident than in the powerful description of du Bellay's ghost—nevertheless it is equally important not to exaggerate its value in comparison with the more emphatic and consistent consolatory and euphemistic attitudes, in our opinion the expression of Ronsard's 'authentic voice'. It is not merely that references to a gothic vision of death are relatively rare. It is also significant that the vast majority of the allusions to physical decay are brief, lacking in visual emphasis and realism, and, apart from the very last years of Ronsard's career, do not betray obsession or fear.[68] On the contrary, his allegorical account of Death is more akin to Sleep than to the frightening figure of Dürer's woodcuts, and the personification reveals much repetition on the commonplaces of Death's heartlessness, blindness and deafness (XII, 266–7; XIII, 184; XV, 296; 297; 302; XVII, 81). Similarly in his evocations of the *Parcae* and the Underworld, realistic detail is conspicuously absent, and nowhere do we find the grotesque and horrific portrayals of medieval literature and art. Neither is death envisaged as a tragic rupture for always there is continuation of existence beyond death, be it in the Elysian Fields (or, much more rarely, in the Christian heaven), in memory, poetry and intellectual activity, or in regenerated matter. The void is peopled with all the figures of mythology, with lovers, poets, friends, with the mass of immortal souls which wait on God, or with the numberless spirits of the Underworld. Even though death looms so large in his work, in the final analysis Ronsard is to be celebrated as the poet of life.

NOTES TO CHAPTER SEVEN

1   On the diffusion of neo-Platonism throughout France in the sixteenth century, see J. Festugière, *La Philosophie de l'amour de Marsile Ficin et son influence sur la littérature française au XVIe siècle* (Paris, 1941); R. V. Merrill with R. J. Clements, *Platonism in French Renaissance poetry* (New York, 1957); A. H. T. Levi, 'The Neoplatonist Calculus. The exploitation of Neoplatonist themes in French Renaissance literature', in *Humanism in France*, pp. 229–48 (and note 2 for fuller bibliographical references, especially to works by F. Yates and D. P. Walker).

2   Cf. Ficino, *Commentary on Plato's 'Symposium'*, Seventh Speech, Chapters XIII–XIV.

3   Cf. Pontus de Tyard, *Œuvres. Solitaire Premier*, éd. critique par S. Baridon (TLF, Geneva, 1950), p. 3.

4   This work can be read in an English translation in E. Cassirer, P. O. Kristeller, J. H. Randall Jr. (editors), *The Renaissance Philosophy of Man* (University of Chicago Press, 1948), pp. 223–54. For the *dignitas hominis* theme, see H. C. Baker, *The Dignity of Man. Studies in the Persistence of an Idea* (Harvard Univ. Press, 1947); L. Sozzi, 'La "Dignitas Hominis" dans la littérature française de la Renaissance', in *Humanism in France*, pp. 176–98.

5   On this work, see E. F. Rice, *The Renaissance Idea of Wisdom*, pp. 106–23. An edition of the *De Sapiente* by R. Klibansky can be read in E. Cassirer, *Individuum und Kosmos in der Philosophie der Renaissance* (Leipzig and Berlin, 1927), pp. 299–412.

6   Cf. Tyard, *Le Premier Curieux*, in *The Universe of Pontus de Tyard*, ed. Lapp, pp. 4–5.

7   VIII, 86–7. For the theme of the cosmic voyage of the mind, see R. M. Jones, 'Posidonius and the Flight of the Mind through the Universe', *Classical Philology*, XXI (1926), 97–113; B. S. Ridgely, 'The Cosmic Voyage in French Sixteenth century learned poetry', *Studies in the Renaissance*, X (1963), 136–62.

8   *Astronomica*, IV, 875–9. Du Bellay's translation is found in Chamard's edition (STFM), VI, 440–1, together with the Latin text.

9   VI, 194. For the relationship between *savoir*, *gloire* and *vertu* in Ronsard's conception of poetry, consult H. Franchet, *Le Poète et son œuvre d'après Ronsard* (Paris, 1923), pp. 43–175.

10   For further details concerning these neo-Platonic commentaries and the wider implications of this theory of divine inspiration in the aesthetic of the Pléiade, consult H. Franchet, pp. 1–42; G. Castor, *Pléiade Poetics* (Cambridge Univ. Press, 1964), chapt. 3; I. Silver, *The Intellectual Evolution of Ronsard*, vol. II: *Ronsard's General Theory of Poetry* (St Louis, Washington Univ. Press, 1973), chapt. XII; A. H. T. Levi, 'The role of neoplatonism in Ronsard's poetic imagination', in *Ronsard the Poet*, pp. 137–49, together with their bibliographical references.

11   Cf. Ficino, *Commentary on 'Symposium'*, Seventh Speech, chapt. XIV; Tyard, *Solitaire Premier*, ed. Baridon, pp. 17–19.

12   For Ronsard's association of the Orpheus myth with this neo-Platonic doctrine of poetic fury, see E. Kushner, 'Le personnage d'Orphée chez Ronsard', in *Lumières de la Pléiade*, pp. 280–4, 286–9, 301. In assimilating Orphism and neo-Platonism Ronsard was typical of the Renaissance (pp. 271–4).

13   On the neo-Platonic basis of the Pléiade's musical humanism, consult in particular the important articles of D. P. Walker, 'Musical Humanism in the Sixteenth and Early Seventeenth Centuries', *The Music Review*, II (1941),

1–13; 111–21; 220–7; 288–308; III (1942), 55–71; 'Orpheus the theologian and Renaissance platonists', *JWCIL*, XVI (1953), 100–20; 'Le chant orphique de Marsile Ficin', in *Musique et poésie au XVIe siècle* (Paris, 1954), pp. 17–34.

14 R. J. Clements, *Critical Theory and Practice of the Pléiade* (Harvard Univ. Press, 1942), pp. 51–83.

15 That it is misdirected intellectual curiosity rather than knowledge *per se* that is under attack, can be deduced from yet another passage from the *Remonstrance* (XI, 76) where Ronsard draws the distinction between those men 'D'un jugement rassis, & d'un sçavoir profond' who remain faithful to Catholicism, and those 'qui sçavent un peu' who are abused by the Reform movement.

16 That Ronsard's questioning of these aspects of neo-Platonism is neither complete nor permanent can be demonstrated by the fact that some of his enthusiastic statements concerning progress, intellectual activity and encyclopedic knowledge occur in collections of verse written after 1560 (cf. the publication dates given in the references, above pp. 174–7 : apart from these references, see also XVII, 212, s. XIX, for a eulogy of the intellect in Platonic mode). It is perhaps not without significance that two of the longer passages devoted to man's misery and inferiority to the animals were suppressed in the course of subsequent revision (X, 309–10, ll. 27–42; XIV, 182–3, ll. 35–52).

17 *Commentary on Plato's 'Symposium'*, Speeches II; IV, chapt. vi; VII, chapts. xiii–xv. Cf. Castiglione, *Il Cortegiano*, IV, lxv–lxx.

18 For Ronsard's antipathy, see P. Laumonier, *RPL*, pp. 467–559 (study of erotic ode); J. Festugière, pp. 138–40; A. W. Satterthwaite, *Spenser, Ronsard, and du Bellay*, pp. 171–200; W. A. R. Kerr, 'The Pléiade and Platonism', *Modern Philology*, V (1907–8), 407–21; H. Weber, 'Platonisme et sensualité dans la poésie amoureuse de la Pléiade', in *Lumières de la Pléiade*, pp. 157–78; A. H. T. Levi, 'The role of neoplatonism', in *Ronsard the Poet*, pp. 128–37.

19 The *Cartel* is immediately followed by an *Autre Cartel fait promtement pour l'Amour* (XV, 114–20) which develops into a hymn to the popular, terrestrial Venus. The two *cartels* are clearly written for court festivities and form a stylised poetic debate of diametrically opposed arguments which in no way transcend the circumstantial. Such poems *Pour Amour* and *Contre Amour* are commonplace in the sixteenth century. The *Discours* falls into the same poetic convention (cf. Laumonier's note, XV, 85). More significantly the final lines of the *Discours* cast serious doubts on the conviction of the neo-Platonic expression, for in these Ronsard states that his poem is merely a concession to the Platonising Scévole de Sainte-Marthe, to whom it is dedicated, and that he has written it purely to acquit himself of a literary debt.

20 XVII, 118. For other aspects of this theme of illusion in Ronsard's verse, see G. Castor, 'The theme of illusion in Ronsard's *Sonets pour Helene* and in the variants of the 1552 *Amours*', *Forum for Modern Language Studies*, VII (1971), 361–73; I. D. McFarlane, 'Aspects of Ronsard's poetic vision', in *Ronsard the Poet*, pp. 43–8.

21 XIV, 151. Cf. XII, 222; 268; 270; XVII, 119–20; 123.

22 See especially, V, 155, s. CCVIII (1584 text). Cf. Propertius, I, xix, 5–6, 12; Petrarch, *Rime*, s. XC, 'Erano i capei d'oro . . .', tercets. See also Ronsard, II, 67–8; IV, 6–7, s. II; XV, 191–3; XVI, 270.

23 XVII, 8–9. See also, II, 140 (and n. 1 for the Ovidian sources); XII, 125; 271; XV, 300.

24 XV, 298–9 (the appeal to the myth is seen as ineffectual in ll. 143–8 of the poem); XVII, 121–2; 128.

25 'Le personnage d'Orphée chez Ronsard', p. 292. On Ronsard's treatment of

the Orpheus myth, see also F. Joukovsky-Micha, *Orphée et ses disciples dans la poésie française et néolatine du XVIe siècle* (Geneva, 1970), pp. 62–103.

26 XV, 220–1 (1584 text). See also XV, 121; XVIII, 308–9. Cf. *The Greek Anthology*, vol. I, p. 169, no. 85. For Ronsard's debt to this Greek text throughout his work, see J. Hutton, *The Greek Anthology in France and in the Latin Writers of the Netherlands* (Ithaca, Cornell Univ. Press, 1946), pp. 350–74.

27 *La Gloire dans la poésie française et néolatine du XVIe siècle* (Geneva, 1969). This section owes a substantial debt to Joukovsky's book. See also H. Franchet, *Le Poète et son œuvre*, pp. 43–175; R. J. Clements, *Critical Theory and Practice*, chapt. II.

28 For some of his most emphatic and developed statements, cf. I, 138–44; 226–8; II, 31–3; 148–51; 152–3; VII, 30–2; X, 105; XIII, 256–9; XVII, 248–9, s. II; XVIII, 60–1.

29 I, 139–40, ll. 19–30 (var.); 176–7, ll. 41–50 (var.); 215, ll. 14–20 (var.); XV, 180, l. 34 (var.).

30 I, 131, ll. 37–40 (var.); II, 105, ll. 19–24 (var.); III, 29, ll. 391–4 (var.).

31 II, 43; VI, 114.

32 II, 152 (var.). See also II, 202; XII, 36; XV, 210. Cf. Horace, *Odes*, II, XX, 9–12; IV, ii, 25–7.

33 Pindar, *Olympian*, IX, ep. 1; *Nemean*, VI, str. 3; VII, str. 2; *Isthmian*, IV, antistr. 1; V, ep. 3; *Pythian*, VIII, antistr. 5; Virgil, *Georgics*, III, 9; Horace, *Odes*, II, XX; IV, ii, 25–7; Ovid, *Metam.*, XV, 875–9; Propertius, III, i, 9–18.

34 Cf. *Olympian*, II, str. & antistr. 5; IX, str. 1; *Nemean*, VI, str. 2; *Isthmian*, II, str. 1. Pindar also uses the metaphor of throwing the javelin (*Olympian*, XIII, str. 5; *Pythian*, I, str. 3; *Isthmian*, II, str. 3), which is echoed in turn by Ronsard (III, 159).

35 Cf. *délivrer* (II, 202); *font oultrage à* (VII, 229); *pren ... la vengence* (V, 251); *donter* (II, 110); *allonger* (XVIII, 61); *chasser* (I, 98); *tromper* (I, 131); *frauder* (V, 246); *pousser* (II, 38, var.).

36 Pindar, *Olympian*, IX, ep. 1; *Pythian*, I, str. 4; VI, str. 1; *Nemean*, I, antistr. 1; VIII, antistr. 3; IX, str. 8; X, antistr. 2; *Isthmian*, VI, antistr. 1; Horace, *Odes*, I, xii, 45–6.

37 See XVIII, 249, where poets are compared to oxen '... labourant les champs, / Sillonnant par rayons une germeuse plaine'. Note also the comparison which equates creative energy and poetic genius with periods of natural fertility and fallow (above, p. 42).

38 II, 104. Cf. I, 203–5; II, 105–7; 129–32; V, 241–2.

39 III, 81–2; 100; 150; 167; VII, 108–9. On this theme, see F. Joukovsky-Micha, *Poésie et mythologie au XVIe siècle. Quelques mythes de l'inspiration chez les poètes de la Renaissance* (Paris, 1969), pp. 103–18.

40 Writer compared to a bee (Pindar, *Pythian*, X, ep. 3; Plato, *Ion*, 534A–B; Horace, *Odes*, IV, ii, 27–32; Seneca, *Epist.*, LXXXIV, 3–5): poetry seen as honey (Pindar, *Nemean*, III, antistr. 4; *Isthmian*, II, str. 1; Lucretius, IV, 22). Cf. Ronsard, II, 36; VII, 140, s. XXII; VIII, 350; XI, 161; XV, 252; XVI, 336. See also R. J. Clements, *Critical theory*, pp. 163–75.

41 Cf. Pindar, *Olympian*, VI, str. 1; *Nemean*, IV, str. 10–11; VIII, ep. 3; Horace, *Odes*, III, xxx, 1–5; Virgil, *Georgics*, III, 13–39; Ovid, *Metam.*, XV, 871–9; Propertius, III, ii, 19–26.

42 For a close comparison of the Latin and French texts and for an analysis of Ronsard's originality, see M. D. Quainton, 'Ronsard's *A sa Muse* and Horace's *Exegi monumentum*', *Pegasus*, University of Exeter, VI (June 1966), 3–9.

43 I, 87. Cf. I, 125; 236–7. Verbs of sound are to be found everywhere: among the most common are *bruire, crier, chanter, sonner, résonner, publier, fre-*

donner, parler, raconter, trompeter, retentir. For this theme, see also Joukovsky, pp. 339–47, 498–515, 601–5.

44 II, 151. For the theme of the poet's participation in the Divine Banquet, see
Joukovsky, *La Gloire*, pp. 547–56.

45 *Iliad*, XIV, 231; XVI, 672 and 682. Cf. *Iliad*, XI, 241; XVI, 454; *Odyssey*, XIII 79
(where death is described as a sleep). For Death and Sleep as children of Night,
cf. Hesiod, *Theogony*, ll. 211–12; 756–66; Pausanias, V, xviii, i.

46 Daremberg and Saglio, s.v. *Mors* and *Somnus*; Tervarent, s.v. *Femme avec ses
deux enfants*, I.

47 Cf. Ronsard, VII, 94; 284; X, 99, s. XIV, var.; 337; XVII, 70. On occasions
(VII, 199) Ronsard recalls Homer directly.

48 Part of Ronsard's description of Death in the *Hymne de la Mort* reads '... &
les piedz par-à-bas / Luy calfeutra de laine' (VIII, 175). This detail is echoed in
an evocation of Sleep in the *Hymne de l'Hyver* of 1563: '... le Sommeil ... /
Prist des souliers de feutre' (XII, 81), and is borrowed, suggests Loumonier,
from Ariosto's description of Silence in his *Orlando Furioso*, canto XIV,
stanza 94. This motif is not found in iconographical representations of Death
in either the classical or medieval tradition. A literary equivalent of this
visual detail is found, however, in Tibullus, I, x, 33–4.

49 XVII, 67. Cf. W. B. Cornelia, *The Classical Sources of the Nature References in
Ronsard's Poetry*, pp. 55–7. On the death of the Dauphin, see especially V.–L.
Saulnier, 'La mort du Dauphin François et son tombeau poétique (1536)', *BHR*,
VI (1945), 50–97.

50 XVII, 125. For detailed textual commentaires, consult L. Spitzer, 'Explication
linguistique et littéraire de deux textes français', *Le Français Moderne*, IV
(1936), 37–48; M. Raymond, *Baroque et Renaissance poétique*, pp. 111–15;
M. Remacle, 'Analyse du sonnet de Ronsard *Comme on voit sur la branche*',
Cahiers d'Analyse Textuelle, I (1959), 15–54.

51 XII, 267. For the possible sources see Laumonier's notes, VII, 285–6. For images
of snow and wax to evoke transience, cf. VI, 81; X, 347; XII, 125. On this
technique of stylistic diversion via developed nature imagery, cf. VII, 57; XII,
195; XV, 297–8; 301–2.

52 F. Joukovsky-Micha, 'Tombeaux et offrandes rustiques', pp. 237–43.

53 See in particular VI, 29–30; VII, 100; VIII, 231; X, 314. Cf. also III, 84–5; V,
248–9; 257; X, 144; XVII, 388.

54 Cybele, or Rhea (Roman: Ops), Mother of the Gods, often identified with the
Earth and associated with plenitude and fecundity (Daremberg and Saglio,
s.v. *Cybele* and *Ops*). Cf. Lucretius, II, 598–660. For Ronsard's descriptions of
Mother Earth and her productivity in terms of sexuality and human conception, cf. I, 150; VIII, 192; XII, 27–34 (and especially ll. 117–20); XII, 282; XVII,
237. On the iconographical tradition relating to the goddess Earth, see Tervarent, s.v. *Femme aux nombreuses mamelles*, II.

55 II, 61; 99; VI, 30; VII, 95. Common source, noted by Laumonier, is *The Greek
Anthology*, vol. II, p. 15, no. 22. Cf. also, nos. 23–4, 31, 36, 222, 321.

56 *Aux cendres*, ll. 61–6. Cf. ll. 37–42; *Election*, ll. 17–24, 73–6. On Ronsard's use
of the word *emmurer*, see E. Armstrong, 'Ronsard and the "Wall of Water" ',
in *Renaissance Studies in Honor of Isidore Silver*, pp. 21–8.

57 II, 101; III, 85; V, 251. See also, F. Joukovsky-Micha, 'Tombeaux et offrandes
rustiques', pp. 243–7. On Latin sepulchral poetry and rites, consult E. Galletier,
Etude sur la poésie funéraire romaine (Paris, 1922).

58 Ronsard, V, 258; X, 143–4 (cf. III, 83). Cf. Horace, *Odes*, I, xxviii, 15–16; *The
Greek Anthology*, vol. II, p. 25, no. 36. See Galletier, p. 226ff. for the funeral
inscription.

59   III, 85; V, 251; XII, 124; XIII, 101. Cf. Homer, *Iliad*, XXIII, 140–2; *Odyssey*, XXIV, 54ff.; Virgil, *Aeneid*, III, 63; 300–5; V, 58ff. The full classical obsequies are reproduced in the *Franciade* (XVI, 204–9) from Virgilian reminiscences (see Laumonier's note 2, p. 208).

60   III, 81; 84; XIII, 99. Cf. Virgil, *Ecl.*, V, 13–14; 40–4; X, 53–4; Tibullus, I, iii, 53–6; Sannazaro, *Arcadia*, fol. 27v.

61   Cf. VII, 46; VIII, 84 (wrong function assigned to Lachesis); VIII, 270; XII, 267–8; XIII, 107; XVII, 67; 71; XVIII, 175.

62   I, 156, l. 33 (var.); II, 110; 128; VI, 60; XIV, 117; XV, 89. For the classical reminiscences, see Laumonier's notes.

63   X, 369; XII, 138; 222; XIV, 118; XVI, 127 (see note 4 for the classical references). For *idole* and *image*, see III, 68; VI, 43; XII, 137.

64   Although Ronsard imitates Virgil in order to describe the entrance to the Underworld (XVI, 273–4: cf. *Aeneid*, VI, 237–42), the propitiatory ceremony (pp. 274–5: cf. *Aen.*, VI, 243–58) and the doctrine of metempsychosis (pp. 283–9: cf. *Aen.*, VI, 719–51), he ignores the descent and the evocation of Hades proper.

65   'The Forces of Flux and Stability', p. 17; 'Contraries...', p. 365.

66   Cf. XII, 299–300; XIII, 182–8; 188–94; XV, 1–12; XVII, 3–10; 65–84. On Ronsard's narrative epitaphs, see Schweinitz, pp. 62–87.

67   'La Pléiade et le Maniérisme', in *Lumières de la Pléiade*, pp. 403, 421. See also, J. Rousset, *La Littérature de l'âge baroque en France* (Paris, 1954), pp. 93–100; M. Raymond, *Baroque et Renaissance poétique*, pp. 121–3.

68   In a recent study of 'Le Baroque et la Pléiade', André Baïche, *La Naissance du baroque français* (Toulouse, 1976), pp. 23–111, has argued against the idea of a 'Ronsard baroque'. His conclusion to a brief study of Ronsard's vision of death (pp. 88–93) is that even in the *Derniers Vers* 'on y cherche en vain la richesse du baroque, son dynamisme, son tourment'.

Conclusion

This present study has demonstrated that the twin concepts of flux and stability represent an important and continuing source of inspiration for Ronsard. These concepts do not merely result in a poetic rejuvenation of certain lyrical commonplaces concerning time's flight, the omnipotence of death and the inconstancy of Fortune, but they have widespread consequences which encompass a diversity of attitudes and perspectives—allegorical, mythological, ethical, philosophical, cosmological, theological and aesthetic. These different visions are not distinct, however, but are interdependent in that they often centre on a common core of preoccupations. These central concerns operate simultaneously on the level of theme, style and structure and frequently find expression in antithetical patterns of rich suggestivity : preservation/destruction; movement/lethargy; activity/stagnation; fertility/sterility; youth/old age; *vray/faux*; harmony/discord; unity/diversity; *copia*/measure; *libre contrainte*.

On the scientific level Ronsard constructs a cosmology which clearly revolves round the notions of change and order, for the universe is envisaged as a complex and delicate balance of opposing forces (a *discordia concors*). This harmony of contraries is seen in the arrangement of the four elements, in the diversity of heavenly movements, in the division of the cosmos into sublunar and extralunar regions and in the balanced pattern of corruption and generation which characterises the sublunar world. As so often in Ronsard's verse this scientific vision is complemented by an allegorical perspective, for the cosmic roles of Peace and Discord are seen to be an expression of this same equilibrium. Moreover the flux and movement of the universe, and especially of the sublunar region, is preserved in a state of stability by a complex system of natural and divine laws, by a dynamic, cohesive pantheism, as well as by a host of allegorical figures, personifications and intermediary divinities (Eros, Bacchus, Nature, Peace, Eternity, Time and its component parts—Youth, the Hours, the Seasons—*Vertu, Puissance*, Destiny and Fortune). Whilst the hierarchy of these cosmic forces may be inconsistent and ambiguous, their function—to combat the enemies of disorder and destruction (*Vieillesse, Maladie*, Discord, Opinion) and to preserve the universe in harmony—is never in doubt. The stability of the sublunar world is similarly achieved by the enduring transformations of matter, the perpetual intermovements of elements and the cycles of corruption and regeneration. Such patterns are controlled, as in Aristotle, by the rotatory motion of the 'le ciel premier-mouvant' which provides the dynamic measure of time within eternity.

The human consequences of this scientific perspective become in turn a fundamental concern of the Pléiade poet. A constant effort is made both to explain flux as a necessary part of a rational order (natural or divine), and, more significantly, to integrate man into this pattern, to fuse him with the wider forces to transience and to introduce him as a vital factor of the cosmic mechanism, subjected to the same processes, the same laws. Indeed the ability or failure to create such a link between microcosm and macrocosm is seen to dictate the mood of Ronsard and to explain a duality in his vision. On those occasions when he fails to look beyond fluctuating phenomena and perceive the cyclic patterns behind the moments of vicissitude, Ronsard experiences a momentary feeling of isolation from the cosmic scheme which reinforces his sense of human fragility and misery. This short-lived pessimism, essentially foreign to his temperament as he defines it (XII, 7), inspires beautiful lyric poetry based on a series of melancholy contrasts—between, for example, the sublunar and extralunar worlds, eternal Nature and transient man, mortality and immortality, the imperfect human conceptions of time and the all-embracing vision of Eternity. Such moments of alienation, however, are relatively rare and there is no discernible pattern of evolution or development of attitude based on chronological reference. More generally Ronsard visualises the forces of flux as an essential aspect of a universal order, and he consistently and emphatically preaches lessons of stoical resignation and joyful submission to human fragility in the name of this cosmic necessity and the rule of Nature.

In his attitude to the concept of Change, for instance, Ronsard commonly looks beyond the Ovidian illustrations of metamorphosis and the isolated moment of flux to the regularity of an ordered pattern ('En son inconstance assuré'). Behind the transience of forms he emphasises the endurance of matter and discovers a stability and fertility preserved, as in Seneca, by Nature and natural cycles. It is precisely the permanence and fecundity of the spiritual forces of Nature which enable Ronsard and the Pléiade to elaborate an aesthetic theory based on imitation, a transference of cultures (*translatio studii*) and a defence of the vernacular. For Ronsard, mutability bears witness to the world's vitality, dynamism and continuity. Change is a prerequisite for existence and preservation, and the absence of change is equated with sterility, stagnation and death : '«Car qui voudroit tousjours en un point se trouver / «Il ne pourroit durer . . .' (VIII, 225). Invigorated and fascinated by the variety of flux, Ronsard constantly explores the aesthetic possibilities of changing phenomena and records the precise moment of metamorphosis—synonymous with life in his materialistic, transformist definitions—in descriptive and visual detail. He proposes a conception of beauty and an aesthetic theory which mirrors Nature's fluctuating variety, with the proviso, however, that as in Nature, society and the universe the diversity and *copia* must be controlled, measured and harmonised (an aesthetic *discordia concors* in fact). Likewise his philosophy of history often relates to the concept of cyclic change and to the transformist principle of the *translatio imperii*, although in the context of France's religious conflict the historical experience of the destruction of empires, and of Rome in particular, attains contemporary significance in that it is used to draw attention to the danger that

> . . . l'empire de France
> . . . mourra, imitant l'inconstance
> De toute chose née . . .
>   (VII, 310)

An identical process of thought can be seen in Ronsard's treatment of Fortune. Although he continues the medieval tradition of the pagan goddess by describing her physical and mental portrait and by emphasising her omnipotence, inconstancy and hostility, nevertheless Fortune is equated with the prudence and wisdom of Divine Providence and, as Nemesis–Fortune, is the instrument through which a moral order of the universe is administered. As a corrector of excess and abuse and as a cosmic force for retributive justice, Fortune is fundamental in preserving the precise and fragile balance between microcosm and macrocosm. His conception of Time reveals a similar attempt to explain transience as an important aspect of cosmic stability and conservation, although here, as with Fortune, there is evidence of a duality in his vision. It is true, on the one hand, that he is obsessed with time as a linear and destructive force, the mobility of which juxtaposes youth and old age in a dramatic antithesis and intensifies the awareness of human fragility. However his allegorical and cosmological visions of Time (and its component parts—the Hours, Youth, the Seasons) concentrate entirely on the dynamic and constructive nature of its role : time—its measure defined by the movement of the outer heaven—is seen to embrace cycles of growth, fecundity and preservation. Human happiness resides in an

acceptance of this dynamic rhythm of time, in a full and lucid utilisation of the variety of opportunities and experiences offered by a continuous stream of present moments.

Whilst the abundance and consistency of references to death in Ronsard's verse suggest a genuine and lasting preoccupation with human
mortality, nevertheless death is not considered as a painful, irrational
accident, as an absurdity which emphasises man's contingency or
negates the significance of life. The anguish of the existentialist has no
part in Ronsard's vision of mortality. On the contrary man's death is
introduced into a universal pattern, a natural order, and forms part of
the cosmic mechanism. Defined in terms of a philosophy of change,
human mortality is integrated into the transformist cycles of matter,
into a dynamic process of regeneration, and if Ronsard prudently
exempts the soul from a cyclic pattern of metempsychosis it is only
with regret and after serious temptation. Similarly mortality is accepted
as a natural part of a balanced scheme of corruption and generation, and
the death of individuals is deemed necessary for the preservation of the
species. Moreover the Pléiade poet finds constant consolation in the
thought, expressed so frequently in the work of Seneca, that death is no
tragic accident but a natural law applied universally and equitably.
Again the correspondences and sympathies established between human
mortality and the wider processes of cosmic order are attested by the
manner in which the divine and natural worlds participate in human
bereavement by presaging, mourning and lamenting man's death.

Within this general context of integrating man into a universal order
and of fusing him with the wider forces of transience, the concept of
hubris gives a theological and moral dimension to the poet's considerations, for arrogant excess is invariably seen as a dangerous threat to
cosmic and social stability. Not only does Ronsard consider the division
of the world into sublunar and extralunar regions as specifically designed to act as a barrier against human hubris and a renewal of Titanism, but man's limited temporal vision, his imprisonment in a transient
present, his subjection to seasonal fluctuation and his mortality are all
traced to the original sin of presumption. Moreover Change, Destiny,
Fortune–Nemesis, Time and Death are attributed with the cosmic function of retaining man within the limits of his fragility and of counter-
acting his tendency to arrogant conquest, and they do so in order to
maintain the correct balance between microcosm and macrocosm. It is
in the name of this universal order that the poet resigns himself to the
mortality of his condition and to the transience of human endeavour,
finding consolation in the fact that the cosmic hierarchy depends on the
submission of man to a series of equitable divine and natural laws. A
precise contemporary illustration of this moral concept of hubris is provided by France's civil wars, for Ronsard—in an argument from which

tactical expediency and personal interest are perhaps not wholly excluded—discovers the same disruptive arrogance in the Reformist theologians who seek the divine mysteries and threaten the social and cosmic
balance. Fearing that France may destroy herself Ronsard redefines the
limits of intellectual enquiry to exclude the divine, and adapts the
theme of *translatio imperii* and the historical example of Rome to
strengthen his polemic and patriotic arguments and to awaken France
to her folly.

Thus, although Ronsard is clearly preoccupied by the consequences of
flux and human mortality, he constantly emphasises the naturalness of
changing phenomena and the most common note struck is one of optimism and resignation, not of despair:[1] he has

> ... peur de rien
> Tant que le fort lien
> De la saincte Nature
> Tient ce monde arresté.

(XVII, 42)

His attitude, in the face of the accidents and vicissitudes of life, is to a
large extent typified by the joyful stoicism of Seneca and Horace[2] and
by his frequent recourse to those comforting arguments expressed in the
classical *consolatio*.

Moreover remedies and compensations for transience are discovered
within man himself, for there are adequate means of extending and surpassing the limitations of man's condition and of transcending sublunar
change, time and death. On the ladder of being man is also a balance of
opposites, poised as he is between the divine and the animal, the mortal
and the immortal, the spiritual and the physical, and Ronsard's solution
to human transience is to utilise both aspects of this duality to the full
in order to transcend man's essential fragility. It is by the fervent
activity of the intellect and the creative mind, by poetry and knowledge,
that man surpasses himself and the sublunar world and assures his immortality and divine apotheosis. It is not merely that the creative act is
equated with the transcendental and liberating force of divine 'madness',
but also that the written word itself conquers the powers of flux, sterility, darkness and torpor in a struggle which finds its poetic expression
in a developed and dramatic antithesis. Similarly encyclopedic knowledge—limited to physical and natural mysteries after the outbreak of
religious hostilities in 1560—gives man mastery over the terrestrial
regions, and it is by a cosmic voyage of the mind, by intellectual and
spiritual elevation, that he attains communion with perfect knowledge,
with the extralunar world and with all that is divine, immutable and
eternal. Even those mythological narrative poems devoted to human

metamorphosis not only visualise change as a victory over time and death by emphasising man's participation in an eternal, natural order and in the divine world, but they also invariably have associations with the surpassing of human mortality by the transcendental values of the creative mind, and by poetry and divination in particular.

In the same way as the intense activity of the creative intellect is an assurance of immortality, so too is the *intensity* of love which is seen to survive time and death by imprinting itself indelibly on the memory. However Ronsard more commonly attributes love's victory over transience not to the artificial *concetti* of Petrarchism or to the nebulous and mystical spiritualism of neo-Platonic doctrine, but rather to the tangible and realistic epicurean philosophy which guarantees present physical satisfaction and which acknowledges the natural inconstancy of human emotions and the necessity of change.[3] Although expressing serious and continuing regret for passing time and an inevitable death, Ronsard is nevertheless willing to accept the fragility of his estate and to reject the more durable status of inanimate matter because, as a sentient being, he can enjoy to the full 'La Dance, le Vin, le Repas / . . . les Instrumens de la vie' (XVIII, 419). Human fulfilment and compensation for mortality are found not only in intellectual activity but also in the gratification of man's senses, in the enjoyment of the present moment, an attitude which expresses itself not only in the popular erotico–bacchic refrains, but also in the allegorical personification of *Kairos–Occasio* and in a series of philosophical arguments (many of them Horatian and Senecan in inspiration) which reconcile epicureanism with Christianity, associate the value of experience with mental awareness and conscious lucidity and judge the worth of life by its quality and intensity and not by its measure of years.

Within this generally optimistic perspective the anguish of the Christian is almost totally absent and is restricted to prudent and conventional reservations concerning theologically dangerous classical doctrines (metempsychosis, Lucretian materialism). Whilst Ronsard's belief in God is not in question, religion is never seriously considered as a consolation for terrestrial flux and mortality, and indeed the theme of God's stability in a mutable world is submerged in an exploration of the aesthetic possibilities of developed images of transience; the religious idea is clearly an apologetic addendum and of minor importance to him. Furthermore he is relatively uninterested in the destiny of the soul after death and his vision of an after-life is more emphatically pagan than Christian, being an extension and an idealisation of life's physical and mental processes. It is true that Fortune and Destiny (and, more ambiguously, Nature) are equated with Divine Providence on numerous occasions and that Ronsard peoples his scientific vision of the universe with multiple personifications and intermediary deities, but here again his interest is primarily cosmological rather than religious and his perspective pantheistic rather than monotheistic. In Ronsard's work there is comparatively little sense of the personal presence and comfort of God: salvation is sought, and found, in this world not in the next.

However, the concepts of flux and stability do not merely present the reader with many of the fundamental areas of Ronsard's inspiration (for example, his vision of the universe and of the microcosm–macrocosm relationship, of society, history, aesthetics, love, mythology), but, equally important, they also introduce him to some of the poet's most beautiful collections of verse and to a good number of his most rewarding individual poems. The balance of opposing aesthetic concepts which Ronsard defines in his theoretical writings, are constantly illustrated throughout his work on structural, stylistic and lexical levels, and the creative principles of diversity in unity, of *copia* and measure, of *libre contrainte*, are everywhere apparent both in the overall architecture of poems and in the richly woven textures of individual movements and fragments. It is rare that one finds the unrestrained exuberance and dynamism of the baroque imagination without the classical principles of measure, balance and control. Thus it is through the thematic diversity and the poetic quality of this concept of *discordia concors* that the reader receives a wide and general contact with the essential concerns of the best verse of the greatest poet of Renaissance France.

NOTES TO CONCLUSION

1 'At no time, except in his declining days, was pessimism the constant attitude of Ronsard's mind' (I. Silver, 'Ronsard's Ethical Thought', p. 371). Cf. Laumonier, *RPL*, pp. 630–3.
2 See, for instance, his personal declarations: XII, 7; XIII, 248–9.
3 Cf. VII, 125–6, s. IX; 127–8, s. XI; 142–3, s. XXV; XIII, 255–6.

Bibliography

In order not to lengthen the bibliography unnecessarily, only primary and secondary material which has contributed substantially to the book in one way or another is included here. Works to which the reader is referred in notes for further information on associated subjects are not recorded, unless they fall within this category. For abbreviations see above, p. ix.

All works by the following classical authors—unless listed below in the bibliography—have been read in the Loeb Classical Library edition (London, Heinemann; Cambridge, Mass., Harvard University Press): Ammianus Marcellinus, Apollonius Rhodius, Aristotle, Athenaeus, Ausonius, Boethius, Callimachus, Callistratus, Catullus, Cicero, Claudianus, Diogenes Laertius, Hesiod, Homer, Horace, Lucretius, Menander, Ovid, Pausanias, Pindar, Plato, Pliny the Elder, Plutarch, Propertius, Seneca, Tibullus, Valerius Flaccus, Virgil. The following collections and anthologies have also been read in the Loeb edition: *Elegy and Iambus* (volume II contains the *Anacreontea*), *The Greek Anthology*, *The Greek Bucolic Poets* (Theocritus, Bion, Moschus), *Lyra Graeca*.

I CLASSICAL, MEDIEVAL AND RENAISSANCE SOURCES

Alciati (Andrea). *Emblemata D. A. Alciati, denuo ab ipso autore recognita, ac, quae desiderabantur, imaginibus locupletata*, Lyon, Bonhomme, 1551.
—— *Andreae Alciati Emblematum Fontes Quatuor*, ed. Henry Green. London, Trübner, 1870.
Baïf (Jean-Antoine de). *Euvres en rime de Jan Antoine de Baïf*. Edition de Charles Marty-Laveaux, 5 vols., Paris, Lemerre (La Pléiade Françoise), 1881–90.
Belleau (Rémy). *Œuvres Complètes de Remy Belleau*. Nouvelle édition publiée d'après les textes primitifs avec variantes et notes par A. Gouverneur, 3 vols., Paris, Franck; Nogent-le-Rotrou, Gouverneur, 1867.
Boccaccio (Giovanni). *De Casibus Virorum Illustrium liber repurgatus studio et opera Hieronymi Ziegleri*, Augustae Vindelicorum, P. Vlhardus, 1544.

Bouelles (Charles de). *Caroli Bovilli. Que hoc volumine continentur: Liber de intellectu . . . Liber de sapiente . . .*, Paris, H. Estienne, 1510. An edition by R. Klibansky is included in Ernst Cassirer, *Individuum und Kosmos in der Philosophie der Renaissance*, Leipzig & Berlin, Teubner, 1927, pp. 299–412.

Brués (Guy de). *The Dialogues of Guy de Brués* (Paris, 1557). A Critical Edition, with a Study in Renaissance Scepticism and Relativism by Panos Paul Morphos, Baltimore, Johns Hopkins Press, 1953.

Cousin (Jean). *Le Livre de Fortune: recueil de deux cents dessins inédits de Jean Cousin*, publié d'après le manuscrit original de la Bibliothèque de l'Institut par Ludovic Lalanne, Paris & London, Librairie de l'Art, 1883.

Du Bellay (Joachim). *Œuvres poétiques*, édition critique par Henri Chamard, 6 vols., Paris, Droz (STFM), 1908–31.

—— *La Deffence et Illustration de la Langue Françoyse*, édition critique par Henri Chamard, Paris, Didier (STFM), 1948.

Emblemata. Handbuch zur Sinnbildkunst des XVI. und XVII. Jahrhunderts. Herausgegeben von Arthur Henkel und Albrecht Schöne, Stuttgart, J. B. Metzlersche Verlagsbuchhandlung, 1967.

Epicurus. *Epicurus: the Extant Remains.* With short critical apparatus, translation and notes by Cyril Bailey, Oxford, Clarendon Press, 1926.

Ficino (Marsilio). *Opera Omnia*, 2 vols. (in 4), Turin, Bottega d'Erasmo, 1959. Facsimile reprint of 1576 Basle edition.

—— *Marsilio Ficino's Commentary on Plato's 'Symposium'.* The text and a Translation, with an Introduction by Sears Reynolds Jayne, Columbia, University of Missouri, 1944 (The University of Missouri Studies, vol. XIX, no. 1).

Jodelle (Étienne). *Les Œuvres et Meslanges poétiques*, éd. Charles Marty-Laveaux, 2 vols., Paris, Lemerre (La Pléiade Françoyse), 1868–70.

Leone Ebreo. *Philosophie d'Amour de M. Leon Hebreu, Traduicte d'Italien en Françoys, par le Seigneur du Parc, Champenois*, Lyon, G. Rouille & T. Payen, 1551.

Le Roy (Louis). *Le Sympose de Platon, ou de l'Amour et de Beauté, traduit de Grec en François, avec trois livres de Commentaires . . .* , Paris, Jehan Longis and Robert le Mangnyer, 1558 & 1559.

—— *De La Vicissitude ou varieté des choses en l'univers*, Paris, L'Huilier, 1576.

Marullus (Michael). *Michaelis Marulli Carmina*, edidit Alessandro Perosa, Zurich, Thesaurus Mundi, 1951.

Petrarca (Francesco). *The Triumphs of Petrarch*, translated into English by E. H. Wilkins, University of Chicago Press, 1962.

Ripa (Cesare). *Iconologia*, Padua, Tozzi, 1611.

Roman de la Rose, le. Par Guillaume de Lorris et Jean de Meun, éd. Ernest Langlois, 5 vols., Paris, Firmin-Didot then Champion (Société des Anciens Textes Français), 1914–24.

Ronsard (Pierre de). *Œuvres Complètes*, édition critique par Paul Laumonier, 20 vols., Paris, Hachette, then Droz, then Didier (STFM), 1914–75. Vols. XVII–XX revised and completed by I. Silver and R. Lebègue.

Sannazaro (Jacopo). *L'Arcadie de Messire Jaques Sannazar . . . mise d'Italien* en Françoys par Jehan Martin . . . , Paris, M. Vascosan & G. Corrozet, 1544.

Secundus (Joannes). *Les Baisers et l'Epithalame suivis des Odes et des Elégies*. Traduction nouvelle de Maurice Rat, Paris, Garnier, 1938.

Stobaeus (Joannes). *Dicta Poetarum quae apud Io. Stobaeum exstant. Emendata et Latino Carmine reddita ab Hugone Grotio* . . . , Paris, Buon, 1623. Contains *Ioannis Stobaei Florilegium ad Epimium*.

Tyard (Pontus de). *Œuvres Poétiques Complètes*, édition critique par John C. Lapp, Paris, Didier (STFM), 1966.

—— *Sceve ou Discours du Temps, de l'An, et de ses parties* in *Discours Philosophiques*, Paris, Abel L'Angelier, 1587.

—— *Œuvres. Solitaire premier*, éd. critique par Silvio F. Baridon, Geneva, Droz; Lille, Giard (TLF), 1950.

—— *The Universe of Pontus de Tyard (Premier et Second Curieux)*, critical edition by John C. Lapp, Ithaca, New York, Cornell University Press, 1950.

2   MODERN WORKS AND ARTICLES

Allègre (Fernand). *Etude sur la déesse grecque Tyché, sa signification religieuse et morale, son culte et ses représentations figurées*, Paris, E. Leroux, 1889.

Allen (Don Cameron). 'The rehabilitation of Epicurus and his theory of pleasure in the early Renaissance', *Studies in Philology*, XLI (1944), 1–15.

Antonioli (Roland). 'Aspects du monde occulte chez Ronsard', in *Lumières de la Pléiade*, Paris, Vrin, 1966, pp. 195–230.

Armstrong (Elizabeth). *Ronsard and the Age of Gold*, Cambridge University Press, 1968.

Baïche (André). *La Naissance du baroque français: poésie et image de la Pléiade à Jean de la Ceppède*, Université de Toulouse–Le Mirail, 1976.

Bensimon (Marc). 'Ronsard et la Mort', *Modern Language Review*, LVII (1962), 183–94.

Bing (Gertrud). 'Nugae circa Veritatem', *JWCI*, I (1937–8), 304–12.

Blechmann (Wilhelm). 'Imitatio Creatrix bei Ronsard (zum sonnet 'Quand vous serez bien vieille'—*Sonnets pour Hélène*, II, 43', *Zeitschrift für Französische Sprache und Literatur*, LXXIII (1963), 1–16.

Bright (James W.). 'The *ubi sunt* formula', *Modern Language Notes*, VIII (1893), cols. 187–8.

Brunel (Pierre). *Le Mythe de la métamorphose*, Paris, A. Colin, 1974.

Busson (Henri). 'Sur la philosophie de Ronsard', *Revue des Cours et Conférences*, XXXI (1929–30), 32–48, 172–85.

—— *Le Rationalisme dans la littérature française de la Renaissance (1533–1601)*, 2nd edn., Paris, Vrin, 1957.

Callahan (John F.). *Four Views of Time in Ancient Philosophy*, Cambridge, Mass., Harvard University Press, 1948.

Canter (Howard V.). ' "Fortuna" in Latin Poetry', *Studies in Philology*, XIX (1922), 64–82.

Carter (Jesse B.)   'The Cognomina of the Goddess "Fortuna" ', *American Philological Association Transactions*, xxxi (1900), 60–8.

Cassirer (Ernst).   *Individuum und Kosmos in der Philosophie der Renaissance*, Leipzig and Berlin, Teubner, 1927 (Studien der Bibliothek Warburg, x). Translated into English by Mario Domandi as *The Individual and the Cosmos in Renaissance Philosophy*, New York, Barnes and Noble, 1964.

Cassirer (Ernst), Kristeller (Paul Oskar), Randall (John H.):   editors of *The Renaissance Philosophy of Man*, University of Chicago Press, 1948.

Castor (Grahame).   *Pléiade Poetics: a Study in Sixteenth-century Thought and Terminology*, Cambridge University Press, 1964.

Cave (Terence).   'Ronsard's mythological universe', in *Ronsard the Poet* (ed. T. Cave), London, Methuen, 1973, pp. 159–208.

——   'Mythes de l'abondance et de la privation chez Ronsard', *CAIEF*, xxv (1973), 247–60.

——   'Copia and Cornucopia', in *French Renaissance Studies, 1540–70* (ed. P. Sharratt), Edinburgh University Press, 1976, pp. 52–69.

——   *The Cornucopian Text: Problems of Writing in the French Renaissance*, Oxford University Press, 1979. Unfortunately, no account could be taken of this book for it did not appear until after my own study was completed and submitted for publication.

Chamard (Henri).   *Histoire de la Pléiade*, 4 vols., Paris, Didier, 1939–40.

Clements (Robert J.).   *Critical Theory and Practice of the Pléiade*, Cambridge, Harvard University Press, 1942.

——   'Ronsard and Ficino and the Four Furies', *Romanic Review*, xlv (1954), 161–9.

Cornelia (William B.).   *The Classical Sources of the Nature References in Ronsard's Poetry*, New York, The Institute of French Studies, Columbia University Press, 1934.

Creore (A. E.).   *A Word-Index to the Poetic Works of Ronsard*, 2 vols., Leeds, Maney, 1972.

Curtius (Ernst-Robert).   *European Literature and the Latin Middle Ages.* Translated from the original German by Willard R. Trask, London, Routledge and Kegan Paul, 1953.

Daremberg (Charles V.) and Saglio (Edmund). Editors: *Dictionnaire des antiquités grecques et romaines*, 5 vols. (in 7), Paris, Hachette, 1877–1919.

Demerson (Guy).   'Le mythe des Ages et la conception de l'ordre dans le lyrisme de la Pléiade', in *Humanism in France at the end of the Middle Ages and in the early Renaissance* (ed. A. H. T. Levi), Manchester University Press, 1970, pp. 271–94.

——   *La Mythologie classique dans l'œuvre de la 'Pléiade'*, Geneva, Droz (THR), 1972.

——   'Poétiques de la métamorphose à la Renaissance', in *Poétique de la Renaissance et poétique du XXe siècle, Revue de Littérature Comparée*, li (1977), 152–7.

Desonay (Fernand).   *Ronsard, poète de l'amour*, 3 vols., Brussels, Gembloux J. Duculot, 1952–9.

Doren (Alfred). 'Fortuna im Mittelalter und in der Renaissance', *Vorträge der Bibliothek Warburg*, I (1922–3), 71–144.

Dubruck (Edelgard). *The Theme of Death in French Poetry of the Middle Ages and the Renaissance*, The Hague, Mouton, 1964.

Duhem (Pierre). *Le Système du monde; histoire des doctrines cosmologiques de Platon à Copernic*, 10 vols., Paris, Hermann, 1913–59.

Eliade (Mircea). *Le Mythe de l'éternel retour*, Paris, Gallimard, 1949.

Festugière (Jean). *La Philosophie de l'amour de Marsile Ficin et son influence sur la littérature française au XVIe siècle*, Paris, Vrin, 1941.

Fraisse (Simone). *L'Influence de Lucrèce en France au XVIe siècle. Une conquête du rationalisme*, Paris, Nizet, 1962.

Franchet (Henri). *Le Poète et son œuvre d'après Ronsard*, Paris, Champion, 1923.

Gadoffre (Gilbert). *Ronsard par lui-même*, Paris, Editions du Seuil, 1960.

—— 'Ronsard et la pensée ficinienne', *Archives de philosophie*, janvier 1963, pp. 45–58.

—— 'Ronsard et le thème solaire', in *Le Soleil à la Renaissance: sciences et mythes* (Colloque international, 1963), Brussels, Presses Universitaires de Bruxelles; Paris, Presses Universitaires de France, 1965, pp. 501–18.

Galpin (Stanley L.). 'Fortune's wheel in the *Roman de la Rose*', *PMLA*, XXIV (1909), 332–42.

Gendre (André). *Ronsard poète de la conquête amoureuse*, Neuchâtel, Editions de la Baconnière, 1970.

Gilson (Etienne). *Humanisme Médiéval et Renaissance dans les idées et les lettres*, Paris, Vrin, 1932.

Glasser (Richard). *Time in French Life and Thought*. Translated by C. G. Pearson, Manchester University Press, 1972.

Goldschmidt (Victor). *Le Système stoïcien et l'idée du temps*, Paris, Vrin, 1953.

Gordon (Alex L.). *Ronsard et la rhétorique*, Geneva, Droz (THR), 1970.

Greene (David M.). 'The Identity of the Emblematic Nemesis', *Studies in the Renaissance*, X (1963), 25–43.

Greifenhagen (Adolf). 'Zum Saturnglauben der Renaissance', *Die Antike*, XI (1935), 67–84.

Hallowell (Robert E.). *Ronsard and the Conventional Roman Elegy*, Urbana, University of Illinois Press, 1954.

Hornik (Henry). 'More on Ronsard's philosophy: the hymns and neo-platonism', *BHR*, XXVII (1965), 435–43.

Huizinga (Johan). *The Waning of the Middle Ages*, London, Arnold, 1924.

Hutton (James). *The Greek Anthology in France and in the Latin Writers of the Netherlands to the year 1800*, Ithaca, New York, Cornell University Press, 1946.

Janson (Horst W.). 'The Putto with the Death's Head', *The Art Bulletin*, XIX (1937), 423–49.

Joukovsky or Joukovsky-Micha (Françoise). 'Tombeaux et offrandes rustiques chez les poètes français et néolatins du XVIe siècle', *BHR*, XXVII (1965), 226–47.

—— *La Gloire dans la poésie française et néolatine du XVIe siècle*, Geneva, Droz (THR), 1969.

—— *Orphée et ses disciples dans la poésie française et néolatine du XVIe siècle*, Geneva, Droz, 1970.

Keller (Luzius). *Palingène, Ronsard, Du Bartas. Trois études sur la poésie cosmologique de la Renaissance*, Bern, Francke, 1974.

Kittredge (George L.). 'To Take Time by the Forelock', *Modern Language Notes*, VIII (1893), 230–5.

Klengel (Alice). *Pierre de Ronsards Hymnedichtung*, Leipzig, Vogel, 1931.

Krappe (A. Haggerty). 'Pierre de Ronsard's *Hymne de la Mort* and Plutarch's *Consolatio ad Apollonium*', *Modern Language Review*, XVII (1922), 150–6.

Kristeller (Paul Oskar). *The Philosophy of Marsilio Ficino*. Translated into English by Virginia Conant, New York, Columbia University Press, 1943.

Kushner (Eva). 'Le personnage d'Orphée chez Ronsard', in *Lumières de la Pléiade*, Paris, Vrin, 1966, pp. 271–302.

Lafeuille (Germaine). *Cinq hymnes de Ronsard*, Geneva, Droz (THR), 1973.

Laumonier (Paul). *Ronsard, poète lyrique*, 2nd edn., Paris, Hachette, 1923.

Leclerc (Hélène). 'Du Mythe Platonicien aux Fêtes de la Renaissance: "L'Harmonie du Monde." Incantation et Symbolisme', *Revue d'Histoire du Théâtre*, XI (1959), 105–71.

Lévêque (Pierre). *Aurea catena Homeri: une étude sur l'allégorie grecque*, Paris, Les Belles-Lettres, 1959.

Levi (Anthony H. T.). 'The Neoplatonist Calculus. The exploitation of Neoplatonist themes in French Renaissance literature', in *Humanism in France at the end of the Middle Ages and in the early Renaissance* (ed. A. H. T. Levi), Manchester University Press, 1970, pp. 229–48.

—— 'The role of neoplatonism in Ronsard's poetic imagination', in *Ronsard the Poet* (ed. T. Cave), London, Methuen, 1973, pp. 121–58.

Lovejoy (Arthur). *The Great Chain of Being*, Cambridge, Mass., Harvard University Press, 1936.

Matzke (John E.). 'On the Source of the Italian and English Idioms meaning "To Take Time by the Forelock" ', *PMLA*, VIII (1893), 301–34.

McFarlane (Ian D.). 'Aspects of Ronsard's poetic vision', in *Ronsard the Poet* (ed. T. Cave), London, Methuen, 1973, pp. 13–78.

—— 'Ronsard's poems to Jean Brinon', in *Renaissance Studies in Honor of Isidore Silver: Essays on French Renaissance Literature* (ed. F. S. Brown), *Kentucky Romance Quarterly*, vol. XXI, Supplement no. 2 (1974), 53–67.

Merle (Raimond van). *Iconographie de l'art profane au Moyen Age et à la Renaissance*: vol. II, *Allégories et symboles*, The Hague, Martinus Nijhoff, 1932.

Merrill (R. V.) and Clements (R. J.). *Platonism in French Renaissance Poetry*, New York University Press, 1957.

Moreau (Joseph). *L'Ame du monde de Platon aux Stoïciens*, Paris, Les Belles-(1953), 88–112; 324–43.

—— 'L'idée d'univers dans la pensée antique', *Giornale di metafisica*, VIII Lettres, 1939.

Morin (Edgar). *L'Homme et la mort dans l'histoire*, Paris, Editions du Seuil, 1957.

Morrison (Mary). 'Ronsard and Catullus: the influence of the teaching of Marc-Antoine de Muret', *BHR*, xviii (1956), 240–74.

Mourgues (Odette de). *Metaphysical, Baroque and Précieux Poetry*, Oxford University Press, 1953.

—— 'Ronsard's later poetry', in *Ronsard the Poet* (ed. T. Cave), London, Methuen, 1973, pp. 287–318.

Nolhac (Pierre de). *Ronsard et l'humanisme*, Paris, Champion, 1921.

O'Brien (Denis). *Empedocles' Cosmic Cycle*, Cambridge University Press, 1969.

Panofsky (Dora & Erwin). *Pandora's Box: the Changing Aspects of a Mythical Symbol*, London, Routledge and Kegan Paul, 1956.

Panofsky (Erwin). *Albrecht Dürer*, 3rd edn., 2 vols., New Jersey, Princeton University Press; London, Oxford University Press, 1948.

—— *Studies in Iconology. Humanistic Themes in the Art of the Renaissance*, New York, Harper Torchbooks, 1962 (The Academy Library).

—— ' "Virgo et Victrix", a Note on Dürer's "Nemesis" ', in *Prints. Thirteen Illustrated Essays on the Art of the Print*. Selected by Carl Zigrosser, London, Peter Owen, 1963, pp. 13–38.

Patch (Howard R.). 'The Tradition of the Goddess Fortuna in Roman Literature and in the Transitional Period', *Smith College Studies in Modern Languages*, Northampton, Mass., iii (April 1922), 131–77.

—— 'The Tradition of the Goddess Fortuna in Medieval Philosophy and Literature', *Smith College Studies in Modern Languages*, iii (July 1922), 179–235.

—— 'Fortuna in Old French Literature', *Smith College Studies in Modern Languages*, iv (July 1923), 1–45.

—— *The Goddess Fortuna in Medieval Literature*, Cambridge, Mass., Harvard University Press, 1927.

Pietsch (Karl). 'On the Source of the Italian and English Idioms meaning "To Take Time by the Forelock" ', *Modern Language Notes*, viii (1893), 235–8.

Posnansky (Hermann). 'Nemesis und Adrasteia', *Breslauer Philologische Abhandlungen*, v (1890), 1–184.

Poulet (Georges). *Etudes sur le temps humain*, Edinburgh University Press, 1949.

—— *Les Métamorphoses du cercle*, Paris, Plon, 1961.

Quainton (Malcolm). 'Some classical references, sources and identities in Ronsard's *Prière à la Fortune*', *French Studies*, xxi (1967), 293–301.

—— 'Ronsard's philosophical and cosmological conceptions of time', *French Studies*, xxiii (1969), 1–22.

Quinones (Ricardo J.). *The Renaissance Discovery of Time*, Cambridge, Mass., Harvard University Press, 1972.

Raymond (Marcel). *L'Influence de Ronsard sur la poésie française (1550–1585)*, 2 vols., Paris, Champion, 1927.

—— *Baroque et Renaissance poétique*, Paris, Corti, 1955.

——— 'La Pléiade et le Maniérisme', in *Lumières de la Pléiade*, Paris, Vrin, 1966, pp. 391–423.

——— *La Poésie française et le maniérisme*. Selected with an Introduction by Marcel Raymond, University of London Press, 1971. Also published by Droz (Geneva) and Minard (Paris) in 1971 (TLF). Notes and bibliographical index by A. J. Steele.

Remacle (Madeleine).   'Analyse du sonnet de Ronsard *Comme on voit sur la branche*', *Cahiers d'Analyse Textuelle*, I (1959), 15–54.

Rice (Eugene F.).   *The Renaissance Idea of Wisdom*, Cambridge, Mass., Harvard University Press, 1958.

Roubichou-Stretz (Antoinette).   *La Vision de l'histoire dans l'œuvre de la Pléiade. Thèmes et structures*, Paris, Nizet, 1973.

Rousset (Jean).   *La Littérature de l'âge baroque en France: Circé et le paon*, Paris, Corti, 1954.

Saxl (Fritz).   'Veritas filia temporis', in *Philosophy and History: Essays presented to Ernst Cassirer* (ed. by R. Klibansky and H. J. Paton), Oxford, Clarendon Press, 1936, pp. 197–222.

Schmidt (Albert-Marie).   *La Poésie scientifique en France au seizième siècle*, Paris, Albin Michel, 1938.

Schweinitz (Margaret de).   *Les Epitaphes de Ronsard. Etude historique et littéraire*, Paris, Presses Universitaires de France, 1925.

Schweitzer (Bernhard).   'Dea Nemesis Regina', *Jahrbuch des Deutschen Archäologischen Instituts*, XLVI (1931), 175–246.

Seznec (Jean).   *La Survivance des dieux antiques*. London, The Warburg Institute, 1940.

Silver (Isidore).   'Ronsard's Early Philosophy', *Studies in Philology*, XLV (1948), 119–33.

——— *Ronsard and the Hellenic Renaissance in France*, vol. I: *Ronsard and the Greek Epic*, St Louis, Washington University Press, 1961.

——— 'Ronsard's Ethical Thought', *BHR*, XXIV (1962), 88–117; 339–74.

——— 'Ronsard's Reflections on Cosmogony and Nature', *PMLA*, LXXIX (1964), 219–33.

——— 'Ronsard's Reflections on the Heavens and Time', *PMLA*, LXXX (1965), 344–64.

——— *The Intellectual Evolution of Ronsard*, vol. I: *The Formative Influences*, St Louis, Washington University Press, 1969.

——— *The Intellectual Evolution of Ronsard*, vol. II: *Ronsard's General Theory of Poetry*, St Louis, Washington University Press, 1973.

Solmsen (Friedrich).   *Aristotle's System of the Physical World. A Comparison with his Predecessors*, Ithaca, New York, Cornell University Press, 1960.

Sozzi (Lionello).   'La "Dignitas Hominis" dans la littérature française de la Renaissance', in *Humanism in France at the end of the Middle Ages and in the early Renaissance* (ed. A. H. T. Levi), Manchester University Press, 1970, pp. 176–98.

Spitzer (Leo).   'Explication linguistique et littéraire de deux textes français', *Le Français Moderne*, IV (1936), 37–48.

——— '«Sonnets pour Hélène», Livre II, 43', in *Interpretationen zur Geschichte der französischen Lyrik*, Heidelberg, 1961, pp. 20–4.

Stegmann (André). 'L'Inspiration Platonicienne dans les *Hymnes* de Ronsard', *Revue des Sciences Humaines*, Fasc. 122–3 (1966), 193–210.

Stone Jr. (Donald). *Ronsard's Sonnet Cycles: a Study in Tone and Vision*, New Haven and London, Yale University Press, 1966.

Storer (Walter Henry). *Virgil and Ronsard*, Paris, Champion, 1923.

Swain (Joseph Ward). 'The Theory of the Four Monarchies: Opposition History under the Roman Empire', *Classical Philology*, XXXV (1940), 1–21.

Tervarent (Guy de). *Attributs et symboles dans l'art profane* (1450–1600), 2 vols. (in 1), Geneva, Droz (THR), 1958–9. *Supplément et index*, 1964.

Tillyard (Eustache M. W.). *The Elizabethan World Picture*, Harmondsworth, Penguin Books, 1963.

Tournier (Edouard). *Némésis et la jalousie des Dieux*, Paris, Durand, 1863.

Trousson (Raymond). 'Le mythe de Prométhée et de Pandore chez Ronsard', *Bulletin de l'Association Guillaume Budé* (1961), 351–9.

Varga (A. Kibédi). 'Poésie et cosmologie au XVIe siècle', in *Lumières de la Pléiade*, Paris, Vrin, 1966, pp. 135–55.

Viarre (Simone). *L'Image et la pensée dans les 'Métamorphoses' d'Ovide*, Paris, Presses Universitaires de France, 1964.

Walker (Daniel P.). 'Orpheus the theologian and Renaissance platonists', *JWCI*, XVI (1953), 100–20.

——— 'Le chant orphique de Marsile Ficin', in *Musique et Poésie au XVIe siècle*, Paris, Editions du CNRS, 1954, pp. 17–34.

Weber (Henri). *La Création poétique au XVIe siècle en France, de Maurice Scève à Agrippa d'Aubigné*, 2 vols., Paris, Nizet, 1956.

——— 'Platonisme et sensualité dans la poésie amoureuse de la Pléiade', in *Lumières de la Pléiade*, Paris, Vrin, 1966, pp. 1577–94.

Wilson (Dudley B.). 'The Forces of Flux and Stability in Sixteenth Century Thought and Literature in France', *Durham University Journal*, XLVIII (December 1955), 13–20.

——— 'Contraries in sixteenth century scientific writing in France', in *Essays presented to C. M. Girdlestone*, University of Durham, 1960, pp. 351–68.

——— *Ronsard, Poet of Nature*, Manchester University Press, 1961.

Wind (Edgar). *Pagan Mysteries in the Renaissance*, Harmondsworth, Penguin Books, 1967.

Wittkower (Rudolf). 'Patience and Chance', *JWCI*, I (1937–8), 171–7.

——— 'Chance, Time and Virtue', *JWCI*, I (1937–8), 313–21.

INDEX

(Includes names of persons, mythological and biblical figures, anonymous works, places, personifications, historical events, characters of sixteenth-century and classical texts, contemporary critics, and major thematic and stylistic areas)